Reputation, Image and Impression Management

Reputation, Image and Impression Management

D. B. BROMLEY
University of Liverpool, UK

JOHN WILEY & SONS
Chichester · New York · Brisbane · Toronto · Singapore

Other Wiley Editorial Offices

John Wiley & Sons, Inc., 605 Third Avenue,
New York, NY 10158-0012, USA

Jacaranda Wiley Ltd, G.P.O. Box 859, Brisbane,
Queensland 4001, Australia

John Wiley & Sons (Canada) Ltd, 22 Worcester Road,
Rexdale, Ontario M9W 1L1, Canada

John Wiley & Sons (SEA) Pte Ltd, 37 Jalan Pemimpin #05-04,
Block B, Union Industrial Building, Singapore 2057

Library of Congress Cataloging-in-publication Data

Bromley, D. B. (Dennis Basil), *1924–*
        Reputation, image, and impression management / D. B. Bromley.
            p.   cm.
        Includes bibliographical references and indexes.
        ISBN 0-471-93869-6 (cloth)
        1. Impression formation (Psychology)   2. Social perception.
    3. Corporate image.   4. Public opinion.   I. Title.
    BF323.S63B76   1993
    302'.1—dc20   92–44134
                                                                        CIP

British Library Cataloguing in Publication Data

A catalogue record for this book is available from the British Library

ISBN 0-471-93869-6

Typeset in 10/12pt Times by Dobbie Typesetting Limited, Tavistock, Devon
Printed and bound in Great Britain by Biddles Ltd, Guildford, Surrey

Contents

Preface

I first became interested in the social psychology of reputation in the 1960s, but put the topic aside in favour of other research areas. Having returned to the topic in recent years, I was surprised to find that it still did not feature prominently in the literature of social psychology. It turns out to be a multidisciplinary area, and readers will form their own views about its importance for social psychology. I have not attempted to delve deeply into the technicalities of other disciplines. Limitations on the length of the text have obliged me to curtail discussion of several topics. Nevertheless, I have aimed to cover the main areas of interest.

I considered referring to published examples of the phenomena of reputation, but realised that such examples are soon outdated and of little current interest. I decided instead to describe the types of phenomena that are widely reported in the media or observable in ordinary social interaction, and readers are invited to find their own contemporary examples.

Acknowledgements

I wish to thank the many students who showed interest in the course, from which this book has arisen, and who struggled through earlier versions of the text. I also wish to thank those people and organisations who helped in connection with the associated university course: D. Bamber (Public Relations Officer, University of Liverpool); Royal Insurance; Saatchi and Saatchi; British Nuclear Fuels; Granada TV Tours; Boots the Chemists. Many authors were kind enough to respond to requests for reprints of their articles, although I have not been able to incorporate references to all the material I received. Naturally, I am entirely responsible for the contents of this book. The University of Liverpool has provided important research facilities, especially library support and office facilities.

My wife Roma continues to provide the necessary life-support systems, and regularly brings home examples of reputation in the politics of everyday life, all of which is gratefully received.

1 Definition and Usage

Dictionary Definitions

The word 'reputation' is well known and widely used. *The Concise Oxford Dictionary of Current English* (Sykes, 1976) defines it as follows:

> Reputation—*n*. what is generally said or believed about a person's or thing's character (*has not justified his reputation; has a reputation for integrity; place has a bad reputation*); state of being well reported of, credit, distinction, respectability, good report, (*persons of reputation*); *the* credit or discredit *of* doing or *of* being (*has the reputation of swindling his customers, of being the best shot in England*). [ME, f. L *reputatio* (as foll.; see -ATION)].

No indication is given as to 'how general' what is said or believed should be. The implication is that it is *extensively* said or believed. In fact, the things that are said or believed about people and things vary from those for which there is unanimous agreement, through those for which there is some agreement, to those for which only one person's agreement can be found. Where the reputation of a person is concerned, there are usually several communities (social groups). What is generally said or believed about a person in one group may not coincide with what is said or believed in another. In other words, a person or thing may have more than one reputation. In so far as there are channels of communication and overlapping membership *between* groups, information and influence are likely to be transmitted from one group to another and diffused throughout the wider community. It is possible, however, for opinions and beliefs to circulate among members *within* a group without people *outside* the group being party to them.

The above definition does not distinguish what is *said* from what is *believed*. Beliefs can remain unspoken, and what is said need not correspond with what is believed. Moreover, neither what is said nor what is believed need correspond to the truth about a person or thing. Finally, one must not confuse (a) what is *in fact* generally said or believed with (b) what people *think* is generally said or believed. People can be mistaken in their appreciation of group opinion.

Social evaluation plays a prominent part in reputation. This is clearly apparent in the above definition. A person's reputation is often taken to mean the esteem or standing that they have in their main social groups. Conversely, reputation can reflect general discredit or ill favour. Reputation can be spoken of metaphorically as black, white, pure, sullied, sick, bankrupt, wounded, doubtful, unsavoury, and so on. Such metaphors usually express a value judgement along the dimension good–bad (Chapter 16).

Reputations (public images) are formed not only about people but also about other things—including organisations (corporate images), and commercial products and services (brand images). Reputations are formed about classes of things—Alsatian dogs, Rolls-Royce products, English pubs. The word 'reputation' refers most frequently to particular people, but can refer to classes of people—politicians, university students, psychologists, and so on. The phrase 'reputational entity' will be used to refer to anything that can have a reputation.

The above definition shows that a person can have a reputation for a particular characteristic—of having done something, of being able to do something, or of having some outstanding attribute. The *Shorter Oxford English Dictionary* (Little, Fowler and Onions, 1984) gives a more detailed definition, but it does not clarify the issues raised in connection with the first definition, although it illustrates the way the word has been used, for example, 'The reputation of the state was the first consideration' (Buckle), 'At every word a reputation dies' (Pope).

Common Usage

The word 'repute' is not often used as a noun nowadays; 'He is a person of good repute' sounds rather archaic. The word 'reputation' is used more often. Reputation is assumed to refer to the general opinion about or impression of something, or to the evaluation of it, for example 'He has a good reputation'. Unless the word is qualified in some way, and depending upon the context, the implication is that the impression is widespread, and that public estimation (in terms of value or esteem) is high, as in 'He has a well-established reputation'. The word 'reputation' is often used to indicate fame, honour or good report. So, for example, we might say 'He has an enviable reputation'. The associated adjective 'reputable' means in good repute, respectable, honourable.

The media provide diverse examples of the use of 'reputation' and 'public image' in ordinary discourse. The widespread and easy use of the word 'reputation' and its associates suggest that it is a fundamental and well-recognised phenomenon, even if the processes and technicalities involved are not well understood.

The word 'reputation' can be used to refer to an entity's social impression as a totality, or to some specific aspect of that impression, as with 'professional reputation' or 'reputation for getting things done'. The San Francisco Golden Gate Bridge, for example, developed a reputation as a location for suicidal behaviour (Seiden and Spence, 1983–84).

The word 'reputably' functions as an adverb, as in 'This book is reputably the best for beginners'. The word 'putative' means by repute, as in 'The putative father of the child'. The word 'reputatively' has the same meaning but is rarely used nowadays. The adjective 'reputed' means by repute, or supposed, or generally reckoned to be so, as in 'The reputed owner of the goods'. One can say that an article is reputed to be a person's own work, but is not necessarily so. Similarly, the adverb 'reputedly' means by reputation or common estimation, but with no implication that the claim to validity or genuineness is correct. These words derive from the Latin *reputare, -atum -putare*, meaning to reckon.

The following examples further illustrate common usage:

She is a dancer with an international reputation.

He has a shocking reputation.

'Shall we go into this pub for a drink?' 'How about your professional reputation?' 'Oh, I think I can stand it.'

The following example illustrates indirect usage:

'They say he doesn't like Obstacle Golf.' 'They say, they say,' mocked Lenina.
[Aldous Huxley, *Brave New World*].

There are many examples of common usage. They suggest that:

- people (and other entities) *have* reputations
- reputations are *important*, or *valued*
- reputations vary in *extent*
- people have reputations *for* various things, or *of* being or doing something
- people have various *kinds* of reputation
- reputations can be *manipulated*.

An analysis of common usage illustrates common-sense notions that see person and reputation as separate but interrelated phenomena. Three basic features of reputation can be discerned. The first is the nature of the opinions about the person in a community. The second is the extent and distribution of those opinions. The third is the evaluation of the person (or other entity) and associated attributes.

Some facts about a person can be assembled with a fair degree of objectivity, others not. The things that are generally said or believed about a person, however, depend not only upon these facts but also upon complex processes such as the spread of information (and misinformation) and social influence, and on coincidental circumstances. It is not always easy to make a clear distinction between factual and value judgements where interpersonal relationships are concerned. Value judgements play an essential part in the organisations of social activities and relationships, and many attributes such as intelligence and extraversion—which can be validly assessed by psychometric or controlled clinical methods—are socially evaluated. Allport and Odbert (1936)

showed that evaluative terms have a large share of the vocabulary of interpersonal assessment, and, in many instances, only a careful examination of the
context in which a word or phrase is used (or of the intention of the user) reveals
whether it is used objectively or evaluatively. Terms such as 'conservative',
'shrewd' and 'independent' fall into this category. Other terms, such as 'good',
'bad', 'nice' and 'nasty', are clearly socially evaluative judgements.

Common sense suggests that there is no hard and fast line to be drawn between
people who are widely known and people who are not, or between characteristics
that are more generally known and those that are less generally known. What
is said or believed about someone varies from one group or class of people to
another. Such groups or classes can be part of the same community, because
even if there are channels of communication between all its members it does
not follow that information and influence spread equally throughout the social
network. Moreover, there are serial changes in (a) the *extent* to which a person
is known by repute, and (b) the *amount of agreement* among individuals about
his or her attributes. Reputations can change over time, becoming larger or
smaller, better or worse, or different in some ways from what they were before.

The word 'reputation' is used mainly, but not entirely, about persons. Certain
types of consumer goods—motor cars, cameras, computers—can have a
reputation, known as a 'brand image'. The companies that manufacture or
market them, as with Ford, Pentax, or Marks and Spencer, can have a
reputation, known as a 'corporate image'. Other sorts of things, such as the
Lake District, Benidorm or Liverpool, have a reputation. Activities, such as
smoking, jogging or sailing, and events, such as Munich, the Battle of Britain
and the assassination of President Kennedy, could be said to have a reputation
in so far as there is a shared or 'collective' set of beliefs about them in a given
community. Some of the impressions that people have of these activities and
events circulate within a social network and become consolidated into a simple
schema or stereotype shared by many of its members. The resulting image then
helps to determine their attitudes, expectations, choices and actions. The
reputation of a book or author influences the readership positively or negatively.
People form erroneous impressions by being exposed to indirect and invalid
opinions, and they react inappropriately.

There is a considerable area of common ground between these sorts of
collective or social representations, and it will be useful at times to compare
them, and to use some of the terms interchangeably. An 'extended analogy'
will be used to explore the similarities between different sorts of reputational
entity.

We are mostly concerned with individual persons, groups of people,
organisations, products and services. In practice, the distinction between
different sorts of reputation is sometimes lost, as when the public image of
Dr Somebody (the psychiatrist) merges with or overlaps the public image of
the profession (psychiatrists) or the discipline (psychiatry), or is confused with

psychology or psychoanalysis. Sometimes, the brand image of a product merges with the corporate image of the firm that produces it.

How do we distinguish between social representations (public images) that are regarded as 'reputations' and those that are not so regarded? For example, can we say that marijuana has a reputation or a public image? It is certainly possible to compare marijuana with other drugs, and it has certain properties that are reasonably well known. People differ in their beliefs about it. To this extent it has a reputation. The reputation it has among the general public is, of course, likely to be different from the reputation it has among drug users, drug enforcement personnel and other 'interest groups' involved in the drugs scene.

There are other entities about which the public form beliefs—babies, the Hubble telescope, electricity privatisation, suicide, recycled paper, and so on. But do these public beliefs, and the opinions to which they give rise, mean that these entities have a reputation? The answer is probably given by the acceptability of any phrase which attempts to link an entity to the word 'reputation'. So, for example, we could say 'Recycled paper has the reputation of being expensive'. Even if the statement were untrue, it might still be a common opinion. In contrast, 'Babies have the reputation of attracting the attention of females' sounds odd even if true. Statements about reputation usually make sense only if they refer to individual entities or to homogeneous subclasses of entities rather than to large heterogeneous classes. Thus, 'Low birth-weight babies have the reputation of being more at risk than babies of normal weight' seems more acceptable than the statement about babies in general.

The *collective* view of a person, or other entity, can be strongly evaluative (in a positive or negative way), or ambivalent or neutral. The immediate positive associations with the word 'reputation' have to do with authority, credit, influence, prestige and fame, i.e. with having a 'good name'. But the word can be used to indicate the absence or the opposite of these attributes, for example when used in connection with a 'bad' or 'poor' reputation, or with not having established a reputation, or with being 'in disrepute'. Thus disrepute is the negative pole of reputation. The evaluative aspects of reputation—its worth— are easily recognised in familiar quotations:

> 'Good name in man and woman, dear my lord,
> Is the immediate jewel of their souls;
> Who steals my purse, steals trash; 'tis something, nothing;
> 'Twas mine, 'tis his and has been slave to thousands;
> But he that filches from me my good name
> Robs me of that which not enriches him,
> And makes me poor indeed.'
>
> [*Othello*, III.iii]

> '. . . Then a soldier, . . .
> Seeking the bubble reputation
> Even in the cannon's mouth'
>
> [*As You Like It*, II.vii]

Reputation as a social phenomenon itself has a mixed reputation. The second quotation illustrates the ambivalence we feel towards reputation: it is worth striving and fighting for because we value it; at the same time, it is evanescent or trivial. Personal reputation is the focus of ambivalent feelings and attitudes. The way the word is used in daily life, and the folklore that has grown up around it, illustrate a diversity of beliefs: that reputation is valuable and important; that it can be magnificent but fragile; that it is empty and based on hypocrisy; that it reflects virtue, work and justice; that it depends upon accident and the fickleness of other people.

The concepts of 'reputation' and 'public image' are virtually identical. The main difference is that reputation usually implies an evaluation, whereas public image is a fairly neutral term. There are cultural differences in the social functions of reputation, but, in general, reputation ('face', 'good name', 'honour' 'credit', 'respect' or 'standing') is highly valued. Its main function, however, is to maintain the social order (Chapter 9).

Proverbs and Maxims

Reputation has been the subject of many wise and witty sayings, and a theme for historians and writers from the beginning:

> 'I am a long-suffering man. I pay heed to my reputation; it shows what is in my heart.'

Reputation has been regarded as a basic feature of a person's existence, and a measure of his or her place in society. Persons and their reputations are clearly distinguishable. Their relationship is neither simple nor direct, like that of an object and its reflection; it is complex and indirect, like that of an organism and its effects on the ecological complex of which it forms part.

There has been little systematic study of reputation by social scientists—partly, perhaps, because we acquire an intuitive grasp of the concept through social interaction (the politics of everyday life) and do not feel the need for further enlightenment. Reputations are an integral part of the social process. They help to make history, politics, science and the arts. Legends about people become part of the cultural heritage and help to shape people's attitudes and values. Success in government, business, entertainment, science and the arts depends partly on the aura of reputation that surrounds a person. In some instances, it is the reputation itself—the 'public' image—rather than the person that produces results, for example in politics and show business. This is because reputation has a much wider range of influence than have the actions of the individual. Moreover, reputations can be 'managed', and to some extent detached from the entities to which they refer.

Even in densely populated societies, the number of people with whom we are acquainted is small, although we have to interact superficially with many.

We know some people through direct, face-to-face interaction; we know others scarcely at all (in the sense of having any understanding of their personal qualities and circumstances). Many of these people are known to us only by 'reputation', that is, by hearsay; others are known to us only as ciphers—as people having a certain position in society with associated roles and statuses. We know our relatives, friends, colleagues and close neighbours reasonably well. There are many people we have heard about but never actually met; we believe that they exist and they are reputed to have certain characteristics. We do not know anything about them at first hand, and may not know anyone who does. Thus our knowledge of other people varies from zero up to some unknown limit. In studies of reputation and personality assessment, it is possible to devise operational measures for translating our knowledge of others into judgements about them.

From birth until death (and later!) people attract some social attention and interest for:

'No man, however great, is known to everybody, and no one, however solitary, is known to nobody.'

There is usually some agreement about what is said or believed among the people who know of a person's existence. The behaviour of individuals and their relationships with other people set in motion a widely spreading pattern of consequences and reactions—consequences that interact and produce further consequences, often of an unpredictable sort, and reactions that reflect back upon individuals, changing their behaviour and altering their relationships with others.

In large communities, few individuals are widely known. In small communities, however, people can be known at first hand or by repute throughout that community. Research suggests that in urban areas an average adult encounters about 50 different people in a week, and knows most of these informally or knows who they are (see Emler, 1990). Encounters with 'strangers' are rare.

First hand, direct acquaintance and word of mouth are the usual ways of getting to know about people in small face-to-face social settings. The mass communication media, however, make it possible for large numbers of people to know about a person (or product or organisation) indirectly. The reputation of a person or thing can expand quickly, so that certain things are then said or believed by 'people in general'. Some people—public personages—become the focus of attention and interest for thousands or even millions of people; they are watched, talked about, assessed, copied and caricatured. The ability to focus public interest is generally what is meant by the term 'personality' in the context of politics and entertainment. Reputations of this kind are often superficial, simple and stylised. They can be used to express—at a concrete and literal level—certain abstract and general aspects of human existence—integrity, beauty, courage, evil, virtue or diligence. Eponyms, such as Christian, Stalinist and Freudian, show how ideological principles can be personified.

Less widely known, but perhaps equally important, are the reputations of people in authority—people whose attributes and actions have considerable significance for those in subordinate positions. Managers, heads, officers, chairmen, and others with power and prestige, are a natural focus of social interest because their actions and personal qualities often have more consequences for more people than those with less standing. What is generally said or believed about such people constitutes a frame of reference within which certain actions and events derive their meaning. The same action or decision may be interpreted quite differently depending upon the reputation of the person concerned. People of high social status often set standards, communicated through their reputation, to which others must conform. They can exert considerable influence on the behaviour of others, for example through the exercise of leadership, through their prestige, by their example, and by their behaviour towards and comments about people. The phenomenon of reputation is thus associated with the social psychology of leadership, prestige, charisma, authority and social control. People in high-status positions can rarely afford a loss of social esteem.

Reputation is a phenomenon of considerable social and scientific importance, but the interest shown in it by writers and by ordinary people has not been paralleled by an equivalent degree of interest shown by social and behavioural scientists. The word 'reputation' rarely appears in the titles of technical reports and books, and the main textbooks of social psychology find no place for it. Yet it can be argued that reputation is an important variable in—perhaps one of the main determinants of—social behaviour. This suggestion can be tested at a common-sense level by observing one's own behaviour and the behaviour of others.

One of the reasons why this important phenomenon has been neglected by social scientists is that social processes have been studied by somewhat contrived methods—experimental studies of small groups, surveys using interviews or structured questionnaires, and so on. Methods like these do not necessarily give an accurate picture of what *actually* goes on in normal interaction, though they help to identify important variables and throw light on what *may* go on in the conditions specified by the controlled investigation. The systematic study of naturally occurring social activities and social relationships, especially if this could be combined with a rigorous examination of people's aims, motives, attitudes and expectations, would also show whether reputation plays an important part in a person's dealings with other people. Relevant research studies are mentioned throughout this book.

The clearest expression of reputation in daily life is the exchange of information, news and opinions about people or things. Gossip and hearsay play a prominent part in 'micro-politics' or the 'politics of everyday life'. Our opinions about other people express attitudes and feelings, though not necessarily directly. The underlying beliefs and values are important because they contribute to our perceptions of others and our reactions to them. It is a common experience to meet someone and to be surprised at the discrepancy between what we expected that person to be like (from his or her reputation) and the impression created through first-hand acquaintance. We normally approach another person for the first time with expectations based on hearsay, i.e. secondary reputation. The standards of evidence and argument people use in daily life leave much to be desired, and are subject to a variety of fallacies and biases (Nisbett and Ross, 1980). Certain kinds of fact, however, can be verified by personal observation, by consulting reliable public or private records, or by corroborative evidence from credible observers.

Literature and Folklore

Individuals vary in the extent to which they seek to develop or modify their reputation. They vary too in their success, because the factors that determine reputation are complex and interdependent, and are not entirely under the control of the individual. Several proverbs and maxims draw attention to the ease with which reputations can be lost or destroyed, and to the effort that is required to achieve and sustain one's good name.

It is not unusual to find that modern ideas, especially in the social sciences, have been anticipated by earlier thinkers. The ideas become part of our cultural heritage and are expressed in proverbs, maxims and cliches. A systematic survey by the author provided a sample of 122 quotations. These were classified as general statements about reputation, giving 12 major propositions and several minor ones. The sources were Bartlett (1980), Benham (1948), Stevenson (1949, 1974), and the *Oxford Dictionary of Quotations* (Oxford University Press, 1979).

The following examples illustrate the nature of the material:

I have offended reputation,
A most unnoble swerving.

Who can see worse days than he that yet living doth follow at the funeral of his own reputation?

Conscience and reputation are two things. Conscience is due to yourself, reputation to your neighbour.

Many of the items sampled are accounted for by two general propositions:

1 To have a bad reputation, or to lose a reputation (or be in danger of losing it), is to suffer feelings of guilt and anxiety.
2 To have a good reputation is to be in possession of something valuable and to feel happy and secure. It will compensate for anything that was lost in attaining it.

Some are accounted for by seven further propositions:

3   A good reputation is an ideal that one must live up to.
4   It is difficult to make and keep a good reputation or to repair a damaged one.
5   A good reputation is easily lost or damaged.
6   Reputations are sometimes empty and worthless and based on hypocrisy.
7   Reputations are sometimes not merited, and depend upon accidental circumstances or corruption.
8   Persons and their reputation are separate, and sometimes difficult to reconcile.

Most of the remainder are accounted for by five minor propositions:

9   A good reputation is potentially immortal and has an existence independent of its owner (see 8 above).
10   It is immoral deliberately to seek to establish reputation.
11   To lose a good reputation is not important (contradicts 1 and 2 above).
12   Most people want to be well thought of.
13   Reputation is a necessary part of social life.

Proposition 11 is a special case which seems to apply to a situation in which (a) what is lost is the cheap approbation of a large number of people who are not in touch with the facts, or (b) self-respect is retained.

These 13 propositions summarise common-sense views about reputation. Some of them could be regarded as basic assumptions or value judgements. The apparent contradictions disappear when the context of use is taken into account. They are not easily translated into scientific hypotheses because some are value judgements, some are vague and general, and others are not testable in real-life conditions.

In addition to the 13 proposals listed, the study of quotations, proverbs and sayings suggested a number of other proposals that provide assumptions or leads for research:

1   Reputation centres on those qualities of people that distinguish them from others, and are salient attributes.
2   Reputation sometimes concentrates on minor features of the personality.
3   Reputation selectively emphasises a person's good and/or bad points.
4   Reputation focuses on defects of character.
5   The esteem in which a person is held is lower among close acquaintances than among those who are more distant.
6   Popular (widespread) and rapidly acquired reputations are short lived. Reputations that are deliberately cultivated are likewise more vulnerable than those that are not.
7   Individuals vary in their ability to establish and maintain a good reputation, and in their ability to rehabilitate themselves following a fall in esteem.

8   Reputations vary in size or extent.
9   Reputations are determined not only by the actions of the person but also by the consequences of those actions, the circumstances surrounding the actions and their consequences, the person's relationships and personal qualities, and by many other factors, including chance.
10 Reputation (the collective expression of opinion) affects several social and psychological functions, including social control and self-esteem.
11 Individuals value their own reputation more highly than that of others.

These issues are dealt with in one way or another in the chapters that follow.

Although reputations are simplified and distorted representations of persons, they describe people's social identities. They provide an external standard or criterion against which, through social 'feedback', we try to assess our social identities. Reconciling personal identity and social identity is a continuing problem of adjustment. Family, school and neighbourhood life is much concerned with training children to conform to community standards and values. Ridicule and humiliation on the one hand, and approbation and admiration on the other, are powerful external constraints on our behaviour.

Failure to meet the standards set by society normally means lower self-esteem as well as lower public esteem. Having to account to others for our behaviour is an important and sometimes stressful aspect of social adjustment. Hypocrisy, denial and rationalisation are examples of common methods of evading the conflict between personal and social identity. Social accountability may be involved in a variety of psychological disorders. In extreme cases, it can lead to suicide. In some circumstances, however, the individual's values with regard to a particular course of action do not correspond with those of the community. In this case, reputation presents the person with the problem of reconciling conflicting social and personal values.

Common sense, as judged by popular quotations, proverbs, and other sayings, recognises that persons and their reputations are interdependent entities and need not correspond in the way a map corresponds to the territory it represents. Reputation is determined by many factors other than the qualities, actions and circumstances of the person concerned. Apart from the foreseeable and intended consequences of a person's actions, all kinds of factors contribute to the making of a reputation, including coincidental circumstances, the natural flow of communication and influence through a social network, and other people's deliberate interventions. People do have *some* control over what is generally said or thought about them. One frequently observes individuals 'putting their side of the case' to others in the community, especially to those in key positions in the network of communication and influence in that community.

The autonomy of reputation, as a process distinct from the personality it is supposed to reflect, is the cause of much ambivalence. We are not responsible for the unforeseeable and uncontrollable consequences of our actions or our reputation, yet we are brought up to believe that our reputation (what other people think) is our responsibility. It is not surprising that this contradiction finds expression in ambivalent attitudes towards reputation, as has been illustrated here. The apparent contradictions disappear when the context of attitudes towards reputation is taken into account.

Varieties of Reputation

As normally understood, the essential features of reputation, whether of a person, a group, an organisation, an object, an event or an activity, are that there is a some sort of estimation of its nature and value, and that this estimation is widely shared in a group of people. Reputations are collective systems of beliefs and opinions that influence people's actions with regard to persons and things. Reputational entities range from those that engage the wider public interest to those that affect small groups of people. To some extent, reputations are self-validating, in the sense that beliefs derived from one source of opinion are confirmed by another source, even though the sources are not independent and not based on first-hand information.

To illustrate the various factors that influence reputation, consider two examples. (1) Restaurants develop a reputation by word of mouth among customers and their acquaintances, by word of mouth among sectional interests (suppliers, neighbours, competitors or relevant professional associations), by reports in the local or national media, by reports in good food guides, by individuals wishing to boost or lower a restaurant's reputation through unfair means, by sheer chance, i.e. accident, infection, theft or coincidence. (2) Scientists develop a reputation by word of mouth among colleagues and their acquaintances, by word of mouth or the publication of opinions about them or their work at conferences and in technical or semi-technical journals, by the circulation of referees' reports on job or grant applications, by the publication of citation counts, by the publication of reviews putting a scientist's work into perspective, by the publication of more personal accounts (profiles, reminiscences), from close acquaintances, by publication of criticisms from competitors or enemies, by sheer chance, i.e. available funding, strong or weak support from individuals, accidental meetings or observations, illnesses, absences, coincidences, and eventually (but not finally!) by obituaries.

Subreputations

Large entities, such as commercial organisations, social movements and cities, have reputations that incorporate the subreputations of their constituent parts. Thus, Liverpool's reputation in 1990 incorporated the subreputations of its constituent parts: its people, location, socio-economic structure, University, architecture and history. It also incorporated: the local authority—its personnel and policies—as the body responsible for managing the city's affairs; the Militant Tendency as a local political movement in conflict with the Labour Party; the local trades union branches as sources of power and conflict.

The analogy between personal reputation and corporate image is that large entities have subreputations, the reputations of its constituent parts, which is like the way personal reputations incorporate particular attributes. For example, a personal reputation usually consists of a configuration of beliefs about several aspects of a person's existence—his or her appearance, achievements or failures, social relationships, life-style, defects of character, personality traits, and so on. One or more of these aspects of reputation can become prominent at a particular time, or for a particular audience, whilst other aspects remain in the background.

Reputation is not static; it changes in response to the demands of the situation, i.e. the social circumstances in which information is conveyed and influence exercised. In the UK in November 1990, the leadership contest between John Major, Douglas Hurd and Michael Heseltine gave rise to considerable public discussion regarding their personal attributes. Different aspects of their personalities were emphasised by supporters and detractors, and according to the context of the discussion—policy on Europe, defence, popularity, leadership style, and so on.

Personal Reputation and 'Public Image'

Personal reputation is usually perceived as *belonging* to the person, and in some sense their responsibility, so that they tend to get the blame or the credit for having it. In the law on defamation, people are presumed to have a good reputation, so the burden of proving statements that damage reputation rests on the defendant (Chapter 9). The term 'public image', on the other hand, seems to emphasise the distinction between persons and their reputation. A person's 'public image' is not a genuine reflection of the person (mirrored in the public gaze), but rather a social product related only indirectly to what it is supposed to represent, and capable of being manipulated in all sorts of ways. The word 'reputation' emphasises ownership peculiarity; the term 'public image' emphasises the collective representation. The word 'reputation' and the term 'public image' can both be used about corporate bodies—firms, social organisations—hence the term 'corporate reputation'. They tend to have the same meaning when so used, without the distinction drawn above.

Both personal reputation and public or corporate image can be managed. As far as the individual person is concerned, this requires forms of behaviour that are called self-monitoring, self-presentation and reputation management (Chapter 7). Large organisations usually rely on public relations activities, which include a variety of promotional schemes, such as advertising, sponsorship and lobbying (Chapter 12). Recent years have seen many examples of corporations refurbishing their public image by means of renaming, new logos and livery, and other public relations activities.

One's public image can be adversely affected by the spoiling tactics of competitors and enemies; this sort of reputation wrecking or character assassination uses propaganda, rumour and 'dirty tricks' of one sort or another.

The mass media provide many examples of the use of 'reputation' and related words in ordinary discourse. Readers may be surprised at their frequency and diversity. Some examples can be found in the social and behavioural sciences' research literature.

Real and Apparent Characteristics

Persons and organisations have *real* characteristics, whereas reputations are *representations* of real or imaginary characteristics. Some real characteristics may not enter into reputation. For example, a bank has real assets, branches, policies, and so on, but these may not be represented in the reputation it has among holders of small accounts. A bank's reputation(s) is only one factor, although often a critical factor, affecting its success as a commercial venture. Similarly, a person has real physical and psychological characteristics, possessions, friends and enemies, and so on, but these may not be represented correctly or at all in his or her reputation. Reputation is only one factor affecting a person's adjustment. Some real characteristics form part of an entity's reputation, particularly those concerned with personal or corporate identity, but some do not. This is particularly important in situations where identities have been confused (Fiske, Haslam and Fiske, 1991), or where there has been a deliberate attempt to impersonate people (the author having suffered one such!), or to falsely represent an organisation or product.

Impression Management

We are most likely to be aware of the impression we make on *particular* people, not people in general. These are the people about whom we are most concerned, or who are most concerned about us. They are often the people with whom we are in close and frequent contact. This leads to the distinction between primary and secondary reputation (Chapter 3). We are likely to become aware of the impression we are making on others on those occasions when we realise that our behaviour appears to be different from what we or other people expect it to be—for example, when we are not in our usual frame of mind (depressed, anxious, annoyed, or whatever). Similarly, we sometimes realise that we have made a mistake, or that someone is trying to make out that we have made a mistake, and that others have formed an unfavourable impression of us. Another example would be when we anticipate having to make a good impression to achieve an important goal—at a selection interview, for example, on a 'date' or at a public meeting.

Impressions are normally 'managed' by preparatory, concurrent or subsequent efforts to influence particular people (or an entire audience in the case of a public performance). We do this by voicing certain opinions, intentions, expectations, explanations, apologies, and so on, and by our demeanour and actions. If we feel we have been successful in presenting ourselves to the people we feel are important to us, we can to some extent ignore the impressions that others might have formed, because the people who are part of our wider social network are likely to share the impressions formed by the people we regard as important and influential. We normally assume that those who are not part of our social network will probably not be interested or, if they are interested, that their opinions are likely to be irrelevant or only marginally significant.

A related issue is that in our dealings with other people our immediate concern is with their behaviour or state of mind—what it signifies, what effects it is likely to have, how we should respond to it. Any inferences we draw about their personality are likely to be secondary reflections—impressions of their strengths and weaknesses, attitudes, values, motives, traits, social relationships, and so on. These impressions are used in anticipating and dealing with the person on future occasions. Such knowledge is relevant to self-presentation because we anticipate having to deal with other people by presenting ourselves to them in certain ways, by giving warnings or promises, by expressing certain feelings and expectations, by disclosing or concealing significant personality characteristics, such as determination, patience, distrust or dislike. The aim is to elicit from them the response we desire; this may be of mutual benefit.

Scientific Approaches

From the point of view of basic science, the study of reputation is concerned with elucidating the social and psychological processes that make (and unmake) reputation. A better understanding means describing the processes more fully, and finding valid explanations for what appears to happen. From the point of view of applied science, the study of reputation is concerned with practical applications in various fields—personality and social adjustment, public relations and advertising, politics and economics, for example.

Scientific research requires operational definitions of reputation; these are definitions in terms of explicit measures. Reputation is essentially a collective system of subjective beliefs among members of a social group. The problem is how to assess it in ways that are scientifically meaningful and useful. For example, Covington, Spratt and Omelich (1980) examined the possibility that students who do not make an effort to achieve good results do so to avoid a reputation for low ability. So, suppose one were to hypothesise that students with a reputation for not working had low self-esteem or had doubts about their academic ability relative to their peers. One way of defining reputation would be to identify an appropriate 'public' (interest group), for instance students taking a particular course or sharing the same accommodation, who rate or rank each other in terms of work effort. A student's overall rating or ranking on this attribute would provide an operational definition of his or her reputation. Alternatively, the students on a course could be asked to give free descriptions of their impressions of other students, or to mark a checklist of attributes. The number of mentions of particular attributes provides another operational measure of reputation. The ethical problems of research on naturally occurring reputations are obvious.

Teacher evaluation exercises are now a regular feature of higher education. Teacher evaluation questionnaires contain about 20 standardised items. Circulation of the results is usually restricted to those who 'need to know'. In other words, students may be unaware of how other students have responded, and there may be wide individual differences. This illustrates the problem of investigating *collective* representations (see also Hewstone, 1989). Perry *et al.* (1979) defined teachers' reputation in terms of students' expectations about a teacher's ability to teach, and found that students' judgements of videotaped lectures were influenced by the teacher's expressiveness. Leventhal *et al.* (1975, 1976) argued that teachers' reputations based on students' ratings may be distorted and resistant to change because students are not randomly distributed across courses. The most frequent sources of information about teachers' reputations were reports from other students and published ratings.

Measurement issues, including reliability and validity, have to be attended to. The question of the validity of measures of reputation should not be confused with the question of whether a reputation is a valid representation of the entity to which it refers. Reputation can be defined in several ways. For the time being, it will be defined as the sum of *all* the opinions expressed about an entity in a particular community. These opinions are shared to a greater or lesser extent. The extent of sharing of any one opinion can range, in theory, from 1 to n, where n is the number of people in the community or group, and 1 refers to an idiosyncratic opinion, i.e. an opinion that is not shared with any other member. This range can be divided, for convenience, into three sections: high, middle and low. These sections can be defined arbitrarily, in terms of percentages, to suit one's theoretical or applied purposes, since the observed empirical distributions vary from one investigation to another (Chapter 14).

The range of opinions can be represented in tables and figures. For example, Figure 1.1 shows the frequency distribution of attributes over the high, middle and low sections of a child's reputation. It illustrates the reversed-J frequency distribution described and discussed in Chapters 14 and 15. Figure 1.2 shows a set of overlapping ellipses. Each ellipse represents a member of a social group. The dots represent the different characteristics attributed to a person by a member of the group.

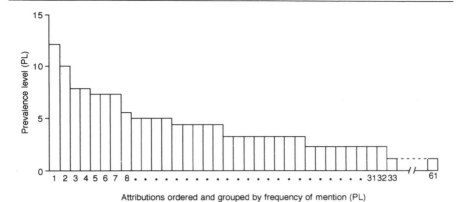

Attributions ordered and grouped by frequency of mention (PL)

Figure 1.1. A typical reversed-J frequency distribution of attributions for the reputation of one schoolchild from a class of 29 schoolchildren. There are 173 attributions altogether, ordered and grouped by frequency of mention (prevalence level—PL). There are 61 different attributions (DAs). The number of DAs tends to increase at successively lower PLs

Thus some attributions are common to several members, whilst others are idiosyncratic. A person's reputation can be defined either as the sum of all the attributions, including those that are idiosyncratic, or, more simply, as the attributions that are widely shared. This aspect of the problem of definition is dealt with in detail in later chapters.

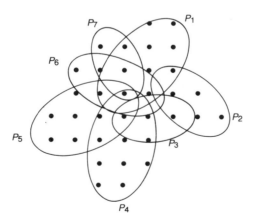

Figure 1.2. A schematic representation of the distribution of beliefs about a person or other reputational entity among members of a seven-person group. Each ellipse represents a member of the group (P_1 to P_7). Each dot represents a different belief or attribution. Note that there are differences between individuals in the number of attributions mentioned, and that whereas some attributions are common to several members, others are idiosyncratic, i.e. made by one member only. In a large, heterogeneous group, one would not expect any attributions to be common to all the members

2 Historical Landmarks and Further Guidelines

HISTORICAL LANDMARKS

Introduction

A convenient point of departure for a brief review of the history of reputation as a topic of interest to social and behavioural scientists is a quotation from Volume 1 of *The Principles of Psychology* (1890: 293–296) by William James, a psychologist of outstanding reputation. The best-known quotation is the clause beginning '. . . we may practically say . . .', but for the present purpose the section is worth quoting in full, except for the footnotes signalled here by asterisks, as follows:

> '*A man's Social Self* is the recognition he gets from his mates. We are not only gregarious animals, liking to be in sight of our fellows, but we have an innate propensity to get ourselves noticed, and noticed favourably, by our kind. No more fiendish punishment could be devised, were such a thing physically possible, than that one should be turned loose in society and remain absolutely unnoticed by all the members thereof. If no one turned round when we entered, answered when we spoke, or minded what we did, but if every person we met 'cut us dead,' and acted as if we were non-existing things, a kind of rage and impotent despair would ere long well up in us, from which the cruellest bodily tortures would be a relief; for these would make us feel that, however bad might be our plight, we had not sunk to such a depth as to be unworthy of attention at all.
>
> Properly speaking, *a man has as many social selves as there are individuals who recognize him* and carry an image of him in their mind. To wound any one of these his images is to wound him.* But as the individuals who carry the images fall naturally into classes, we may practically say that he has as many different social selves as there are distinct *groups* of persons about whose opinion he cares. He generally shows a different side of himself to each of these different groups. Many a youth who is demure enough before his parents and teachers, swears and swaggers like a pirate among his 'tough' young friends. We do not show ourselves to our chidren as to our club-companions, to our customers as to the laborers we employ, to our own masters and employers as to our intimate friends. From this there results what practically is a division of the man into several selves; and this may be a discordant splitting, as where one is afraid to let one set of his acquaintances know him as he is elsewhere; or it may be a perfectly harmonious division of labor, as where one tender to his children is stern to the soldiers or prisoners under his command.
>
> The most peculiar social self which one is apt to have is in the mind of the person one is in love with. The good or bad fortunes of this self cause the most intense elation and dejection—unreasonably enough as measured by every other standard

than that of the organic feeling of the individual. To his own consciousness he *is* not, so long as this particular social self fails to get recognition, and when it is recognized his contentment passes all bounds.

A man's *fame*, good or bad, and his *honor* or dishonor, are names for one of his social selves. The particular social self of a man called his honor is usually the result of one of those splittings of which we have spoken. It is his image in the eyes of his own 'set,' which exalts or condemns him as he conforms or not to certain requirements that may not be made of one in another walk of life. Thus a layman may abandon a city infected with cholera; but a priest or doctor would think such an act incompatible with his honor. A soldier's honor requires him to fight or to die under circumstances where another man can apologize or run away with no stain upon his social self. A judge, a statesman, are in like manner debarred by the honor of their cloth from entering into pecuniary relations perfectly honorable to persons in private life. Nothing is commoner than to hear people discriminate between their different selves of this sort: "As a man I pity you, but as an official I must show you no mercy; as a politician I regard him as an ally, but as a moralist I loathe him;" etc., etc. What may be called 'club opinion' is one of the very strongest forces in life.* The thief must not steal from other thieves; the gambler must pay his gambling-debts, though he pay no other debts in the world. The code of honor of fashionable society has throughout history been full of permissions as well as of vetoes, the only reason for following either of which is that so we best serve one of our social selves. You must not lie in general, but you may lie as much as you please if asked about your relations with a lady; you must accept a challenge from an equal, but if challenged by an inferior you may laugh him to scorn: these are examples of what is meant.'

The above quotation anticipates some of the important social and psychological issues in the study of reputation. Another favourite quotation with regard to reputation is from *Human Nature and the Social Order* (1922: 184) by C. H. Cooley:

'A social self of this sort might be called the reflected or looking-glass self:

'Each to each a looking-glass
Reflects the other that doth pass.'

For Cooley, this sort of social self is how we *imagine* we appear to other people, not how we actually appear to them. It has three components—our appearance, the other person's judgement and our reaction to that judgement. These imaginings are adapted to what we believe about the other person. We manage our impressions accordingly, and we imagine the other person's reactions accordingly. We 'share' his or her impressions of us, at least momentarily. The self is thus a social product—a set of self-attributions prompted by social interaction. Like William James, Cooley (1922: 240–241) agrees that in some circumstances honour is more important than survival, and quotes:

'Mine honor is my life: both grow in one;
Take honor from me and my life is done.'

The relationship between the self-concept and social identity was a focal issue in the work of G. H. Mead (1934). Briefly, Mead's argument is that the child's self-concept is shaped by the attitudes taken towards the child by its care-givers. Young children have strong needs for the attention of their care-givers. As they develop, their behaviour evolves in response to the contingencies of reinforcement, and on the basis of individual differences in temperamental and cognitive characteristics. Young children's attitudes towards themselves are strongly influenced by care-givers' attitudes towards them. The child eventually develops a notion of the 'generalised other' that shapes its social identity. The self's 'me' is what the person assumes to be that set of attitudes other people adopt towards the self. By contrast, the self's 'I' is the person's reaction to that set of attitudes, for example 'I think they don't like me' or 'I am annoyed with myself [me] for what I have done (what others blame me for)'. As Mead (1934: 174) puts it, 'The "I" does not get into the limelight'. It reacts to the self as object (the 'me'). The self is both the 'I' and the 'me'. Interestingly, the concept of reputation as such appears to have no place in Mead's writings.

For both Cooley and Mead, therefore, the point seems to be that we do not have direct access to other people's impressions of us. We imagine what their attitudes are, presumably on the basis of the inferences we make about their behaviour. The question of how we monitor our reputation is considered in Chapter 7.

Attempts to measure reputation date back to the work of Hartshorne, May and Shuttleworth (1930). In their 'studies in the organization of character', Hartshorne et al. concentrated on four criteria of character: reputation, social adjustment, judges' ratings of 'pen pictures' of schoolchildren, and self-consistency. They developed four measures of reputation derived from teachers and classmates: teachers' deportment marks, a conduct record (a check-list of 20 items dealing with persistence, cooperativeness, control of temper and so on), a check-list of 160 'good' and 'bad' words, and a 'Guess Who?' test (Chapter 16). Their methods and results have been debated at length. Their work has featured prominently in the controversy over the extent to which behaviour is determined by personality and situation.

Moreno (1934) developed sociometry. This was a method of mapping social relationships (friendships, likes and dislikes, and so on) and was widely used in education. It is one way of investigating reputational networks, and has developed into a more sophisticated theory of social networks (Chapter 6).

Tuddenham (1951, 1952) developed the 'Guess Who?' test as a device for studying the social aspects of personality development and adjustment in large samples of children of elementary school age. It contained bipolar items such as 'Doesn't get mad easily—Gets mad easily', 'Acts like a little lady—Tomboy'. The test was popular with younger children but tended to make adolescents uneasy. Tuddenham found clear gender differences in the children's attributions reflecting cultural factors. At older ages, the gender difference was less marked, and unfavourable nominations were fewer. The girls were less favourable in their self-evaluations. Both teachers and children made more favourable than unfavourable nominations. Self-nominations were mostly favourable. The reliability of the measure appeared to be higher at older ages, although nominations by teachers, classmates and self did not show good agreement. Different items in the test elicited different degrees of agreement between respondents, such as 'quiet' (good agreement) and 'good sport' (poor agreement). Cluster analysis of some of the data revealed a strong 'evaluative' (like/dislike) factor; other factors were differentiated in older age groups, reflected gender differences and social values.

Jones (1958) studied the reputation of high-school students by calculating their frequency of mention (of contributing to the school's social life) in the school's daily newspaper. Five hundred and forty issues of the newspaper over a 3-year period were examined. The total number of mentions ranged from zero to 112. Jones contrasted high- and low-mention groups with regard to physical maturity, behaviour ratings, 'Guess Who?' nominations, drive ratings, intelligence, physical abilities, socio-economic status, attitudes, self-concept and role pattern. A long-term follow-up revealed some of the factors affecting social prominence (see Jones, 1958, for details).

The main aim of the early work on the psychology of reputation was not to study reputation as such, but to use measures of reputation to assess personality. The traditional methods were ratings and check-lists (Chapter 16). The difficulty of obtaining direct, objective indices of personality explains why we resort to evidence about reputation in scientific research—through observers' ratings—as well as in daily life—through gossip, voting and referees' reports. Cheek (1982) re-examined the issue of assessing the extent of agreement between observers—this is what reputation normally refers to.

The work of Allport and Postman (1947) was an historical landmark in the study of rumour. Rumour and gossip are important in the spread of information and influence through a network of social relationships (see Emler, 1992, for a brief review; see also Chapter 6).

The works of Ichheiser (1943–44, 1949–50) were historical landmarks in the study of attribution (the way we assign characteristics to, and interpret the behaviour of, ourselves and others). Reputations can be regarded as the extent to which people share the same impressions of a person or other entity.

Personality as Social Stimulus Value

May (1932) defined personality in terms of the responses people make to a person, i.e. the person's 'social stimulus value'. Craik (1985, 1986) drew attention to the history of research methods in the study of personality. He reminded us that Allport (1937) explicitly rejected the view that 'social stimulus value' was a useful approach to the study of personality, on the grounds that observers would be overwhelmed by considerations of gossip, rumour, misjudgement, social effectiveness and reputation. Allport's view has something in common with the objections to reputation as evidence in judicial investigations: to introduce such evidence would open up a multiplicity of inconclusive lines of inquiry (gossip, hearsay).

It is reputation rather than personality that reflects a person's 'social stimulus value'. The difficulty arises because although there is a clear difference between personality and reputation, there are important connections between them. From a theoretical point of view, other people's reactions to us establish a relationship between our personal identity (self-concept) and our social identity (reputation). From a practical point of view, a good deal of our social behaviour is governed by considerations of reputation management (Chapter 7).

The philosophical point is that our beliefs about the world do not necessarily correspond with what the world is really like. Similarly, our beliefs about persons do not necessarily coincide with what persons are really like. Many beliefs can be tested against external, independent criteria; contradictory beliefs about something, or about a person, cannot all be true. The problem is how to make an *objective* assessment of a person or other reputational entity. An objective assessment, however, is simply an inter-subjective assessment, an agreement between competent observers based on the best empirical evidence and cogent argument. Our understanding of personality, like our understanding of anything else, is *socially constructed*; it reflects our current state of knowledge. Unfortunately, it is sometimes difficult to find valid objective criteria against which we can test our beliefs about persons—hence our reliance on reputation. Measures based on reputation (in the sense of agreement between judges' subjective impressions) have been and continue to be substituted for objective criteria in personality research.

Craik (1989) presented a conceptual analysis linking personality assessment, personal reputation and self-assessment. Craik's (1989: 7) remarks remind us that biographical inquiries, those of for instance Longmore (1988) and Taylor (1989), are based on methods drawn from history and the humanities, and help to define reputation as a distinct and important area of study. There are many studies of famous people—artists, politicians, scientists, soldiers, and so on. The question is whether the information provided is largely biographical, with asides on public reactions, or whether it is an account of reputation as a phenomenon in its own right. If the latter, then the methods used to collect and analyse the data should have some scientific interest.

Looking at the historical background to the psychology of reputation, Craik says that the distinction between individual and collective representations was made by Durkheim (1898), who argued that social interaction between individuals gives rise to social products or social facts that are different from those produced by individuals acting alone; they are *collective* phenomena, such as religions and trading relationships. Any system of beliefs, values and practices that emerges as a consequence of collective action (social interaction) can be looked at in this way. As social products, reputations (public images) are collective representations of persons and other entities.

The work of Hartshorne, May and Shuttleworth (1930) continues to be of interest in the controversy about the relative importance of dispositional and situational factors in behaviour. Their work continues to be of interest in connection with the developmental aspects of social behaviour. Surprisingly, however, the study of reputation did not develop as a distinct area of interest to social and behavioural scientists, and there appears to be no clear historical pattern in the research on reputation. The items in the following sections give some further guidelines on the social and psychological issues in the study of reputation. These and others are dealt with in more detail in the following chapters, where further references are cited.

FURTHER GUIDELINES

Expectations and Anticipatory Reactions

In the formation of social relationships, persons are often preceded by their reputation. When we join a group or interact with someone for the first time, people will have heard something about us and will have formed attitudes and expectations on the basis of that information. These attitudes and expectations are likely to vary from one person to another. In some circumstances these impressions are detailed and well established, but usually they take the form of simple stereotypes encapsulated in a few words or phrases; 'A hard-working, no-nonsense chap', 'A real bitch', 'Quiet and aloof'. A newcomer might arrange for word of his or her reputation to be spread in advance, so that people are prepared for what is to come. This state of affairs is more likely to be found in organisations where firm leadership and discipline are called for—military establishments, commercial take-overs and the like. First-hand acquaintance, however, is likely to quickly dispel any disparity between expectation (reputation) and actuality (personality, performance).

The effect of reputation is that our expectations about other people, based on hearsay, influence our behaviour when we come into face-to-face contact with them. In turn, our behaviour has effects on them, possibly in a way that makes our expectation a self-fulfilling prophecy. For example, if we expect the person to be aggressive or uncooperative then we may act aggressively or uncooperatively in anticipation, or conversely we may act submissively or be too conciliatory. In either event, this could have the effect of provoking the behaviour we expected. There are many psychological and situational factors influencing interpersonal encounters of this kind. Social identities are 'negotiated' in interactions that have not become routine.

Persons and organisations risk failing badly if they do not live up to their reputation, because their public react adversely if their expectations are frustrated. If a person or organisation is unaware of their public image, then such failures are more likely; hence the need for individuals to monitor their reputation(s), and for large organisations to maintain a public relations facility.

Lazar (1973) cited teachers' reputation as a factor influencing students' choice of courses. Bowers and Pugh (1973) found that the two most important reasons given by students and parents for choosing a college course were the academic reputation of a college and the reputation of particular departments. Thoreson, Cox and Krauskopf (1975) found a 'halo' effect in professionals' ratings of doctoral programmes in counselling psychology. Littrell, Caffrey and Hopper (1987) found that students' preferences for a counsellor were influenced by information about reputation, but that a negative reputation could be countered by more direct evidence of the counsellor at work. White (1985) reported on the way the reputation of an institution and a department affect students' choice of a counsellor education programme. Bloom, Schroeder and Babineau (1981) showed that reputation is not the only factor influencing subjects' perceptions of therapists. Objective information (or information presented as objective), such as fees and personality, had more influence. Several other authors have remarked on the way reputation affects the relationships between therapists and their clients and colleagues (see King and Blaney, 1977; Lewis and Lewis, 1985; Guillebeaux, Storm and Demaris 1986; Haas-Wilson, 1990; Uribe, 1988). Young (1984) has suggested that practitioners of rational emotional therapy could use their reputation to influence lower-class clients.

Interaction Between Self and Reputation

Reputations have a positive or negative value. Consequently, in the event of a mismatch between people's actual characteristics and the characteristics attributed to them via their reputation, people are under some obligation to 'live up to' that reputation or to 'live it down'. For example, a delinquent youth with a reputation for taking risks feels some obligation to take up a particular challenge, on the grounds that not to do so would detract from the favourable reputation he has among his delinquent reference group. A politician who has failed in some respect—said the wrong thing, broken a promise—will have lost support and will feel under some obligation to make up for that loss of social esteem by succeeding in other ventures: looking after his or her constituents, or seeking compensatory media exposure or public statements of support from influential people.

Forming Impressions

Through social interaction, we form schemata, or impressions, representing other people. These schemata function like maps or conceptual routines guiding our behaviour in matters relating to them. The present account emphasises the rational aspect of impressions; there is an equally important 'affective' (emotional and motivational) component in impression formation. First impressions of other people are fairly immediate and not obviously the product of rational judgemental processes. First impressions are often important in the development of an impression. On the other hand, first impressions are likely to be rapidly dispelled by countervailing direct experience with a person or other entity.

The point is that processes outside conscious awareness influence people's behaviour. We are often influenced to buy something or to accept a point of view because it is endorsed by a person with a good reputation. Editors of some scientific journals require submissions to be anonymous because of the biasing effect of an author's reputation on peer reviewers. These and other heuristics and biases are studied under the general heading of social cognition (Nisbett and Ross, 1980) and obviously have a bearing on the formation of shared impressions in reputations.

Reputations Formed for Professional Purposes

In a scientific or professional context, detailed technical information of the sort compiled as a case-study, medical history, political profile, assessment centre report or criminal record, could be regarded as a special category of reputation. In theory, each member of the investigatory team has access to all the information, although some may have a better grasp of some parts than of others. In so far as a group of investigators share a collective impression of a client, this is one of the client's reputations. That reputation, like others, would be partial and selective, but presumably more firmly based on empirical data and rational inference through documentation and case discussions. The information may be highly confidential and for limited circulation; it is compiled for a special, limited purpose—medical examination, state security, management recruitment or police investigation, for example.

Some of the information may be known outside the professional group charged with collating the information; some of it may 'leak out' into the wider community. The main differences between these professionally contrived reputations and natural reputations in the wider community is that they are more sharply focused and systematically organised, and usually recorded in a permanent form; they are formed for a special purpose. They are, nevertheless, collective or shared impressions, known as 'social representations', of the person under investigation. They can, of course, be mistaken.

A different kind of professional assessment occurs when assessors independently observe a person behaving, or have access to information about a person's behaviour. Their *independent* ratings can be averaged over each of a number of characteristics, usually traits. Alternatively, after discussion they can agree on a group rating for each trait. The difference between an 'averaged' impression and a 'collective' impression is that a collective impression is *shared* following a mutual exchange of information and influence. Reputations are collective impressions that combine the effects of conformity and diversity. Averaged impressions that are made public, as in opinion surveys, can become reputational attributes to the extent that people believe that information.

Attributes of Reputation

As with personality impressions, reputation can be specified in terms of a number of features or attributes. The nature of these attributes varies from one sort of reputational entity to another. The 'image attributes' of a type of motor car differ from the image attributes of a politician or a university. Within these general categories, however, we normally find a limited range of attributes. These attributes are not distributed equally across members of a particular sector of the community, but rather follow a reversed-J curve of conformity. Many people cite the same few attributes, fewer people, or perhaps only one person, cite other attributes. This is essentially the form of a stereotype (see Chapter 5). The contents of a reputation tend to become consistent. The reasons are that individuals are naturally inclined to hold consistent beliefs (Maddi, 1980), that conformity reduces the range of individual differences, and that the social sharing of ideas leads to shortening and simplification.

Any consumer article, even something like a psychometric test, can develop a reputation, for example the Repertory Grid Technique (Easterby-Smith, 1980). Its reputation consists in what the relevant social groups believe about it, which affects how they behave towards it. In this, as in other cases, the reputation has been influenced by experts and opinion leaders (not necessarily the same people!) whose views are accepted by others in lieu of first-hand experience with the entity. Sometimes people misunderstand and misuse instruments and techniques with the result that they acquire a 'bad name'. The reputation of the social services in the UK has suffered as a consequence of the mishandling of cases of child abuse. Some breeds of dog—Alsatian, Rottweiler—have acquired a bad reputation on account of adverse publicity not compensated for by publicity about the merits of these breeds.

Extent and Duration of Reputation

Reputations vary in extent from little known to widespread, and vary in duration from brief to enduring. Extension and duration are not entirely independent of one another. Longstanding reputations are likely to be widespread, as with famous names in history. Reputations vary from being fragmented to being cohesive, in the sense that what is believed about a person may consist of a collection of unrelated items of information, or a more coherent, interdependent set of ideas. In practice, we are likely to find a small but coherent core of high-frequency items together with a wide range of items with lower frequencies of occurrence. This can be represented graphically as a reversed-J curve of conformity or as a set of overlapping ellipses, as illustrated in Figures 1.1 and 1.2.

The size, shape and content of an individual's reputations vary. A reputation in one group can be extensive and coherent compared with that in another group. In so far as members of different groups interact and communicate with one another, information and influence will spread. The reputation developed *within* one group is likely to be different from that developed in other groups, firstly because the social impact a person makes differs from group to group, and secondly because the membership characteristics, and the networks of communication and influence, vary from one group to another.

Comparisons Between Reputations

An interesting aspect of the life-history of reputations is that reputations are not independent entities, they interact with each other. A clear example of interaction is the way judgements about one person are made by comparing one person with another. This commonly occurs in newspaper reports about people in the public eye; and it ties in with what is known about the way people ordinarily describe themselves and others (Bromley, 1977).

Another form of interaction is that in some circumstances there is an ecological relationship: as one reputation increases in extent it tends to do so at the expense of another in the same area of public interest, as if there were factors limiting the kind and amount of interest and information that a public can sustain. Initially, competition may increase the size of competing reputations, but as one develops the others tend to fade (Chapters 14 and 15). The availability of reputations that compare and contrast can help or hinder the development of a reputation. Consider, for example, a situation where three or four politicians are competing for a leadership position, as compared with a situation where there is only one contender; similarly, consider competition for high-level appointments where several candidates have to be recruited and short-listed.

An example of the interdependence of reputations is seen in a voting system. An electorate distributes its votes, in theory at least, as signals of approval for this or that candidate. The 'candidate' could be a person, organisation, product, service or policy proposal. A vote for one is a vote withheld from another.

Members of an electorate can vote without knowing what other members of the electorate think, i.e. without any clear idea of the reputation of the entities being voted on. Nevertheless, the results of the election will be taken as evidence of the reputation of the entities involved. This illustrates one aspect of the 'collective' nature of reputation; but reputation is not something in the minds of individuals acting alone, it is the outcome of what is in the minds of individuals acting collectively. The effects on voting produced by bribery or intimidation give rise to an 'apparent' or 'pseudo-' reputation that masks an underlying 'real' reputation.

An ecological perspective is relevant and useful because it focuses attention on the way a person's social interactions give rise initially to individual (first-hand) impressions; but the social context (interpersonal communication and influence) gives rise to collective impressions (reputation or public image) that become an important part of a person's social environment, part of the 'ecosystem'. The person's social adjustment now depends on appreciating the nature and extent of his or her reputation (strictly speaking, reputations, plural), and acting accordingly. This means understanding how their reputation is helping or hindering them in their endeavours, and 'managing' their reputation in ways that further their life goals.

Some reputational attributes are more prevalent than others, as illustrated in Figures 1.1 and 1.2. The word 'prevalence' suggests an analogy with epidemiology. That is to say, beliefs or social representations can be thought of as spreading like an infection. Their distribution might be limited or diminished subsequently because of resistance, countermeasures, and so on. The metaphor is useful in drawing attention to the different ways in which beliefs can spread and evolve, and to the 'virulence' of some beliefs.

League Tables

Public images can be enhanced or diminished by an individual's or an organisation's standing in a league table. Not only football teams, but many other sorts of groups compete with each other for a higher position in the relevant league table. Thus we refer to 'top' people or companies, to the results of public opinion polls, and to the rankings of individuals or institutions published in the media. Sometimes such rankings can be misleading even when they appear to be based on objective criteria, as with the rankings of university departments based on research output or student applications. On one occasion, it was found that departmental size had not been taken into account, and on another occasion that the date when a survey was made affected the outcome. When these sorts of adjustments are made, league table ranks can change.

Cultural and Subcultural Factors

Some reputational attributes are more important than others in a given set of cultural conditions, for example, gender (Long, 1984; Kelley, 1991); consider also factors such as premarital virginity, scientific rigour and commercial and political acumen, in particular social contexts.

Workplace reputations are important in organisations because they contribute to industrial relations and managerial effectiveness. We try to associate with people whose reputations promise to provide benefits rather than costs, in both workplace and leisure settings. A person's or an organisation's reputation is an important factor affecting the extent to which other people are prepared to associate with them.

The concept of reputation has a place in anthropology. Studies of witchcraft and faith-healing illustrate the ways in which reputation influences people (Henry, 1977; Lewis, 1974). The study of social movements and political behaviour illustrates phenomena such as charisma, leadership, personification, and the power of identification with a person or ideology, conveyed through stereotypes and slogans.

The reputation of an advisor—therapist, lawyer, teacher, dentist—is likely to influence the clients' decisions to seek help, to accept or reject advice, and the client's subjective evaluation of the outcome. The more 'psychological' the condition, i.e. the more it is based on subjective factors, the more influential the effect of reputation is likely to be. It seems that there is a strong placebo effect from the reputation of the source of advice and treatment (as with various spas, religious shrines and faith healers). Some organisations, such as financial institutions, industrial and commercial organisations, charities, and so on, have a favourable or unfavourable social image that influences clients' and supporters' preferences and actions, and affects relationships between organisations.

Reputation as Process and Product

Reputation is a social process as well as a social product. As a product, according to one definition, it is the sum of the relevant opinions held by members of a specified interest group at a particular time. Some interesting aspects of reputation are associated with stability and change over time (Chapters 14 and 15). Hence the need for longitudinal studies with their attendant procedural and statistical complications. In some circumstances, reputation lags behind the character of the entity with which it is associated. The initial reputation, like a first impression, is sometimes resistant to change. This notion is captured in the maxim, 'Give a dog a bad name, and it sticks.' The time-span over which a reputation can be studied varies greatly from one area of inquiry to another. Changes in the reputation of political parties span years or decades. Changes in the reputation of someone involved in a disagreement at work can occupy a few days or weeks.

Audiences and Interest Groups

The word 'audience' is sometimes used as an alternative to 'public'. Audiences can be family groups, guests at dinner parties, classes of students, viewers of party political broadcasts or any other interested party. The people who register our behaviour are an audience. An 'audience' does not imply mere passive observation of a person's behaviour, without direct interaction. 'Live' audiences react; they signal approval or disapproval, or a mixture of both. The actor, the person to whom the audience is attending, tries to register the audience's reactions and to interpret them one way or another, and tries to foster a particular kind of impression. Interest groups comprise those people who, for one reason or another, have an 'interest' in a reputational entity, for example football supporters, employees in a firm or airline passengers.

Biosocial Basis of Reputation

Where animals interact with each other through recognition of individuals, they learn to coordinate their behaviour in particular situations, particularly those involving food, sex and territory. These mutual recognitions and coordinations give rise, for example, to dominance hierarchies, bonding, cooperation and territoriality. Thus recognition of individual identity could be regarded as an evolutionary precursor of reputation. If it were not for human individuality, there would be no reputations.

Reputation in higher primates is expressed in dominance hierarchies and alliances. There is some evidence that chimpanzees are capable of tactical deception (Byrne and Whiten, 1988). Tactical deception, Machiavellism, is one aspect of impression management in humans (Ickes, Reidhead and Patterson, 1986). In chimpanzees, tactical deception refers to forms of behaviour that mislead a competitor or an aggressor so as to secure an advantage or avoid attack, for example by distraction, by concealment and by making indirect approaches to goals.

In human societies, however, cognitive and linguistic abilities, together with complex forms of social organisation, give rise to highly sophisticated forms of social identity (reputation or public image) and interaction. In Western democracies, individuality has a prominent place in political philosophy (Lukes, 1973).

Demographic Factors

Reputation is affected by demographic variables—age, gender, social class, and so on. These variables are associated with particular sorts of interests, patterns of communication, and degree of exposure to the person or organisation concerned. Consider, for example, how the reputation of a doctor might be affected by the way he or she deals with men as compared with women, or with patients in different age groups or different socio-economic strata. A pop group could have a well-defined and extensive reputation among teenagers, and a non-existent one in, say, upper–middle class professional groups.

End Note

Reputation is closely associated with many aspects of social psychology, including interpersonal relationships, attitudes, stereotypes and prejudice,

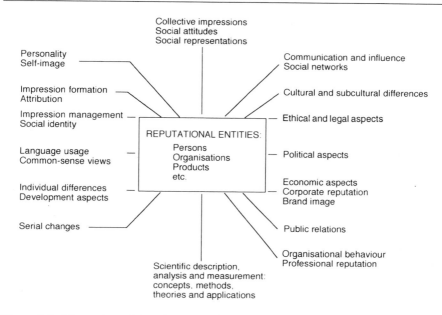

Figure 2.1. The main social and psychological aspects of and approaches to reputation

deviant behaviour, communication and influence, public opinion, the mass media, social interaction and conformity, personality, and social cognition. Knowledge about reputation has applications in organisational behaviour, public relations, propaganda and advertising, and consumer research. Reputation is the key concept in the law on defamation. The scientific study of reputation is a multidisciplinary enterprise.

Limitations on the length of this text mean that the developmental aspects of reputation and a variety of minor issues will not be examined. The main aspects of and approaches to reputation are illustrated in Figure 2.1.

3 Assumptions and Issues

Introduction

Much of what we know about reputation is based on common knowledge rather than on empirical research findings. Once this knowledge is examined critically and constructively, however, many of the ideas interlock, and some can be put to the test. This increases our confidence in the resulting framework, but leaves open the question of further rigorous testing, especially of those ideas that are counter-intuitive.

The concept of reputation has much in common with the concepts of public opinion, collective belief and social attitude, in so far as these notions refer to a collective representation of whatever the notion refers to. For a review of the psychology of widespread beliefs, see Fraser and Gaskell (1990).

The psychology of human social life includes three important areas of interest. The first is personality (the study of persons as individuals, and the study of differences between individuals). The second is the relationships between people and between groups. The third is reputation (the study of persons and other entities as represented collectively). The methods used to study reputation range from the traditional experimental and survey methods to the methods used in the humanities. They include both quantitative and qualitative methods, such as content analysis and case-studies, as well as the psychometric methods used in personality research (Chapter 16).

Self-esteem and Social Approval

Most people like to think well of themselves and like to be well thought of by others (Crowne and Marlowe, 1964). Some people seem careless of or insensitive to the impression they make on others, but closer observation usually shows that they are capable of monitoring other people's reactions and managing the impression they wish to make. A few, for one reason or another, have low self-esteem, and feel depressed, guilty or anxious. Schlenker and Weigold (1990) argued that some of the problems of having to account to others for one's actions may cause serious psychological disorders.

People generally prefer respect and esteem to be enduring and firmly based on genuine personal qualities and real achievements. They vary in the extent to which they enjoy the capacities needed for effective adjustment—intelligence, experience, emotional stability, social skills. Such capacities are regarded as socially desirable, and people like to feel that they possess them. They are often assumed by default, in attributing characteristics to people.

The relationship between reputation and self-esteem depends more on the 'relevance' of a particular public image than on the total size and content of a reputation. In other words, individuals and organisations are more concerned with some publics than with others, namely those that would bring about adverse consequences if reputation were not maintained. So, for example, as scientists or professionals we are more likely to be concerned with our reputation among fellow scientists or professionals than with what the public at large think. These key groups are called 'reference' groups; they are the groups that have the values and life-style to which we aspire. A reputation for delinquency may be exactly the reputation a youth wishes to maintain among his delinquent reference group. Barry (1984) argued that therapists might mistakenly view a client's suicide as harmful to their professional reputation and sense of competence. We are usually most concerned with the impressions we make on *individual* people, namely those with whom our fate is closely tied, those with whom we have significant emotional ties and those whom we regard as influential in our social life.

It is possible to get along without social approval. History records cases—in science, religion and politics—of individuals who have managed to sustain their activities, reach their goals and maintain their self-respect, not merely without social support but in spite of active ridicule, hostility and deprecation associated with severe damage to reputation. Membership of a minority group of like-minded individuals can be an effective buffer against a hostile majority.

Person Perception (Impression Formation)

Person perception deals, among other things, with what attracts our attention about people, how accurately and rapidly we process information about them, how we retain, recognise or reproduce that information in the short term and in the long term, and what inferences we draw from what we observe and remember (see, for example, Hastie et al., 1980 and Jones, 1990). For example, from a person's facial expression and tone of voice, we immediately suppose, possibly mistakenly, that they are angry; or, because of a person's behaviour and circumstances, we later conclude that they are intelligent and well adjusted. We retain an impression of the incident for a time, and possibly give a vague and distorted account of it later to other people.

Livesley and Bromley (1973), Bromley (1977), Schneider, Hastorf and Ellsworth (1979), and Jones (1990) have dealt with person perception. The perception and understanding of other reputational entities—organisations, social institutions, products, and services—appear to have received little attention until the recent emergence of studies in social representations and everyday understanding (Semin and Gergen, 1990). These sorts of perceptual and cognitive processes are central to person perception (impression formation) and central to the formation of primary reputation, which consists of shared impressions based on direct observation of the target person.

Person perception is concerned with the factors affecting our impressions of ourselves and other people. Person perception can be compared and contrasted with the perception of objects and events in the natural world. Bromley (1977) argued that experience with people (as contrasted with experience of objects) in infancy and childhood strongly conditions the development of our perception and understanding of the world. As a result, we are naturally inclined to attribute psychological characteristics to inanimate objects, to think in animistic ways. Such tendencies are commonly observed in adults.

The study of person perception is part of the wider area of social cognition. This includes attribution, social categorisation and schemata, attitudes, the self, and social identity, all of which are relevant to reputation. Fiske and Taylor (1991) have provided a comprehensive review of social cognition and an extensive list of references.

Anthropomorphism

There is a widespread tendency to attribute human characteristics to non-human objects and events. Barker and Miller (1990), for example, described how hurricane Gilbert, which devastated Jamaica in September, 1988, was subsequently talked about in personal terms by the people caught up in the event. The tendency to anthropomorphise in this instance was no doubt strengthened by the practice of using personal forenames to label hurricanes. This practice, according to Barker and Miller, had its origin in World War II when US meteorologists used the names of their wife or girl-friend to identify tropical storms. The advantage of anthropomorphism seems to be that it is a familiar, well-practised and natural tendency that offers a simple, socially acceptable framework for understanding and communication. So, for example, the complex nature and effects of the hurricane could be attributed to Gilbert's arrival, his rage, his destructiveness and even his 'respect' for certain types of roofing. Some of the effects took on political significance—for some, hurricane Gilbert personified social equality because all social classes were affected.

The tendency to attribute psychological characteristics to entities other than people is so ingrained and widespread that it is not surprising that collective entities, such as political parties, nations, firms and institutions, are referred to in terms of their supposed psychological attributes, or are identified with a particular individual. Hitler personifies Nazism and the Nazis: Florence Nightingale personifies care and compassion. It is easier to blame a tyrant than to blame the complex events and power structures that support such a person. Credit for an organisation's success (or blame for its failure) tends to be assigned to the person who is held to be ultimately responsible, rather than to the wider membership. The risk of incurring blame if things go wrong is balanced by the chance of receiving the credit when things go well. It is possible that attributing praise and blame to organisations is affected by the bias that looks for internal causes when explaining the behaviour of others, but looks for external causes when explaining our own behaviour.

The perceptual and cognitive processes underlying the phenomena of reputation are not confined to those involved in person perception. Reputation—including personal reputation, corporate image and brand image—involves a variety of social processes. Reputation has to be examined in the wider context of social psychology. Often, the role of direct observation and inference in the formation of impressions of personality is small compared with the role of indirect influences. Indirect influences operate, for example, when our impressions are formed through hearsay, gossip, rumour and other people's opinions, or by information conveyed through the media. We sometimes accept such information uncritically, paying little attention to the credibility of the information or its source. Reputation reflects the way social factors generate shared (collective) perceptions of and beliefs about people, organisations, products, services and other sorts of entity, especially those that can be assigned human-like attributes metaphorically—for example diseases, social movements and supernatural agencies (holy places, saints, idols, talismans, and so on).

The special features of person perception that call for comment regarding reputation are as follows. First, persons are reactive—their characteristics alter in response to, or in anticipation of, attention from others. Second, persons are proactive—they can command the attention of others, and 'present' themselves in ways calculated to foster a particular sort of impression. Third, persons can dissimulate—they can conceal their true state of mind and simulate another. Fourth, persons can sometimes detect dissimulation in others. Fifth, persons are causal and moral agents—their behaviour has consequences, and they can be held responsible for those that are intended or foreseeable; indeed, actions may not be comprehensible without the agent's account. Sixth, social learning enables most people to acquire the knowledge, language and social skills needed to understand and interact with others. It does not follow, of course, that the processes involved in perceiving *persons* are exactly the same as the processes involved in perceiving other types of entity, for example social groups. The exact processes at work are a matter of empirical enquiry (Hamilton, 1992).

We share various beliefs, values, attitudes and forms of conduct with other people, although there are wide differences between individuals. A reputation comprises a complex changing system of impressions shared among members of a social network. It is embedded in a wider system of impressions and information covering all aspects of life.

People observe others and interact with them. They register not only the other person's coping behaviour (what they do or say, or fail to do or say), but also the person's expressive behaviour (how they behave—their demeanour, posture, gestures and so on). They assume that certain outward characteristics—accent, appearance, or whatever—indicate other characteristics, such as social class, social attitude, personality traits or life-style. Through conversation, including the associated nods and winks, and the many ways in which ordinary language can convey implicit meanings, information is transmitted and influence exerted.

People can look at the same information selectively from different perspectives, and so interpret it differently. A person's nonverbal expressive behaviour—facial expression, eye contact, posture and gesture, and so on—carries considerable weight in the impressions we form of their personal characteristics and state of mind. We sometimes regard people's spontaneous expressive behaviour as more 'revealing', in some ways, than what they actually say or do. There is no limit to the significance we can read into such behaviour or into the reactions it elicits. Reactions such as like/dislike, trust/mistrust, dominance/submission and intimacy/distance are particularly important.

There are modes of communication other than those associated with face-to-face interaction. There are the mass media and the more specialised media, such as conferences, lectures, circulars, articles, books and pamphlets, associated with particular sectors of the public—political associations, professional organisations, religious groups and so on. These too play a part in the formation of impressions.

Agreement between observers does not necessarily validate the attribution made, although it has long been used in this way. Interactants in daily life sometimes form the same impression of a target person independently of each other. These facts link personality with primary reputation. Kenrick and Funder (1988) reviewed the person–situation controversy and concluded that personality assessments can be valid, and can be distinguished from shared impressions (see also Park, 1986). The point to remember is that shared first-hand impressions provide provisional evidence of a person's actual characteristics, but not *conclusive* evidence.

First Impressions

We sometimes make snap judgements of people—initial impressions based on fragmentary evidence. Such judgements depend upon pre-existing frames of reference built up through experience, possibly without a substantial rational basis. For example, we make snap judgements based on physical appearance, accent, demeanour and expressed opinions. First impressions can have considerable effects on person perception, but such impressions are unlikely to persist for long in the face of counter-evidence from closer acquaintance. Vonk and Heiser (1991) have studied the effects of familiarity on observers' descriptions of others. Paradoxically, perhaps, superficial acquaintanceship could lead to a high-consensus type of reputation based on common stereotyped judgements, such as those based on physical appearance, nationality, accent, colour or creed (Chapter 5). Closer acquaintance, however, is likely to reduce consensus because of the diversity of information available to different observers and interactants.

Attribution

Attribution is a word used in social cognition to refer to inferences in which actions are interpreted in terms of personal characteristics or circumstances, to provide a causal exlanation for or a moral judgement on that behaviour (Shaver, 1975; Jaspars, Fincahm and Hewstone, 1983). For example, a person's success might be attributed to his or her ability and determination, or conversely to situational factors, such as help from others. The moral judgement might approve or disapprove of the person's motivation, depending upon the observer's ethical standpoint. We might attribute a firm's success to its research and development or to its public relations, and we might hold a person or company morally responsible for an accident or failure.

Attributional processes are part of our natural inclination to impose a 'pattern of meaning' on what we observe, to make sense of the world. We need to do this to anticipate events, and to react adaptively to events as they occur. The processes are no doubt influenced by motivational and emotional factors but are generally analysed in cognitive terms. For example, the expression on someone's face may be taken to mean that they are not pleased, and that it is something we have done that has caused the displeasure. This leads us to anticipate questions and accusations, and to come up with the appropriate apologies, excuses or denials. In this situation each party is engaged in attributing characteristics to the other.

Concerning reputation, the most obvious effect of attribution is on consistency and coherence. Having learned about some characteristics of a person through social interaction, we are likely to infer associated characteristics. For example, on hearing that you are a psychologist, people are inclined to assume that you can make an instant personality assessment. Such effects are produced by people's 'implicit personality theories' (Schneider, Hastorf and Ellsworth, 1979).

A major feature of attributional processes is the division of the causes of behaviour into two kinds: internal (within the person) and external (in the outside circumstances). For example, we can lay the blame for an accident on the person, because of fatigue, or on the situation, because of faulty equipment. In practice, of course, events that call for explanation often have complex, interacting internal and external causes. Some external factors are important in explaining people's behaviour, for example threats, promises and opportunities. If we are unable to find a rational explanation, we are likely to categorise people as 'strange', 'eccentric', 'insane' or 'not themselves'.

A person's reputation is usually described in terms of stable, internal attributes, although an attribute such as 'lucky' suggests that some people enjoy more favourable circumstances and life-chances than do others. In some professions, such as sport, stockbroking, or scientific research, competition is strong and chance plays an important role. But success or failure is likely to be attributed to ability rather than to luck.

Attribution plays a part in reputation when we falsely assume that the characteristics expressed in social role behaviour are spontaneous expressions of personality characteristics. It is clearly wrong to confuse an actor's personality with the roles the actor plays. On the other hand, some social roles cannot be enacted effectively if the person lacks certain personal qualities—ability, temperament, or whatever. Many social roles—teacher, physician, sales representative—require the player to 'put on an act' at times; thus observers and interactants form a false impression of the person enacting the role.

Research into attribution shows that people are not always aware of the factors that influence their behaviour or the factors that influence their interpretation of other people's behaviour. Attributional processes are important in self-perception. In 'person' perception, attention is focused more on the person than on the situation—hence the tendency to attribute someone's behaviour to personal characteristics rather than to the circumstances he or she is facing. In 'self' perception, on the other hand, attention is focused more on the circumstances facing us and how to respond, hence the tendency to account for our own behaviour in terms of circumstances rather than in terms of our personal qualities.

Stable personal qualities, such as temperamental traits and abilities, are taken for granted. Explanations in terms of inner personal characteristics are more likely to refer to temporary states of mind, for example feelings, expectations and desires. The observer's assumption about personal or situational factors is easily challenged by drawing attention to the alternative type of explanation. The 'fundamental attribution error' is the common tendency to attribute other people's behaviour to internal factors and to attribute one's own behaviour to external factors. Internal and external attributions can be made for either actor or observer, but, in general, internal attributions tend to be preferred for both actor and observer. This is relevant to reputation because information about a person's behaviour often comes to us indirectly, through hearsay. Such reports are likely to include attributional information supplied by informants, where inferences are confused with observations. Journalists, like scientists, are supposed to distinguish between news (observations) and comment (interpretation).

The fundamental attribution error, or actor–observer effect, is most likely to affect our perception of the people we know least well or know only indirectly through hearsay. Having little or no information about the circumstances affecting the target person's behaviour, and being driven by our 'effort after meaning', we are inclined to attribute their behaviour to internal characteristics, their traits or states of mind. When we make judgements about people we know reasonably well or empathise with, we are more likely to take account of the way situational factors affect their behaviour. The initial discrepancy between actors and observers in their explanations of behaviour means that it is sometimes difficult for them to agree about what should be done to improve performance.

By definition, we have little experience of why people behave as they do in unusual circumstances. As a result, we are more likely to attribute distinctive behaviour to internal factors, as in awards for gallantry or charges of dereliction of duty, which would naturally feature prominently in reputation; non-distinctive behaviour would be attributed to the external situation, because the common internal characteristics would be taken for granted.

We respond to our own behaviour by way of self-criticism or self-congratulation; but such accounts often have to be negotiated with others who sometimes hold different views from ourselves. If we are held responsible, we have to justify our behaviour. Less problematically, we may reluctantly accept other people's acclaim.

Behaviour that is regarded as normal or expected does not usually call for comment, it is self-explanatory. Behaviour that is deviant or unexpected, on the other hand, is more noteworthy and calls for comment or explanation. Such behaviour is assumed to reveal more about the person. reputations, therefore, are likely to contain a high proportion of features that distinguish one individual from others, and indicate deviation from what is regarded as normal or expected.

In ordinary discourse, much information is implicit and taken for granted, as with a person's age, sex and social role. These details might have to be spelled out only to someone who was totally unacquainted with the person being referred to.

Reports about people in daily life commonly contain no behavioural data in the strict sense, but rather generalisations and interpretations. Consider the difference between 'He insulted me' and 'He said, "You are talking too much" '. If a report does describe actual behaviour, it is likely to describe the circumstances in which the behaviour occurred. Listeners will then make whatever attributions seem appropriate, depending upon their own personal qualities, circumstances and point of view.

Attributions depend upon background knowledge and belief. Cultural factors and experience are relevant here. For example, beliefs in witchcraft influence attributions regarding the cause of an accident or illness. The words used in attributional statements may reveal cultural assumptions. Different experiences with and attitudes towards delinquents influence the attributions made by the police and by counsellors regarding delinquent behaviour. Information about reputation is processed (interpreted and transformed) by the receiver according to his or her belief system, and subsequently transmitted to other people, for example in casual conversation or at a case conference. Background assumptions and local circumstances can distort the transmission of information.

Attributions are important in connection with primary reputation. Primary reputation is the consensus built up from direct contact with the target entity through observation and interaction. Here, the behaviour itself is observed, and the attribution of cause, reason or responsibility follows immediately if the person and the circumstances are familiar to the observer. In secondary reputation, however, information about the target entity is often pre-packaged, as it were. The behavioural information, if reported at all, is usually interpreted in an attributional framework.

Attributional frameworks are often simple mental models: stereotyped interpretations of behaviour. We can attribute a person's behaviour to snobbishness, carelessness, grief, affection, compassion, poverty, illness, unforeseen circumstances, or a host of other factors available from common sense and expressed in the ordinary language of daily life. For example, we usually attribute grief to the loss of an object or person of great affection. The importance of this point is that our 'effort after meaning' inclines us to jump to conclusions; commonly accepted attributional frameworks enable us to do this. Attributional analyses of a more sophisticated sort require time, effort, ability and detailed information.

The salience of behaviour is important in reputation, as mentioned elsewhere. Normal behaviour is uninformative in that it is self-explanatory. Behaviour that is out of the ordinary captures and holds attention, and provokes 'effort after meaning'; it is the *behaviour* that calls for explanation rather than the *circumstances*. Of course, circumstances that are out of the ordinary capture and hold attention.

The attributional process known as the 'self-serving bias' (Schlenker, Weigold and Hallam, 1990) is the tendency to give credit to ourselves for our successes but to blame our failures on external circumstances. It is relevant to the issues of self-esteem and self-presentation in the accounts we give to ourselves and others by way of explaining or justifying our behaviour (Chapter 7). The self-serving bias is pervasive: some students attribute their poor performance to poor teaching, library facilities, financial circumstances, and domestic problems; business people blame the unions, the economy, the government; sports people blame the temperature, the altitude, the referee.

Another bias in attribution is for the observer's attention to be drawn to the more dramatic, vivid or salient features of a situation. Salience is the extent to which a person or other reputational entity stands out from other entities of the same sort, or the extent to which a particular attribute stands out among others. Salience is determined by many factors—physical appearance, proximity, importance, and so on. Some factors are coincidental, others are deliberately arranged. In social interaction, we attend more to some people than to others, and we attend more to some of their attributes than to others. But the factors that make some people and some characteristics more salient than others are likely to be common to large numbers of people, thus fostering consensus on at least some attributes of reputation. This sort of perceptual focusing makes the observer more likely to take account of these features when offering an explanation. Reputational information, therefore, often refers to behaviour characteristics that are unusual or unexpected. That is to say, normal behaviour is literally 'unremarkable'.

Another bias is the tendency to jump to conclusions, making inferences on the basis of insufficient evidence. This bias is strong where observers have well-established frames of reference for dealing with particular kinds of situations, as in stereotyped reactions to ethnic, religious or occupational characteristics. There is a tendency to simple categorisations of other people—to label them, to see them in terms of one dimension only, as warm or cold, sociable or unsociable. By contrast, we tend to think of ourselves as complex or multi-dimensional. A difference is seen in ratings of the self and others (Sande, Goethals and Radloff, 1988).

The types of attributes assigned to entities depends to some extent on the age, sex, ability, experience and other characteristics of respondents. Young children, for example, are more inclined to refer to concrete, surface attributes, such as physical appearance and actions, whereas older children and adults are more inclined to refer to abstract, underlying attributes, such as traits, values and motives. The exact ways in which the characteristics of respondents affect their understanding of reputational entities has to be determined empirically for particular classes of entity; the effects are likely to depend on contextual factors. The point is that an entity's reputation in an audience comprising people of a similar sort will be strongly influenced by their common characteristics, as shown elsewhere in connection with teachers' reputations among students (Chapter 14).

Manifest and Latent Reputations

One person's knowledge of or opinion about another person may be correct but unimportant; reputational attributions are usually interesting or important. Sometimes a person's ideas are vague and unformulated. This makes it convenient to distinguish between the *manifest* and the *latent* content of reputation. The manifest content consists of those ideas and feelings that we make explicit spontaneously as statements or opinions. The latent content consists of those ideas and feelings that we are prepared to agree with when we are given the opportunity—for example, in a conversation or in response to a survey questionnaire—but would not normally express spontaneously. Although we cannot always recall information from memory or find the words to express an attitude, we can usually recognise an item of information and agree with a statement that seems to accord with our attitude. In other words, reputation has a foreground (manifest content) and a background (latent content). The manifest content consists of those impressions that are voiced because they are interesting, unusual or important. Only those impressions that are voiced are communicated to others; they contribute to a reputation, and may eventually become widely shared—either because other observers form the same impressions independently and voice them, or because other people feel inclined or are persuaded to agree.

The latent elements in a reputation include individual impressions that are not shared with others. People have ideas and feelings that they regard as trivial or private, or that they are afraid to express. Their status and position in the social network may prevent their ideas from circulating. If circumstances change, however, impressions that were formerly latent or implicit can become manifest. Low-frequency attributions can increase in frequency, and high-frequency attributions can decrease. Given the appropriate operational definition, opinions expressed by just one person, i.e. idiosyncratic opinions, can be counted as manifest parts of a reputation. Normally, however, reputational attributes are assumed to be those that are shared, usually widely shared, in an audience or interest group. The latent contents of reputation comprise those items of information that respondents cannot or choose not to put into words. Such items are potentially manifest contents awaiting the circumstances that will make them explicit and communicable.

Collective impressions, like individual impressions, can incorporate a number of attributions. These attributions tend to be psychologically consistent, but can be logically inconsistent, as with social stereotypes and prejudices that combine and rationalise contrasting negative attributions, for example meanness and lavish lifestyle.

The main structure of personal reputation consists of a nucleus of interconnected impressions shared and expressed by a high proportion of members of a defined social network. These central, manifest impressions occupy the foreground of the collective impression, the background of which usually consists of a larger and wider range of impressions that are less widely shared and less systematically connected. If there are distinct subgroups within the social network, then a person's reputation consists of a number of subreputations. Shared reputational attributions form what is called a 'social representation', i.e. a collective image of the entity referred to (Chapter 5). The collective image is shaped by the social processes at work in and on the interest group.

Primary and Secondary Reputations

Under one set of conditions, beliefs about a few key attributes of the target person are widely known among members of a group. This reflects the standard definition of reputation as 'What is generally known or believed about a person'. Over time, however, additional information seems to dilute reputation in the following ways.

First, one peculiar feature of primary reputation (reputation based on direct, first-hand acquaintance) is that the information in circulation can be more diffusely spread than for secondary reputation (reputation based on hearsay). This could be a consequence of the target person being or becoming known as an *individual person*, rather than as a *type of person*. In other words, direct, first-hand contact leads to highly individualised impressions, whereas indirect contact based on hearsay leads to stereotyped impressions. Formal interaction with a person in a role relationship restricts the expression of individual personal characteristics, and the impression formed tends to be stereotyped. Public personages, people with high status or well-known personalities, are likely to behave in a stereotyped way appropriate to the situation, so that, again, a widespread, stereotyped impression is formed by others.

Second, reputations that for any reason occupy the attention of an audience over a considerable period of time can become more diffuse rather than more concentrated (more widely shared). This might be because time allows more information to filter into and through a communication network. In theory, given enough time, the information should spread throughout the group; so, if the group were composed of people of the same sort, equally exposed to information and influence, then each person would have roughly the same set of views about a target entity. In practice, human groups contain different sorts of individuals, unequally exposed to information and influence; each of them is likely to form a somewhat different impression of the target entity, and that impression is likely to vary from one occasion to another.

The variation in the frequency of occurrence of characteristics attributed to an entity by a group of people can be seen as the result of competition between the contrasting pressures of conformity and diversity. Moreover, the group as a whole is likely to contain more information than any one individual can conveniently handle. Consequently, individuals assimilate and retain information selectively according to their particular abilities, interests and circumstances. Over time, under stable conditions, these individual impressions reach an optimum size, have their individual contents and organisation, and contribute to a greater or lesser extent to the *collective* representation.

Circumstances connect the activities and welfare of the individual members of primary groups. In a primary group, individuals interact frequently in a direct person-to-person way, so that interpersonal relationships are established, such as dependency, family partnerships and working relationships, as well as relationships of dislike or affection. The members of a primary group are to some extent emotionally involved with each other because their 'fates' are bound up together.

Members of a primary group form impressions of the persons with whom they interact. They normally try to establish and maintain a good reputation within it; informal mechanisms of social control reinforce this tendency. The impressions they form have idiosyncratic features because of the unique patterns and circumstances of direct person-to-person interaction. Each member's direct first-hand impression is likely to be modified by indirect information and influence coming from other members of the group, whose impressions of people are formed in a similar way.

A 'primary reputation' can be defined in a number of ways. First, it can be defined by the totality of opinions circulating within a primary face-to-face group. This takes account of idiosyncratic impressions. Second, it can be defined by those opinions that are fairly widespread within the group; this takes account of the 'collective' character of reputation. People normally belong to a number of different primary groups, so that they have a number of primary reputations. Third, it can be defined by the set of shared attributions, excluding only idiosyncratic beliefs.

The concept of 'primary reputation' is linked with the concept of 'secondary reputation'. Secondary groups consist of sets of interrelated primary groups forming a larger extended social network, such as a business organisation, a religion, a university, a local community, and so on. Primary groups are interlocked in a functional sense in secondary groups and have overlapping membership, so people belong to several primary groups in several secondary groups. The point is that information and influence are generated in and flow through these social networks. Information about a particular person is likely to be concentrated in local (primary group) areas of an extended network; but information and influence can spread. Whether it does so depends upon a variety of circumstances (Chapters 5 and 6).

Secondary reputation refers to those opinions in circulation in an extended social network that are not based on, or closely connected with, direct face-to-face contact with the person concerned. Unlike the members within a primary group, people outside have little or no chance to test their opinions about a person (known only at second hand, by hearsay) through direct person-to-person interaction. Their impressions are likely to be simple and stereotyped—conforming to prevailing opinion. The people within the primary groups usually generate information about a person, whereas the people outside relay it. There are complications, however, because information can be lost or distorted in transmission, and misinformation can be accidentally or deliberately introduced by various sources.

Multiple Reputations

A person has as many reputations as there are distinct social groups whose members interact with him or her or for some reason take an interest in that individual. It follows that the image formed in one group is likely to be different from the image formed in another group, because the factors that influence the formation of the image are different. The person behaves differently in different groups; different groups are composed of different categories of person with different expectations and with different sorts and levels of interaction with the person; different groups have different communication networks and opinion leaders, and are exposed to different sorts of coincidental influences affecting the impressions they form of the person.

If our associates fall into distinct groups, for instance colleagues at work or political associates, we are likely to foster different impressions in those different groups. The people in those groups are likely to form different impressions of us because they have somewhat different frames of reference, different concerns, different sorts of background information, and are exposed to different aspects of our behaviour.

For both persons and organisations, the question is 'Does our reputation in this or that social network matter?' A social group that has little or no influence on one's fate is of little or no consequence. One's fate, of course, is tied up with the fate of other people (and various social organisations); the reputation one has in a particular group could have consequences for other people's reputations (and therefore their fate), just as their reputation could have consequences for oneself. Goumaz (1982) discussed the way that children with behaviour problems can damage a school's reputation unless they are effectively integrated. From a marketing point of view, and from a reputation-management point of view, the question is the same. An organisation's main public relations effort has to be directed at those social groups whose behaviour, directly or indirectly, affect its fate.

Some large organisations, such as commercial conglomerates, consist of a large number of interrelated subsidiary organisations. Each subsidiary has its own localised reputations in its geographical region and in its sector of the market. The question is 'How do these subsidiary reputations add up or average out to an overall reputation?' Each group or level within the conglomerate develops its reputation in its relevant audiences. At the highest level, the organisation has a reputation based on its overall effects on interested parties—politicians, unions, the financial market, and so on. In other words, whereas a single entity, such as a person, might be said to have different reputations indifferent groups, a complex organisation, such as a conglomerate, is best thought of as a system of interrelated entities, each with its own identity and reputations. The organisation as a whole might find it difficult to coordinate a multiplicity of activities, identities and reputations. Indeed, there could be advantages in maintaining separate identities and reputations.

Restricting Reputation

Under normal circumstances, people do not try to restrict the extent of their reputation; on the contrary, most people like to be widely known. In other circumstances, however, people deliberately avoid direct or indirect contact with people outside a small trusted circle. This could be the case, for example, with people who for one reason or another have changed their identity, or people engaged in espionage or terrorism or other criminal activities, or reclusive people who feel threatened by publicity, or members of minority groups whose activities are not approved of by the wider society. The methods used to restrict the extent of reputation include avoidance of people outside the trusted circle, the use of 'gate-keepers' to block inquiries, the use of public relations personnel to 'put up a front' or to present a pseudo-reputation.

International Reputation and National Character

Consideration of a country's reputation abroad, or its international reputation, raises the question 'Which sets of people or organisations provide a basis for an international reputation?' These could be opinion leaders with access to the mass media, they could be members of foreign governments, or spokespersons for business, scientific, cultural or sporting interests. Their views are assumed to represent informed opinion.

Communication and influence at an international level are different, in some ways at least, from communication and influence at lower levels of social organisation. In particular, the barriers to effective communication and influence are greater because of differences in language and culture, and because even high-technology communication cannot substitute fully for direct face-to-face interaction. Advertising and propaganda, for example, have to be carefully adjusted to the language, culture, beliefs and values of the people at whom they are directed.

The phrase 'international reputation' or 'international image' is commonly used in journalism. The difficulty of assessing a country's international image, or the international image of any person or entity—scientist, musician, nuclear power, religious movement—is obvious. Common usage indicates that it is usually personal impressions based on selected data sources (other journalists, foreign correspondents, government officials, opinion leaders and media output). The phrase refers to a convenient fiction; the problem is to work out what importance to attach to such impressions.

A nation's 'national character' can be viewed from the inside or the outside, as it were. A nation's internal view of itself, its 'self-image', is largely favourable; the external view, the view from another country, is likely to be less favourable and more variable (Wilterdink, 1992). For example, in 1992, the importance of national stereotypes was shown at a UK Government meeting on relations with West Germany, and the subsequent resignation of a government minister over remarks about the German national character.

Validity of Reputation

An interested investigator who wants to understand what an entity is really like, i.e. what is known about an entity, as opposed to what is believed from hearsay, has to make direct observations, or find objective evidence, or discover who the key informants are and what value to place on their information—important skills for a detective, an investigative reporter, a biographer, and so on. The important thing is to appreciate the difference between, and the relationship between, an entity and its reputation.

Some reputations may be invalid, exaggerated and otherwise ill founded. Consider, for example, the reputed aphrodisiac effects of rhinoceros horn, the quality of Liverpool humour (among Liverpudlians!) or the chronicity of schizophrenia (Zubin et al., 1985).

It is natural to assume that a good reputation is valid evidence of the character of the entity it represents; and a good reputation is a presumption in law (Chapter 9). There are instances, however, where this assumption proves false. This is easily seen in instances where, say, someone of good standing is found to have done wrong, as in a financial or political scandal. Consider a different sort of example: Fox (1977) reported that the charity, the Samaritans, had a favourable public image. Fox seemed to regard this as evidence that the Samaritans contributed significantly to the reduction, by one-third, of the suicide rate in Britain since the Samaritans had been nationally organised. The argument could be the other way round: a reduction in suicides since its inception could be cited as objective evidence that justifies the Samaritans' good reputation, provided independent evidence of a causal link could be established. The introduction of North Sea gas, and greater care in dispensing medicinal drugs, could have been contributory factors reducing the number of suicides. *Post hoc, ergo propter hoc* is not a valid form of argument.

The representational validity of reputation refers to how truly it represents the entity to which it refers. This has to be established empirically, which can be difficult. The relationship between evidence of reputation and evidence of performance is likely to vary from one set of circumstances to another. The law deals with the difficulty by considering evidence of 'general reputation', obtained from credible informants, without entering into detailed arguments about the validity of their testimony.

For practical purposes and in research, however, information about reputation should be checked against evidence that is more objective. For example, when selecting a university, joining a company, or buying a product or service, one needs to go beyond advertisements, brochures and word of mouth, to criteria such as staff/student ratios, library facilities, conditions of service, guarantees, and so on. An organisation making decisions about appointments is likely to rely heavily on the reports of 'experts' (referees, head-hunters, former employers) but will also take account of objective evidence of performance. Referees' reports are, as in law, statements of reputation from what are regarded as the best-informed sources. They may or may not reflect the individual's wider reputation(s). The reputations of academic institutions, in the USA at least, as judged by peer ratings or nominations, are fairly closely correlated with their research productivity, as judged by citation counts. But there are shifts over time in both indices. Over (1982) demonstrated a durable link between psychologists' reputation (peer ranking) and their citation counts. Golden, Kuperman and Osmon (1980) assessed the relative standing of clinical psychology programmes by counting the publications of staff. Howard, Cole and Maxwell (1987) found a strong relationship between reputation and research output for psychology institutions, but the relationship varied with the size of the institution and the journals in which the research was published. Sindelar and Schloss (1987) found a relationship between rankings for citation count, reputation and number of publications.

The relationship between a reputation and what it is supposed to represent raises a scientific question. Is it possible to identify objective criteria that would (a) establish the nature and scope of a reputation, and (b) test the representational validity of that reputation, i.e. test the extent to which the public image corresponds to the real entity it represents? The nature and extent of a reputation can be investigated in a number of ways (Chapter 16). The validity of some types of reputation can be assessed against objective criteria, such as citation counts for scientists, votes in an election, nominations for office or an award. These and other 'performance criteria' are not substitutes for data on reputation; they indicate the extent to which a person's reputation corresponds with inferences (or implicit expectations) based on reputation. A company might enjoy a favourable public image (sponsoring the arts, making donations to charities) but engage in doubtful trading practices and exploit some sections of the public. If performance criteria are made public, however, they contribute to reputation and so are no longer *independent* criteria for representational validity.

Receiving information about an entity's reputation enlarges the recipient's knowledge of that entity and normally facilitates effective action. The distribution of information about an entity in a group gives individual members access to a much wider range of information and influence than would be possible on the basis of direct personal contact with the entity.

Posthumous Reputation

Lang and Lang (1990) studied nearly 300 men and women who had pursued artistic careers in print-making and identified factors affecting posthumous reputation. These included: education, family circumstances, social relationships and sponsorship, apart from coincidental (chance) factors. It is important that some actual products or records of achievement survive as criteria for historical judgement. These and other factors are likely to affect posthumous reputation in other areas such as science, politics, religion and military affairs.

Objective public records normally provide good evidence of reputation, but public records and other sorts of objective data can be lost, destroyed, ignored, altered or fabricated. These are people, organisations or events of historical or social significance. It requires painstaking historical research to confirm or refute the supposed connections between personality and performance. Without detailed records and research, it may not be possible to be sure of the facts. The reputations of ordinary people are relatively simple social representations shared among the people who know them, directly or indirectly. These impressions may survive a generation or more, especially if they are associated with memorabilia—photographs, letters, awards, and so on.

Reputation in History, Fiction and Biography

People are remembered in different ways. For some, the salient features of the impression are concrete, particular images—faces, names, logos, slogans—or simple anecdotes. These may be the sorts of impressions kept alive by the media and by other cultural institutions, such as schools, festivals and ceremonies. They remain prominent in collective memory. For others, those interested in social history or the particular individuals remembered, the impressions are more complex and propositional. They include more information on the person's character, life and achievements, with interpretive and evaluative judgements. The better-known personages come to symbolise or personify important cultural values—courage, intelligence, sacrifice, and so on. Thus we have the collective posthumous reputations of Napoleon, George Washington, Joan of Arc, Machiavelli and Al Capone, for example.

Individuals who are well known during their lifetime may leave little or no residue in the collective memory. Social changes can shift the focus of public interest away from some people towards others, or away from one sort of attribute to another. Deliberate attempts to destroy a person's good reputation may be successful.

We must not neglect the role of fiction (in books, magazines, films, television) in presenting images of various kinds—of peoples, countries, disasters, individuals or companies. Some sections of the public confuse factual reporting and fictional stories, especially when the factual reporting is fragmented and unconsciously selected or distorted. Thus we may wrongly expect a film star or an historical figure to have been the sort of person portrayed in a work of fiction (consider Shakespeare's Richard III, or Schaefer's Mozart). Similarly, our beliefs and expectations about politicians and other people in the public eye are likely to be biased by satire and by thinly disguised fictions.

In some circumstances, over time, a 'story' can develop into a powerful myth or legend, as with political and religious ideologies. In some instances, the central feature of the ideology is entirely fictitious, although its originators may have thought it to be a matter of fact, as with belief systems involving magic and the supernatural. King Arthur and other legendary figures are personifications of abstract and general beliefs and values of cultural importance, such as love, honour and chivalry. The idea of reputation as honour or name features in Celtic myths. Behaviour was regulated partly by taboos (geis). To break a taboo meant not only loss of honour, but possibly misery and death. Banks and Zil (1980) cited Ibsen's supposedly autobiographical character Peer Gynt as a fictional example of character disorder and resentment resulting from society's lack of social recognition of a person.

Simonton (1991) examined Galton's question as to whether reputation is a fair test of natural ability. Galton (1869) was interested in eminent people whose eminence lay in the social recognition of their achievements. Although reputation undergoes serial changes during the lifetime of an individual and subsequent to his or her death, agreement about posthumous reputation is reached in time, although as Simonton shows, agreement can be reached through different causal paths.

It is possible to quantify reputation in various ways. One can measure the space allotted to people in history books and works of reference, one can count citations, or obtain ratings from experts. According to Simonton (1991), there is usually considerable agreement between different measures of posthumous reputation, and considerable stability over time.

Achievement depends, to a greater or lesser degree, on ability, experience, effort and circumstances—familiar concepts in the study of attribution. Clearly, achievements that bring social eminence require ability of sorts, depending upon the nature of those achievements. Simonton examined several measures of reputation spread over several years for large samples of eminent people— Presidents of the USA, philosophers, artists and composers of classical music. The correlations between different measures of reputation for each of these groups supported the idea of an underlying common factor or set of factors.

One advantage of studying reputation in historical perspective is that one is more likely to separate the personality from the achievements. Contemporary reputations, on the other hand, are more likely to conflate personality and achievement. Simonton reminds us that eminence associated with achievement usually depends on high productivity. Lehman (1953) showed that quantity and quality of intellectual achievement are associated. Simonton's main point seems to be that although posthumous reputation is the product of a complex social process it is firmly anchored in a basic set of personality attributes.

The controversy surrounding the late Sir Cyril Burt is an example of a radical shift in historical reputation (Hearnshaw, 1979), and there are many other examples. Skanes (1984) commented on how Francis Galton's views on heredity had diminished his reputation in psychology. Coleman (1982) has described B. F. Skinner's life and reputation. Morrant (1985) has defended Freud's reputation following Masson's (1985) criticisms.

Many famous people, in the arts, science, literature, religion and politics, have been closely investigated, but these studies are biographical. They investigate the person rather than the reputation, although they make considerable use of the impressions of key informants, and comment on the person's reputation(s). Crick (1980) wrote a biography of George Orwell but found that he had to describe how Orwell appeared to different people at different times, because the accounts he obtained were contradictory. Some biographies possibly avoid such contradictions by their selective use of material.

End Note

Throughout the text, I make comparisons between different sorts of reputational entity, which together amount to an 'extended analogy', with a view to exploring what might be called the 'dynamics' of reputation for different sorts of entity.

4 Personality, the Self, Social Identity and Social Deviation

PERSONALITY, THE SELF AND SOCIAL IDENTITY

Introduction

In psychology, the word 'personality' is used to refer to those personal characteristics that bring about consistencies and regularities in a person's behaviour over time and across different situations. The concepts of 'personality' and 'reputation' are closely linked. May (1932) went as far as defining personality as 'social stimulus value', i.e. reputation (Chapter 2). This view was subsequently rejected, but it survives in the sense that, in the absence of more objective evidence, evidence of reputation is assumed to indicate personality. The conceptual and methodological problems associated with the study of personality continue to be the subject of debate and research. The literature is extensive.

The problem of consistency in personality and behaviour has been a major focus of research in psychology, and has led to contradictory and inconclusive results. The safest conclusion is that although people strive for consistency, claim to be consistent and expect others to be consistent, they are nevertheless sometimes aware of inconsistencies in their beliefs and attitudes, and behave in ways that others regard as inconsistent.

Personality and Reputation

Personality can be studied as a process over time or as a set of characteristics present at a particular time. There are limits to the relevance of life-history information, but if such information is widely known or easily available, it finds its way into the person's reputation because the contents of people's impressions of others are governed by factors such as availability, simplicity and consistency, and by social processes, such as audience interests, beliefs and attitudes, that operate independently of the target person. Reputation too can be studied as a process (serial changes in attributions over a period) or as a product (a set of attributions at a particular time for a particular interest group) (Chapter 14). Changes in reputation and changes in personality take place with some degree of independence. It takes time for information about changes in personality to spread through a social network. It also takes time for a person to become aware of changes in his or her reputation, and to adjust to them.

Craik (1989) summarised an investigation made by Peterson in 1965 in which Q-Sort personality assessments were made of US Air Force captains by panels of judges and based on their performance in a variety of circumstances. It was reported that the composite panel judgements were reliable (+ 0.83), although there was considerable variation in the individual judgements for particular items. A second independent assessment using an adjective check-list correlated reasonably well (+ 0.73) with the first assessment. These results indicate variations in agreement among observers given access to the same behavioural data and using common methods of assessment, but forming their impressions independently of each other.

The consensus found in studies of reputation in the normal circumstances of daily life is not achieved in this way. Personality research of the sort mentioned above has little relevance to the study of reputation. What it indicates is that observers' impressions of an individual differ even when they observe the same behaviour and use the same method of recording their judgements. It also indicates that reliable judgements are possible only when results can be averaged over several similar observers working in standard conditions. The circumstances governing the formation of reputation are clearly different.

Personality can be assessed in several ways—by self-report inventories or other personality tests, and by ratings (or other indices) made by observers using standard procedures. These observers do not represent the person's social contacts, and usually operate independently of each other. Their judgements are averaged to obtain a single measure of each attribute assessed. The result says nothing about the person's reputation outside the laboratory. The averaged measures do not index the person's reputation, except in a special sense, in the group of assessors. Reputation can be represented by a single index, but is best seen as a *distribution* of attributions among a group of assessors or repondents— an attribute × assessor matrix—as in Table 4.1 (see also Chapters 1 and 14).

The relationships between reputation and the target person can be better understood if we shift the emphasis from the target's 'personality' (usually

Table 4.1. A hypothetical attribution × assessor matrix showing the distribution of attributions for a target

Assessor	Attributions					
	a	b	c	d	e	etc.
1	+		+		+	
2	+		+	+	+	
3		+	+			
4		+	+	+	+	
5		+	+		+	
etc.						

defined by traits) to the target's characteristics and circumstances. The rarely used word 'personalia' covers virtually everything that might pertain to a person—observations, anecdotes, circumstances, states of mind, dispositions, future prospects. Almost any item of personal information can find its way into reputation: for a review of the sorts of information typically found in free descriptions of persons, see Bromley (1977); for the inference of traits (dispositions) from everyday actions, see Buss and Craik (1983a, 1983b).

Although a person's reputation can be summed up in a word or phrase, this summary statement can usually be 'unpacked', at least by a first-hand informant, to yield details, examples, sources, justifications and other personalia. Sometimes, however, details are lacking, and the source or basis of the information is omitted, presumably because it is regarded as less relevant than the focal information. The difficulty of tracing sources or validating information about reputation explains why evidence about reputation presents problems in civil and criminal trials (Chapter 9).

Representative observers from one of the target person's reputational communities may not collectively provide a reliable and valid personality assessment. This is because their knowledge of the person is restricted to particular behaviour settings, and because social factors influence the transmission of information.

Cooley and Seeman (1979) used a Personality Integration Reputation Test to show that personality integration was related to subjects' social relationships. The confusion between personality and reputation arises because when *close* acquaintances are used as assessors, their impressions seem to be fairly accurate and stable (at least for those aspects of the person's behaviour to which they are privy). Minor biases and slight differences in perspective are assumed to cancel out, given several different observers, so that the average impression gives a reasonably valid assessment of an individual's personality. We fail to recognise the limited amount of credible, first-hand data circulating among our acquaintances, as compared with hearsay and guesswork. Moreover, close acquaintances are likely to have shared their impressions with each other, further increasing the likelihood of agreement and the elimination of errors of judgement. In these circumstances, reliability and validity could be high.

A person's reputation among close acquaintances is often the only available 'personality' assessment, and is useful in some research and applied settings. The danger is that if close acquaintances are drawn from a narrow section of the person's reputational community, they may share certain judgemental biases about the person (see Craik, 1989). In this case, the assessment would be highly reliable but invalid in some respects. So, what is confusing is that reputation may or may not correspond with 'What the person really is', namely, personality. Another source of confusion is that personality assessments are notoriously weak. Those based on self-reports, objective tests or projective tests need not correspond closely with each other, or with assessments of reputation.

Self-assessment is notoriously weak (see Wylie, 1979). This creates confusion because it is difficult to see how people can develop effective techniques of self-presentation unless they can make reasonably realistic and comprehensive self-assessments. If they can make adequate self-assessments, it is difficult to see why self-report measures of personality are not more reliable and valid. Perhaps the way through this confusion is to suppose that self-appraisal and self-presentation are associated. Given wide differences between individuals in their understanding of themselves, and in their understanding of the impressions they make on other people, there is considerable scope for misunderstandings.

Reputation can shape personality and the self-concept, and these in turn shape reputation; these phenomena are interdependent. For example, if we discover that we are more highly regarded than we had supposed, our self-esteem increases, leading us either to strive even more to justify that regard or possibly to relax our efforts and 'rest on our laurels'.

Craik (1989) reminded us of a peculiar difference between positive (socially desirable) and negative (socially undesirable) attributions about traits. Positive traits are generalisations that are easily proved false—one negative instance is sufficient. Traits that are stated negatively, such as, 'He is a poor manager', 'She does not have much patience', run counter to expectation because, in the absence of other information, we assign 'default characteristics' to people; these are normal role characteristics or socially desirable traits. Hence, more instances are required to confirm negative traits, and one counter-instance is not enough to falsify them. This issue is relevant to defamation, and to less serious attacks on reputation, because of the difficulty in falsifying negative attributions.

Terms such as 'frightening' and 'intimidating' do not, strictly speaking, refer to personality traits, but to the effects that one person has on others. This is their 'social stimulus value' (May, 1932; Allport and Odbert, 1936), and corresponds to their reputation if such attributions are common within a particular interest group. Terms denoting social judgements are used loosely in ordinary language, and have implications for personal qualities. Evaluative terms, such as 'good' and 'bad', are social judgements, not traits; so these terms too form part of a person's reputation if the attributions are widely shared.

It is not difficult to show that personality impressions are selective, possibly distorted, subject to change over time, and subject to influences independent of the person to whom they refer. Thus, although observers' impressions can be used in the assessment of personality, their value, compared with other forms of assessment, such as self-report or objective test, varies from one set of conditions to another. For example, observers' impressions formed under standard conditions, such as a selection board, are likely to be different from observers' impressions formed in the normal circumstances of everyday life. Moreover, different observers are likely to form different impressions because of their different psychological characteristics. The different methods used to record impressions of people are likely to produce different results even for the same observers. This has led to the multi-trait/multi-method approach to personality assessment, which aims to separate out the effects attributable to methods of assessment from effects attributable to the traits being assessed (Sullivan and Feldman, 1979). This increases the likelihood of identifying and measuring distinct attributes of personality.

Person Perception in Everyday Life

Burroughs, Drews and Hallman (1991) have shown that personal characteristics, as judged by self-ratings, can be predicted at better than chance levels by observers who have information only about the target person's possessions (clothing, record albums). They have also shown, by multi-dimensional scaling, how some cues are more salient than others for some observers. Observers have a tacit understanding that some kinds of information are more revealing than other kinds when making inferences about people.

Swann's (1984) view was that accounts of person perception based largely on laboratory and paper-and-pencil studies, and using an information processing approach, underestimated the accuracy found in real life. Experimental studies have focused on errors in person perception, such as the halo effect, first impressions and attribution errors. Clinical judgements have proved to be generally inferior to actuarial judgements. Research into social cognition has revealed various heuristics and biases that lead to errors. First, some observers are inclined to rate other people's personal qualities higher or lower, on average, than other observers. Second, they are less inclined than other observers to recognise the full range of differences between people, and so fail to make the necessary discriminations. Third, they are better at judging some kinds of attributes and some kinds of people, as compared with other observers. Fourth, observers' judgements of others are biased by the judgements they make about themselves, for example their self-ratings; this can lead to errors or to spurious accuracy. These biases are clearly seen in quantitative studies in which observers rate themselves and other people on a variety of attributes (see Cronbach and Gleser, 1953; and Cronbach, 1955, 1958; see also Poulton, 1975, on biases in subjective judgements).

Swann (1984) presented a detailed argument in favour of the view that the processes of person perception have a close functional relationship with the practical aspects of social interaction. If person perception is liable to so many sources of error, how is effective social interaction possible? Swann (1984) argued that it is possible because the people engaged in social interaction are assessing whatever is relevant to the immediate situation, so that they can fulfil their aims. Accurate assessment of others is socially adaptive. The process of 'negotiating social identities' means that people present themselves in certain ways to each other, to create certain impressions and attain certain ends, such as asserting themselves, making themselves attractive to others, or whatever.

The presentational behaviour of one person constrains the presentational behaviour of the other. People, however, may present themselves in different ways in different social situations and in response to different people, although they may believe that they are conveying the same impression. It is as if we presented 'edited' versions of our self-concept to different audiences. Our behaviour appears to us to be consistent, but it may not appear consistent to others, especially across different situations. So inferences about personal qualities tend to be context-dependent. Observers may forget this and over-generalise from insufficient evidence.

In real life, observers are not usually concerned with assessing attributes that are stable across situations and over time. The search for stable personality traits is a mainly academic pursuit with limited practical uses—in selection for example. In real life, observers (interactants) usually want to understand or predict the target person's behaviour in a current circumscribed situation. This situation typically includes the presence of one or more interactants, related circumstances and expectations. Accuracy increases because people tend to exhibit habitual patterns of behaviour, occupy a limited range of behaviour settings and associate with similar sorts of people (because of social segregation). An observer is often an associate of the target person, or familiar with persons of that sort. This usually enables people to present themselves to each other in standard ways that are readily interpreted and responded to.

Deception may take place; attempted deception may be recognised as such. Misunderstandings occur, but may be counteracted by more vigorous self-presentation (identity negotiation), for example by correcting a person's mode of address, or by making excuses (Chapter 7). An observer may explore the other person's social identity by acting in certain ways or by asking questions, for example by being flippant, by refusing to accept an excuse, by challenging their views. We may choose to make a point of behaving in ways that contradict an observer's assumptions, for example by expressing homosexual characteristics or minority political views.

People try to behave consistently with regard to *their* expectations about themselves (their self-concept). Observers look for behaviour that is consistent with *their* expectations about the target person. These perspectives may not coincide, in which case the expectations have to be reconciled or the interaction breaks down. Self-definitions (people's beliefs about their social identity), in adults at least, are usually firm; but people can be dominated by others, for example in conversion experiences or 'brain washing'.

We sometimes under-estimate the influence we have, as interactants, on the behaviour of the person(s) with whom we are interacting, forgetting that they behave differently with other people. Experience of a person in a variety of situations, however, or in the same sort of situation over several occasions, should enable us to form an impression that is less dependent on social context. The point is that circumstances and people's expectations exert considerable influence on our behaviour, making it more stable and predictable than it would otherwise be. So observers who are well acquainted with us are likely to be more accurate in their assessments of us than people who are not.

Our self-assessments are based on long and varied personal experience. What we tell ourselves and what we tell others depends on the nature of the situation; they need not coincide. In any event, the self-concept changes with experience, and we are aware of different aspects of the self at different times. Experimental studies have been done on the effects of other people's impressions on self-attributions (see Lord et al., 1992). Occasionally, situations arise that bring conflicting aspects of the self into awareness, but normally our behaviour seems to us to be internally consistent.

Concerning reputation, Swann's (1984) view was that our assessments of people tend to be shared by others. We commonly seek out confirmation of our impressions and commonly find it among like-minded associates. Another point is that where we form negative (unfavourable) impressions of people we tend to avoid them. We are therefore less likely to encounter further direct, first-hand information about them that might counteract the initial impression. So, for example, people who give the impression of being aggressive, aloof, uninteresting or unreliable may find it difficult to correct that initial impression. Conversely, more frequent interaction and closer acquaintance should increase the amount of direct, first-hand knowledge, and so increase the accuracy of our impressions.

When we interact with another person we normally consider how that person will behave in relation to us in this situation. We are less likely to consider how they react to other people or in other situations. We can, if necessary, extend our range of inquiry by observing how a target person behaves with other people and in other situations. We can also obtain information from other observers. Observers lacking direct, first-hand knowledge of a target person may find their indirect, hearsay, views confirmed by other observers, who also lack direct, first-hand knowledge.

If people wish to break free from a particular social identity, they need to break free from the constraints of social circumstances, and the influence of particular people. Some people appear to change radically following a period away from their usual social surroundings, for example in military service, in higher education or abroad. Conversely, if people want a particular sort of social identity, they need to submit to social constraints and influence. Failure to do so may result in their being rejected by others, for example by being obliged to leave a community or political party.

Albright, Kenny and Malloy (1988) drew attention to the way obvious facts about a person, such as physical appearance and gender, may influence first impressions. Some characteristics are more obvious than others, for example age or extraversion. Although there may be good agreement between observers for some traits, the question is how accurate (valid) these judgements are.

Albright et al. (1988) compared observers' ratings of acquaintances with observers' ratings of non-acquaintances (based on physical appearance only). Observers agreed moderately well in their ratings of sociability and responsibility for non-acquaintances. These ratings correlated with the target persons' self-ratings, and with ratings made by observers acquainted with the target persons. Physical attractiveness made for positive (favourable) ratings on certain traits, such as sociability, talkativeness and good nature, but not on others. Other influential characteristics—posture and gesture, eye contact, responsiveness—are likely to have effects, especially on initial impressions (see also Kenny and Albright, 1987).

Funder and Colvin (1988) commented on the paucity of investigations examining the relationship between judgements of personality and direct observation of the behaviour of persons (but see Wright and Dawson, 1988). The question is whether judges who are well acquainted with a target person, and therefore more likely to make valid judgements, agree with each other more than do judges who have only superficial or indirect acquaintance with a target person. A sample of male fraternity members gave self-descriptions based on a variation of the California Q-Sort (Bem and Funder, 1978; Block, 1978). Two of their close acquaintances also assessed these subjects. These acquaintances also assessed members of the sample, with whom they were not acquainted, from brief videotape recordings of them in conversation. The results showed significantly higher agreement between the judgements of self and close acquaintances than between self and non-acquaintances. There was, however, considerable agreement between the judgements of acquaintances and non-acquaintances. Agreement varied widely across the 100 items of the Q-Set. The higher levels of agreement were associated with personality characteristics independently judged to be more visible, i.e. more easily detected. The implication for reputation is that direct, close acquaintance enhances inter-judge agreement in person perception. This probably reflects more valid judgements. Even if it does not, it means that social consensus among acquaintances will give the appearance of validity and a more well-defined, consistent reputation. Funder and Colvin (1988) did not claim that their results proved that judgements based on close acquaintance are more accurate, because agreement can arise through shared misapprehensions. Still, valid judgements must show agreement.

Wright and Dawson (1988) considered the possibility that certain kinds of behaviour, such as aggression and sexuality, are naturally more salient than other kinds because of their adaptive importance. They also considered the question of how observers perceive behaviour that is consistent within but not across situations. Observers rated children's general behavioural tendencies, and their behaviour in different kinds of situation, over several weeks in a field setting. The results showed that observers were more sensitive to some kinds of behaviour, such as aggression and compliance, than to other kinds, such as withdrawal and refusing to respond. This differential sensitivity occurred across and within different situations. The implications of this study for reputation are as follows. First, some personality characteristics are more overtly expressed, more noticeable, and therefore more likely to lead observers to make associated attributions. Second, some personal characteristics are more important than others in a given social context, and are more likely to become the focus of interest and attention. Third, observers in different interest groups or audiences have different interests and priorities, and so are more sensitive to some aspects of a reputational entity than to others. In a commercial organisation, for example, the attributes that concern the employees are somewhat different from the attributes that concern suppliers, customers and investors.

Reputation and the Self

People take action to enhance and protect their reputation because it has value for them; it is an important 'concern'. Reputation is, in effect, an extension of the self—something that is peculiarly one's own—Allport's (1955) notion of the 'proprium'.

In a given area of social interaction—at work, for example, or at leisure—our social identity is defined by the relevant attributes assigned to us collectively through conformity effects in the various groups with which we have dealings. It does not follow that a person's self-concept corresponds to any one of his or her several social identities. It is likely, however, that these social identities have characteristics in common. The individual's self-concept is likely to consist of these core features (because personal identity is constrained by biological characteristics, shaped by social interaction especially in the early years, and continually subject to life-history events). In addition, the self-concept is likely to include a selection of socially desirable characteristics appropriate to the relevant membership and reference groups. Naturally, we can expect people who are socially isolated or deviant, or otherwise out of touch with people, to have a self-concept that does not match their reputation.

We can expect some discrepancy between our self-concept and our reputation(s) (Orpen and Bush, 1974). The image we have of ourselves is associated with self-esteem (or lack of self-esteem). Some aspects of the self, or the self as a whole, are positively or negatively evaluated by the person. Awareness of a disparity between our self-image and our perceived public image is often a signal that action is needed to resolve it. Inability or unwillingness to change one's self-image means restricting oneself to those circumstances to which one's identity is adapted. This makes one vulnerable to changes in circumstances, and inhibits personal (or corporate) development. On the other hand, too great a readiness to adapt one's identity to changed circumstances suggests a lack of firm beliefs and values. Political behaviour illustrates these points.

Names

An entity's name is not merely an identifying label, it evokes strong associations with the salient attributes of an entity. In some cultures it is thought to have magical properties. Names can be assigned in all sorts of ways—they can be inherited, arrived at casually or by whim, they can be worked out rationally, or agreed as a compromise. As circumstances change, a name becomes more, or less, suited to the entity to which it refers. Some women retain their maiden name in their professional capacity, but use their married name in other contexts (an example of negotiating social identity). Some persons' names cause great amusement, especially among schoolchildren; middle names are often a source of embarrassment, presumably because they are less common and not normally associated with the bearer. Nicknames often draw attention to an important reputational attribute. Foreign names are often difficult to pronounce and sometimes have unfortunate associations in another language. The widespread and frequent use of a name restricts and stabilises its meaning. Names are important in corporate identity and brand image.

Self-disclosure

Disclosures that appear to demean the self are more readily believed than disclosures that promote the self. This is presumably because we take account of the effect of self-interest in disclosures promoting the self. In law, statements against one's own interest are taken as evidence that a witness is telling the truth.

Emler (1990) reports that in conversations with informal contacts (mutual acquaintances) the most common topic is self-disclosure, and the next most common topic is named acquaintances. This sort of face-to-face social interaction is part of the *process* of reputation—conveying information. Social interaction involves the effects that one person has on another, possibly through overt action and nonverbal (expressive) behaviour; this too is part of the process of reputation—exerting influence. Reputation pervades social interaction.

Social identity

Emler (1990) argued that people define themselves, i.e. express their social identity, in particular ways—as liberals or conservatives for example, or as law-abiding persons. They behave in ways appropriate to their conception of that identity. At least they claim or appear to behave appropriately, because their success (their social identity) depends on ensuring that other people form the impression that they are behaving appropriately. In other words, we need others to confirm the way we define ourselves; this calls for negotiation—some measure of accommodation between people regarding appropriate behaviour. For example, we learn through interaction with others how to behave as professional people, as members of the armed forces, as Catholics, or whatever.

The norms appropriate to the occasion specify the standards used in judging the appropriateness of the behaviour of a person belonging to a particular category—psychologist, Methodist or policeman. The judgements are likely to vary with the social context and the occasion. A disciplinary committee investigating a complaint against a member of a professional organisation might judge that the behaviour complained of was within the normal range of acceptability. A policeman's actions might be judged to be contrary to accepted practice.

Social identity theory (Abrams and Hogg, 1990) emphasises the collective characteristics of members of a group, and de-emphasises the distribution of differences between individuals within that group. This distribution is important in the theory of reputation. It helps to explain the distinction between manifest and latent reputation, the reversed-J distribution of reputational attributions, and serial changes in reputation. The distributive view shows how the 'collective' and 'individual' aspects of social phenomena can be reconciled.

SOCIAL DEVIATION

Delinquent Reputation

Emler (1990: 171) adopted the received view of reputation as, '. . . that set of judgments a community makes about the personal qualities of one of its members'. He was concerned with the moral aspects of reputation in politics and delinquency. He connected reputation with social identity, the self, impression management (self-presentation) and behavioural consistency. He saw reputation as central to collective existence.

Reputations are involved in deviant behaviour. For example, public recognition for bad, eccentric or unusual behaviour might be preferred to no recognition, as with certain kinds of social disorder. Lack of reputation (recognition) might lead to feelings of disappointment, depression, and possibly even a wish for revenge. The need that some individuals have for public recognition is expressed in deviant modes of appearance and behaviour, usually with support from a minority group. We try to develop a particular sort of reputation by acting in ways we think will lead other people to form a particular sort of impression. For example, we might give the impression of efficiency as a guise for seeking increased control over others.

There are two reasons why deviant behaviour need not have adverse effects on reputation. The first reason is that it might be so well concealed as to be undetected—behaviour that appears to be normal or expected does not raise questions or suspicions. Deviant behaviour that involves other people cannot, by definition, be totally concealed. There is the risk that information will be passed on, even by people sworn to secrecy. Information about deviant behaviour, however, tends to be confined to one other person—partner or accomplice, or to a few co-transgressors, as in a group of people involved in child abuse, fraud or crime. Thus the second reason why deviant behaviour need not have adverse effects on reputation is that a person could have different reputations in different groups with no overlapping membership; a delinquent reputation in a delinquent group is normal. Emler (1984) pointed to the apparent paradox that most antisocial behaviour is social behaviour! Children disposed to delinquency do not normally conceal their minor misbehaviours from their friends, and sometimes they openly boast about them.

Emler (1990) reported that some delinquents advertise certain personal attributes, such as toughness and vindictiveness. These signal likely consequences to opponents. The principle involved can be generalised to other areas of social life. Thus a reputation for sexual availability, managerial efficiency, financial weakness, single-mindedness, legal acumen or other special characteristic, advertises opportunities for social interaction that interested parties wish to pursue (or to avoid). Emler seems to argue that social values are internalised through social learning, and that this explains some kinds of moral conduct; other forms of misbehaviour, however, are influenced more by immediate social influences, such as pressures within a delinquent group or a political caucus. This does not mean that the effects of immediate influences are short-lived, rather that they constitute a *continuing* social context within which the individual operates—a sort of schedule of reinforcement that shapes behaviour.

It is possible that making reparations is more effective than punishment (fines, imprisonment) in dealing with some offenders. This should have the effect of making good, where possible, the damage done, and of making the offender more aware of and responsive to reputation in the wider community. Failure to establish an approved role in society, through educational failure and unemployment for example, leads some people to suppose that they have little to lose from antisocial behaviour. This applies especially if their social network consists of people of a similar kind. Consequently, threats to their wider reputation through misconduct may have little or no effect on behaviour. Conversely, people with an established approved role in society have a lot to lose.

Reputation affects deviant behaviour in other ways. In a prison, for example, the formal and informal incentives normally used to persuade prisoners to conform to prison requirements are sometimes removed or break down for some reason, perhaps because of staff shortage, or a change of staff or policy. In these circumstances, if normal social control becomes ineffective, this could lead some inmates to compete with each other in establishing local control of the situation through rational persuasion or more likely by violence. Violence seems a basic instinctive mechanism for achieving status, and survival.

Emler (1984) pointed out that educational achievement reflects a whole range of socially desirable characteristics—mental ability, good working habits, good relationships with others, and so on. It thereby serves as a formal public marker of a good reputation, with an implied moral basis. Delinquency, as commonly defined, is associated with low educational achievement. Inability or unwillingness to give an appropriate account of delinquent behaviour when challenged by those in authority is associated with continued delinquency, perhaps because the delinquent is unable to distinguish between the norms of the delinquent group and the norms of the wider society. Emler suggested that a delinquent career could be a positive choice, not just a side-effect of not having the good reputation that accompanies educational achievement.

Some conditions encourage people to develop a reputation for delinquency. The argument is that whereas a reputation for being law-abiding is acquired passively by default, by not transgressing social rules, other sorts of reputation are more exciting and attention-getting. This calls for action and achievement of some sort—heroism, daredevilry, clowning—as well as antisocial behaviour and rebellion. These sorts of actions make a definite impression, whereas law-abiding behaviour does not.

The word 'default' used in the previous paragraph reminds us that many of our social routines are governed by 'scripts' and 'schemata'. We learn routine ways of understanding and dealing with the world and the people in it, as in attending concerts, travelling by train or celebrating Christmas. If a situation seems *not* to call for an interpretation or response that is out of the ordinary, we assume the appropriate default value; this is the standard interpretation or response in that sort of situation. The impressions we form of other people are based on schemata that assume default values in the absence of alternative indications. Thus, we need positive indications that someone is delinquent, otherwise we assume, by default, that he or she is law-abiding. There is normally no need to prove a default characteristic. For example, the plaintiff in an action for defamation is not required to disprove a defamatory statement; the burden of proof is on the defendant. In daily life, however, we may feel obliged to prove that accusations or other criticisms are false. Persons and organisations normally take positive action to counter such denigration.

5 Group Factors

Introduction: Primary and Secondary Groups

References to 'the general public' or to 'people in general' ignore the fact that most people belong to many interlocking social groups with overlapping memberships. There are small, primary, informal, face-to-face groups—family, friends, work groups; there are larger, more formal, secondary groups—public and private sector organisations, commercial conglomerates, religions, and charities. Social interaction, communication and influence occur through various forms of association, from the most private and intimate to the most public and formal, leading to the manifold structures and functions of society and the economy. In modern large-scale societies there are many different sorts of secondary groups. These organisations are often large and require complex administrative structures to coordinate the diverse activities needed to reach the organisation's objectives.

In the secondary groups and in social interaction generally, people interact indirectly, at a distance as it were, through intermediaries, notices or other means. Consequently, a person's reputations spread well beyond his or her immediate contacts, creating secondary (indirect and extended) images different from the primary images. Primary images have been regarded as valid data for assessing personality—'What the person really is'—according to Allport's (1937) definition. Secondary images have not been so regarded, and they correspond more closely to the common-sense notion of reputation.

There is usually some flexibility and ambiguity in the social roles that people occupy in organisations, especially as circumstances and memberships change. Individuals receive feedback from others about their own behaviour and respond to the behaviour of other members by offering praise, criticism, guidance, and so on. This sort of information and influence occurs in both primary (informal) and secondary (formal) groups. An organisation's effectiveness depends on the coordination of formal and informal group processes.

Members of an organisation communicate with each other and develop a shared point of view about a person or an issue. The target person often participates in this process. Members with similar interests and roles establish a common point of view different from that of the other members who have different interests and roles. The homogeneity and the density of social networks affects reputation (Chapter 6).

The greater the level of communication and influence, the more likely it is that conformity (shared beliefs, common standards of behaviour, common interests) will increase. Cohesive groups have high levels of interpersonal communication and influence, and well-coordinated role relationships. Primary groups are thus likely to be highly influential, especially in the early stages of the development of secondary levels of organisation, and when a large organisation has to deal with non-routine business, as in crisis management. Formal administrative arrangements for communication and influence (management) are set up to deal with routine business. To the extent that some non-routine business—accidents, crises, and so on—can be anticipated, the necessary administrative procedures can be set up and tested by simulated exercises. In real life, however, initial reactions to non-routine eventualities occur at the primary group level, where communication and influence are faster and more direct. In such situations, individual differences in performance are more obvious and contribute to individual reputations. Even in routine situations, individual differences in performance are likely to be more obvious at the primary group level simply because of the more frequent interaction and closer physical proximity of primary group members.

Group Morale

In our 'extended analogy', group morale is analogous to individual self-esteem and self-confidence. Self-esteem and self-confidence refer not to every aspect of the self but to a broad range of attributes that the individual feels are important. These attributes differ in some respects from one person to another, because people have different abilities, interests and values, and because they face different sorts of circumstances. Some attach importance to physical appearance, job performance or social relationships; others attach importance to artistic achievement, social prestige, wealth, or whatever. By analogy, then, the factors affecting morale vary from one sort of group to another, as for example, in military units, commercial firms, voluntary organisations and juvenile gangs. It is possible that individual self-esteem and group morale differ in that self-esteem is more retrospective. That is to say, self-esteem depends more on life-history influences, whereas, in a social group with a turnover in membership, contemporary circumstances and future prospects are likely to be more influential in raising or lowering morale.

The importance of self-esteem and group morale for reputation is that they affect performance, and performance will in time affect reputation. Similarly, reputation, whether deserved or not, affects self-esteem and group morale, which in turn affect performance. In one case, lower self-esteem or morale could have an adverse effect on reputation. In another case, a decline in reputation could have an adverse effect on self-esteem or morale, or it could stimulate efforts to improve performance and re-establish reputation.

Interest Groups

The name 'interest group' is apt because it describes how members of a group see their future as tied up in some way with the target entity. They are, therefore, 'interested' in protecting and enhancing its reputation (or, conversely, in derogation of its reputation). The name 'interest group' can be applied to a collection of individuals each of whom has a personal 'interest' in the target entity. They need not necessarily communicate with and influence each other directly as interacting members of a social network. Interest groups include those who are for the most part spectators taking a vicarious pleasure (or displeasure) in the fate of the target entity. That is to say, they feel emotionally involved in the fate of the entity without necessarily being functionally involved. Their interest probably reflects their conformity to the social norms of their membership or reference group. This provides a psychological basis for a good deal of media coverage of public figures, such as royalty, of deviant behaviour, for example scandals or criminal acts, and of ordinary people and their special circumstances, for example human interest stories. Vicarious involvement provides a psychological basis for the reputations of fictional characters and organisations—in novels, films and soap operas.

Social Support and Opposition

How does the notion of social support relate to that of reputation? Social support normally refers to a primary group—a small group of people closely involved with a dependent target person needing help or advice. They normally share some important common beliefs about and attitudes towards the person in need; they normally have an altruistic commitment to the health and well-being of the person. Therefore, they constitute a particular sort of interest group. The problem is that they know the target person intimately, but in different ways, so that their impressions may have little in common save the basic attributes related to identity and dependence.

We can contrast social support with social opposition, in the sense that some individuals and organisations are subject to systematic attack and denigration by groups in competition with them. Members of an opposition group are unlikely to know the target person intimately, so they are more likely to share common stereotyped beliefs about and attitudes towards the object of their attack.

Exchange Relationships

Emler (1990) explained the function of reputation in terms of social reciprocity. Many sorts of social exchange take place—of money, goods, affection, information, protection, and so on. Exchange relationships operate within a system of values, beliefs and social norms appropriate to the prevailing cultural circumstances. People try to establish acceptable cost–benefit relationships in their dealings with others (Thibaut and Kelley, 1959). From this perspective, reputation is the collective outcome of individual appraisals of an entity based on expected exchange relationships. This seems reasonable, at least at the level of established, informal, face-to-face relationships—at work, for example, or among friends. This perspective is less helpful, however, when we consider extended (secondary) reputations; here the cost–benefit relationships are obscure, and people are more likely to be influenced by the many factors affecting reputation discussed elsewhere.

Social Visibility

Emler (1990) pointed out that people who do not interact much with other people, who have a low 'participation rate' or low 'visibility', are unlikely to have an extensive or well-defined reputation. Moreover, their reputation is likely to be less valid than that of people known more widely and more fully. This is because there is less information based on first-hand observation in circulation, and fewer opportunities for corroboration. A person with low 'visibility' can behave less consistently and more deviantly. Organisations that are not well known sometimes take advantage of this fact, at some cost to clients and creditors. The investigation into serial changes in reputation offers further comments on the effects of 'visibility' on reputation (Chapter 14).

Social Control

Although many actions produce a range of social impressions, individuals are not fully known by others. There are significant aspects of the self that the individual discloses to no-one, and actions that are completely private.

Confession is a technique of social control (or counselling) adopted by some religious and political organisations. Confessions can be extracted from people by force if no other 'proof' of guilt is available. Such confessions are used to damage the individual's reputation and to justify the sanctions imposed to maintain the social order. The recent political history of Eastern Europe illustrates the extent to which individuals have to conceal aspects of the self even from close acquaintances if political surveillance is an extensive and persistent element in social life. In daily life, we often use confessions and admissions in 'negotiating' our 'social identity' with other people, and when we are obliged to account to others for our behaviour.

Emler (1990) explained that even in large industrial societies, people interact mostly with a few fairly well-known acquaintances. This contrasts with the large number of people known indirectly and met infrequently. The problem faced by an authoritarian regime is that it cannot function effectively if its surveillance activities seriously interfere with the natural processes of social interaction. If people cannot express their individuality for fear of persecution, and if the main means of communication and influence are controlled by the state, then reputations will form but most will not be distinctive. People's reputational attributes will emphasise those used for identification and routine social interaction (age, gender, occupation, address, leisure interests) and reputational differences will be greatly reduced.

Fame

Famous people have widespread reputations that are more like corporate images than ordinary personal reputations. The reason for this is their high exposure in the media and their need to exercise control over this publicity through public relations (PR) activities, or other efforts at self-presentation. The wider reputation of famous and infamous people is likely to be stereotyped and subject to the presentational effects of commentators and propagandists operating in the media.

Fame means that a large number of people have at least heard of the target person—'Reputation is measured by the acre' (Sir Thomas Overbury, 1613). This sort of fame depends upon information that is widely broadcast—over short periods by the mass media, or over longer periods by historical records, legends or social movements. One can, in a sense, be famous within a circumscribed social nexus—among chemists, for example, or librarians or safe-breakers. Here, fame depends on being well known within the circumscribed audience.

Social Attitudes

The way that beliefs and attitudes are formed, and the effects they have on our behaviour, are central topics in social psychology. Beliefs and attitudes are important in the study of reputation, for several reasons. They are subject to social influence, and they affect the way we react to information and influence regarding a reputational entity. They affect the way we react to an entity in a direct encounter. An entity's reputation is likely to produce certain sorts of attitudes in certain kinds of people. The way people express their attitudes is likely to influence their reputation.

The difference between 'reputation' and 'social attitude' is blurred because in one sense an entity's reputation can be defined by the prevailing attitude of a particular audience towards that entity. An attitude, after all, consists of a system of beliefs, values and intentions. So, for example, we could conceivably refer to the 'reputation' of the physically disabled or the mentally ill, meaning the prevailing social attitude towards people with these conditions. It would be convenient to use the word 'reputation' for social attitudes (especially the belief component) that refer to individual entities, and to avoid using it to refer to ill-defined, heterogeneous categories, such as those just mentioned. Unfortunately, this recommendation would not allow us to refer to the reputation of 'psychologists' or other professional groups. The comparison between 'reputation' and 'social attitude' is complicated by the way the words are used in ordinary discourse, and by the way they are defined and measured in scientific research (Chapter 16).

Corporate bodies have 'attitudes' in the sense of having beliefs about, and being ready to react in certain ways towards, matters of interest to them. The collective character of corporate attitudes depends on the conformity that arises through the interaction and the shared interests of members of the organisation, especially the leading members.

The Media

One should not confuse media reports with the facts. The facts can be established, if at all, only by a systematic objective inquiry. Reports by credible journalists, however, may be the best evidence available in the circumstances, given the pace at which newsworthy events occur and the absence of fast, flexible methods of surveying the relevant social groups. Even good reporters who are trying to be objective can be misled or make mistakes. Their reports may become self-fulfilling prophecies because of the influence they have on viewers and readers. Cottle (1991) examined the Salman Rushdie affair as a case-study of the way that public opinion can be shaped by those responsible for collecting, selecting, packaging and presenting television news. Social attitudes and the reputations of individuals and groups can be influenced by news gathered under time pressure, by normal journalistic practices, and the wish to construct a coherent (if erroneous) story about a controversial social issue (see Graber, 1988; Chen and Meindl, 1991).

Third-Person Effect

Davison (1983) used the term 'third-person effect' to refer to the way people tend to over-estimate the effect of media information on others as compared with themselves. This bias affects their behaviour. Gunther (1991) tested and developed the idea. The theory underlying the third-person effect is as follows. First, one's personal involvement in an issue encourages the belief that one's own attitude is soundly based and resistant to change. People who are less involved have attitudes that are more susceptible to change. Second, one assumes that biased or unreliable sources of information influence others more than oneself. Third, attribution bias inclines us to attribute causality of responsibility to external factors (circumstances) for our own behaviour, and to internal factors (dispositions) for other people's behaviour. We tend to ignore the possibility that other people adjust their behaviour to the circumstances, as we do, even if other people are similar to us in many respects.

Gunther's (1991) experiment simulated defamation. Subjects read a report about the target person in either a high-credibility newspaper or a low-credibility newspaper. They rated their opinion of the target person and the opinions of other groups of people who had read the report. They were influenced more by the high-credibility report. They rated other people as more influenced than themselves, especially by the low-credibility source. After being informed that the news item was false (libellous), subjects estimated what compensatory and punitive damages should be paid by the newspapers. They penalised the less credible newspaper more with punitive damages, but penalised both sources equally with compensatory damages. One would expect the high-credibility report to cause more actual harm.

A third-person effect in reputation means that we are likely to overestimate the effect of public information and influence on the reputation of people we know well (including ourselves!). This helps to explain the high expectations of people who take action for defamation, and the high damages awarded by juries. It also helps to explain the degree of distress felt by people whose reputation has been damaged. Although the third-person effect is a widespread bias, there may be differences between individuals.

Conformity and Minority Opinion

The effect of conformity is to reduce the range of differences between individuals in their beliefs, values, attitudes and behaviour; this produces 'collective' effects—public opinion, social movements and, of course, reputation. People usually conform to majority opinion, but majority opinion operates within the social networks to which people belong. Consequently, a minority group within a wider community can exert a powerful influence on its members, for example ethnic or religious minorities, factions within a political movement or professional organisation. Through its activists and opinion leaders it may inform and influence majority opinion.

Social influence is exerted by most people but especially experts, opinion leaders, and those in positions of power and authority. One aim is to manage the social process, for example by controlling the flow of information and the occupants of key social positions.

Conformity to prevailing beliefs is sometimes maladaptive for individuals or for the group as a whole. The existence of differences between individuals in their personal characteristics and circumstances provides a basis for the emergence of minority views. These can, in some circumstances, overturn majority opinion, as is the case with innovations in science, changes in political or economic policy, and religious conversions. Minority views within a group tend to become more prevalent to the extent that they are consistent and vocal enough to raise doubts and questions among the majority. On reflection, some members will perceive that they have more in common with the minority than with the majority position. The views of minorities outside our membership and reference groups are likely to be ignored or rejected. This is because they are seen as falling outside our general framework of beliefs and values.

We have referred to the tension between the pressures towards conformity and the pressures towards individuality (or away from the prevailing consensus). This tension is shown in the typical reversed-J distribution of opinions about an entity in a social group. The tension is a permanent feature of social life because social groups have to adapt to changing circumstances and to changes in membership.

Turner (1991) reminded us that we do not value expert opinion because it is valid (we cannot judge its validity). We value it because the social institutions that we accept and value define the expert as someone whose opinions we can trust. Our uncertainty is reduced by social influence in the guise of expert information.

Social information and influence do not necessarily flow in one direction from informant to recipient. Informants may be contradicted or questioned. Social influence is exerted through the exchange of information and value judgements. It is also exerted through the familiar techniques of rewards and punishments, promises and threats, i.e. through negotiations between people that explore and define social issues and aim to reach agreement and cooperation. If persuasion and negotiation fail, it may be possible for those with power to enforce compliance.

Stereotypes and Stigmatisation

Stereotypes are simple mental models. They over-generalise in that they minimise or ignore individual differences by concentrating on superficial common features. They identify targets by attributes that are highly visible, and associate them with positive or negative evaluations that are highly polarised. A negative reputation and stigmatisation usually go together, leading to prejudice, discrimination and labelling, for some minority groups.

There are wide differences between individuals in the extent to which their ideas are shared with others. Some of their ideas are idiosyncratic. For many reputations, perhaps most, the extent to which beliefs and attitudes are shared is small (Chapter 14). The ideas that are widely shared are simple and few in a typical reputation or collective image. They correspond to what is called a stereotype. A stereotype enables us to react quickly to a stimulus, and involves little mental effort; it is often shared by many people with whom we associate, which gives us confidence that our reaction is appropriate. The identifying characteristics of the targets of stereotyped attitudes elicit a pre-established frame of reference (mental model) consisting of beliefs, feelings and motives that process information about, and organise behaviour towards, the target. This behaviour may provoke the target into exhibiting the characteristics attributed to it, such as hostility, defensiveness or dependence. Typical stereotypes include those connected with age, race, religion, occupation and nationality. Arluke and Levin (1984) regarded stereotyping as an integral part of the public image of the aged, perpetuating the notion of 'second childhood'.

Stereotypes are categories we use to attribute some socially salient characteristics to diverse individual entities. The danger, of course, is that the stereotype over-simplifies the stimulus and prevents us from recognising the complexities and variations in the class of persons or objects to which we are reacting (Tajfel, 1981). For example, a stereotype such as 'psychologist' categorises a wide range of persons deemed to be psychologists (whether or not they are properly qualified). Some supposedly common characteristics, such as the ability to read people's minds, or to explain unusual forms of human behaviour, are attributed to them. The individuals identified by social stereotypes are often easily recognised by their appearance, accent or occupation. Such identification is then associated with a variety of attributes, usually prejudicial. Stereotypes can be favourable rather than prejudicial, as when people refer to the social groups to which they belong or to which they aspire.

Stereotyped attitudes can be formed in different ways and fulfil a variety of functions. For example, they can be formed indirectly through socialisation or through false inferences. Attitudes and expectations influence the way we interpret and react to information. Stereotypes provide us with simple cognitive frameworks that are fast and require little mental effort. We rely on these conceptual routines in organising our behaviour when dealing with objects, people and events.

Stereotypes are clearly over-simplified views, and are likely to permit individual exceptions to the general rules they imply. Thus we can hold an over-simplified and negative view of old people in general, but tacitly exclude some that we know personally who do not fit the stereotype. Otherwise, stereotypes are thought to be resistant to change.

Stereotypes fulfil an affective as well as a cognitive function. They act as vehicles for the expression of racial and religious hostility, political allegiance and attitudes to minority and disadvantaged groups and the opposite sex. Stereotypes are often thought to have an irrational basis. They are the result of pressures to conform to pre-existing social values in the family and in the wider culture. They can express unconscious feelings of guilt, anxiety and aggression displaced from their proper target. Stereotypes, of course, can be based on personal experience. Widely held social stereotypes, however, are usually too simple and too inclusive to be justifiable on rational and empirical grounds.

Human beings are prone to some cognitive biases when making social judgements. We are inclined to be unduly influenced by 'first impressions'.

We neglect alternatives to the interpretations we have put on people's actions. We recognise the differences between individuals more readily among the sorts of people we are familiar with than among those we know less well.

Stereotypes are socially learned categorical forms of judgement that lead us to have expectations about and attitudes towards various classes of people. Some play an important part in the social psychology of reputation because they are widely shared. Indeed, if we exclude medium- and low-frequency attributions, a social stereotype and a reputation (collective representation) are conceptually similar. In other words, the amount of information about a person or issue held *in common* by a 'public' or 'audience', i.e. an identified section of the community, is usually quite small compared with the total amount of information in circulation. This small element commonly takes the form of a 'stereotype', which is a fixed, simple idea or small set of ideas, well established in the minds of individuals and resistant to change. One person's stereotype is reinforced by those of other people.

There are many examples of persons, categories of persons, and other entities, that have stereotyped public images. They include psychologists and psychiatrists, prostitutes, social workers, stockbrokers, the mentally ill, the disabled, the elderly, political parties, homosexuals, AIDS, drug abusers, and members of the Royal Family.

The tendency to conform, and the tendency to simplify the process of attribution, lead naturally to stereotyping—over-generalising from initial impressions, exaggerating the differences between one class of people and another. So, for example, we perceive a noisy football-team supporter and classify him as a football hooligan, we attribute various distinctive 'hooligan' characteristics to him whilst neglecting all the other attributes he shares with people who are not hooligans.

Individuals who are perceived as belonging to an identifiable group for which a stereotype is available are likely to have the characteristics associated with the stereotype attributed to them. Charactertistics that do not fit the stereotype are discounted—as 'exceptions proving the rule' or as 'untypical'. The reputations of stereotyped groups are resistant to change, as illustrated by the persistence of ethnic and religious prejudices. Another way of discounting is to refine the stereotype by subdividing it or adding further discriminatory characteristics. Thus, the political labels 'Conservative' and 'Labour' can be modified by the words 'right' and 'left'. Characteristics can be described differently, thus Jewish in-group solidarity might be described as out-group prejudice.

The currency of ordinary language changes over time because of technological and cultural changes, so that the attributes used by one generation go out of fashion in subsequent generations, and new attributes make their appearance. For example, the attribute 'ladylike' is not much used today (and might not be regarded as a compliment!); the words 'punk', 'wally' and 'yuppy' were used in the 1980s and are examples of social stereotypes.

Stereotyping is a major area of interest in social psychology. It is particularly concerned with group differences—national and racial stereotypes, for example. Ordinary language abounds with references to stereotyped entities, as if Blacks, Jews, Arabs, Irish, Northerners and Southerners were each homogeneous collections of people each sharing a distinct set of characteristics such as sexual prowess, religiosity, friendliness, or whatever. Where stereotypes of this sort are fairly widely shared in a community, they constitute one type of group reputation. Naturally, different sections of a community have different impressions of a target group, depending upon the nature and extent of their exposure to members of the target group and the consequences that such exposure has had for them.

The minority status of groups subject to prejudice, discrimination and stereotyping means that their reputation is likely to be of the secondary sort, based on hearsay and other indirect influences. Controlled face-to-face interaction is thought to be an effective way of breaking down stereotypes, because it makes people more aware of the range of differences between members of the stereotyped group. It makes them more aware of the similarities between the stereotyped group and non-stereotyped groups, and encourages the development of a group reputation of the primary sort, based on first-hand knowledge through direct interaction.

Prototypes and Personality

Almost any trait can be inferred from almost any behaviour by interposing a reason or cause to explain the connection (Gergen, Hepburn and Comer, 1986). Human actions are often the result of multiple causes, so that people's behaviour in a particular situation cannot necessarily be attributed to their personal characteristics. Nevertheless, we are usually inclined to attribute other people's actions to their internal dispositions.

The prototype, act-frequency, approach to personality assessment is highly relevant to reputation. It assumes that traits are attributed to people on the basis of the frequency with which they exhibit certain patterns of behaviour. The good agreement between observers in deciding which actions go with which traits means that there is a firm basis for the collective character of person prototypes. It is not just our unique personal act-frequency experience of others that underpins the way we attribute traits to people. We are strongly influenced by the way other people attribute traits—the sorts of traits they use and the actions they associate with traits. The information comes to us through ordinary language and common sense (Bromley, 1977), and the influence is exerted through social interaction. We are 'socialised' into thinking about people in the way we do during the juvenile period and throughout adult life.

Broughton (1990) provided a useful review of the concept of 'prototype' in personality assessment. We shall use the concept to link personality and reputation to social stereotypes. A prototype is a clear or typical member of a category that contains some diversity. For example, the M6 is a prototypical motorway; my friend S. is a prototypical amateur photographer. Broughton (1990) has developed a method of personality assessment based on vignettes that describe 'a day in the life of' some fictional characters. Each character's actions are based on the 20 most typical actions for one trait, such as dominance. Subjects are asked to rate how similar they are to each character. The data are handled by multi-dimensional scaling.

This approach is an improvement on the traditional self-report approach to personality. In particular, the cognitive processes involved seem closer to those that operate in person perception in daily life, whereas rating an adjective check-list seems remote and artificial.

When one examines the actual descriptions that people give of others and of themselves, however, one rarely finds a clear-cut description of a person's traits, and those that are mentioned are usually qualified in some way. What one does find is a selection from a variety of descriptors ranging from statements about a person's physical appearance to statements about his or her motives or future prospects.

Personality stereotypes are learned in the usual way through socialisation. We categorise people as 'high flyers', 'cranks', 'dickheads', 'tarts'. Similarly, on an act-frequency basis, we categorise some forms of behaviour as 'motherly', 'rude', 'reckless', 'friendly'. Some people in the person categories, and some actions in the trait categories, are more typical of the category than others. These categories, however, are not clearly defined. I can ask 'What do you mean— reckless?' I can argue that the person's actions are not 'reckless' but 'adventurous'. Although there is considerable agreement about the context-free meaning of commonly used trait terms, there may be considerable disagreement about their applicability in an individual case.

An interesting comment in Broughton (1990: 35) reveals that the fictional characters in the vignettes are seen by subjects as more like caricatures than real people. The reason is that the characters' behaviour is one-dimensional. In fiction, these are called 'flat' characters (Bromley, 1977: Ch. 10). Broughton hopes that adding neutral contextual material to the vignettes will make them more realistic.

Inter-subjectivity

We cannot acquire all we need or want to know through direct, first-hand experience. We have to rely on others to give us the benefit of their experience, through education and social learning. Also, because individual assessments and evaluations may be wrong, they need to be corroborated by independent observers. Thus, inter-subjective negotiations and agreements are essential for personal adjustment and social organisation. To a large extent, inter-subjective agreement defines reality. It does so partly through an evolutionary process in which some issues, but not others, become the focus of public interest. We could say that reality imposes itself on society (through natural causes), but society interprets reality through a process of inter-subjective negotiation and agreement between its members. Reputations reflect this process, and it reflects the conflicts, disagreements and individual differences that accompany it.

The feeling of certainty about a belief for which there is some inter-subjective agreement depends upon several factors. These include how much agreement there is (this reflects the proportional rather than the absolute number of contacts holding the belief); whether the social contacts are in-group or out-group members; the personal importance of accepting the belief; and the availability of independent evidence.

Information that runs counter to pre-existing beliefs has the effect of alerting recipients to the risk of error, i.e. it increases uncertainty (raises doubts and questions). This motivates a search for more information. An alternative or supplementary view is that social influence limits and reduces conflict between individuals and between groups. Persuasive information enables people to perceive and interpret facts in almost the same way, and so reduces the grounds for disagreement.

By definition, information about entities with small, localised reputations tends not to flow through the public media. It flows mainly by word of mouth, through the interpersonal networks concerned with those entities. There is likely to be more direct, first-hand, experience of the entity. This first-hand information is likely to be widely shared within a small well-connected network, and therefore is less likely to contain contradictions or raise false expectations. Although the information may be selectively biased and subject to value judgements, these biases are likely to be shared within the group and so cause little disagreement or uncertainty.

Reputations as Social Representations

The study of social representations (Farr and Moscovici, 1984) emphasises the extent to which our understanding of the world is socially conditioned—through socialisation, education, common sense and ordinary language, and conformity. Social representations provide frameworks of understanding for most people in a society; consider, for example, common-sense understanding of the seasons, agriculture, political organisation, disease and death. No doubt many, perhaps most, of our representations are socially derived or influenced. First-hand experience of entities, however, can provide people with unique experiences that are different from or even conflict with the prevailing social representations (widely held or official views, or 'common sense'). The history of ideas is virtually the history of how *individuals* helped to shape society's understanding of the world, including human nature.

Within a given society, however, social groups differ with regard to certain kinds of social representation. For example, there are wide differences in group ideas about religion, politics and race. Some groups have special interests and beliefs that set them apart from, or even bring them into conflict with, other groups, for example those for or against abortion. Membership of such groups contributes to a member's social identity.

Social representations have an evolutionary history. They are subject to the pressures of selection through competition with alternative representations put forward by sectional or minority interests following individual insights or claims. Representations that confer less advantage on a society in adapting to its environment give way to those that confer greater advantage. This takes time, of course, and has to be studied in historical perspective. Some social representations are capable of providing realistic accounts and accommodating to new findings; others prove maladaptive and are abandoned. Reputations, as social representations or shared opinions and attitudes, have an evolutionary history; we deal with short-term effects under the heading of 'serial changes', later in this book (Chapter 14).

Reputation can be defined as the sum of members' beliefs about an entity. This combines the distributive and the collective views on social representation. The distributive view focuses on the distribution of beliefs in the group, i.e. how many members hold each belief. The collective view focuses on the *social system*, in particular how the more widely held beliefs interlock. It takes account of the interdependence of members' beliefs.

The main point about a social representation, as opposed to an individual representation, is that the social representation is a shared, collective product; it is produced through social interaction. A social representation, of course, cannot exist without individuals' representations. It is best regarded as the internalised 'norm' that arises because of conformity among members of a group. Sherif's (1936) classic experiments illustrated the phenomenon. One could define a person's reputation in a group as the group's social representation of that person, in the sense that the members of the group conform to certain beliefs about and attitudes towards that person. Reputations are collective attempts to make people, and other entities, comprehensible and manageable.

The external reputations of individual members of a group enhance or diminish the image that other publics have of that particular group. For example, the behaviour of schoolchildren affects their school's reputation. The same applies to football fans and their club, citizens and their city, professionals and their profession, delegates and their parties.

Since Durkheim's (1898) work on individual and collective representations, the study of 'social representations' has developed considerably in recent years (Farr and Moscovici 1984; Potter and Litton, 1985; McKinlay and Potter, 1987). We somehow construct 'mental models' (mental maps or schemata) to represent aspects of the world with which we have to deal. These enable us to impose patterns of meaning on the world, so that we can reason things out and act appropriately. Through the processes of assimilation and accommodation, we modify our mental models to bring them into line with reality, or use them to engineer changes in the real world. Individual representations (impressions of people, objects, and so on) can be shared with others through the normal processes of communication and influence.

Galam and Moscovici (1991) have offered a quasi-mathematical account of the tendency of social attitudes and group decisions to polarise around extreme views rather than around average views. Social interaction often substantially reduces the individual differences in behaviour that were apparent before interaction. In other words, there are strong social conformity effects. Deliberate social influence can alter attitudes that are not strongly held or for which there is little or no objective evidence. People often justify their beliefs and actions by reference to majority opinion. In circumstances where there is no objective reason for acting one way rather than another, the tendency to conform combined with the tendency to yield to even small social pressures should gradually lead to a polarisation of attitudes. In large, open, democratic societies, people belong to different groups and are exposed to contrasting influences, so that shifts in public opinion may be difficult to forecast. In authoritarian societies, the expression of unofficial minority opinions is discouraged, thus promoting conformity to the official view.

In groups exhibiting attitudes that have become fairly extreme and widely shared, we have what is called an emergent 'collective' or 'group' phenomenon, which is the result of social interaction between individuals. The change in attitude is internalised, and persists even when the individual member is acting alone. Galam and Moscovici (1991) draw the conclusion that the best way to promote a particular point of view is to preach to the converted, thus strengthening their conviction, and presumably strengthening their influence on people whose views are undecided.

Social representations are systems of belief, and so play a part in attribution, i.e. explaining behaviour or assigning responsibility. Social representations are 'constructions' that fulfil social functions without necessarily being valid accounts of the entities to which they refer. Thus a political ideology or a scientific theory helps people to 'make sense' of the world for a time; it can motivate them to act in accordance with their expectations, even if subsequent events prove them wrong.

The studies in personal reputation described in Chapters 14 and 15 show that the distribution of attributions is not what one would expect on the basis of the theory of social representations outlined above. In theory, the extent of agreement in a group of n people can range from 1 to n, but typically reaches only about 30% for the most widely shared attribution. Moreover, most attributions are idiosyncratic, i.e. not shared. Social surveys normally use simple words and phrases for ease of comprehension and scoring. The categories used depend upon assumptions about the nature and distribution of opinions in a sample. Such surveys may fail to uncover relevant views and the wide range of opinions among respondents.

Where does the information about reputation come from? In the first place, it comes from people who have observed or interacted with an entity and therefore have first-hand knowledge. They convey their impressions selectively to others—to people who also have first-hand knowledge and to people who do not. They may be influenced by the information that others bring to their attention. In conveying their impressions, informants do more than simply transmit their observations. They select, edit, invent and otherwise manipulate the information they convey to an audience in response to the constraints and opportunities available to them. People who do not have first-hand knowledge of a target person or other entity must base their ideas and opinions on other people's impressions. The point is that personal views are socially conditioned. Diverse individual mental representations are transformed into a collective or shared social representation that exhibits the characteristic reversed-J distribution of attributions. This distribution expresses the tension between the pressures of conformity and the pressures of diversity in social interaction. Social representations are ways of understanding that some people share with each other. This definition emphasises that social representations vary in the extent to which they are shared—from simple dyadic agreements to widespread belief systems. Social representations help like-minded people to understand and communicate with each other, and hinder those who have different assumptions and views. Sentences beginning 'We think . . .' or 'We believe . . .' express the individual's understanding of the social representations referred to. Policy documents and codes of conduct attempt to formalise 'What is agreed or understood.'

Sometimes, unspoken or tacit agreement between people on matters that are 'obvious' or 'basic' means that they are accepted without question. For example, social structure, religion and customs are taken for granted by people in a community at a particular time. The main point about social representations is that they help to explain that people behave in similar ways because they perceive things in similar ways. They impose similar patterns of meaning on a situation. Social representations impose order and familiarity on our world. They enable us to identify things as usual or unusual, acceptable or unacceptable. Social representations that are widespread are regarded as social facts, and as aspects of reality. These patterns of meaning need not be correct. The history of ideas provides many examples of widespread but false beliefs. The 'shared' aspect of social representations does not preclude individual differences. Consider, for example, the way different people understand matters such as work, crime, loyalty and illness. Individual diversity limits the effects of social conformity, and vice versa.

The words 'social' and 'collective' overlap in meaning. The word 'social' emphasises that representations are (a) social in origin (the individual acquires them through social learning), (b) social in the sense of being shared (the extent of sharing is a matter for empirical inquiry), and (c) social in the sense that they refer to matters of social interest or importance. The word 'collective' emphasises the social, as opposed to the individual, character of representations. It draws attention to the widespread systems of belief that play a major role in the organisation of society—its traditions, myths, values and institutions. We note in passing that the word 'representation', like the word 'belief', emphasises cognitive, as opposed to affective and motivational, processes. The word 'attitude' by comparison is more inclusive in its meaning. The word 'value' emphasises the affective and motivational aspects of an attitude.

Cultural Aspects

The attributes of reputation are likely to vary considerably from one culture or 'subculture' to another. In cultures where religious and supernatural beliefs are prevalent, people and other entities may be seen in this perspective as holy or sinful, as a witch or witchdoctor. In Argentina, apparently, certain people are reputed to be 'movers', and association with them is supposed to bring bad luck, even serious misfortune.

Henry (1977) has described the public image of a healer in a cultural context of magic and religion. Lewis (1974) described the wide reputation of a Teton Dakota Indian healer and the associated cultural context. Ritter (1973) described the history of social prejudice towards epilepsy, and the part played by religious doctrines and social factors influencing the public image of epileptics. Davis (1984) reported that a physician who does not appreciate local cultural factors can make a wrong diagnosis and undermine a patient's reputation in the community. Ruiz-Ruiz et al. (1986) surveyed attitudes towards suicide in a large sample of subjects, and showed how the 'public image' of suicide varied with cultural, social and professional factors. For Peretti, Brown and Richards (1979) reputation was one of 10 value criteria that discriminated between female virgins and non-virgins. Shapurian and Hojat (1985) commented on virginity and family loyalty as factors affecting the reputation of women in Iranian culture. Dorn (1986) described the role of gossip, proverbs and reputation in Turkish Jewish culture. Bailey (1971) gave an anthropological account of reputation as it operates in the daily life of the inhabitants of a French alpine village.

The moral and legal norms of a society affect the way a person's behaviour is judged—as good or bad, right or wrong. These norms affect the individual's self-concept and self-esteem. Failing to be strong and brave in a culture that prizes these as virtues is likely to lead to guilt and low self-esteem. Gender differences in social training illustrate the point. Burt and Albin (1981) examined female reputation as a factor in the social definition of rape. Findings by Kanekar et al. (1981) suggested that being the target of female aggression could damage a man's reputation.

Social status is a cultural aspect of reputation: a person of higher status can choose to ignore people reputedly of lower status (caste or class), thereby refusing to recognise them as equals. People of lower status have to follow certain rules of etiquette or 'form' to interact effectively with people of higher status, as with forms of address and salutations.

Cultures differ in their folklore—their widely accepted beliefs about the way the world works, expressed in proverbs, maxims, superstitions, clichés, and the like (Chapter 1). Well-worn, familiar sayings enable us to express socially acceptable opinions about almost anything. Thus, a person's achievements can be attributed to ability, chance, circumstances, social connections, or whatever, according to preference, within the prevailing system of beliefs. Attributions based on beliefs in astrology or magic are accepted in some cultures or subcultures but not others. The point is that a person's reputation is constructed within a particular cultural or subcultural framework, and in relation to important concerns in a particular community—whether it is an academic, military, political, delinquent or isolated rural community.

Excessive concern with one's reputation can inhibit action. One is unable to change for fear of making a bad impression. If such concern is widespread in a community, there is likely to be social stagnation, a strong conservatism that resists change. Bailey (1971) suggested that this is characteristic of some peasant communities, and of small tightly-knit communities anywhere. It represents one sort of outcome of the conflict between self-interest and the public interest, between freedom and security. Change comes about because some people are prepared to break with traditional forms of social behaviour and promote changes in the structure of society.

Fischer and Finkelstein (1991) commented on the way that the reputation of various family members influences a Pakistani woman's chances of marriage in an urban development area near Lahore. They report that statistically the mother's reputation is most important, followed by that of older sisters, younger sisters, then brothers and, lastly, the father. There is considerable variation, however, and the women's reputations are influenced by the brothers' and the father's reputation. This interdependence illustrates that reputation constitutes a form of social control limiting or enhancing the chances of marriage. Even in a society dominated by men, the reputation of female family members affects the reputation and therefore the social status of the male family members (see Fischer, 1991, cited in Fischer and Finkelstein, 1991). We have already generalised this idea by saying that any individual member of an identifiable social group contributes to the reputation(s) of that group, *and* that the reputation of the group contributes to the reputation of its members. Clearly, reputation is a powerful social influence that can, in some circumstances, counteract other important influences, such as age, status or gender.

6 Social Networks, Communication and Influence

SOCIAL NETWORKS

Introduction

Social networks generate and transmit information and influence that affect reputational entities. Information itself is a form of influence if it changes the behaviour of the recipient towards the target entity. For example, if I am told that someone disapproves of my work, this is likely to decrease my regard for that person, leading me to react antagonistically. Social behaviour is influenced by a variety of factors, so attitudes towards a person can change without noticeable changes in people's reactions to that person. Thus, unless we monitor our reputation carefully, we remain unaware that people's regard for us has changed or is different from what we suppose.

Influence can be exerted not only by passing on true or false information, but also by the manner in which the information is conveyed—in public or in private, neutrally or emotionally. In a work situation, for example, public praise from a superior would be interpreted as credible, whereas praise given in private might raise the suspicion that it was not genuine (Kydd, Ogilvie and Slade, 1990). Influence can be exerted by threats, promises, hints and bribes. These change the recipient's behaviour without necessarily changing their impression of the target entity.

There are many examples of networks. Knight (1984) investigated freemasonry among the police and the Conservative Party in the UK. Freemasonry is an example of a network of communication and influence. Kaplan (1984) discussed the importance of corporate social networks of communication and influence in relationships with trading partners at the managerial level. LaBarbera and Wolfe (1983) reported on an illicit social network in the manufacture and distribution of a drug (fentanyl), and on the reputation of the drug.

Interpersonal communication and influence are major factors affecting an individual's behaviour regarding a variety of issues, including political and consumer issues. It is reasonable, therefore, to assume that the impressions contributing to reputation are affected by the characteristics of the relevant social network(s). The characteristics of social networks most likely to affect attitudes are homogeneity and density. Homogeneity is defined by the extent to which members of a network share one or more relevant characteristics, such as gender, occupation or religion. Density is the extent to which members of a network interact, i.e. communicate with and influence each other. Close-knit, highly interconnected (high-density) groups are likely to have norms that are well defined and well enforced. Network homogeneity and density, however, are likely to have an effect only if an issue appears to be important to members. Homogeneous networks are likely to share attitudes and opinions that are well defined and strong.

The questions are 'What effects do network characteristics have on reputation?' and 'How do they interact with other relevant variables?' The difficulty of research into these questions in natural settings is obvious. Network analysis is a recent development, so it is not surprising that there appears to be no published work relating network characteristics to reputation. Bienenstock, Bonacich and Oliver (1990) studied the effects of network homogeneity and density on social and political attitudes. They confirmed that, in some comparisons, higher density increased the differences between groups with different levels of homogeneity for gender, education and religion. Networks with a greater density of white members were more racially conservative.

Breaugh, Klimoski and Shapiro (1980) found no effect of the reputation of third parties (mediators or arbitrators) on negotiations to resolve inter-group conflict. Rose (1985) reported that women rated their social networks less effective in helping them to build their professional reputation than did men.

The attributes that become incorporated in a reputation depend to some extent on the 'interests' and 'concerns' of the people whose shared images constitute the reputation, i.e. the people in a social network. They attend, perceive and remember selectively. Their particular patterns of interaction and communication determine the rate at which, and the extent to which, various sorts of information and influence are distributed within a group and between distinct groups.

A person's performance is enhanced (or diminished) by his or her participation in a particular social network—for example, participation in an 'invisible college' of research workers, or a political movement, or a hobbyist club. Failure to establish the right 'contacts' can retard a person's career and reputation. Networks of information and influence are particularly important in social groups that have control of large organisations and resources, such as governing bodies, boards of directors and management committees. Putnam and Stout (1985) noted the relevance of social networks and organisational reputation to policy making.

From a sociological point of view, individuals do not act as independent, rational decision-makers, but are strongly influenced by shared beliefs and values that arise through social interaction. Concern for reputation has the effect of inhibiting self-interested but antisocial behaviour, at least within the social networks to which the individual feels bound. Reputation underlies honour among thieves, team spirit, cabinet responsibility, scientific integrity, business relationships, and so on. Of course, people do occasionally cheat, break ranks or otherwise act against the interests of their associates, but in so doing they risk losing other people's trust and cooperation, to their own longer-term disadvantage. Trust and respect among people with good reputations enable them to establish exchange relationships that are cooperative and mutually beneficial rather than risky and costly, and therefore inefficient.

In commercial transactions, the knowledge that someone did not honour their financial obligations, or has cheated or defrauded others, impairs that person's reputation and their future commercial relationships. Reputation thus provides a convenient informal substitute for legally enforceable sanctions against dishonesty. An established firm with a good reputation makes it costly and risky for a potential competitor to enter the market (Chapter 13).

The rate at which knowledge about an entity spreads through the relevant social networks depends upon a variety of factors, such as the frequency and duration of interpersonal contacts and the importance of that knowledge. The effects of a person's actions on his or her reputation can accumulate over time as more people get to know about those actions and make inferences about the person. On the other hand, a person's past actions can have a diminishing effect on reputation as time passes because the information becomes out of date and so less relevant to current concerns about that person. Reputational attributions, however, often refer to stable personal dispositions, rather than to particular actions, so that reputations persist long after the actions that gave rise to them.

Network Theory

Rogers and Kincaid (1981), Knoke and Kuklinski (1982) and Scott (1991) have reviewed the concepts, theories and methods of social network analysis. Software packages are available for computer-assisted analysis. For example, networks can be analysed for gender, age and social role. Modern social network analysis is not limited to the examination of interpersonal relationships, which originated in sociometry. It can deal with the relationships between categories of people, social roles and social organisations.

The density of a social network can be thought of as the ratio of the number of actual links to the number of potential links between persons. The calculation of the ratio varies according to what density is supposed to measure. Some high-density networks show many members with kinship connections. It does not follow, however, that the flow of information and influence about an entity depends on the density of a social network. Much depends on the importance of that entity to the people in the network, and on the nature of the information and influence flowing through it. Confidential information and influence is supposed to be restricted in circulation, although 'leakages' occur especially in large, well-connected social networks. Modern technology offers new methods of communication, new methods of tapping into restricted networks and new methods of detecting surveillance.

Individuals in a social network differ in the extent of their direct contacts with other members. Individuals with many direct contacts (forming a sociometric 'star'), for example leaders, opinion-makers and popular people, are said to have high local centrality. A network with many 'stars' would have high global centrality, provided the 'stars' were closely linked.

There is a clear difference between a fully connected, or generally well-connected, network and a centrally organised network, such as a hierarchy or star, especially if the relationships are not reciprocal. Cliques and other subgroups in a social network can be identified by graphical or matrix methods of analysis. This requires basic information about persons and their affiliations, for example scientific authors and their citations, kinship or friendship relations, borrowers and their lenders.

Some individuals occupy key positions in a network linking otherwise separate groups of people (factions and subgroups). Some individuals have few or no substantial relationships with others in the group. Other individuals, by contrast, have multiple links with others that increase the likelihood that they will be subject to the flow of information and influence between members. The significance of one's position in the network depends partly on direct contacts, and partly on indirect contacts (contacts of contacts).

Individuals who are aware of the structure of a social network may position themselves in a way that increases their information and influence, as in politics and commerce. Those in authority may 'place' preferred people in positions (roles) that further strengthen their authority. In commerce, for example, directors may sit on the boards of several companies. The exchange of information and influence helps to determine the strategies and tactics of commercial enterprises, for example, through trading relationships, financial arrangements, agreements, cooperation, negotiation, and so on. Analogous effects occur in other kinds of corporate bodies—in education, religion, and national and local government.

Social network analysis is relevant to the study of reputation because it offers a systematic and quantitative approach to the way that information and influence spread through members of a group. The level of analysis varies with the size and type of reputation under examination. Sociometric diagrams may be sufficient for small-scale studies, but groups larger than, say, 10 usually require matrix methods. The basic data for an interpersonal network can be arranged in a rectangular incidence matrix in which the rows correspond to persons and the columns correspond to their characteristics. The cells show which persons have which characteristics, such as gender, age and role. This incidence matrix can be transformed into two different symmetrical adjacency matrices, for persons or for characteristics; one shows how many characteristics each person has, and the other shows how many persons have a particular characteristic. Methods of rearranging the rows and columns or transforming a matrix may reveal relationships not discernible in the original data. For example, the persons may fall into distinct subgroups, some persons may occupy central positions, and there may be cliques, isolates and unexpected links through intermediaries.

Raub and Weesie (1990) offered an analysis of reputation as a factor in the effects of social networks, with special reference to the Prisoner's Dilemma game and to associated economic relationships. They begin by defining reputation as an effect that emerges if a person's future associates are given information about his or her present behaviour. Raub and Weesie (1990) mentioned the interesting point that, in game theory at least, even a small amount of information can bring about significant effects in reputation. They show how the Prisoner's Dilemma model with repeated trials can be modified to take account of reputation among a group of individuals. The rational strategy is to cooperate conditional upon others' continuing to cooperate, even though the risk of non-cooperation (exploitation) by others remains. In connection with game theory, Wilson (1985) has argued that '. . . the player's reputation is the history of his previously observed actions' (see also Rosenthal and Landau, 1979). As we have seen, however, reputation is not a passive, objective record of the attributes or actions of an entity, but an active, subjective reaction by others to the perceived attributes and actions of that entity. Moreover, reputations can be 'managed' and 'damaged' deliberately; an entity and its reputation are distinct, each influences the other.

Raub and Weesie (1990) raised another interesting point, namely the costs of monitoring information circulating in the social network. Failing to know about the poor reputation of a person, organisation, product or service can be costly. On the other hand, it is costly to be constantly on the alert for information. People differ in their ability and in their desire to monitor the effects of their behaviour on others (Pozo et ai., 1991).

Extent and Degrees of Acquaintance

We interact mostly with people we know reasonably well on a regular, frequent, and informal basis, particularly those within our primary groups. Social acquaintance varies from frequent, direct, intimate contact to infrequent (perhaps single occasion) contacts of a highly formal, indirect sort. Husband/wife and parent/young child relationships typify one extreme; manager/worker and commander/soldier relationships typify the other. Close relationships between people are usually complex. They have many inter-dependent aspects, as in family, friendship or business relationships. Furthermore, relationships are affected by factors such as age, sex, seniority and personality.

Reputation is not confined to interpersonal contacts of a direct sort. Many social relationships are indirect and distant. Information and influence can spread well beyond their origins in primary groups, and information and influence that originate in extended secondary groups can penetrate primary groups. Malicious rumours, infiltration, as well as sheer weight of external opinion can lead to changes in reputation even within closely knit primary groups. Thus, members of a person's reputational community include close and distant acquaintances, supporters and detractors, central and peripheral members of the total network of information and influence.

A person under investigation as a matter of public interest, for instance the victim of an accident or crime, brings together several 'interested parties', such as the police, social workers, relatives and friends. The information available to one party may be different from the information available to another. The overlap between different interest groups concerning information relating to a person is analogous to the overlap between individuals in their beliefs about a reputational entity (see Chapter 1 and Figure 1.2).

Methodology

The original work on social networks—sociometry—was carried out by Moreno (1934) who made considerable use of sociograms. Sociograms are diagrams in which points represent persons, and the lines connecting them represent relationships of one sort or another. Small-scale sociograms are easy to construct and useful in educational and other applied social settings. Besides providing a basis for the study of reputational networks, they can be used to identify popular or isolated children, bullies, preferred and non-preferred co-workers, cliques, and exchange relationships.

Social network analysis is now much more sophisticated (Knoke and Kuklinski, 1982). It attempts to deal with large-scale social networks, and with multiple relationships between people or types of people, or between organisations, rather than with dyadic relationships such as like/dislike or preferences. Social relationships can be represented as a matrix, where the numbers 0 or 1 in the cells show the relationships between the entities listed in the rows and columns of the matrix, as illustrated in Figures 6.1 and 6.2. Matrix algebra can be used to analyse such data. In this way, one can examine direct and indirect relationships, and sets of relationships between sets of entities. Other analytic techniques—directed graphs, multi-dimensional scaling, cluster and factor analysis—can be used to identify latent variables.

Knoke and Kuklinski (1982) described how large-scale social networks can be investigated. They do not catalogue every individual's direct and indirect relationships, but instead sample the population of interest and establish the relationship, if any, between all pairs of members of the sample. This reveals the density of the network. Another method is to classify respondents on relevant variables, such as age, sex, residence and political affiliation, and similarly to classify the people with whom each respondent has a specified relationship (friend, co-worker, and so on). This shows the extent to which such variables, in isolation or in combination, account for the observed relationships in a

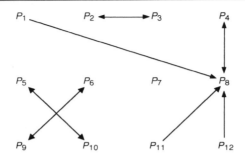

Figure 6.1. A simple single-choice sociogram representing a group of 12 persons (P_1 to P_{12})

network. Knoke and Kuklinski (1982) argued that the traditional sampling techniques used in social survey work are not suitable for investigating social networks.

Research into social networks has increased greatly in recent years. The main issues appear to have been those of definition and measurement. There are many kinds of social network. For example, there are family networks, professional networks, support networks and social networks associated with leisure, friendship, neighbourhood, crime, and so on. A person's social networks can be combined into a global network. Some networks are long lasting, others are

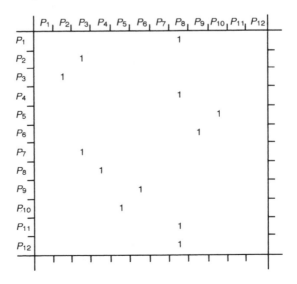

Figure 6.2. A sociomatrix representing the same set of interpersonal choices as those shown in Figure 6.1

short lived; some have a stable membership, others fluctuate. The problem is to define the nature of a network. This is sometimes implicit in the sorts of questions asked of respondents. For example: 'Who have you interacted with directly concerning your work in the last week?', 'Which of your neighbours have you acknowledged recently?', 'Who would you turn to for help about a personal problem that you did not want to become widely known?' The answers to each question reveal different networks.

Social networks can be measured in several ways. For example, respondents can be asked to identify the people they know in samples of names and addresses from a *Who's Who*, electoral roll or professional register. They can be asked to name the people who might help them to contact someone with whom they are not acquainted, or who might be willing to take part in a joint venture. Different questions tend to yield different names, but questions that yield similar networks help to define the nature of those networks.

Bernard et al. (1990) compared four different methods for measuring personal social networks. They found wide differences between individuals, but few substantial factors to account for the variation. Travel increased network size; their middle-aged respondents had larger networks than younger or older people. There were more men in the global networks, but more women in the support networks. Bernard et al. (1990) raised the interesting question of how social networks are stored in memory, and how names are accessed when required, for example, in response to questions of the form, 'Do you know anyone who . . .?'

Personal social networks and reputational networks no doubt overlap, but the essential feature of a reputational network is not who the person knows, but who knows the person. Some of the links in the reputational network of communication and influence are remote or tenuous. The emphasis in the study of reputational networks is on the distribution of information in fairly well-defined social groups or 'audiences'. This is because some social groups are more significant than others for reputation, and because remote low-frequency attributions are of little practical importance.

There are risks in relying on verbal reports of social relationships. Nevertheless, retrospective reports, log-book entries, and other methods of recording interactions and relationships, can be used to trace the sources and recipients of the information and influence that spread through a network. Where possible, direct observation is preferred. The difficulties associated with direct observation in real-life settings are well known. In real-life settings we are unlikely to be able to monitor the behaviour of all the people all the time even if we could delimit the network realistically. Moreover, information about reputation is often confidential and unavailable to an outside observer and the reputee.

If we had information on the characteristics of respondents, this might help to explain the distribution of beliefs. For example, how does the reputation of a financier or a commercial organisation spread through the stock market? How does the reputation of a new psychological technique spread through the community of psychologists? How does the brand image of a perfume spread among the women in a city?

Social network analysis is not confined to interpersonal relationships. It can be applied to inter-organisational relationships. Organisations exchange information, goods and services; they sometimes share managers and other staff. Organisations influence each other; they participate in large, complicated, secondary networks of business, educational, scientific, cultural and other relationships.

Much is known from ordinary experience about the spread of information and influence in social networks. The question is what might be gained from more rigorous investigation using modern techniques of network analysis. Economists and sociologists are interested in mapping large-scale social structures because of the light this might throw on economic, technological and cultural developments. The police and investigative journalists are interested in linkages of a political or financial sort that appear to work against the public interest— illegal arms sales, financial swindles, political subversion, drug trafficking.

It is important to recognise the scale and complexity of social networks even for ordinary people in the activities of everyday life. Burt's (1982) analysis of social networks included estimates of (i) the total number of people with whom a person interacts directly; (ii) the diversity or heterogeneity of the person's social contacts; (iii) the extent to which members of a person's social network interact with each other; (iv) the extent to which the person has different sorts of relationships with people in the network. Boissevain (1974), Burt (1982) and Bernard et al. (1991) have attempted to specify particular networks (see also Burt and Minor, 1982; Fischer, 1982; Burt, 1990).

The question is, 'What purposes are served by this kind of research?' Emler (1990) argued that it demonstrates the importance of primary social relationships even in large industrial societies, contrary to some sociological views. Emler (1990) studied the social contacts of students over a 7-day period. He reported an average of 50 (for men) and 49 (for women) *different* people contacted, most of whom were informal contacts—friends and casual acquaintances. In a different study, Emler found that, in industry and the public sector, managerial staff aged 30 to 50 years had a higher proportion of formal contacts but about the same number of *different* contacts. Even the formal contacts were known fairly well.

Boissevain (1974) estimated that the adults in his sample knew and were known by perhaps 3000–5000 people, and that the numbers of people known personally by ordinary adults ranges from several hundreds to several thousands. Individuals know some people who do not know them, and do not know other people who do know them. If these balance out, on average, we can begin to appreciate the quantitative scale of reputation. People who are identified and 'known' through the media are likely to have a large-scale reputation, meaning that a large number of people are at least aware of their existence. They are often 'known' briefly and superficially. Widespread access to the media led to Warhol's comment that, 'In the future, everyone will be famous for fifteen minutes'! We have argued elsewhere that public interest and attention, as the sum of individual interest and attention, has an upper limit, so that some reputations decrease in size in response to the emergence of competing reputations. Social network analysis has been used to study the transmission of information and money between organisations. Thus, apart from networks concerned with information and influence, there are networks concerned with the exchange or transfer of goods and services, financial transactions, kinship and friendship, functional interaction, and emotional involvement. Although social network analysis appears not to have been applied to the study of reputation, it is clearly relevant.

Reputational Networks

The essential ingredients of reputational networks are persons and relationships. In situations where organisational rather than interpersonal networks are being investigated, it is *individuals* within the organisations who are at the receiving end of information and influence. They, in turn, transmit information and exert influence in the name of the organisation. People are the organisation's agents. This is clearly seen in situations where persons *represent* organisations or *embody* them. People control organisations not only by controlling the flow of information, but also by holding key positions in the network that enable them to allocate resources, block interference by others and negotiate relationships with other organisations.

At a community level, many people have a multiplicity of formal and informal relationships with various others. Social network analysis tries to capture and analyse this complexity. The usual aim is to understand why people or organisations behave in the way they do, for example, in business matters, politics, leisure activities and consumer activities. In other words, network analysis deals with the structure, content and process of social interaction.

Reputation entities (organisations, persons, products and services) have characteristics attributed to them by interested parties (groups of people sharing a common concern with an entity). These attributions need not correspond to an entity's actual characteristics. Relationships too are characteristics; so relationships can be misconstrued. For example, respondents might say, 'Their relationship is reputed to be more than friendly'. This might or might not be true, but the belief forms part of the reputation of each of the persons referred to, and illustrates the interdependence of some reputations.

The information in circulation usually tells us something interesting or useful about the target entity—for example, that Smith is thinking of leaving his job, that Smith and his neighbour are not on friendly terms, that Smith devotes much of his time and money looking after his elderly infirm mother. Some information in daily life is commonly regarded as gossip or rumour (Rosnow and Fine, 1976); it may or may not have functional significance, for example, information to the effect that someone cannot be trusted or is promiscuous. It can be believed or not; it can be passed on to others or not. Reputational information is part of the politics of everyday life—the business of monitoring and managing our relationships with the people with whom we interact and with whom our fate is, or seems to be, intertwined (see Bailey, 1971; Emler, 1990).

Within a social network some individuals are better informed than others, and have more influence on opinions within the network. This may be associated with gossip or with better means of observation and communication. Most adults have many social contacts if one counts both direct (face-to-face) contact and indirect (at-a-distance) contacts (friends of friends, contacts of contacts at further levels of remove). These contacts provide the basis for primary and secondary groups, cliques, factions, pressure groups, and so on.

COMMUNICATION AND INFLUENCE

Introduction: Information Pathways

Many interpersonal pathways of information and influence connect people in social networks. Information can be transmitted by word of mouth or other means. Social networks are often well connected, so that one person can usually communicate with an identifiable stranger some distance away, with just a few intermediate contacts (Milgram, 1974). People are socially segregated in many ways. Gate-keepers and modes of access sometimes restrict communication and influence. Even so, the well-connected nature of communication networks means that persistence and ingenuity should enable contact to be made even with reclusive and protected persons.

It is impossible to say how information and influence diffuse through a social network. We assume that information flows more readily between people who would nominate each other as confidant(e), colleague or friend. The rate and pattern of diffusion, however, depends on the nature of the information and influence, on the receptivity of the people concerned, and on a host of coincidental circumstances.

Communication in Everyday Life

Conversations about oneself or other people, as well as more serious discussions, are familiar to most adults. As Emler (1990) pointed out, they are the commonest topics of conversation. Information can be transmitted casually, inadvertently, or deliberately; it can be registered by the recipient, but not retained for long;

it can be misunderstood or deliberately misconstrued; it can be 'filed away' for possible future use. Information transmitted and received in these ways might or might not spread through part or all of a social network. Much depends on the perceived importance of the information, and the receptivity of the audience. Information can be broadcast to large numbers of people through the mass media of communication.

Information is communicated in a context that affects its meaning. For example, spoken words are often accompanied by paralinguistic signals—facial expression, tone of voice. Similarly, one can 'read between the lines' of a written statement, and realise that it means the opposite of what it seems to say, or that it is not to be taken seriously. Coded messages refer to the practice of saying something in such a way as to convey a secondary message, such that a remark or an action should be regarded as a joke or, conversely, as serious. Information is conveyed by what is *not* said.

The main point, however, is that individual representations enter the public domain via a common language and shared frames of reference for understanding the world. These individual representations are subject to social conformity, and some features converge in time to form a collective representation, a representation common to most members of the relevant community. It incorporates shared beliefs, values, attitudes and opinions. The extent of sharing is a matter for empirical inquiry.

The extent to which some social representations are shared is considerably less than one might suppose. The phrase 'What is generally believed', defining reputation, is misleading because the extent of agreement may be less than a simple majority. This raises the question of how best to define reputation. We have argued elsewhere that reputation can be defined as the sum of shared representations at a given time and in given circumstances. This collection of shared representations can be transformed into a 'collective representation' and acted upon by whatever means a community adopts to 'represent' their common view. The means adopted may be fairly rational and straightforward—majority voting on a motion, the views expressed by an elected delegate or spokesperson, or tacit acceptance of what is perceived to be the majority viewpoint. On the other hand, collective action may be irrational and indirect—directed by minority activists, and the slogans of agitators or state propagandists or self-appointed opinionists.

Polarisation

Turner (1991) has reviewed classic and recent attempts to analyse the processes of social influence. It is not possible to describe this work in detail, but it is worth rehearsing some key ideas. The exchange of information in a group may lead to conformity, such that members whose views were not typical for the group gradually bring their views more into line. Widely shared views are more likely to be encountered, so that people with deviant views will often feel under some obligation to conform. Prototypical members are those whose views are more widely shared within their in-group and more sharply differentiated from the views in a contrasting out-group. In circumstances where some members have initial views closer to one standpoint whilst others are closer to the other standpoint, group opinion may split or polarise. This may be because members see themselves as having more in common with one subgroup than with another or become aware of the costs and benefits of different standpoints. Much depends on the extent to which contrasting views can be tolerated within a group. The threat of social division may lead to compromise. On the other hand, a minority may break away from or be expelled by the majority, as with political or religious dissidents.

In analysing reputation, we are concerned with conformity rather than with compliance or with the social influences and power structures that produce compliance. Opinions about entities expressed in compliance with external constraint result in *pseudo-reputations*. It is, of course, possible, given a lack of counter-information and counter-influence, for people to believe what they are told to believe. As we have seen, much of what we believe is socially constructed and taken on trust. It is not that we have been forced to believe, it has simply not occurred to us to question what we have been told.

Discussion about a reputational entity can have two effects. It can draw members' attention to issues they had not previously considered, and it can give a rough indication of the extent of agreement within a group. These two effects in combination may lead not to conformity but to polarisation. The polarisation of views under certain conditions helps to explain the different impressions formed of an entity, even within a well-connected social network. It also helps to explain why some members change their point of view in response to a challenge. The challenge offers a contrasting view, and a member may modify his or her view to accommodate or deflect the challenge. For example, challenging a person's impression that a political candidate is left-wing might make that person search for evidence to the contrary and so shift their impression in that direction.

Combining Attributions

Although particular attributes (for persons, products or organisations) can be defined and assessed, they are expressed in combination with other attributes. The question is 'What impact does a particular attribute have on an observer when it is perceived in association with other attributes?' It can be shown that some attributes are more 'central' than others, in the sense of facilitating associated attributes. Individuals are likely to differ in the way attributes are associated in their implicit theories about persons, products and organisations. In any event, in normal discourse, attributions are usually qualified and assigned in a particular context that restricts their meaning.

In some instances, people's general attitudes towards an entity can be influenced by having them attend to particular attributes, rather as one's attitude towards a food can be influenced by having one's attention drawn to the ingredients. People differ in their reactions to this sort of information, as they do when their attention is drawn to a person's attributes. Another problem is that the attributes people assign to others sometimes refer to imaginary characteristics. Market research into brand image considers the effects of various combinations of product attributes on consumer behaviour, and calculates the relative importance of the attributes.

Opinion Leaders

Opinion leaders are persuasive to the extent that they are perceived as credible, i.e. seem to be experts in their area, trustworthy, truthful and well intentioned. It also helps if they are attractive, have attributes in common with the listener, and appear to have little or nothing to gain personally in voicing their opinions. In law, as in daily life, opinions that go against the speaker's interest are regarded as more credible than opinions that serve the speaker's interest. An opinion leader for one issue or in one social context need not be an opinion leader for another issue or in a different context. The opinions of celebrities, however, often carry weight even on issues outside their range of competence. Preston and Guseman (1979) considered reputation to be one factor in the problem of identifying community leaders.

People differ in their willingness to interact with others and to voice their opinions, especially when the issue is novel or controversial. For example, in the UK in the Conservative leadership election of November 1990, some people were prepared to proclaim their support publicly for one candidate or another. Other people were reticent or completely silent on the issue. Similarly, because of their personal qualities, some were more effective than others in explaining and justifying their opinions, and in convincing others to think likewise. Circumstances play a part too, for there are occasions when a person's views are influential and other occasions when they are not. For example, voicing criticism of someone who has just suffered a misfortune might have the opposite effect to that intended.

Direct, first-hand personal experience is normally the most influential factor in forming an impression, whether of a person, organisation, product or service. Perhaps the next most influential factor is direct exposure to the opinions of respected or admired people who claim to have direct personal experience of an entity. Many of us, for example, are inclined to take a friend's first-hand opinion about a make of car or household appliance more seriously than, say, a consumer report based on a survey of anonymous users. It seems to follow, therefore, that some sources are more important than others in the spread of information and influence (Kadushin, 1968; Brody, 1991). This affects the study of reputation.

Opinion leaders do not necessarily exercise their influence only by word of mouth; their behaviour sets an example and they provide a role model for others to imitate, perhaps in ways that their followers misunderstand or take to extremes. This ranges from simple copying of appearance and mannerisms to identification with a 'cult figure' or 'hero worship', with its attendant uncritical acceptance of the hero's pronouncements.

Opinion leaders, by definition, become the focus of attention from others, and so develop a more extensive reputation. This is likely to induce a certain amount of anxiety in some and euphoria in others, leading to changes in their behaviour—generating more moderate or more extreme opinions. Opinion leaders must be willing and able to operate at the focus of public attention. This is easy on a small social scale but becomes more difficult as the scale of public attention increases, especially when opposition emerges. Consider, for example, dealing with hecklers at a political meeting, answering critical questions at a scientific meeting or coping with the media's attempts to ridicule a point of view.

Opinion leadership is clearly relevant to the study of reputation. A few important people figure prominently in the media over long periods of time—celebrities, television 'anchor men', politicians and political commentators, experts of different sorts, newspaper correspondents and leader writers—and their opinions are likely to be influential and widespread. At the other extreme, in everyday life, the opinions of some people are more influential than those of others. Most people express their opinions, if at all, and are influenced in their opinions, by word of mouth through a network of social relationships. From time to time, an issue figures prominently in the media, but the widespread effects on opinion and behaviour that follow may be superficial and temporary, particularly among people who have no great interest in that issue. The people who are influenced tend to forget how their opinions were formed.

Experts differ. The information and opinion available from one expert does not necessarily represent the views of the general body of people in the expert's field of interest, for example nursing, education or manufacturing. The expert might well over- or under-estimate some features of an entity and not have the benefit of current first-hand knowledge in a key area.

Turner (1991) reminded us that we do not value expert opinion because it is valid (we cannot judge its validity). We value it because the social institutions we accept and value define the expert as someone whose opinions we can trust. Our uncertainty is reduced by social influence in the guise of expert information. The issue of opinion leaders in advertising is taken up in Chapter 13.

Scandal, Rumour and Gossip

The importance of scandal in reputation is that, by definition, scandal is about something important to society generally, or is made to appear so to a section of society (see Rost, 1990). Consequently, people feel free to pass on information about a scandal, unless their fate is linked with that of the person concerned. There are, however, legal restraints on the sorts of things that can be said or written about people (Chapter 9). Scandals provoke rumour and gossip with their attendant inventions and distortions. For a recent brief review, see Emler (1992).

Rumours abound in situations where the future is uncertain and people feel vulnerable or excited about it. They become sensitive to signals that seem to show how things might work out. They are inclined to attach firm meanings to ambiguous circumstances or events, and to communicate their views to others in the same situation. This information is likely to be passed from one person to another. In the process, it becomes shorter and more concise as details are dropped, it becomes distorted by invention and transposition. Rumour and gossip can be malicious or criminal, for example in attempts to manipulate the stock market.

Rumour and gossip contribute, temporarily at least, to a person's reputation. Similarly, information about other sorts of entities circulate as rumour or gossip with little foundation. People entertain all sorts of untruths or half-truths that they convey to others who often accept them uncritically and pass them on. As more people accept an idea, it appears to be more valid than it really is.

Rumour and gossip enter into national politics, and into the 'politics of everyday life' in every sphere of social relationships. They provoke political leaders into issuing statements that, directly or indirectly, lead to clarification of a situation, as in an internal policy dispute or a leadership contest. At whatever level of participation in this political process, people seek to protect and enhance their reputation and the reputation of their social contacts and organisations. This is achieved through the content of relevant statements and the style of their presentation.

In some circumstances, people are prepared to put their reputation at risk, for example by voicing their personal opinions, in the interests of moral principles or social objectives. This kind of self-assertion usually requires the confidence that some social support will be forthcoming.

We need to distinguish between three related phenomena: rumour, gossip and hearsay. Rumours were studied intensively during World War II in connection with the maintenance of morale. Rumours are unattributable reports that circulate rapidly in communities that face an uncertain future and lack reliable information from credible sources about what is likely to happen. Thus rumours spread in the stock market in conditions of economic uncertainty; rumours spread among troops when things are not going according to plan. Rumours can be spread deliberately, or they can arise accidentally through speculations, misunderstandings and partial 'leaks' of confidential information. As they spread through a social network they become self-reinforcing, because the more people that hear the rumour the more reliable it appears to be. Rumours tend to disappear as their improbability becomes increasingly apparent, or when reliable information is available.

Hearsay is simply information received indirectly from a third party. Hearsay is not 'good' evidence in the legal sense. Good evidence is testimony based on direct observation and documentary or material records.

Gossip refers to the casual exchange of information usually about people and their circumstances. Gossip can include passing on rumours. The information in gossip is quasi-confidential in that it usually takes place between people who are on close, friendly terms with each other. Each understands the extent to which the gossip can be passed on. The deliberate introduction of false, malicious, unattributed information would not count as gossip, since gossip normally has an attributable, if remote, source. Gossip is likely to include information that is socially significant or stimulating. Therefore, scandals, secrets and revelations—matters normally restricted in circulation—are important.

Impressions based on rumour, hearsay and gossip are likely to exhibit several features associated with the serial transmission of information from one person to another. Such impressions are likely to show good continuation (coherence or consistency), assimilation to expectation (information is remembered better if it fits in with what is already believed), condensation (information is abbreviated into key words and phrases), sharpening (some information is highlighted), and levelling (some details are omitted).

The relevance of rumour, gossip and hearsay to reputation is that these sorts of information circulate in social networks. They influence reputations by adding to, subtracting from or otherwise modifying the distribution of beliefs about a person (or other entity) in a social group.

Malicious rumours can be spread in the interests of political, financial or social gain. In everyday life, suspicions, guesses, assumptions and deliberate lies occur in conversations and are passed on as true or likely to be true. Rumours and gossip are sometimes prefaced by qualifying statements, such as 'I understand that . . .', 'I believe . . .', 'Don't quote me but . . .', 'Is it true that . . .?' and 'People say . . .'. These phrases enable the speaker to engage in rumour and gossip without checking the evidence or being held responsible for the information.

The word 'gossip' refers to conversations about people carried on in the absence of the person being talked about. Remarks would probably not be made if the person were present. These are disparaging, derogatory remarks, or items of information that the person being talked about does not want to be made public. The motivation behind gossip varies. The speaker may want to show their 'insider' status, or may want to damage the reputation of the person referred to, or may simply want to amuse their audience. The listener also may be keen to hear 'inside' information, or may be interested or amused by the reported doings and scandal. Gossip fulfils several functions. It satisfies personal needs, however trivial. It sets up exchange relationships between the people who are gossiping—they are, in a sense, conspiring, and entering into mutual obligations. Gossip is a way of trading information. Gossip exerts control over people—the gossipers and the person being talked about. This is because it is likely that the reputation of the person being talked about will, in time, have effects on that person. The effect of reputation usually brings his or her behaviour more into line with social expectations. Those taking part have an implicit understanding of the effects of gossip, and the possibility that they too may become the subject of gossip. Gossip has its dangers. Passing information to 'outsiders' may bring retribution from within the group or from the person who feels offended or betrayed.

Some newspapers and magazines carry 'gossip' columns that inform and entertain readers with stories about the behaviour of well-known people. Newspapers also devote space to 'human interest' stories about unusual episodes in the lives of otherwise ordinary people, or about the unusual behaviour of some individuals. These are examples of the way the press and other media manage the news.

Rumours are more likely in conditions of perceived threat and lack of credible information. Rumours tend to circulate mainly within the social groups that have a strong interest in certain kinds of information, for example, rumours within a company about company affairs and personnel. At some stage in their spread, rumours may provide reasons for decisions and actions—to retreat or not, to buy or sell. If this effect spreads quickly, we have a collective or general reaction, the group or organisation reacting like a single entity.

People who are more familiar with or closer to the situation, or better acquainted with the entity that is the subject of rumours, will adapt to the perceived threat. In comparison with those who are less familiar or less well acquainted with it, they will perceive it as less threatening. They have learned to discount rumours.

AIDS Rumours

Kimmel and Keefer (1991) examined rumours about autoimmune deficiency syndrome (AIDS). The first point to note is that a disease can be a reputational entity. That is to say, it can be identified as a specific thing or condition (here, HIV infection) with various attributes (symptoms, risks). It is the focus of a distribution of attributions in social groups. Kimmel and Keefer (1991) reported that there are many misconceptions about AIDS. Some groups, including college students, tend to get their information informally by word of mouth or from the media, not from 'official' sources. This illustrates a general point about reputation, namely that the main flow of information and influence is through informal channels. Information from official sources, experts and opinion leaders usually flows mainly through these channels.

Many people under-estimate their risk of infection, perhaps because they contrast themselves with high-risk groups. Some people have false beliefs—for example they believe that sex with a healthy, attractive partner is safe. Rumours about AIDS seem to operate in much the same way as rumours about other matters. Rumours are unverified reports about matters that people regard as interesting or important, and particularly about matters about which they feel anxious or uncertain. Rumours spread because they provide information where more credible information is lacking. Rumours about AIDS include reports that it can be transmitted by kissing, spitting, sneezing, insect bites, and surgical and dental treatment.

Kimmel and Keefer (1991) found wide differences between individuals in the number of AIDS rumours they had heard (averaging about seven), and in the number of sources from which they had received information about AIDS. They found that college students who were more anxious about AIDS were more likely to spread a rumour. The AIDS rumours that raised high levels of anxiety were the ones most likely to be transmitted. The self-reported level of anxiety was high. Although respondents reported changes in their *attitude* towards AIDS, this did not seem to correspond with reported changes in sexual *behaviour*.

Rumour transmission has a dual function. It conveys information that senders' social contacts want. It enables senders to test the credibility of their information against that available to their social contacts (who may refute the rumour). The media have a responsibility to publicise correct information about matters of public concern, and to do so promptly, widely and repeatedly. This should have the effect of limiting the spread of rumours and ill-advised behaviour.

7 Impression Management

Introduction

There are many questions of interest related to impression management (including self-presentation and reputation management). How do people assess their reputation in daily life, or their professional reputation? What methods do they use to manage their reputations? How does the self-image affect impression management? What factors affect individual differences in the management of reputation? Can one draw a useful analogy between self-presentation and public relations work? The related topic of person perception (impression formation) is dealt with in Chapter 4.

The proverb, 'Many a man would not recognise his reputation if they met on the street', reminds us that our knowledge of what other people think about us is at best partial and indirect. We may be fortunate in having personal contacts who are well informed and honest enough to tell us what other people think. Or we may be unfortunate in being surrounded by flatterers and 'gate-keepers' who select and distort the realities of our social image. We may be to some extent socially isolated and so be ignorant of the image of us that others share. Our psychological defences may prevent us from seeing ourselves as others see us.

Most adults have at least a limited tacit understanding of reputation and related processes (impression management, social networks, and so on). At times, we sense the impression we are making on other people, and try to change our behaviour (Scheier, 1980). People who have a lot to gain or lose through reputation—celebrities, people in prominent social positions, entertainers, criminals, and so on—are usually sensitive to and active in managing their reputation. Some employ public relations personnel to manage their public image; they are obliged to restrict their ordinary behaviour to safe settings that exclude access by the wider public or investigators of one sort or another.

Awareness of Reputation

DePaulo et al. (1987) investigated several aspects of person perception, including how we are viewed *generally* by others, and how we are viewed by *individual* others. These two forms of understanding do not necessarily coincide. The investigation used the Social Relations Model (Kenny and La Voie, 1984) to separate three effects: first, a subject's general impression of other people (within a restricted range); second, other people's general impression of a target person;

third, a subject's impression of a particular target person. The same effects presumably play a part in metaperspective impressions, i.e. how people judge the impressions they make on others.

The subjects in the experiment interacted in different pairs on four different tasks and completed a set of ratings of themselves and their partners. The ratings combined to produce two composite scores: liking and competence. The subjects' self-ratings were consistently lower than their partners' ratings of them. That is, subjects under-estimated the impression they made on others (perhaps because of the demand characteristics of the situation). Subjects could not accurately judge how well their partners judged them overall on either likeability or competence. There was little agreement between subjects in their impression of a given partner. Subjects correctly judged that the impressions they made improved from one occasion to the next.

Socially anxious subjects believed they gave the impression of being incompetent and not liked. Extraverts believed that they gave the impression of being likeable and competent. Subjects generally believed that those whom they perceived as likeable and competent viewed them in the same way.

DePaulo et al. (1987) made the point that self-monitoring and self-presentation are more likely when the motivation to impress is high but confidence is not. This would be the case when we know we are being evaluated by influential people whose reactions towards us are not easily discovered or changed. DePaulo et al. (1987) also mentioned the difficulties in assessing the accuracy of person perception identified by Cronbach and others, such as the effects of assumed similarity. We tend to assume that other people see us as we see ourselves, although the relationship between self-perception and perception by others is not as close as we assume. A key finding in relation to reputation was that partners did not show consistent reactions to the same partner. This confirmed the view that reputation is a distribution of different attributions (Chapters 1, 14 and 15). Target persons, however, believed that they had conveyed broadly the same impression to different partners (thus confirming the view that people tend to over-estimate the *generality* of their reputation).

Monitoring Reputation

The idea of self-monitoring refers to the process by which we evaluate our own performance. The standards against which we judge ourselves need not be entirely rational, as with people whose anxiety, depression or perfectionism is partly a cause or consequence of unrealistic self-appraisal. In the normal course of events, we compare our behaviour and characteristics with those of certain other people. These 'self–other' comparisons lead to different sorts of reactions depending upon the outcome. For example, if we feel dissatisfied with the outcome, we feel despondent or, conversely, determined to improve our appearance, work performance, morality, education, or whatever. Faced with conflicting standards, for example at work, we judge our own behaviour against that of our colleagues, or against some ideal standard (maximum performance), or by what we can get away with (minimum performance). Normally, the standards against which we judge ourselves are socially prescribed and widely recognised in the communities to which we belong.

Biggs, Rosen and Summerfield (1980) reported on the use of video-feedback to explore subjects' awareness of their public image by observing changes in subjects' self-appraisal. Feedback increased self-esteem in normal subjects but decreased it in anorexic subjects. Self-esteem remained negative before and after feedback in depressed patients. Bond (1982) argued that under certain conditions social facilitation can be accounted for by self-presentation, but loss of public esteem can cause embarrassment and a fall in performance. Baumeister (1982a) investigated the effects of self-esteem on self-presentation. Subjects with high self-esteem showed increased self-esteem in response to bogus information about their personality. Effects depended on whether the information was public or confidential (private), and on whether future interactions were expected. For a self-presentational view of social behaviour, see Baumeister (1982b).

Pozo et al. (1991) used bogus video responses, and showed that subjects with high or low social anxiety did not differ significantly in their responses to changes in the facial expression of an evaluator. Subjects with high social anxiety, however, believed others viewed them more negatively (were less interested and less accepting) than did subjects with low social anxiety. Pozo et al. pointed out that their results could be interpreted as bias on the part of low social anxiety subjects to believe that others view them more positively.

Deluga (1991) used self-report measures to investigate how people in subordinate roles try to influence their supervisors and managers. The scales purport to measure self-monitoring (behaving in a way that fosters a particular impression), deception of others (dissembling) and organisational influence strategies. Deluga identified a number of impression management strategies, for example, reasoning and bargaining, friendliness (ingratiation and flattery), and the use of assertiveness, power, authority and coalition. Subjects who scored higher on self-monitoring and deception of others appeared to be more effective in influencing their supervisors. Deluga also drew attention to the difference between motivation and skill in impression management.

In a free society, considerable choice is available to individuals regarding their standards of conduct. In authoritarian societies, there are severe sanctions against deviations from the prevailing code of conduct. Self-monitoring is reinforced by monitoring by others. Deviations from what is normally expected of us are likely to elicit questions, criticisms, warnings or more severe penalties. Self-monitoring takes account of the likely reactions of other people, especially the key people in our social network. This is how individuals and society reach an accommodation between the self-concept and reputation (Chapter 4).

People have several reputations, and these reputations change with circumstances over time and may be quite unstable. So, strictly speaking, we do not normally, and maybe cannot ever, become aware of the full nature and extent of our reputation(s). Instead, we pay attention to the reactions our behaviour gets from those people we regard as important or influential. Their reactions signal approval or disapproval, like or dislike, or indifference, as well as specific impressions. In theory, the procedure known as 'performance evaluation' in organisations provides opportunities for frank and confidential exchanges of views between superiors and subordinates. In the process, subordinates are made more aware of the impressions that other people have formed of them.

So, in one sense, our general reputation is less important than the specific impressions formed by key associates. Two assumptions are possible. One is that the impressions formed by our key associates influence our general reputation. The other is that our general reputation is simply less accessible and less important than these key impressions. Both assumptions seem likely to be correct. The people with whom we are closely associated, through frequent, direct interpersonal contact, are likely to be fairly closely associated with each other. This comes about because of the way social relationships are organised. We behave, with varying degrees of individuality, in extended networks of social relationships. We contribute to, and are subject to, the information and influence that flow through these networks (Chapter 6).

In the interests of economy of effort (optimal self-monitoring) most people note the reactions of a few key informants and key influencers rather than try to find out what everyone thinks about them. Some individuals in some circumstances actively monitor and manage their reputation(s); but this sort of behaviour is not without its costs and risks. Indeed, people who are unduly concerned about what other people think of them are regarded as lacking in self-confidence and self-esteem. Questions such as 'What are people saying about me?' and 'What is your opinion of me?' are likely to be met by evasive or non-committal statements if the truth is likely to be unpalatable. Lack of confidence and lack of self-esteem (social anxiety) handicap a person's public performances; this leads to a worsening of reputation and a further weakening of confidence and esteem.

In our culture it is normally impolite to tell people that the impression you have formed of them is in some ways a poor one. Even a counsellor is circumspect in drawing attention to a client's socially undesirable characteristics. On the other hand, there are circumstances in which telling someone what you really think of them, and what other people think of them, is regarded as socially acceptable, even laudable. Consider, for example, a teacher admonishing a child who has misbehaved badly, a judge commenting on an offender, or one person berating another for serious misconduct (betrayal, negligence, unprofessional conduct). There are, of course, legal restraints on saying publicly what you think of someone—the laws of libel and slander (Chapter 9).

Our understanding of other people's impressions of us depends upon being able to make the appropriate inferences from their behaviour: what they do, what they say, and what they do not do and do not say, in a given set of circumstances. People's expressive behaviour provides important clues about their attitudes towards us. However, their more deliberate actions may disguise their real feelings and intentions. We can be mistaken even about the true views of the people we know best, because there are circumstances in which people feel it would not be prudent to disclose their true nature. This is familiar to all of us in the case of people we feel it would be unwise or cruel to offend. So it is not easy to monitor one's reputation(s). One can be led astray by misleading indications—by people telling us what they think we want to hear. We may be afraid to expose ourselves to criticism through performance evaluation, peer evaluation or open discussion. It follows that we may know little of what other people think of us, not only those with whom we have no direct face-to-face contact but also those with whom we interact frequently. In managing reputation, one needs to define the target audiences (publics) because it is usually necessary to cultivate different reputations in different groups, and to use appropriate methods in each.

Large-scale organisations deal with the problem of reputation monitoring and reputation management by using a wide range of professional public relations techniques (Chapter 12). A public 'personage'—in politics or entertainment—uses similar techniques. Persons who do not have a well-developed reputation can employ techniques to enhance their image, such as circulating a *curriculum vitae* or references from credible sources, or by finding sponsors, or by advertising. A damaged reputation can sometimes be repaired by reputation management and public relations efforts.

Diamond (1991) in a technical contribution to the literature on banking concluded that, where there is some risk of default, new borrowers form their reputation under supervision. They borrow from banks and the banks monitor their performance. Their reputation is established by performing well and meeting their obligations. The same borrowers may then issue debt directly, without monitoring, or borrow more with less collateral. Economic events in the UK in the late 1980s illustrated the risks associated with excessive borrowing and inadequate monitoring. By analogy, we could say that personal reputations are formed under the supervision or protection of people with established reputations. That is to say, people who are not yet established socially are backed or sponsored by those who are established. Personal recommendations, school reports, letters of reference, and so on, make this possible. Exceptions include innovators lacking socially acceptable backers, whose achievement makes so great an impact that it overcomes initial lack of social support or even opposition. Sponsorship and protection, of course, make it possible for some people to develop a spurious reputation, one that precedes or exceeds demonstrable achievement, as in nepotism.

Self-presentation (Impression Management)

Self-presentation means that our actions are constrained by our awareness of the effect that our behaviour might have on the person or persons with whom we are interacting, or on the 'audience' that witnesses, or might hear about, our performance. Shimanoff (1985), for example, described the expression of emotions in marital relationships as 'face' or impression management. Tunnell (1984) claimed that female undergraduates who were particularly concerned with their public image were more variable in the way they presented themselves in social situations. They also showed a greater discrepancy between their self-image and the public image they projected. They scored higher on conformity, 'exhibition' (probably extraversion), anxiety and social recognition, and lower on self-esteem, risk-taking and innovation.

Self-presentation affects reputation because of the way one person conveys information to another, and tries to exert influence. Self-presentation is also apparent in a person's reactions to the information conveyed and the influence exerted. For example, an attempt by one worker to convince another worker that a supervisor is incompetent might elicit a reaction that gives the impression that the listener has a high regard for the supervisor. This impression then forms part of the *listener's* reputation. The flow of information and influence in social interaction shows reputation in the making, as it were.

Impression management pervades social interaction. Terminal social actions—retiring, resigning, breaking off a friendship, divorce, leaving a neighbourhood, even dying—may be intended to take credit or lay blame, or to signal a change of attitude. Obituaries provide intermediaries with opportunities to promote posthumous reputation and perhaps to associate the intermediary more closely with what the deceased stood for.

Impression management raises ethical issues in the sense that the motivation behind impression management could be regarded as immoral. This includes lying to gain personal advantage, and being disloyal to an organisation. Much immoral and criminal behaviour, by definition, depends upon impression management, in the sense of misleading other people. This does not mean that all impression management behaviour is wrong. On the contrary, much impression management is for the public good because it helps social interaction and personal adjustment.

Unsuccessful impression management does not merely fail to create the intended impression, it can have the opposite effect. Unconvincing friendliness may be seen as ingratiation, unconvincing assertiveness may be seen as weakness.

The idea that we try to influence the impressions other peope form of us is not as simple as it appears to be at first sight. To begin with, there is the problem of distinguishing between actions motivated by a deliberate attempt to manage the impressions people form, and actions motivated by other concerns—cognitive consistency, exchange relationships, moral values, and long-term or indirect consequences. The degree of motivation (arousal) may make a difference to self-control. Second, personal characteristics such as extraversion, autonomy, social anxiety and self-monitoring, and social habits such as deference or suspicion, are likely to lead to individual differences in impression management behaviour. Third, different social circumstances impose different demands; actions that make the desired impression in one situation need not do so in another. Fourth, individual differences in social skills mean that some individuals are less able than others to make the desired impression, less able to work out what impression an audience expects or deserves, or less able to recognise the impression they have made. Fifth, socialisation has effects on behaviour even when the individual is acting alone, and trying to convince himself or herself that they are what they claim to be.

Impression management can be reflexive. We can engage in behaviour aimed at changing the impression we have of ourselves (our self-image) to bring it closer to our ideal self. Assertiveness training and role-rehearsal using feedback enable trainees to try out new forms of behaviour and learn habits of social interaction that change their self-image.

The main issue in impression management is understanding the conditions under which certain kinds of social behaviour occur, especially deceptions, mistakes, misunderstandings and social identifications. Consider, for example, the problem of deciding whether the statement 'I was only joking' is a genuine self-attribution or a way of disguising an inappropriate action. Johnson (1990) concluded that the statement is likely to be sincere, but not likely to be believed by others!

Tetlock and Manstead (1985) regarded impression management ideas as a metatheory or research programme based on certain assumptions. They think that the ideas do not add up a well-defined theoretical model, and that they are not clearly different from ideas derived from other approaches to social behaviour. There are difficulties in experimental studies in constructing valid and discriminating measures that are not confounded with related variables.

Individuals have different reasons for wanting to make a given impression on other people. They may need to make an impression to establish or confirm their impression of themselves. Impression management behaviour can be expected to vary from one audience to another. This is so at least for individuals who are sufficiently sensitive to impression management factors (high self-monitors) and have the ability and inclination to foster a particular impression. Different audiences have different expectations about a person. This person may or may not be aware of those expectations, or willing or able to fulfil them.

Gangestead and Snyder (1985) developed an 18-item measure of self-monitoring that was in some respects an improvement on Snyder's original 25-item measure (Snyder, 1974). It contained items such as 'I'm not always the person I appear to be' (keyed as True), 'I find it hard to imitate the behaviour of other people' (keyed as False). They concluded that self-monitoring could be regarded as a categorical variable rather than a dimensional (continuous) one.

Impression management aims to promote an impression in others that the actor believes will be effective and personally beneficial. Impression management behaviour usually conforms to generally accepted norms, values and expectations, but it need not do so because at times self-interests and social interests conflict. Most adults have a well-developed social identity (or set of social identities) that guides social interaction. If social identities are not routinely understood or taken for granted, then they have to be negotiated. People have to come to some sort of understanding and to define the situation they are in, otherwise there will be confusion.

Impression management concerns our 'public self', i.e. the impression we wish others to form. It also concerns our 'private self', i.e. our self-image, because impression management can produce different behaviour for different audiences, and sometimes outright deception. Impression management is not simply social conformity. Impression management is a way of negotiating our social identities in relation to other people who are also concerned to protect and enhance their social positions. This results in exchange relationships that reflect the kinds and degrees of power and dependence that people have in different areas of social life, such as pupil–teacher, professional and family relationships.

The concept of impression management can be used to explain various social phenomena. The main problem, however, is to identify the specific factors that lead to forms of social behaviour. These include modesty, altruism, surveillance, conformity, autonomy, expressive behaviour, ingratiation and cognitive consistency.

The importance of impression management in the study of reputation can hardly be exaggerated, because self-presentation presents an 'edited' version of the personality to a particular audience. Observers may fail to 'see through' self-presentational behaviour and so form incorrect impressions. The relationship between our private self and our public self may not be clear. So, the relationship between 'What the person really is' (Allport's phrase) and 'What is generally believed' is likely to be complicated and confusing. For other aspects of self-monitoring and self-presentation, see Funder (1980, 1987), Tedeschi (1981), Danheiser and Graziano (1982), Giacalone and Riordan (1990), Rosenfeld (1990), Cronshaw and Ellis (1991), Martink (1991), Morrison and Bies (1991), Olson and Johnson (1991), Villanova and Bernadin (1991), and Wall (1991).

Methods of Impression Management

One form of impression management is defensive—a response to threats to one's social or personal identity, well-being or reputation. Another form is promotional—an attempt to consolidate or enhance one's social standing generally or with particular people. Tedeschi and Reiss (1981) dealt with the verbal strategies used in the first kind of impression management when people find themselves in 'predicaments' in which they feel obliged to explain or justify their behaviour. These strategies include making excuses, giving reasons, apologising and denying; they are commonly observed in everyday life. Among the many sorts of justification for questionable actions are those associated with reputation. For example, we could say that we acted in defence of our reputation—to repair the damage done and to inhibit further attacks. Defensive forms of impression management include actions such as making a formal complaint or taking legal action.

The nonverbal strategies in impression management include expressive behaviour that communicates one's attitude, such as shaking one's head, tearing up a document or punching someone. It is sometimes necessary to act forcefully to establish or maintain one's credibility. This applies not only at the level of interpersonal relationships, but also at the level of corporate or international relationships. Threatening or actual aggressive behaviour is a common feature of dominance hierarchies in animal as well as in human societies.

Impression management sometimes calls for substantial shifts in behaviour. These include becoming more (or less) friendly with certain people, adopting a different religion, losing weight, or modifying one's style of writing or speaking. Impression management is particularly important in social relationships that are not well defined, and where personality characteristics come into play. Impression management can be taken too far. For example, too obvious displays of status or upward mobility may betray insecurity or selfishness.

Promotional forms of impression management mean that we go out of our way to advertise our aspirations and achievements, or the benefits we can provide for others because of our abilities and circumstances. These strategies too can be verbal or nonverbal. Boasting is a familiar but not always successful strategy in some circumstances; modest, humorous self-deprecation can be more effective. The performances we put on for interviews, weddings, funerals, staff meetings, 'dates' or other public occasions—the way we dress and speak, the action we take—can promote a particular reputation.

In its more extreme form, self-promotion can be stage-managed by professional public relations experts. The methods used to enhance corporate reputation—visual identification, policy statements, public relations activities, personal impression management, and so on—should be tested in field settings with appropriate audiences. The external audience reactions should reveal whether the reputation is enhanced or not by the particular method of promotion used. The internal audience reactions should reveal whether the image being promoted is in the best interests of organisational morale.

Strategies and Tactics

We can distinguish between strategic and tactical self-presentation. Tactical self-presentation refers to the spontaneous or habitual forms of behaviour we use to interact with people in ordinary, routine, face-to-face situations. Strategic self-presentation refers to the deliberate pre-planned actions we take to protect or enhance our self-concept, social position and reputation, as all three are closely interlocked. Strategic self-presentation, under this definition, is an attempt to improve our exchange (cost–benefit) relationships with others. For example, familiar ways of pursuing social status include cultivating useful contacts, achieving higher levels of performance and advertising the risks of non-cooperation.

Impression management refers to the attempt to control the effect one's coping and expressive behaviour have on other people in face-to-face situations. Reputation management refers to the attempt to control the more widespread and longer-term effects of one's behaviour, by deliberately modifying the impressions formed by others, especially others who are influential (see Salancik and Meindl 1984). Impression management is immediate and tactical, reputation management is pre-planned and strategic. Emler (1990) points out that the social repercussions of a person's actions often extend well beyond the immediate audience and the immediate occasion, and that the effects of a person's actions accumulate over time. Thus impression management interacts with reputation. *Impression* management on one occasion with one audience may be carried on in the wider, long-term interests of *reputation* management.

Craik (1989) listed some of the 'tactics' used in reputation management. These include marshalling support for oneself, making use of opportunities for public expression and repairing any damage to reputation. Sometimes, of course, people make mistakes—misunderstanding the audience they wish to influence, and using ineffective methods of communication and influence. The result may not be what they intended.

Emler (1984) reminded us that people have commitments to or investments in particular lines of behaviour. We have used the word 'concerns' elsewhere to refer to emotional involvement in certain kinds of goal-directed behaviour, those that we regard as personally important. These concerns are likely to involve others, or at least to have some social significance, so that they get incorporated into our personal and social identity. They are put at risk by threats to reputation. Furthermore, the people with whom we have strong attachments are extensions of our personal identity (see Allport's, 1955, notion of the 'proprium'). Our attachment to significant others affects our behaviour in the sense that we are likely to take account of its effects on them. The implications for reputation are that people find themselves protecting and enhancing the reputations of others who form part of their extended self.

One strategy of self-presentation conveys specific sorts of attribute: name dropping to show that one is well connected socially; initiating or contributing to conversations in ways that express one's cultural, scientific or political values and interests; dressing to show that one is fashion conscious, or, conversely, that one is unconcerned with outward appearances. Another strategy is to present oneself as a particular 'type' of person—academic, sportsman, businessman, feminist, housewife/mother, career women—or as a member of an in-group—gang member, member of a clique or political faction. Persons in these categories act in ways designed to foster the appropriate impression in others, i.e. they try to negotiate a particular sort of social identity.

Jones and Pittman (1982) listed some ways of presenting oneself to others, including self-promotion, ingratiation, intimidation and dependence. Expressions of opinion can fulfil instrumental functions, by showing independence, conformity or antagonism, for example (Smith, Bruner and White, 1956). Nonverbal behaviour—facial expression, posture, gesture, and so on—plays an important role in self-presentation (Argyle, 1975). Self-presentational actions are deliberate rather than spontaneous, at least until they become habitual. With practice, we develop habits of self-presentation that become an integral part of our personality; we convince ourselves that we are the sort of person we appear to be! A person who has cultivated a particular 'persona' for a time will appear to be spontaneously expressing personal qualities, for example moral rectitude. Self-presentation has all sorts of manifestations: the way we pose for photographs, the photographs we choose to show to others, the way we use our accommodation and display our possessions, the thoughts and feelings we disclose to others, the faults we disguise or disown.

Bennett and Yeeles (1990) said that some techniques of self-presentation, such as ingratiation, appear to be cognitively more complex than others and so appear later in development. They asked children aged 8 and 11 years to explain the actions of characters in stories, and showed that older children were more likely than younger children to refer to attempts to change a character's mental state. They were able to show an improvement with age in interpersonal understanding, but could not confirm that 'ingratiation' was cognitively more complex than 'self-promotion'.

The impression we usually wish to convey is our personal identity or self-concept. This is the long-term or strategic aspect of reputation management. In some circumstances, however, we 'put on an act' temporarily, and pretend to be something we are not—brave, affectionate, honest, or whatever. This is the short-term or tactical aspect of reputation management. Self-presentation is essential for two reasons. First, it helps to confirm the meaning of actions that might otherwise be misinterpreted. Second, it enables people to bring their personal identity (self-concept) and social identity (reputation) into line with each other. This helps to bring about social adjustment and behavioural consistency.

Emler (1984) suggested that responses to self-report measures are influenced by efforts at self-presentation—'faking good' and 'social desirability' response biases are obvious examples. Behaving in a socially desirable way need not be merely a response bias; it could be the expression of a genuine personality disposition.

Self-presentation is motivated in different ways. Some individuals are socially insensitive, or confident enough to ignore other people's reactions to them. Such people would not normally engage in self-presentational behaviour because they would not be concerned to present a favourable image. They would act as they thought fit, despite the impression made on others. To put it another way, such people would not normally hold themselves accountable to others.

Schlenker, Weigold and Doherty (1990) described the complex relationships between self-identity and social accountability, and showed how some psychopathological forms of behaviour can be interpreted as ways of dealing with or avoiding the stresses of being called to account. Social accountability is one aspect of reputation. It is the basis of social approval and disapproval; it is the basis of specific attributions related to success or failure. Schlenker and Weigold (1990) carried out a series of complex experiments on the relationship between personal autonomy and self-presentation. They used spurious feedback to test how subjects would report their opinions under social pressure to change their attitude. They argued that people who are autonomous are not insensitive to the effects of their behaviour on others. On the contrary, such people are prepared to monitor the effects of their behaviour on others and to 'put on an act' in order to present themselves as independent. People who are not autonomous can put on an act to secure the approval of others, and thereby present themselves as cooperative and conforming.

Emler (1984) studied the efforts that people imagined themselves making to describe and explain their actions to other people. The point is that some consequences of our actions become known, and need to be accounted for. Sometimes we need to explain that we were *not* involved in some incident that threatens our reputation. Sometimes we try to show that we were involved if it does credit to our reputation. Emler reported that potentially damaging incidents would be more often discussed with family and close friends. The presence of witnesses increases the effect, as does the interconnectedness (density) of our social network. In other words, we make more effort to protect our reputation if we realise that information about us will be reported and disseminated.

The effect of self-presentation on reputation varies with the situation. We take more care with the impression we are making when interacting with important or influential people. Frequent, routine encounters with people in daily life are governed by role prescriptions, modified somewhat by personal characteristics. Habitual modes of self-presentation are found in routine work situations and other aspects of daily life. Where frequent, intimate relationships occur, in family life for example, self-presentation strategies are so closely integrated with other personality characteristics that they are scarcely distinguishable as exercises in social skills. Failure to present oneself in the usual or expected way raises questions in the minds of others about one's state of mind or circumstances.

We carry out specific acts of impression management to achieve, maintain or improve an image that other people have of us. Impression management can be directed in quite specific ways at particular people—one's partner, colleague, friend, stranger, or whoever. Impression management can be used to create several different social identities (a familiar theme in fiction, especially farce). For example, we find ourselves having to deal with the conflicting requirements of family and work, or of different friendship groups.

One way of managing the impressions we make on others is to segregate the audiences with which we have to deal. Failure to do so may lead to anxiety, guilt, embarrassment and strained relationships. This is an important and widely recognised aspect of social organisation and interaction. People usually adapt their self-presentational strategies to a particular audience. Sometimes, an audience happens to include groups or individuals to whom the self would normally be presented differently. An adulterer might find it difficult to interact simultaneously with spouse and lover! People who habitually interact with a limited range of others might be unable to present themselves effectively to people outside that range.

Goffman (1963) has described how behaviour that goes on 'behind the scenes', i.e. in private or restricted settings, can differ greatly from behaviour 'on stage', i.e. in public. Earlier on, Goffman had described the presentation of self in everyday life, and gave a wide range of examples of the forms that self-presentation can take (Goffman, 1959). Consider, for example, the changes in posture and appearance that take place in a family when visitors arrive. Many social interactions, and accounts (explanations, justifications) of actions, are influenced by the wish to present oneself in a certain way to certain people. Goffman (1959) said that in some circumstances an individual tries to foster the impression among his 'audience' that their conduct in a given situation is their essential or only form of conduct. The audience assume (or act 'as if') the individual's conduct defines his or her social identity. Many schoolchildren, for example, have little interest in, or idea of, their teachers' lives outside the classroom; and teachers tend not to talk to the children about their lives outside the classroom. Goffman says that performers try to foster the impression that their actions are spontaneous, unique and of benefit to the audience, and not calculated, routine or self-interested.

Routine behaviour and good manners are often used to conceal the inner personal state of the performer. This is another illustration of the distinction between 'What a person really is' and the 'Impressions that others form of a person', namely their social stimulus value (Chapter 2). We try to foster a particular impression of ourselves in particular groups; and members of groups, because of their common characteristics and interests, form similar impressions.

Self-presentation can take many forms—ingratiation, intimidation, supplication, and so on—see Jones (1990). The basic aim of these and other forms of self-presentation is to increase the likelihood that we will fulfil our social aims—secure cooperation or support, frighten off competitors or avoid the consequences of our mistakes. These forms of behaviour are not necessarily or even probably stable personality dispositions. They are, rather, tactical adjustments that most people can make to particular people in particular circumstances. They are not necessarily deliberate in the sense of being conscious and pre-planned. They can be routine habits or spontaneous adjustments to a situation. They may incorporate expressive features that betray our temperamental qualities, attitudes and abilities.

Self-presentational actions are sometimes recognised by an observer, particularly the person who is the target of the actions, for what they are, and so are possibly discounted. Observers try to 'see through' the self-presentational strategy to assess the person's underlying aims and personal qualities. It may not be difficult, for example, to recognise flattery or obsequiousness. Self-presentational behaviour is not necessarily intended to deceive but to increase the likelihood of success.

The relationship between what we might call the ordinary forms of self-presentation on the one hand and reputation on the other is as follows. First, observers' first-hand reports of a person's behaviour often include information and comments on the way that person presents himself or herself to others. In other words, self-presentational style can be a characteristic attributed to a person, for example, 'She's inclined to exaggerate' or 'He invariably makes disparaging remarks about himself'. Second, the recipient of information about a person's behaviour may *interpret* that behaviour as self-presentational behaviour even though another interpretation is possible.

Some forms of self-presentation are well-known and widely used; they are 'prescribed' as 'normal' social behaviour. People who fail to present themselves in socially acceptable ways are likely to suffer adverse consequences—they will be said to be rude, insensitive, boastful, pushy, snobbish, or whatever. Thus, self-presentational behaviour is a salient feature of social interaction, and, like appearance—another salient feature—is likely to be incorporated in a person's reputation in the usual way.

Self-presentation can be deliberate and systematic. This is seen most clearly in what is known as the 'cult of personality', whether in politics, religion, science, entertainment or other areas of public life. Personal dominance can be attained by ability and effort, by personal style or 'charisma' (Chapter 8), and by public relations efforts (Chapter 12). History reveals the lengths that people will go to to develop a personality cult; but people who engage too obviously in advertisements for themselves risk social disapproval. Interactants and observers are likely to discount such behaviour, for example, when courting popularity is interpreted as power-seeking.

Self-presentation is linked with attribution. Interpreting the behaviour and circumstances of people is complicated and liable to error (see Jones, 1990). For example, in some circumstances, observers are inclined to over-estimate the part played by personality dispositions and to under-estimate situational factors. They under-estimate the difficulty of a task, and so under-estimate the ability of the person faced with the task. Observers sometimes neglect the effect that their presence has on the person they are observing. Observers' personal perspective, goals and values affect their attention, perception and interpretation of events. This is particularly likely in situations where observers are ego-involved, or where, as in some media reporting, a particular 'story' is wanted.

All parties to social interaction engage in self-presentation, and all parties are aware, to a greater or lesser degree, of the self-presentational tactics that other parties are using. Attempts to disguise the true nature of one's purpose through dissimulation (see later) are more or less successful depending upon one's social skills and those of others. There is a measure of hypocrisy and self-delusion (rationalisation) in the self-presentational behaviour of some people, for example, exaggerating an ailment or difficulty in order to attract attention and gain sympathy.

A person's social behaviour is often open to different interpretations. This helps to explain the *diversity* of low-frequency attributions typical of personal reputations. The *conformity* reflected in high-frequency attributions depends on people sharing some common views about the target entity, or on the availability of unambiguous items of information.

We normally try to enhance or at least maintain our achieved level of self-esteem. Our position in society is a pattern of roles and statuses related to those of other people with whom we normally interact—at home, at work or in our leisure pursuits. This results in a pattern of exchange relationships that contributes to our reputation and our level of social satisfaction and adjustment.

Even within the normal range of social behaviour, however, there is a range of differences between individuals and variations across different situations. This requires participants and observers to exercise a certain amount of intelligence and experience in monitoring the social process—one's own behaviour and that of others. In doing so, we make the necessary adjustments—an allowance for one person's anxiety, a firmer line with another person's repeated deviance, an apology or amends for one's own misunderstanding or fault. Although the general aim is to make such allowances in the interests of smooth social interaction, this aim has to be set alongside the aim of protecting and enhancing social exchange relationships.

Table 7.1 lists some of the strategies used in self-presentation and reputation management. The table should be regarded as a visual aid, not as a definitive or even a provisional taxonomy.

Table 7.1. A selection of reputation management strategies classified as defensive or promotional, and positive or negative

Defensive	Promotional
Positive	
Apologising	Advertising benefits and support
Conforming	Being friendly
Explaining (giving reasons)	Bargaining
Flattering	Boasting
Making amends	Ingratiating
Pleading	Making and keeping promises
Performing better	Performing well
	Seeking opportunities and advancement
	Seeking patrons and advocates
	(proxies)
Negative	
Appealing to authority	Admitting dependence
Appealing to support (coalition)	Deceiving
Blaming others	Derogating competitors
Complaining	Intimidating
Denying	
Excusing	
Retaliating	
Taking legal action	
Threatening harm	

Self Presentation by Proxy

One method of reputation management is to permit or encourage people in our social network to defend, extend and promote our reputation—by proxy as it were. People are usually loyal to their friends and colleagues, even if they have reservations about them.

The person acting as proxy presents an account that is normally his or her version of the collective representation, although it might be a purely personal impression, or an attempt to mislead an audience. Normally, when we introduce one person to another, introduce a visiting speaker to an audience, compose an obituary notice, write a political profile or write a testimonial or reference for someone, we present an image of the person that is received in good faith as a reasonable approximation to an informed collective representation. In these contexts, as opinion leaders (Chapter 6), we are expected to act in the public interest and to represent the community's collective image of the person. A discourse analysis approach to these sorts of communication would show how such presentations can be used to convey certain meanings or produce certain effects—distancing oneself from the other, or enhancing one's own reputation, for example.

Impression management operates by proxy when one person is inhibited or prevented from dealing directly with the third party, and an intermediary can somehow convey the impression more effectively, by speaking calmly, not angrily, for example. The systematic use of intermediaries in this way is one aspect of 'networking', i.e. using exchange relationships to protect and enhance one's social position. Networking may be particularly helpful if it extends beyond the work environment of the organisation and into cultural and leisure activities. This increases the number of acquaintances and so increases the extent and depth of one's reputation through the exchange of information and influence. It may also increase opportunities for the expression of socially desirable personal qualities—humour, public speaking, coping with stress, energy, originality, and so on—especially in public performances. Higher managerial positions call for effective interaction with external bodies—with people in other departments or other organisations.

Reputation Management and Impression Formation

The individual's coping and expressive behaviour, and the consequences of his or her actions, have a direct impact on other people, helping to shape the impression they form, by modifying or consolidating it. Of course, the impression they form is partly determined by their psychological make-up and circumstances; they have certain expectations and concerns about that individual. They are inclined to interpret the individual's behaviour in particular ways, and to attribute certain characteristics to him or her based on their assumptions.

Semin and Manstead (1981) used students' ratings of social transgressions to examine the relationship between intentionality, social emotionality and impression management. They used role-playing to examine the emotions produced by discrepancies between the self-image and the public image. Social emotions arise when social rules are contravened. Emotional reactions were greater when the contravention was public rather than private. Manstead and Semin (1981) reported that subjects over-estimated the negative effect that a social transgression would have on observers, despite the intention underlying the transgression. Ungar (1981) used a 'hidden experiment' to show that people use cues provided by others, interviewers for example, to decide how to manage the impression they wanted to convey.

Bailey (1971), discussing the management of reputation, and social change, mentions the way information shared in social interaction can be labelled as 'my opinion', 'gossip', 'rumour', 'confidential' or 'reliable'. This shows how people wish to present themselves as informants. There are ways of rectifying errors in the opinions we have expressed, to repair any damage to reputation, for example through apologies or excuses.

The changes in observers' impressions brought about directly by the individual's behaviour are then conveyed to a wider circle of people, by report, by gossip and by perceived changes in the behaviour of those directly affected. For example, a newly appointed head teacher about whom the staff have no clear or firm image may make a critical remark or hand out a compliment to a member of staff. His action is interpreted in a certain way and conveyed to other members of staff directly or indirectly. Metaphorically, the head's actions are the seeds of his reputation among the staff; the staff—their personalities, aspirations, interpersonal relationships and circumstances—are the soil in which the seeds grow. To pursue the metaphor, the subsequent growth of reputation can run wild or it can be cultivated, depending upon how effectively the head can manage the impressions he makes on others.

Unless individuals are completely insulated from many people affected by their actions (as sometimes happens in authoritarian regimes), they perceive for themselves, or are told by their immediate contacts and confidants, about the impressions that people have formed of them. They usually modify their behaviour to bring it more into line with the public image they wish to have. There are examples, even in recent history, of individuals in authority, Ceauşescu for example, who appear to have been insulated from political realities by lackeys until the discrepancy was resolved by physical violence. On the other hand, there are cases, such as Stalin, who have such overwhelming social control that almost no adverse comment is allowed to reach the public domain during the individual's lifetime. In these circumstances, surveillance and censorship inhibit the development of a true 'collective' impression, because people's individual impressions cannot be effectively shared, and propaganda has created a pseudo-reputation. Restrictions on the spread of information can be imposed by threats and obligations in the ordinary affairs of everyday life (Chapter 9).

Rosen, Cochran and Musser (1990) examined the effects of applicants' work reputation, self-presentational style, and the interaction between them, on judgements of their suitability for a job. In job selection, work reputation is usually established by internal and external reports of supervisors, former employers and referees. Reputation can be validated by objective information available from performance records of one sort or another. Self-presentational style can be assessed by observers' ratings of certain characteristics, in this case 'boastful–modest'. Reputation reports were rated 'superior–inferior'. The impact of self-presentational style depends on whether observers see it as accurate or justifiable, as matching or failing to match reputation. It is likely to depend on other factors too—cultural expectations, age, gender, and so on. In the investigation by Rosen et al. (1990), four large samples of students read reputation reports and watched a videotaped job interview relating to a job applicant, and then made ratings. Confidence (boasting) coupled with superior work reputation was the most influential of the four combinations of self-presentational style and reputation. The least preferred candidate was the one with an inferior reputation who nevertheless had a confident (boastful) self-presentational style. Surprisingly, 'attraction' as such did not appear to mediate the effects of reputation and self-presentation.

Reputation Management and Self-Image

The relationship between public image (reputation) and self-image is both indirect and reciprocal. It is indirect in the sense that the image we have of ourselves is associated with our behaviour and our experiences, but our behaviour does not necessarily have the effect of creating an impression in others that matches our self-image. Moreover, we may not want other people to know what we are really like; we want people to form a particular sort of image. When we become aware of a mismatch between our self-image and our public image (reputation), we can either try to manipulate public opinion directly (without changing ourselves) or try to change our ways in the hope that people will eventually see us as we really are.

We can manipulate the image that other people have of us. This fact underpins work in public relations, propaganda and advertising. The terms 'brand image' and 'packaging' are associated with advertising consumer products, but similar techniques are used to promote individuals and organisations. Improving the public image of an organisation, for example the police (Arthur, Sisson and McClung, 1977) or a university (Footman, 1986), is not simply a question of using public relations techniques to change public opinion. It is a question of changing the nature of the organisation and its individual members—by changing organisational policy and practices, by training individuals in specific skills (particularly social skills), and by altering the ethos, and even the identity, of the organisation (Chapter 12). Awareness of a disparity between our self-image and our public image is often a signal that action is needed to resolve it. Social approval—the esteem of others—provides a powerful incentive and reinforcement for behaviour, provided the approval comes from the appropriate reference groups, i.e. the social groups we admire or to which we belong. Public recognition is a way of signalling social approval, as in the award of prizes and honours, or receiving favourable mention by people with high status.

It is possible to adapt even if one is held in low esteem and ostracised—isolated or outcast—because of one's beliefs and actions. This is true of some political or religious dissidents, members of minority groups and deviant individuals. Social adjustment is made possible through such social support as is available (family, friends, partners). Considerable strength of purpose is required to withstand public condemnation. In less extreme circumstances, we withstand public disapproval by denigrating the sources of disapproval. This is typical of political and religious conflict and the politics of everyday life.

Reflected Glory and Guilt by Association

The notion of 'reflected glory' refers to the tendency for individuals to identify with, and signal their association with, successful others. The signalling often includes wearing appropriate apparel, badges or rosettes, carrying flags and banners, repeating slogans, being members of associated groups, and showing antagonism or competition with rival groups. Cialdini et al. (1976) described the phenomenon of reflected glory in students' support of their football team, and their strong reactions to threats to their team's public image. Bond, Chiu and Wan (1984) showed that individual members of a group were expected to defend the reputation of the group as a whole (see also Turner et al., 1984).

Political and religious movements usually have a hard core of activists and a larger but more passive body of supporters. Interesting developments occur when the more extreme activists go beyond what most supporters expect. Success shifts the movement in the direction advocated by the extremists; failure can result in the eclipse of the extreme faction or even in retribution. Examples of this can be found not only in political and religious history, but also in small-scale social movements—charitable bodies and pressure groups. Partly because of hindsight (a feature of social cognition), the reputation of individuals and organisations is influenced by the success or failure of their actions. Charisma and support depend on success (Chapter 8).

One's reputation is tied to that of others through 'guilt by association' or 'reflected glory'. We normally try to avoid the former and take advantage of the latter—two more examples of the tactics of reputation management.

Public Relations as Impression Management

Impression management at the corporate level can be subsumed under the heading of public relations, although it may not be managed by, or recognised as part of, public relations work (Chapter 12). Organisations, like persons, make different impressions on different audiences, partly because they present themselves differently to those audiences, and partly because the different audiences—customers, competitors, investors, commentators—are interested in different aspects of an organisation. Some organisations provide reports tailored to particular audiences. For example, small shareholders prefer abbreviated reports omitting complex technical detail. Such reports are more 'expressive' and contain less 'substance' than the full reports preferred by large shareholders. They are partly exercises in public relations—the corporate equivalent of impression management.

A persuasive, charismatic leader supported by public relations efforts (advertising, media coverage) may, for a time, sustain a favourable impression for a failing organisation. Otherwise, rational assessment of its characteristics and performance would produce an unfavourable impression.

Information about an organisation is sometimes difficult for people to understand. This is because there is too much information, or because it is too technical, or because background information is deliberately withheld. This hinders assessment of an organisation based on performance criteria.

Consequently, most people are obliged to rely on secondary sources—opinion leaders, experts, popularisers—for information and advice.

Corporate Image

Groups and organisations that have no clear corporate identity are not likely to be able to promote a clear public image. However, the idiosyncratic behaviour of individual members—directors, managers, party politicians, university students—is perceived by the public as 'representative' of the group or organisation to which members belong. In these circumstances, the public image may be clear and simple, but stereotyped and false.

One aspect of the management of an organisation's public image is that it is reluctant to publicise some aspects of its existence because of the negative effects such disclosure might have. For example, it may discover and rectify errors and take elaborate precautions against hazards, yet not want to dismay or frighten the public by disclosing these aspects of its operations.

Some companies tolerate maladjusted or alcohol-dependent employees (or get rid of them quietly at some considerable cost) because they do not want the adverse publicity that might attend dismissal. Investigative journalism and police inquiries have uncovered many examples of criminal or negligent behaviour that organisations have attempted to cover up. Public relations staff must often be put under considerable pressure to work outside ethical guidelines.

Reputation can affect policy-making in an organisation in that a particular policy might be thought to benefit or harm an existing reputation. This is an area where the need to deal with different publics can bring problems; persons as well as organisations need to cultivate different reputations in different publics.

Impression Management Within Organisations

Giacalone and Rosenfeld (1991) present a variety of approaches to impression management in organisations. As Schlenker and Weigold (1990) point out, people present differently edited versions of themselves to different audiences. This is rarely a deception, usually it is a natural consequence of dealing with different people and different social circumstances. Impression management is not necessarily insincere or selfish (Machiavellian), although it is a social skill that can be used for antisocial purposes.

Impression management underlies the 'self-fulfilling prophecy' effect in the sense that, if people believe that an individual has certain characteristics, they may behave in ways that enable the person to exhibit those characteristics. For example, a new manager's reputation for administrative efficiency may lead staff to improve their administrative practices in anticipation of closer scrutiny. This increases the likelihood that administrative efficiency will improve under the new manager. One technique of impression management therefore is to let people know in advance that they can expect a newcomer to possess certain characteristics. This can be done by intermediaries. Information about reputation will otherwise spread by default. Informants discuss their observations and beliefs with others through their usual channels of communication and influence. This information may not be in the newcomer's interest, and may reduce the effectiveness of his or her self-presentational efforts.

In its crudest form, impression management can be compared with the threats, submissions, courtships and groomings observed in animal behaviour. Such behaviour expresses basic social relationships. In its more sophisticated forms, impression management pervades the complex and subtle social relationships seen in political behaviour, in seduction, in the public appearances of celebrities, in public relations activities, in sales techniques and in confidence tricks such as impersonation. The ability to 'see through' impression management behaviour calls for what is called metaperspective thinking, i.e. appreciating another person's point of view.

The anxiety sometimes associated with a public performance is called 'evaluation apprehension' (Rosenberg, 1965). Conformity of one sort or another and refusing to draw attention to oneself are examples of self-presentation in response to evaluation apprehension. Social skills training (Argyle, 1981) can reduce social anxiety, and enhance the motivation and ability people need to interact effectively with others. Self-presentation is an essential ingredient in social skills training.

Impression management can be used to improve other people's self-image and performance. For example, colleagues and supervisors can give the impression that they are pleased with our performance, or express confidence in us, or show that they like us. This usually has the effect of increasing our self-esteem and raising our aspirations. This kind of impression management sometimes calls for considerable self-control, inhibiting the natural tendency to criticise, punish or lose patience with people who are not behaving as we wish.

Some personal characteristics, such as those commonly associated with gender, age, race, nationality and religion, lead to stereotyping, discrimination and labelling. Impression management can be used to counter these effects. This means behaving in ways that do not fit the stereotype and do not accept the discrimination. It means voicing certain opinions, appearing in certain settings, adopting certain life-styles, and so on. For example, feminist women may choose less 'feminine' accoutrements, act more assertively and react more vigorously to sexual harassment.

Impression management affects organisational behaviour in many ways. For example, job applicants are likely to compose their *curriculum vitae* and job application in ways that make them attractive to employers. Some forms of impression management purport to show that the person's aspirations are legitimate and reasonable. For example, a curriculum vitae or job application will suggest that the post is a natural career development and realistic aim. This is done by suitable phraseology, by preparing answers to expected interview questions, and by including or excluding references to matters other than those pertinent to the job application.

Some selection procedures include informal settings, for example conversations in casual surroundings or over a meal. These settings provide opportunities for observers to make judgements about candidates' personal qualities, and for both candidates and observers to use impression management techniques. The people responsible for selecting applicants will tend to do so in ways that enhance their image within the organisation, for example by selecting the right 'types', by avoiding 'risky' appointments or by strictly following organisational procedures.

Another aspect of impression management in organisations is the way it affects performance evaluation. In theory, performance evaluation evaluates 'performance' independently of the personal qualities of the performer. In practice, performance indicators may be difficult to measure, since performance often depends on circumstances, and circumstances may differ from case to case. So, subjective assessments supplement or substitute for measures of performance. This allows impression management factors to influence the evaluation. To some extent, persons being evaluated can 'present' themselves as hardworking, ambitious, loyal, reliable, and so on. Simply conforming to the organisation's norms should ensure at least an average evaluation. The person carrying out the evaluation can also engage in impression management practices. These include being or seeming critical or supportive, threatening or apologetic, demanding or tolerant. Both parties to the evaluation exercise are negotiating a relationship. The terms of the relationship depend upon the personal qualities of the persons involved and the circumstances in which they are working. There are third parties to the evaluation exercise, i.e. other people in the organisation who may be influenced, directly or indirectly, by it. This affects the way the organisation as a whole deals with performance evaluation.

Impression management behaviour in large organisations often expresses aspects of the corporate culture, for example, in the way people dress, the opinions they express and their life-style. There are, of course, differences between individuals, but conformity arises because of self-selection (different organisational cultures attract different sorts of people) and organisational pressures (through social learning). Also, behaviour that fits the organisation's culture may be for the sake of appearances, not because the individual is committed to the organisation. Impression management can disguise lack of commitment. For applying impression management in organisations, a model that takes account of the context in which impression management occurs has been offered by Martink (1991). How organisations might overcome the disadvantages of impression management in organisational behaviour and career development has been considered by Feldman and Klich (1991).

Dissimulation

Detecting deception in others is unlikely in initial encounters, for example in experimental studies, because we have no frame of reference against which to judge a person's behaviour. Familiarity with a person's expressive behaviour, however, increases the likelihood that small departures from normal patterns of expressive behaviour will be detected, and questioned—a familiar experience between couples who have lived together for a time. Surprisingly, in experimental studies at least, bodily movements and posture seem to reveal deception slightly more than does facial expression (Ekman and Friesen, 1974), perhaps because they are less closely monitored and controlled by the deceiver (see also Ekman and Friesen, 1975; Ekman, 1985).

Society sets legal and moral limits of acceptance to human behaviour, hence the tendency to use indirect, even devious, means to achieve one's aims. One can propose a biological basis for dissimulation—it camouflages both prey and predator. Self-presentational behaviour that is perceived as ill-intentioned dissimulation is likely to have the opposite effect to that intended. People's actions can be misinterpreted because social behaviour is often ambiguous— disagreement is seen as hostility, truthfulness as insensitivity. Some forms of dissimulation can be morally justified, for example 'white lies'.

Social Norms

Our behaviour is under pressure to conform to the patterns prescribed and sanctioned by social norms and values. To this extent normal social behaviour appears to be uninformative—it tells us little that we do not already know. Social prescriptions and sanctions constrain people's behaviour. These are normally fairly stable over time; they have the effect of reducing the range of differences between individuals, and so impose more coherence and continuity on social behaviour than would otherwise be the case. Emler (1990) pointed out that people who behave in socially acceptable and expected ways do not expose themselves to close scrutiny, as do people who behave deviantly. Normal behaviour does not capture our attention, or call for explanation or justification. Successful criminals and terrorists *appear* to behave normally.

Emler (1990) also pointed out that reputations fade if not continually renewed. We raise the same issue when dealing with serial changes in reputation (Chapter 14). Unless people are willing and able to assert themselves, and make some impact on others, either directly in face-to-face situations, or through 'public' performances, then none of their aspirations that depend on collective recognition and support are likely to succeed. Failure to make the expected impression on others can have adverse effects on an individual's career. For example, people appointed to high office are normally expected to be able to make an impact on people. This is often one reason why they have attained high office. Failure to make an impact is likely to be attributed to personal inadequacy.

The view that social controls normally become internalised and part of the self is widely accepted. Such internalisation depends upon successful social adjustment, and should be regarded as an aspect of social skills developed and exercised throughout life. Reputation management reflects the exercise of social skills *and* the existence of a system of social values and aspirations forming an integral part of the self.

Reputation needs to be 'managed', if only in the passive sense of conforming to prescribed forms of social behaviour. If we wish to cultivate a distinctive reputation, then reputation management needs to be more active. This means making ourselves and our achievements known to others, especially influential others. This can, of course, have the opposite effect to that intended! Self-presentation that is not backed up by genuine personal qualities and achievements is likely to fail eventually. Conversely, personal qualities and achievements can count for little or can be ignored in the competition for public esteem; they must be made known through self-promotion, or through advocacy and patronage. Reputation management includes actions intended to derogate and denigrate other people, particularly competitors (Buss and Dedden, 1990).

Individuals differ in their willingness and ability to engage in reputation management. They differ in their awareness of the impressions others form of them, and in their ability to 'see through' the impression management techniques used by others.

8 Politics and Reputation

Introduction

It sometimes seems that the electorate expect political leaders to achieve policy objectives without cost to themselves. Hence people have to be persuaded to cooperate with political leaders, or be coerced, so that policy objectives can be attained, because in the end it is their efforts that produce the desired results. Failure to secure sufficient cooperation eventually leads to the abandonment of policy objectives, accompanied by a loss of public esteem.

People often simplify political issues when trying to understand and deal with them, for instance deciding how to vote in an election. People can base their preference on political ideology, party allegiance or on their impressions of a candidate's personal qualities. Rudd (1986) gives a clear account of how political issues can be used as a vehicle for conveying personality impressions (see later).

When political analysts describe the personalities and the patterns of interaction that determine political manoeuvring and the course of government, they use virtually the same terms of reference and forms of explanation that are used to describe people in everyday life and ordinary forms of interpersonal behaviour. There is little reliance on technical terminology. Thus political reputations are special only in the sense that the people involved have important positions in society, and their actions have, or are believed to have, more impact than the actions of most other people. Political reputation, and to some extent corporate reputation, is about gaining, maintaining, enhancing or losing, status, esteem, trust and support in society generally, as contrasted with personal reputation, which operates in a similar way but on a smaller scale in the 'politics of everyday life'.

Much of what I have to say about political reputation and political marketing applies equally well to reputations in religious movements, and to other movements with a general message and a wide appeal, such as ecology, morality, feminism, anti-abortion and cultural fashions.

Erikson (1990) investigated the relationship between respondents' ratings of US Senators on an 'ideological' scale ranging from 1 (extremely liberal) to 7 (extremely conservative) and Senators' voting record. Although respondents are generally not well informed about their political representatives, the Senators' political behaviour (voting record) has a general effect on their reputation. This could be attributed to the spread of information and influence in the usual way (Chapter 6), and to voters' knowledge of a Senator's party affiliation. Erikson found a moderate correlation between political reputation and Senators' voting record. He found that the reputations of politicians of lower political status were more moderate, they were seen as closer to the centre of the political spectrum than politicians of higher political status. He also found that the distribution of respondents' political ideology tended to occupy the centre ground, whereas political candidates' ideology was generally viewed as more extreme. The political reputation of the Senators was close to the average ideological position of their electorate.

Political reputation

Schwartz (1990) described how Abraham Lincoln's political reputation changed between 1901 and 1921. He examined sermons, newspaper articles, books and other sources. He showed that the frame of reference shared by commentators shortly after Lincoln's death looked towards the past, whereas later commentators looked towards the future. Later generations of commentators received what Lincoln stood for, and his personal qualities, more favourably. In terms of the sheer quantity of material published, Lincoln's reputation soon exceeded that of George Washington. In the process, the characteristics attributed to Lincoln shifted—from those that were homely, even vulgar, to those that were heroic and forward looking. The way Lincoln's reputation was compared and contrasted with that of Washington is of particular interest. Washington provided a standard against which future great Presidents could be measured. The characteristics attributed to them at various times reflected the cultural values and ideologies then in vogue. In Lincoln's case, apparently, ambivalence was produced by the conflict between the need for strong leadership and a structure of authority in a large, diverse, and rapidly developing country, and the need for democratic freedom and equality of opportunity.

Schwartz (1990) made a distinction between folk heroes and epic heroes. Folk heroes are 'familiar' figures symbolising the common weal—the concerns and conditions of ordinary people. Epic heroes are 'remote' figures symbolising what people ought to be—their ideals and aspirations. (See also Schwartz, 1991).

The public images of famous people are in part history and in part social representations that people use to understand and deal with the world in which they live. Cultural changes then lead to changes in reputation. What is collectively remembered has to fit in with the new ideas. When they are retrieved from the past and re-examined, reputations are reconstructed. Reputations that persist unchanged over a long period reflect basic and widespread cultural conditions. Through their characteristics and achievements famous people come to personify (embody) abstract and general social values. These characteristics and achievements are presented to the public in concrete and particular ways, for example as legends or parables, so that ordinary people can appreciate their importance (Longmore, 1988).

As time went by, Lincoln's reputation developed because people who had known him at first hand published their reminiscences. Independent reviewers and commentators based their reports on what they had heard or read about Lincoln. As explained elsewhere, person-to-person contact is the basis of primary reputation; but reputation develops secondary features that arise because of information conveyed and influence exercised indirectly by third parties. In both primary and secondary reputation, information and influence can be 'managed' in strategic and tactical ways, by the target person and his or her supporters, and by competitors and detractors, independently of the true character of the target person. The point is that reputation as 'discourse' is about accounts, arguments and persuasion. Reports of reputation have to be interpreted. Interpretations reflect reporters' ideologies, i.e. the assumptions and concerns that form the basis of their beliefs and expectations. Public acclaim then depends on those reputational attributions that express what the public want and feel— security, freedom, revenge, dominance, or whatever.

Schudson (1990) examined the role of media commentators in forming President Reagan's political reputation. This illustrates two issues: the social construction of reputation and the connection between primary and secondary reputation. The circumstances were that President Reagan had low popularity ratings in public opinion polls at the beginning of his presidency, but had the reputation of being a popular president. Thus, somehow, in spite of the importance of public opinion polls in politics in the USA, these relatively objective survey results appeared to have little effect on President Reagan's reputation. One possibility is that the media, and through them the public, reacted favourably to the President but unfavourably to his policies. The difference between the public's 'personal' and 'job-approval' ratings of President Reagan supported this possibility. Even so, in 1981 the press and Congress members reported that President Reagan had the public on his side (with about 60% approval). Nevertheless, his level of support was *lower* than that for four previous presidents.

Schudson (1990) argued that, in general, US Congress members, political commentators in the media and other 'insiders' allowed their subjective social consensus to override the evidence from public opinion polls. Journalists rely on other journalists for much of their information, so that impressions conform and reinforce common biases. Schudson went on to explain that 'political insiders' in Washington interact closely with each other. Information and influence operate at what we have called the primary group or face-to-face level. These insiders appear to have liked President Reagan personally even if they disagreed with him politically. President Reagan actively cultivated good personal relationships, particularly with political supporters, media representatives and other politically influential people. In this respect he stood in contrast to former President Carter. It seems that his natural affability lent itself to effective reputation management. In any event, President Reagan and his public relations advisors built up a vast network of active political support throughout the country. Schudson (1990) did not believe that the media were deliberately manipulated. He did not comment on the possibility that those with access to the media are on average more supportive of Republican policies. If objective evidence (public opinion) is unclear, then political commentators resort to subjective impressions (their personal estimates and those of their colleagues). Schudson emphasised the extent to which we live in a socially constructed world: a world of myth and illusion; a world of simple generalisations and images (stereotypes). Working with objective evidence and sophisticated modes of reasoning is difficult and time consuming in comparison with social discourse at a common-sense level that confirms our preferences and prejudices.

Although members of an influential person's primary groups can probably make a valid assessment of his or her personality, this information is usually confidential, restricted to these inner circles. People outside have to rely on indirect methods of assessment. Understanding the real character of an influential person is politically important in situations where situational constraints and opportunities do not indicate an obvious course of action. The influential person's motives, beliefs and abilities then have to be taken into account when deciding how to react.

Affective reactions in political reputation

Abelson et al. (1982) compared conventional judgements of politicians in terms of traits (courageous, selfish, and so on) with judgements in terms of subjects' affective reactions (making them feel angry, hopeful, and so on). They found that the affective reactions were clearly either positive or negative, but independent of each other. That is to say, respondents could express both positive and negative reactions to a target politician. Respondents with partisan views were more likely to show consistent affective reactions. They also found that positive and negative traits were less independent of each other than the affective reactions. Subjects tended not to assign both positive and negative traits to the same target politician. Affective reactions appeared to be more predictive of likely voting behaviour. Abelson et al. (1982) implied that the analysis of affective reactions may add to our understanding of person perception in ordinary life. Affective reactions and evaluations are prominent features of reputation.

Political Marketing and Public Relations

Given the way that politics is pursued in Western democracies, public relations play a major role in the fortunes of any serious political party (O'Shaughnessy, 1989). Harrop (1990) drew attention to several types of political campaigning, and to the changes that have taken place in recent history. Nowadays, television, the press and computerised direct mail are widely used. These methods of communicating with and influencing people are not likely to be effective unless they are coordinated by a well-organised marketing strategy informed by a coherent and convincing political agenda.

A party must have a clear identity, different from that of other parties; it must have an easily recognisable symbol or logo, some simple, appealing slogans and a short meaningful name. There are, of course, many other public relations requirements—personal contacts, information about the electorate, spokespersons, literature, funds, and so on. The aim is to attract support for the movement.

There are limits to what public relations and advertising can do to conceal the real character of an entity (including self-presentation by persons). A political party's promotional activities are not likely to conceal its fundamental weaknesses and divisions—poor leadership, disaffected supporters, contradictory objectives, special interests, factional conflicts. The increased attention generated by promotional activities, including attention from independent observers and opponents, increases the likelihood that flaws will be revealed. In a democratic society, there are limits to the extent to which a promotional campaign can control the effects it produces. It may have little effect beyond the effects produced by normal political processes.

In the UK, the use of marketing techniques on a substantial scale in the promotion of politicians and political movements is recent. By 1990, however, all the major political parties had accepted that such techniques were necessary for their survival. One important reason for this has been the vast increase in the influence of the mass communication media, reaching a far wider public than was possible with the earlier forms of persuasion—personal contact, rallies, posters, pamphlets. President Reagan's cultivation of people working in the media could have been partly a natural interest and partly an awareness of the usefulness of the radio and the press by President Roosevelt.

Harrop (1990) reviewed the current situation, raised some issues about the public image of political parties and argued that marketing techniques have improved rather than worsened political communication in the UK. Harrop said that it is difficult to think of any landmark analyses of party images. Another point raised by Harrop is that the marketing perspective emphasises voters' shared interests rather than their conflicts of interest.

Political parties are similar in some ways to other entities that have a corporate reputation, but they are different in other ways. They have, at base, a set of values and aims, an ideology, expressed in political slogans. This produces a set of policies that indicate the means by which certain ends are to be achieved, although often the means are left vague, partly because they are usually less palatable than the ends, partly because they have to be adjusted according to circumstances.

At the strategic level, a political party offers a way of life intended to appeal to most people. At the tactical level, the party engages in various promotional, public relations, activities designed to spread its beliefs and values, and to influence people to support the party. In these respects, political parties are not very different from commercial organisations. Normally, a commercial organisation is at risk if its character is not in the public interest. It is important therefore for a political party to ensure that its strategic aims are realistic and correspond to an objective assessment of what the public want from a political organisation. We need not concern ourselves with cases that go against the public interest; these are matters for historical or legal inquiry.

Spear (1984) gave a detailed account of the relationships between the media, especially the press, and several Presidents of the USA. The Presidents' aim has been to present a favourable, unassailable image to the public. They and their staff went to considerable lengths to persuade, trick and intimidate the press into giving their support or at least avoiding damaging disclosures. Sections of the press, on the other hand, believed they had a duty to investigate political and other wrongdoing. They engaged in investigative procedures and accusations that tested the limits of the law and morality. Television, with its emphasis on the visual image and the spoken word, fulfilled a different function as far as political news and commentary were concerned. It appeared to be more easily manipulated by political pressures and less adept at investigative journalism. Spear's account of the relationships between politicians and the media illustrates the importance attached to political reputation. It also illustrates the need for independent institutions that can expose political and other sorts of corruption.

Political Services

Harrop (1990) drew an interesting distinction between the way the public react to the marketing of goods and the way they react to the marketing of services. He argued that marketing a political movement is more like marketing services than marketing goods. The point is that services are less tangible, and less easy to evaluate. Moreover, services are more closely related to the people who provide them than goods are to those who manufacture them. The analogy, although imperfect, is useful. It draws attention to some key features of political performance—competence, consistency and trustworthiness in governing the country. Once in power, the party is responsible for a wide range of important services—health, education, defence, law and order, and so on. These are matters over which individual members of the public have little control, except perhaps through their involvement in or support of the party, or a pressure group.

The ways in which services of one sort or another are provided to members of the public are complex and obscure. As with medical care, transport, water and electricity supplies, consumers look to those responsible for organising the services to provide them. By analogy, political leaders are held responsible for success or failure in the delivery of services that depend in any way on government policy and machinery. For example, the political leaders of Eastern

European countries were held responsible for the serious social and economic dislocations of 1990.

Persons and Policies

Harrop (1990: p 279) said that political leaders must not only deliver a service, namely government, but *personify* it. They are the embodiment of government. It is worth noting in passing that people perceive and understand persons more easily than they understand abstractions, such as government policies and services. Persons are more tangible, more familiar, and susceptible to influence. It is natural, therefore, and probably more sensible, for ordinary voters to think about persons rather than policies. If we do not understand the complexities of government, we rely on our judgement of the persons or organisation offering to provide it. This makes reputation a major factor in politics.

Harrop went on to argue, however, that it is not 'particular leaders' but 'available leadership' that is important. Political parties need to ensure a steady supply of competent and trustworthy people capable of governing the country. In the UK, the Conservative leadership election in November 1990, illustrated the point.

A party in power has an advantage because it can usually demonstrate continuity in competent government, whereas an opposition party cannot. Harrop suggested that although election campaigns generally make little difference to the distribution of political support, they should benefit an opposition party more if the governing party has experienced policy failures during the pre-campaign period. Election campaigns provide ample opportunities to review and assess political performance.

A political party's image is conveyed mainly through its leaders—the people who hold high office, expound its views and carry out its programmes. This applies to social movements and organisations of other sorts—religious, scientific, professional, cultural. A possible reason, related to the point made earlier, is that we find it easy and natural to form attachments to, and identifications with, persons; after all, that is central to social development throughout life. By contrast, ideologies and policies are abstract and somewhat remote from ordinary life.

With this view, it is not surprising that a party's image has human qualities, and is 'personified' or 'represented' by the attributes of its leaders. The public's tendency to attend to people rather than policies has a psychological basis. In this view, personalities are a major factor in politics. The difficulty is that political leaders tend to be remote from the public, so that reputation intervenes and obscures their true character.

This makes policy issues secondary for ordinary voters, which is perhaps why political leaders are constantly trying to convince us that we should pay more attention to policies and less to personalities. For them, policies have primary importance (except, perhaps, in the micropolitics of party and government!). The policies are supposed to derive from the underlying system of beliefs and values that drives a political movement.

Ideologies provide conceptual frameworks for the expression of psychological characteristics that are basic and widely shared. Ideologies can be interpreted in different ways, which means that all sorts of policy options can be read into them. Ideologies crystallise a particular interpretation that appeals to people with the relevant psychological characteristics. Basic characteristics, such as the need for personal freedom, national or religious identity, security, or prosperity, have a wide appeal; anxiety, hostility and suspicion, too, are common and find expression in certain kinds of ideology. Leaders capable of expressing what many people think and feel thus come to personify or represent a collective view about political ends and means. One could say that all ideologies are corruptible, but some are more corruptible than others!

Different leadership attributes are necessary at different stages in the history of a social movement or political party—at its inception, once it is firmly established, and when it is in power. It goes almost without saying that things can go badly wrong—the founders of a party sometimes prove incapable of managing its policies.

Miller (1990) agreed that the personality of a politician is usually more salient than political issues or parties. Ideological and policy issues, however, can be simplified, and party labels can be attached to politicians; this enables electors to identify a preferred but otherwise unknown candidate. This situation is found in British national and local elections, most voters' knowledge of candidates being small. Public awareness is not simply a function of the political status of candidates; it is more a function of the social circumstances that determine the level of public interest in politics, such as an election or economic crisis.

Different circumstances reveal different facets of personality. For example, a Prime Minister's behaviour in the House of Commons, or in Cabinet, or in informal surroundings, shows different personal qualities to different audiences. So reputational attributes become more salient or less salient according to the occasion, the political circumstances and the changing involvement of various interest groups. This happens at Party conferences, at election times, with the threat of war, or at times of economic growth or decline. As the Prime Minister's actions are observed and reported upon, people's prior impressions are modified. This, in turn, makes it easier or more difficult for the Prime Minister to perform effectively.

In political and probably in other types of voting (Chapter 16), incumbents are usually better known and more positively evaluated than challengers. This is because challengers are less able to point to a previous record in office, whereas incumbents can emphasise their achievements. Depending upon circumstances and individual differences, electors take account of candidates' personal characteristics and circumstances, previous record, ideological position and social group relations. According to Miller (1990), US Presidential candidates are evaluated less on personal characteristics than are Senate or House candidates. Miller identified six substantive personality characteristics that have political appeal for electors: competence, integrity, reliability, charisma, personal identity and responsiveness. Of these, competence, personal identity, and integrity appear to be more important. Surprisingly, charismatic characteristics were not often mentioned by respondents (see later). Comments regarding responsiveness were virtually absent from the assessment of presidential candidates, presumably because voters do not expect to have much if any direct influence on the President as compared with House representatives. House incumbents are more likely to be elected, perhaps because they are perceived as competent and responsive.

Miller's (1990) report revealed some of the factors underlying political reputation. It provided a framework for understanding reputation in quasi-political settings, in professional work and organisational behaviour, where reputations affect behaviour even in the absence of voting in the literal sense.

Political Climate and Interest

In democracies, there are independent, impartial observers capable of commenting on political events. There are spokespersons for special interest or pressure groups, who can comment on particular areas of public concern—law and order, the environment. Harrop (1990) referred to the 'climate of opinion' that develops as political and economic events unfold, leading eventually to a renewal or change of government.

Harrop's view was that a marketing perspective on politics shows how appeals to *common* interests are more effective than appeals to *sectional* interests. He went as far as to say that sectional interests have much in common with the public interest generally. Hence, appeals that succeed with the latter are likely to succeed with the former, provided the sectional interest is not too narrowly defined or deviant. Harrop tried to dispel the notion that the future of political marketing lies in identifying sectional interests, and tailoring information and influence to suit them. In other words, whatever people's political persuasion, most have more interests in common than interests in conflict. This view seems to be contradicted by the failure of centre parties in UK politics in recent years. There are, however, other factors at work—failure to manage their affairs competently, the voting system, and so on.

Harrop agreed that party policies differ, and that individuals agree with one or the other policy. The basic psychological attributes of the parties, however, are not very different from each other, in spite of attempts by party propagandists to make them look different. Supporters of one major party apparently are much the same as supporters of another. A campaign that is effective in influencing one major sector of the electorate is likely to influence another. The question for public relations and advertising then is to weigh up the costs and benefits of targeting a narrow, specialised sector of the public, as opposed to targeting a wider, more general sector.

Politicians who are secure and well supported will be disinclined to advocate minority views or lean far in the direction of sectional interests, because this will jeopardise their wider support. Politicians representing minority opinion are less at risk from such advocacy.

Leadership and Charisma

Gilbert, Collins and Brenner (1990) used 12 leadership attributes to study possible age differences in leadership effectiveness. Subjects rated older leaders slightly lower on friendliness, calming effect and enjoyableness, and slightly higher on delegation. This finding illustrates the effect of contextual factors on interpersonal judgements.

The attributes listed in Table 8.1 could be useful in comparing the reputations of leaders in various fields. The phraseology in Table 8.1 is slightly different from that used by Gilbert et al. (1990).

We can use the analogy of the key and lock to describe charisma. The shape of the key corresponds to the person's characteristics; the tumblers in the lock correspond to the social conditions. The key fits the lock as the 'charismatic' person fits the social conditions. The charisma refers to those attributes of the leader that succeed in recruiting followers in those social conditions. The attributes differ from one set of social conditions to another. Nowadays, public relations techniques make it possible, within limits, to manage public personas, i.e. to manufacture charisma.

For Weber (Gerth and Mills, 1991), charismatic leaders are attributed with quasi-supernatural powers, so that followers tend to accept his or her authority

Table 8.1. Twelve leadership attributes, based on Gilbert et al. (1990)

Number	Category	Attributes
1	Competence	Strong 'presence', commands attention
2		Dependable, responsible
3		Industrious, selfless, high effort
4		Decisive, credible, respect for others
5	Empowerment	Calm, controlled, reasonable
6		Delegates, trusts subordinates
7		Accountable, policy-oriented
8		Straightforward, truthful
9	Relationships	Cares for subordinates
10		Friendly with subordinates
11		Positive affect—good humour
12		External contacts and activities

totally. Charismatic leadership is often associated with 'revitalization movements' (Wallace, 1956)—religious revivals, revolutions, social reforms, and so on. As revitalisation movements develop, authority has to be distributed and delegated because it is not possible for one person to manage a large, complex social organisation. Weber called this 'the routinization of charisma'. The leader's charisma is not necessarily diminished. This is because, in authoritarian organisations particularly, information and influence can be controlled from the centre. The charismatic image of the leader may be maintained even following failure to fulfil promises. Charisma as a function of the relationship between leader and followers is not confined to large social movements. It appears in minor forms in political factions, industrial strikes, social protests and street-corner gangs. For the historical, sociological and political aspects of charisma, see Glassman and Swatos (1986), Lindholm (1990) and Conger (1989). For an account of charisma in organisational leadership, see Bryman (1992).

For Weber, an essential feature of charisma is the fit between the charismatic person, his or her mission, and the duty felt by people to support that person and that mission. Charismatic leadership breaks away from traditional and structured forms of social organisation. There is no procedure for appointment, or training, or career advancement. Charismatic leadership does not recognise external control. It is sustained by success in fulfilling its mission, otherwise it fails. It changes when the mission is accomplished. Naturally, those who have a vested interest in what the charismatic leader has achieved will try to legitimise that authority. House, Spangler and Woycke (1991) carried out a complex investigation into the relationship between charisma and the effectiveness of 31 Presidents of the USA. They could not test possible interactions between presidential characteristics and environmental conditions, although such interaction is likely. Nevertheless, they concluded that there has been an increase over time in the importance of presidential charisma. Charismatic qualities seem to emerge in crises. They emerge when social control is decentralised and when social values encourage personal initiative. The investigators employed many sources of data. Some of these were objective, others involved detailed content analyses or ratings. One issue of particular interest for reputation was called, 'the common pool of historical fact and interpretation'. This refers to widely held and well-established opinions that influence people's attitudes and reactions to some entities, such as famous people and important events. Thus reputation can be regarded as a source of response bias for raters, coders and respondents generally. House et al. (1991) recognised that the attribution 'charisma' provides a convenient *post hoc* explanation of effective leadership. They pointed out that operationally defined charismatic qualities *predict* some kinds of leadership effectiveness (see also Kinder et al., 1980; Kinder and Fiske, 1986).

Leadership characteristics include energy, alertness, originality, integrity, self-confidence, decisiveness, knowledge and fluency. Almost any personal or social characteristic that is high in social desirability is likely to contribute to effective leadership in some circumstances. On the other hand, distinctly undesirable characteristics are not uncommon, in particular, single-mindedness, ruthlessness and deceitfulness. It is people's *perceptions* of leadership qualities that matter.

Charisma and individuality (including eccentricity) are powerful factors in the formation of reputation. Charisma gains and holds attention. Individuality and eccentricity provide the distinctiveness needed for effective recognition and recall. Charisma depends on a degree of remoteness from an audience. Familiarity breeds contempt in the sense that intimate knowledge of another person puts the 'charismatic' aspect of the person into a wider context and diminishes its effect. Remote audiences, however, register only the charismatic aspect, thus magnifying its importance.

Charisma and individuality are expressed in behaviour, and to that extent they are susceptible to training. There is, however, an element of genetic endowment, associated with temperamental and intellectual characteristics, that make it difficult to bring about major changes. The main benefits from training in self-presentation are likely to be gained by those who, for reasons of inexperience or lack of confidence, have not developed the necessary social skills or motivation to interact effectively with others (Chapter 7).

A charismatic figure is supposed to have a special personal quality that sets him or her apart from other people. This quality is a natural (or supposedly supernatural) authority that commands agreement and obedience from followers. A charismatic person is persuasive, attractive, highly motivated and dedicated to certain social values and objectives. Charisma is commonly used to explain the rise to power of people in politics, religion, entertainment, industry and commerce.

However, Spinrad (1991) debunked charisma as an explanatory concept in the study of politics and history. His account shifted the emphasis from personality characteristics to the social conditions that surround the emergence of leaders. Charisma then lies 'in the eye of the beholder', who sees the person as singularly capable of achieving a collective aim. A key quality in charismatic leadership is the ability to identify and express what followers believe and want. Spinrad argued that the widespread image or reputation of charismatic figures is mostly the result of mass persuasion by whatever methods are available to interested parties. Their public image is sometimes transformed over the years, even after the martyrdom or demise of the charismatic person, and becomes largely mythical. Some fictional figures, such as Robin Hood and William Tell, are presented as charismatic leaders, and have the function of personifying collective values.

Although the 'personal aura' of a charismatic leader may not survive close personal acquaintance, close acquaintances recognise the advantages of promoting the public image of someone with popular appeal—a person who can win votes, influence people and get things done. A person's public image can be deliberately orchestrated through propaganda and public relations activities. Recent history and current affairs provide many examples.

After examining various charismatic figures, Spinrad (1991) concluded that most could be explained in terms of the public's perception of the person as the one best able to do what needed to be done—politically, militarily, or whatever—and not in terms of personality characteristics.

A few charismatic figures become symbols or embodiments of large collective enterprises in politics, religion or financial affairs. Others operate on a smaller scale, such as leading fashions in art, leisure and entertainment. Some operate rackets and street-corner gangs. Charisma seems to be a function of three factors. First, particular social conditions generate a demand and support for emergent leadership. Second, someone has the personal qualities that best 'fit' these social conditions. Third, the emergent leader must seem to be succeeding in achieving the collective aim.

Charisma is most clearly seen in individuals who succeed in gaining popular support *in spite of* adverse conditions. Spinrad cited Charles de Gaulle and Gandhi as examples, and emphasised their symbolic identification with a collective entity—a nation or class.

Personalities versus Policies in Political Campaigns

Rudd (1986) examined a political campaign in Idaho, USA, in 1982, with particular reference to television commercials addressing political issues or candidates' personal qualities. The former are supposed to educate the electorate, whereas the latter are regarded as avoiding policy issues by focusing on personalities. Candidates for political office, apparently, are advised to present policy issues in a simple straightforward way, avoiding technical detail. Rudd (1986) used participant observation and in-depth interviews (rarely used methods in research into reputation) to study the relationship between issue-oriented commercials and the candidates' public image. One party produced six television commercials. All addressed political issues, but in so doing they attacked the incumbent politician and attempted to build a positive image of the challenger for office by portraying his family values, personal qualities and leadership potential.

Most ordinary voters cannot properly decide between different policies because they lack the necessary technical understanding or interest. Consequently, they have to rely on a representative who seems credible, who voices opinions they can agree with, and seems capable of taking effective action in office. The television commercials, in effect, presented policy issues in the interests of reputation management, since the candidate's policies were not dealt with in detail. Certain details might not have appealed to some sections of the electorate, whereas the socially approved personal attributes of the challenger emphasised in the commercials would have a wide appeal.

What seems to take place in commercially oriented electioneering is an attempt to convince voters not that certain policies are correct but that certain people have abilities, principles and other personal qualities, and can be trusted to deal effectively with the complex political and economic problems that affect voters.

Television appears to be more effective than the printed word in influencing people through their feelings and emotions. Its messages are simple and direct, and do not rely heavily on language. It can make use of a candidate's appearance and expressive behaviour, and can reinforce the spoken or written word with appropriate visual images. Thus, political broadcasts on television seem to deal with policy issues, but do so in a vague, general way, using the issues as a vehicle for the promotion of a candidate's public image—possibly one at variance with the candidate's actual character. By contrast, broadcasts that deal in detail with policies may avoid important personality issues. Interested parties are bound to present themselves in the best possible light, hence the need for independent and objective commentators.

9 Ethical and Legal Aspects

Introduction

People take action to enhance their reputation and to protect it from harm. This shows its value. Reputation is an important 'concern', a social and even a financial asset. Reputation is an extension of the self—something that is peculiarly one's own. It encompasses the things with which we feel personally involved—our family, friends, achievements, and so on.

Some organisations devote considerable resources to their public image through the efforts of their public relations advisors. Their activities, products and services are extensions of the firm's corporate identity; the firm is held responsible for them and takes legal action to assert rights over them. Protecting one's personal reputation or corporate image may involve denying or excusing shortcomings, hiding unfavourable characteristics and denigrating competitors' reputations. Loss of face (loss of social esteem or reputation) may have to be tolerated in the interests of a higher value, such as protecting others, and requires confidence that esteem can be recovered and in having done the right thing.

The law dealing with libel and slander is designed to protect a person from defamation through the written or spoken word. At the same time, the law tries to protect the social order, and the freedom of individuals to publish the truth about matters of public interest.

What is falsely asserted in acts of defamation must refer specifically to the plaintiff, and must have been communicated to another person, and thereby, possibly, to the wider community. The law on defamation differs somewhat from country to country, as does the law on evidence relating to reputation. Reputation raises some difficulties in law; these illustrate the importance of reputation as a social psychological process and are described below.

Defamation refers to false accusations that damage a person's reputation, making it difficult or impossible for that person to pursue life in the normal way with other people in professional work or in public office. Insults and defamations could be accusations of failure or misbehaviour, such as accusations of negligence, criminal behaviour or prostitution. It is up to a court to decide whether or not the accusation is false, and if so what damage has been done to reputation, and what remedy or compensation is due. The damages awarded reflect not only the seriousness of the particular offence, but also the court's need to show society's abhorrence of defamation.

A positive personal reputation is like a shell of information and social approval that surrounds and protects individual people; it signals their characteristics and their citizenship status. If it is damaged, it has to be repaired, otherwise the individual will suffer. If it is damaged without good cause, then the individual and the community have to take action against the agents responsible for the damage, otherwise the community will suffer.

The law limits the length of time that can intervene between the publication of defamatory material and starting legal proceedings, on the grounds that a person who feels strongly about the material should start proceedings without undue delay.

Reputation can be examined not only from a social or a psychological perspective, but also from a political perspective. The political perspective emphasises that the liberty of the individual is at risk unless his or her character is protected, and that defamation endangers public order. The liberty of the individual and the well-being of society are at risk if people are prevented, by the threat of legal action, from publishing statements of fact and opinion in the public interest.

Reputations can be promoted well beyond their legitimate bounds and status, for example by public relations work, by fraud and deceit, by threats and bribes. Occasionally, even scientists engage in fraud in the hope of making or maintaining their reputation. Clearly, social esteem provides a strong incentive for action, particularly in some areas of life—politics, religion, entertainment, the arts. Reputation affects the behaviour of and relationships between people in virtually every sphere of social life.

People whose misconduct, lapses and mistakes have resulted in an unfavourable reputation have to 'live down' or 'make up for' those errors. Reputations can be repaired, but the scars are likely to remain apparent to the person concerned and to his or her social contacts. People develop a reputation that includes both previous faults and the ways in which they have been atoned for—low school performance is more than compensated for by becoming a Prime Minister, professor or millionaire! Previous reputational merits may go some way to offset subsequent faults, for example when a court takes account of a defendant's previous 'good character'. On the other hand, such merits may make the subsequent faults more reprehensible—a good reputation in business can be destroyed by overstepping the bounds of business ethics. Lapses that would have little or no effect on a person with low social status can make a high-status person's position untenable.

Ethical Aspects

Allport (1937) described the origins of the juristic meanings of personality. In ancient Rome, a slave was not a person. Only freeborn persons had rights and privileges and were protected by law, i.e. enjoyed 'legal status'. The notion of personality extended to the person's material possessions. In civilised countries nowadays, everyone can claim legal protection as a 'person'. Even people who are grossly mentally impaired are given legal protection through a legally recognised advocate.

Craik (1989) outlined the philosophical basis of reputation underlying the law on defamation in the Anglo-American tradition. There are three basic ingredients in reputation: dignity, property and honour. Dignity refers to a person's right to membership of (citizenship in) a community, and participation in it according to reciprocal rules of civility that govern social interaction, role and status. This notion of dignity is difficult to pin down because communities evolve rules that accord more 'dignity' to some people than to others. Dignity is culturally recognised, as in caste, race and class systems. Reputation suffers if people fail to behave in the ways prescribed for people of that sort.

Reputation as property is a possession peculiar to the owner, an extension of the self. Allport (1955) introduced the idea of 'proprium' to describe the scope of the self (whatever is I, me, mine, we, us, our), including, for example, one's achievements, close relatives and possessions. The law seems to recognise that one person's reputation is linked with that of other people—relatives or colleagues. Individuals who are not directly identified or named in a defamatory statement sometimes claim to have been defamed because of their close association with those who are named, or with a named organisation.

In normal circumstances, a personal reputation is assumed to reflect an individual's competence in his or her social position. A corporate image is assumed to reflect an organisation's competence in the manufacture of goods or the delivery of services. A good reputation is an asset in the sense that other people refer to it when establishing or modifying exchange relationships— as in business deals, political alliances, scientific cooperation, and the like. Statements that unjustifiably damage the 'asset value' of a person's reputation—for example false accusations of professional incompetence, misconduct or disloyalty—are therefore a reasonable cause for complaint and legal action.

Reputation as honour (good name) can be looked at in two ways. As recognition of moral worth in a particular community, it refers to the public belief that a person is abiding by the accepted code of practice. Public accusations of failure in this respect might well be a reasonable cause for legal action, as with damage to the 'asset value' of reputation mentioned above. Some people have more to lose than others from damage to their moral creditworthiness (honour) because they occupy important positions in society (central roles, high status), where abiding by the accepted code of practice is essential for the social order. These high-status, central roles permit considerable authority and discretion, which can easily be abused; hence the need for them to be occupied by people who can put the public interest before personal or sectional interests. False accusations of nepotism, corruption or other offences might provoke legal action, depending upon the status of the accuser. Accusations that prove to be true could result in impeachment.

Craik (1989) drew attention to the sources of, and sorts of, information collected for state security investigations—pursued extensively and at considerable social cost in authoritarian regimes. In more open societies, the methods used to collect information and to exert influence, for example by the 'tabloid' press, may go well beyond what is considered reasonable, and the weight of evidence needed to bring about an adverse public reaction is much less than that required in a court of law.

Many personality attributes can be assigned a moral worth—as socially desirable or undesirable in normal circumstances. Moral worth is a prominent aspect of reputation. In other words, characteristics that are especially desirable or undesirable feature prominently in reputation. They are the characteristics most likely to affect, and to come to the attention of, other people.

Blackmail

Further examples of the ethical and legal aspects of reputation are found in the study of blackmail. Hepworth (1975) traced the history of blackmail and distinguished several varieties, including moral or reputational blackmail. This consists in demanding money or other favours from someone in return for not disclosing information that would discredit that person. Disclosed reputational blackmail illustrates a number of social phenomena. It reveals discrepancies between what persons are and what they seem to be. It reveals the worth (price) placed on reputation by the blackmailer and the victim. It reveals the motives of, and the social (exchange) relationships between, blackmailers and their victims.

It seems likely that many cases of blackmail are not reported to the police. Some victims are willing to pay the price for non-disclosure. Some find other solutions to the problem. The legal sanctions against blackmail are strong, possibly because the law-makers belong to that section of society that is more vulnerable to blackmail. Persons of high status have more to lose socially by being discredited, and to blackmailers they appear more profitable. In some instances, discreditable conduct may be well known and widespread in some social circles, but not elsewhere. Successful blackmail, therefore, threatens many in those social circles.

Minor forms of reputational blackmail occur in everyday life: threats to inform on someone for a misdemeanour unless favours are granted; threats to report someone's misbehaviour unless they stop it or make amends. The distinction between socially acceptable and socially unacceptable behaviour changes over time and varies according to the perspective from which it is viewed. Threats to harm reputation are strong incentives to conform. Blackmailers may be able to work out which persons or social groups are most important for the victim's reputation—family members, employer, clients, the police, the media, and so on. Some kinds of reputational blackmail are engineered by tricking victims into behaving in ways that they would not want to be made public, for example sexual or homosexual behaviour or taking drugs. Information disclosed in confidence may also provide material for blackmail.

Prosecutions for blackmail or attempted blackmail usually concern efforts to extort money by threatening to disclose serious immoral or illegal behaviour by the victim, such as sexual perversion, adultery, theft or tax evasion. Threats to reputation might refer to professional malpractice or incompetence, such as plagiarism, scientific fraud or negligence. At the corporate level, the difference between 'whistle blowers' and blackmailers is that blackmailers are acting out of self-interest, whereas whistle blowers are acting in the public interest. Corporate codes of conduct are designed to discourage professional misconduct and to protect those who might be adversely affected by another person's misbehaviour.

Submission to blackmail indicates the value placed on reputation by victims. It may reflect the guilt experienced as a result of their misconduct or, more likely, the anxiety they feel about the consequences, to themselves and others, of disclosure. Blackmail offers opportunities for continuing extortion, virtually depriving victims of their resources and well-being.

The law relating to blackmail recognises that victims have behaved discreditably, even criminally, but regards the attempt by others to profit from the victims' misbehaviour as a serious criminal offence. Blackmail, presumably, compounds the offence against society. Blackmailers may justify their actions by claiming a right to the money or other favour, or by arguing that the victim deserved to be punished. The law tries to protect victims who are prepared to help prosecute blackmailers. People innocent of discreditable behaviour may become victims of blackmail through the circulation of false accusations that the victim might not be able to refute. Anonymous letters, planted evidence, misleading reports and malicious gossip fulfil a similar function without extortion. Indeed, some commercial publications rely heavily on the public's interest in other people's misbehaviour, i.e. scandal. In this light, it has been said that what is of interest to the public is not necessarily in the public interest! Certainly, some protection is given by the law on defamation.

Guilt and Shame

The notions of reparation, penance, apology, punishment, ostracism, rehabilitation, fines, and so on, are familiar in the ethics of everyday life. They refer to the sanctions available to people to enforce conformity to the prevailing moral and legal codes. These codes change over time—behaviour that previously led to social sanctions may become socially permitted, even encouraged.

A distinction can be drawn between guilt and shame in that guilt is an individual reaction to a deviation from an internalised personal code of conduct and can be experienced even in the absence of social blame. Shame on the other hand can be experienced not only when a person's guilt becomes public knowledge but also as a form of vicarious guilt if a person feels associated in some way with the guilty party. The reason, as explained above, is because our sense of self extends into the world and, as it were, we regard parts of it as 'mine' or 'part of me'. Thus we may experience shame if a relative, or friend is found guilty of wrongdoing, or if the organisation we belong to is blamed for negligence or malpractice. Hultberg (1988) contrasted shame as a reaction to loss of social esteem with guilt as a reaction to a loss of self-esteem. Shame and guilt, however, are closely related, and both are consequences of damage to reputation (loss of esteem by others).

Cultural Factors

Different cultural traditions and conditions make for different moral and legal codes. Hence, behaviour that is reprehensible in one culture need not be in another, so that risks to reputation are different. The legal remedies for false accusations are different. In general, however, people proved to have defamed others have to make amends, and may be punished for the offence. For example, they have to retract defamatory statements, offer public explanations and apologies, provide compensation for the plaintiff's financial loss, pay damages for injury to self-esteem and public esteem, or pay damages as a punishment and as a deterrent to others. In a previous age, an insult to one's honour could lead to a duel.

It is sometimes assumed by Europeans that 'face' (personal or family honour) is a peculiar cultural characteristic of Arabs and Orientals; but 'face' is simply another name for 'reputation' or 'honour'. What is different, perhaps, is the value system that attaches greater worth (or discredit) to some attributes of reputation than to others, such as defence of one's extended family or clan, social status, virginity, professional competence, or whatever.

The dearth of empirical studies of reputation contrasts with the great importance that honour, 'face', and reputation generally, have had, and continue to have, in most societies throughout history. The cultural complexities of defamation as a legal issue have been described by Carter-Ruck and Walker (1985). Countries differ in their laws on defamation. They differ about what constitutes defamation; they differ in their legal procedures and in the way they deal with the award of damages or the right of reply by an injured party. Generally, however, defamation means that a published statement was false, and that it was published in the knowledge that it was false or that there were serious doubts about its truth.

Freedom of Speech

Severe legal sanctions against defamation can have a restrictive effect on freedom of speech and therefore on the public interest. It is desirable in some circumstances to investigate suspected malpractices, and to accuse those thought to be responsible for them. The problem is that evidence that makes a good prima-facie case—of say fraud or plagiarism—may not stand up to scrutiny, especially in a court of law, which lays down specific definitions and legal procedures. This might then lead the defendant open to a charge of malicious slander.

In everyday life, minor misunderstandings and disagreements sometimes lead to public accusations—of infidelity, theft, incompetence, laziness, and so on—that harm reputation. If these accusations are false, the person making the accusations is open to counter-accusations of jealousy, deceit, scapegoating or mismanagement. They may be obliged to make amends by offering apologies, explanations and compensatory gifts of one sort or another.

Accusations that come within the ordinary range of interpersonal conflict would not normally lead to legal action for defamation; if they did, they might be quickly disposed of as trivial by a court of law. The assumption would be that the damage to reputation is negligible and easily remedied. At the other extreme, there are published statements that are clearly defamatory if they prove to be untrue. In between the two extremes, there are published statements that may or may not be defamatory until a court has heard both sides of the argument and has reached a decision one way or the other. In spite of the remedies available in everyday life, or in law, it may be difficult or impossible to undo the damage done to reputation by false accusations.

Attempts to prevent publicity are often counter-productive. If made public, the act of trying to prevent it gives the impression that what is being said is true and newsworthy (otherwise why try to prevent it?). Resort to the Official Secrets Act, or to the terms of an employment contract, or to legal action, or to threats, may or may not be effective in preventing disclosure of information unfavourable to a person or to an organisation, for instance malpractice in a bank, drug company or government department. People who disclose corporate malpractice are known as 'whistle blowers'. Their ethical conduct benefits the wider society, often at considerable personal cost.

Defamation

This and the following sections are not intended to be a guide to the legal technicalities of defamation (slander, libel), or to the institutional frameworks within which various legal systems work. The aim is to explore the extent to which consideration of legal issues (in particular, defamation, malicious falsehood and reputation in the law of evidence) helps us to understand the social and psychological aspects of reputation, and to set these legal issues in a more general context of philosophy and ethics. The legal aspects presented in this chapter are based largely on *Legal Aspects of Reputation, Report of the Committee on Defamation* (Faulks Committee, 1975). Watkins (1990) has provided a useful non-technical case-study of a recent libel action. Watkins's book illustrates the ways in which legal technicalities can obscure the main issues; it also illustrates the law's reliance on a somewhat stereotyped definition of reputation. It shows how sensitive people are to adverse comments on their moral and professional standards. The book also contains technical and non-technical references on libel.

There is a difference between damage to reputation and injured feelings resulting from insult—damage to reputation involves a third party. The law on defamation attempts to strike a balance between freedom of speech and the protection of reputation, both of which are in the public interest but sometimes come into conflict with each other. In civil law, defamation is a 'tort', a breach of duty leading to a liability for damages. Although libel (defamatory material recorded in some way) and slander (spoken or transitory defamation) can be distinguished, it is convenient for our purpose to ignore the distinction and let 'libel' include 'slander'. The distinction between libel (defamation published in permanent form) and slander (defamation by word or gesture) has given rise to some interesting and entertaining legal debates but need not detain us here.

Defamatory statements are presumed to be false, so the onus is on the defence to prove them to be true. This goes some way to counter-balance the harm done if the statements are false; if they prove to be true, then the plaintiff has to take the consequences of denying them.

Definition

The legal definition of defamation raises problems because of the need for precision. It is not possible to give an exhaustive and exclusive definition because injury to reputation takes many forms. Some forms are not defamatory in the narrow sense, for example, injury to the reputation of a dead person or malicious falsehood. Circumstances alter cases, and cultural changes affect society's attitude to defamation.

Criminal libel (as opposed to civil action) is concerned with defamation likely to endanger public order. Proceedings for criminal libel are rare in the UK. We need not consider obscene, seditious or blasphemous libel here.

After considering earlier views, the Faulks Committee (1975: 15, 172) proposed the following definition:

> Defamation shall consist of the publication to a third party of matter which in all the circumstances would be likely to affect a person adversely in the estimation of reasonable people generally.

This echoes the earlier test put forward by Lord Atkin:

> 'Would the words tend to lower the plaintiff in the estimation of right-thinking members of society generally?'

Other definitions place the emphasis clearly on damage to reputation, rather than damage to the person, because of published false adverse information. Reputation includes fame, honour and good name. The publication of false favourable information, or information that is merely in bad taste, does not constitute defamation. Bad manners, discourtesy or even somewhat extreme opinions do not constitute defamation. In other words, the law recognises and accepts the normal range of differences between people, and the consequential conflicts of interest and opinion. The law is concerned with public order and freedom of speech, and with the relationship between individuals and the wider society.

The variety of circumstances in which defamation occurs, however, is wide, and a definition in general terms is not much help in deciding particular cases. A minority report (Faulks Committee, 1975: 189–198) by Mr W. Kimber supported by Mr H. Grisewood did not accept the definition of the majority. The minority report listed the sorts of publication that are regarded as defamatory. These can be rephrased as follows: publications that either (a) discredit a person; or (b) lower a person in the estimation of others; or (c) expose a person to hatred, ridicule or contempt; or (d) injure a person's reputation in office, trade or profession; or (e) injure a person financially; or (f) lead others to avoid the discredited person. These effects of defamation are not necessarily exhaustive or exclusive. They represent the more common features of a family of cases of defamation.

The problem in law is not so much the problem of formulating definitions and rules, but the problem of deciding whether a particular case comes within the scope of a definition or rule. Defamations can differ in degree as well as in kind. Some are serious, others trivial, with no clear dividing line between the two. There is the problem of distinguishing between defamation and malicious falsehood (see later).

In law, a balance has to be struck between a plaintiff whose reputation has been damaged, and a defendant who has published material not knowing, and not intending, that it would be taken as referring to the plaintiff, or not knowing that it was false. At the very least, the plaintiff seems entitled to some sort of retraction, apology and explanation.

Facts and Opinions

The Faulks Committee (1975) deal in some detail with the meanings of words associated with defamation. For example, statements of fact have to be proved true, and statements of opinion have to be fair comment on matters of public interest. Statements of fact and statements of opinion have a particular form and content, and they occur in a particular context. Consequently, it is necessary for a court to determine exactly what the statement was, what it meant, whether it was true and, if so, whether and to what extent it was likely to damage the plaintiff's reputation. The meaning of a statement depends upon the framework of understanding of the reader or listener. Different people interpret words differently; this produces effects on reputation and has implications for defamation. Common usage is the main guide to meaning, unless a technical interpretation is clearly appropriate. The question of what a person *intended* to say is a separate legal issue.

These matters are not mere legal niceties; they have their counterpart in interpersonal misunderstandings in daily life, particularly in situations involving reputation management (Chapter 7), when people have to account for their behaviour.

Information that the defendant can show is true is not defamatory; this protects the public's right of access to information of public interest. Particular items of information have to be considered in the wider context of the publication as a whole, because some are true and others false; some are damaging, others not.

The law appears to be generous in its intepretation of what is permitted as 'comment' or 'fair comment' in the expression of opinions. Statements of fact, on the other hand, have to be true for a charge of defamation to be resisted. The statements have to appear justifiable or reasonable in the circumstances, otherwise they might be judged malicious or not genuine. This does not mean that statements have to be relevant to the public interest. The main issue is whether they harm the person they refer to.

Malicious Comments

It is usual to suppose that a person who dislikes you would be acting maliciously in making derogatory statements about you; but this would be difficult to prove. A statement made maliciously cannot be 'fair comment'. The point in law is that a malicious comment does not express a genuine opinion, and that the underlying motivation is improper or indirect. Complications arise if a person motivated by malice somehow involves an innocent party, such as a printer, in the publication of an article. Malice is a state of mind, and difficult to prove. On the other hand, if a co-defendant could reasonably have inferred malice by the main defendant, then he or she might be liable to the charge of malicious comment.

The difference between 'defamation' and 'malicious falsehood' is that malicious falsehood is actuated by malice and harms the plaintiff. The *plaintiff* must prove that what was said is false; this is not required in action for defamation, where the plaintiff is presumed to have a good reputation. Malice (dishonest or improper motivation) is an essential feature of malicious falsehood, and has to be proved by the plaintiff. It appears that malicious intention is the important issue; it might not be necessary to prove that special damage has occurred.

Privileged Statements

Some circumstances are privileged absolutely in law and permit statements to be made without the risk of legal action for defamation—for example statements made in judicial or parliamentary proceedings, or reports of proceedings. This could be regarded as a necessary protection for judicial and governmental processes. There are situations covered by what is called 'qualified privilege'— affecting the reporting of proceedings covered by 'absolute privilege'. These arrangements, however, can be abused. For example, accusations can be made maliciously in circumstances covered by absolute privilege, but not elsewhere. Reports of these accusations, which are also privileged, but to a lesser degree, can adversely affect the person accused and his or her associates.

The main aim is to strike a balance between the public's right to know the truth about matters of public interest and to hear opinions about these matters, on the one hand, and, on the other, the protection of people or organisations against defamation. It will be appreciated that different sorts of published material call for different legal arguments, such as material published in scientific journals alleging fraud or plagiarism, live television or radio broadcasts, or credit bureau reports.

Unintentional Defamation

People can make defamatory statements unintentionally by failing to notice contexts in which statements might take on a derogatory meaning, or by failing to check whether or not they are true. It is sometimes possible to make amends without a full hearing, and to retract the offending statements, although the legal requirements may be difficult to meet. If an offer to make amends is refused by the plaintiff, the case is examined in full. Claiming that the defamation was unintentional may provide a form of defence for defendants whose defamation was intentional.

Corporate Entities

Individuals can combine in collective action, such that no one person is responsible for the actions of the group. Consequently, personality as a legal entity can be extended to incorporate bodies, such as commercial organisations, although the law does not operate in the same way for corporations as it does for individual persons. As we have seen, entities other than persons have reputations, and there are aspects of personal reputation that are not found in corporate, product or service reputations, and vice versa.

A commercial corporation can bring an action for defamation in the same way as a person. Defamation consists in publishing false information, such as accusations of dishonesty or inefficiency, that is likely to injure the corporation's business reputation. Corporations cannot be accused of actions that only individuals can carry out, such as adultery. Recent attempts to bring charges of 'corporate manslaughter', as in the *Herald of Free Enterprise* case (against the owners of the ship, which sank), have failed. Corporations can be injured only through their reputation as a commercial entity (involving money, assets, goodwill). They cannot claim damages for injured feelings or impaired social relationships, although it might be possible for individuals associated with a corporation to bring separate actions on these grounds.

Damages and Other Remedies

The nature and extent of damage to reputation cannot be known for certain. Nevertheless, it is possible to estimate what should be done to make amends for the likely damage caused by making apologies, withdrawing the defamatory material, paying compensation. Compensatory damages are intended to make up for the injury to reputation and to self-esteem (hurt feelings). Punitive damages are intended to deal with special cases, where the defendant stood to gain more from defaming the plaintiff than the plaintiff could obtain by way of compensation. Heavy damages may be awarded by juries to discourage defamation. If a defendant wishes to mitigate damages, one line of argument is that the plaintiff had a bad reputation before the defamation was published.

Defamation and Death

Procedural problems arise if either the plaintiff or defendant in an action for defamation dies before judgment is reached. It might be possible, under some jurisdictions, for relatives of a deceased plaintiff to continue an action already under way, or for a plaintiff to recover damages from a deceased defendant's estate. In the UK, it is not normally possible to bring an action for defamation on behalf of a deceased person.

Evidence of Reputation

Information about specific issues that underlie a person's reputation (as opposed to information about general reputation) is normally excluded because it would introduce merely collateral evidence of doubtful quality, much of it hearsay (Nokes, 1957). Jones, Schwarts and Gilbert (1983–84) reported the effects of first-hand and hearsay information on subjects' judgements of other people's behaviour. The recall of hearsay information was distorted in the direction of the observed behaviour.

In cases of defamation, a person's previous reputation is established by taking evidence of a general sort from a few credible sources; these are people who are presumed to know the plaintiff's reputation. A plaintiff with a poor previous reputation in some respects can still succeed in a defamation case if the defamation is about other aspects of the plaintiff's reputation.

The extent of the damage to reputation by defamation is not necessarily pursued, unless the person has lost his or her social position because of the defamation. The remedies and damages awarded to a successful plaintiff— public apology, resignation, financial compensation—should go some way to offset the adverse effects and compensate for the inconvenience and hurt feelings. The problem is that it is not usually possible to assess the full nature and extent of the damage caused by defamation, or to repair it. Different judges or different juries might come to different conclusions; the public might disagree with the outcome of an action for defamation. It is not the consequences of the act, but the act itself, that is judged to be defamatory because of the damaging effect it is *likely* to have on reputation.

Shotland (1985) considered sexual reputation as a factor in 'date rape'. The defence argument could be that the woman was provocative or willing. A known prostitute might find it difficult to bring a successful prosecution. Reputation may well contribute to the common tendency to 'blame the victim' for their injury.

Juries

A judge or jury form impressions of witnesses based on specific characteristics of which they are unaware, such as appearance and attitude, even though they appreciate the importance of demeanour in assessing the credibility of witnesses. Whobrey, Sales and Elwork (1981) have discussed reputation as one of several factors affecting witness credibility in the American legal system. Witness reputation certainly does affect juries' impressions.

There are arguments for and against using juries to decide cases of action for defamation. These refer, on the one hand, to jury members' supposed familiarity with the ordinary aspects of daily life, language usage and social relationships, and on the other to judges' legal expertise. The debate about the use of juries in civil action for defamation recognises that, logically speaking, a jury should be drawn from those sections of the public in which the reputation in question exists, rather than from the public at large. In the UK, however, special juries are no longer permitted.

Economic and Commercial Aspects

A distinction can be drawn between reputation as an economic asset, in which case damage is equated with pecuniary loss, and reputation as a social and psychological asset, in which case damage is equated with loss of public esteem and self-esteem.

Goodwill is the credit associated with a good reputation. In commercial and legal circumstances goodwill has a financial value. Commercial products or other goods can be defamed if what is published, such as false accusations that a product is dangerous to consumers, is likely to cause financial damage to the plaintiff. This illustrates the way an organisation's social identity, its public image, tends to include everything that is essentially part of, or belongs to, the organisation, including its products.

An example of commercial defamation or malicious comment would be an attempt by one company to malign a product being marketed by another company. The motive might be to reduce the maligned company's market value before a take-over bid.

Other Legal Issues

Material published in good faith is not likely to be actionable on trivial grounds. The reasons for making it difficult to bring an action for defamation based on weak grounds are that it wastes the time of the court and involves considerable expense. A case that fails can do more harm than the publication complained of.

There appears to be little or no research on the longer-term effects of defamation. Courts sometimes seem to assume that the damage done to reputation is serious, and therefore probably long-lasting, hence the severe penalties sometimes imposed, especially by juries, who wish to deter others from making false accusations.

Implications for Everyday Life

Competition and emnity between people means that they sometimes try to spoil a person's reputation, or the public image of an organisation, service or product. This can be done in all sorts of ways—by ordinary criticism, misinformation, distortion, malicious rumour, defamation, or even sabotage or 'framing'. The 'popular' press sometimes use highly intrusive and socially undesirable methods when collecting information and publicising their views. Inferences are sometimes made on slender evidence from sources of doubtful credibility. Character assassination is the deliberate attempt to destroy a person's good reputation by these means. Damaging a competitor's reputation can be an effective way of solving some of life's problems, as in professional advancement, business competition or sexual relationships. This sort of behaviour, however, carries risks of counter-attack or legal action.

10 Corporate Reputation: A General Framework

Introduction

This chapter describes a general framework for the study of corporate reputation similar to that for the study of persons and other entities. Other aspects of corporate reputation are dealt with in Chapters 11, 12 and 13.

One can draw analogies between different sorts of reputational entity. These analogies should not be taken literally; analogies have positive and negative features, and fulfil a heuristic function. The analogies suggest that the 'dynamics' or reputation for organisations, persons, products, and so on, are comparable, although some processes are peculiar to each type of reputational entity.

Organisations have their internal membership groups—management, secretarial staff, production, sales, and so on. These groups do not necessarily work well together. They may be subject to different influences and have access to different sorts of information. Consequently, they have different views of the company. The image prevalent among the members of an organisation is analogous to the self-image of an individual. An individual can have conflicting ideas about the self just as an organisation can have internal divisions of opinion about its structure and functions. Common sense tells us that an organisation's resources, its internal image and esteem (morale), its performance, and its reputation are all interrelated, rather like an individual's personality, self-image, performance and reputation are interrelated. Exactly how these interrelationships work is a matter for research into specific cases.

Consumers expect to pay more for a higher quality product or service—a household appliance or a meal in a restaurant. The quality of a product or service is often judged not only by its cost but also by reference to the standing of the manufacturer or provider. Firms with a good reputation, therefore, can charge a higher price for what is objectively an equivalent (or poorer) product or service. Reports from independent consumer research agencies frequently reveal wide disparities between the prices charged for comparable items. Repeated adverse consumer reports on car servicing, in the UK, confirm the poor reputation of this sector of the economy.

In a free-market economy, commercial and industrial reputations need to be established, protected and, where possible, enhanced. Failure to maintain standards in products and services starts a cycle of decline—reduced sales, lower profits, poorer operating conditions, reduced investment, lower morale, difficulties in recruitment. This is reflected in a less favourable public image, which aggravates the situation. Even monopoly suppliers suffer a loss of reputation if independent commentators and consumer associations voice their criticisms. This has happened in the UK with nationalised (state-run) industries and services (extraction, transport, communications, power, welfare, education). Accidents, scandals and inadequacies provoke negative reactions that spread even to those not directly responsible.

At times, an organisation's corporate reputation is stable, both absolutely (regarding the nature and extent of its public image) and relatively (regarding its public standing relative to comparable organisations). Corporate reputations in a particular sector, like personal reputations for comparable individuals, occupy a position in what is, in effect, a league table of public merit or esteem. At other times, however, a corporate or personal reputation is in a state of flux—increasing or decreasing in size and in esteem. Its character, namely the distribution of attributes assigned to it by interested parties, changes. Some organisations modify their identity, for example by becoming more diversified or by 'going public'. This entails changing their public image—changing their name, address, logo and stationery—and changing the corporate 'subculture' by adopting new aims and methods of operation.

Social and economic conditions can be stable or unstable; in either case, corporate reputations provide important sources of information to people who wish to make political and economic judgements. Different attributes of reputation become more salient for some observers under some conditions. For example, the prospect of a change in national government sensitises investors to the characteristics of firms likely to be affected by government policies.

Organisations, like persons, have as many reputations as there are distinct 'publics' or 'audiences' with an interest in them. In the study of corporate reputation these are sometimes called 'stakeholders' or 'interest groups'. The interest groups in which reputations are formed vary widely, in size, membership, organisation, and so on. An entity's general reputation is shaped by these interest groups, some of which are important in the sense of being large or influential, while others have only a marginal effect. As far as practical applications are concerned, in public relations work for example, it is important to identify these various interest groups. The appropriate information can then be transmitted and the necessary influences brought to bear, making the most effective use of the available resources.

Reputations or public images are part of the total environment, the 'ecology', in which a person or a firm operates. At the corporate level, the wider environment encompasses the economic and political circumstances that affect the firm's performance. At the individual level, the 'micro-ecology' of particular persons refers to the primary groups, social conditions and circumstances affecting them.

The reputation of the head of a department in a company varies because his or her performance affects other people in different ways, and because effects arising from local circumstances are attributed to him or her. Even coincidental effects affecting the spread of information through the communication network affect reputation. Personal reputations, like corporate reputations, provide important sources of information for people who have to make decisions or take action on issues that are important to them. People must decide whether to cooperate, whether to raise sensitive issues, whether to redirect their interests and efforts, and so on.

At higher levels of social organisation, entities such as regions, nations, religions and racial groups have public images that are collective representations amongst the members of other regions, nations, religions, racial groups and other sectors of world society. These large-scale public images are usually 'stereotypes', simple ideas expressed in simple ways (Chapter 5). In some circumstances, these collective images become important factors governing the behaviour of large numbers of people. Consider, for example, the consequences of social disorder associated with political revolution or ethnic conflict. Collective images influence human behaviour at every level, from dyadic interpersonal relationships to mass action at the international level. At these higher levels of social organisation, the mass communication media and propaganda can be used to great effect in shaping public opinion.

The problems of the US National Aeronautics and Space Administration (NASA) with the Hubble Space Telescope and delays in launching the space shuttle are examples of the phenomenon of corporate reputation. These problems have been construed as failures by some observers, and attributed to NASA itself rather than to unforeseen circumstances. This has led to criticism of NASA, and to an apparent loss of public esteem and support compared with the high point of NASA's reputation on completion of the moon project. Loss of public support threatens loss of resources (finance, staff, time), especially if there are other enterprises competing for the same support and resources. Special efforts are needed to repair damage to reputation, and it may take considerable time.

Corporate Identity

An organisation's governing body must have some ideas, however vague or erroneous, about its membership, supporters or customers. Its membership is like an individual's self; the membership's collective view of the organisation, its 'corporate self-image', is like the individual's self-image. The membership's corporate pride and morale are like the individual's self-esteem and confidence. The corporate code of conduct is analogous to the individual's conscience. Corporate identity, the characteristics that distinguish one organisation from another, is analogous to personal identity.

The governors' or managers' 'domestic' policy reflects their assessment of what its members want or will accept. Organisations have aims and use particular methods to reach them. This is sometimes made explicit in a document describing their constitution, although it is not unusual for organisations to deviate from their stated aims and methods. Organisations exhibit certain characteristics in pursuing these aims. These performance characteristics— patterns of organisational behaviour—are perceived and interpreted by interested members of the public. Performance is not necessarily a direct and clear expression of the organisation's nature; and observers do not always interpret the performance correctly. For example, some finance companies administer funds improperly, some members misunderstand an organisation's true character.

There appears to be considerable interdependence between performance and reputation, with mutual positive feedback. There are, of course, instances where interest groups can be seriously misled for a long time, as with outright fraud, impersonation, dictatorial control, and so on. Performance and reputation, however, both depend upon independent external factors, so there is no guarantee that actions will yield the expected effects. Weaknesses in performance and in reputation need to be remedied. If the effect of reputation on performance is marginal, the resources required for public relations can be kept low; otherwise resources have to be geared to the level of threat posed by a damaged reputation. The difficult question is, 'How can the effects of reputation on performance be assessed?'

It is part of the business of public relations to monitor an organisation's reputation in order to protect and enhance it. For this to be effective, there must be a realistic understanding of the organisation's identity, the direction of its development, its publics and the means by which its publics can be informed and influenced. These requirements are separate from but tied in with the organisation's central functions and operations—upholding the law, educating people, transporting people, preaching a faith, playing soccer, or whatever.

Persons and organisations value their reputation, so they have to be alert to risks of harm to reputation and to opportunities for enhancement. This means believing (or pretending to believe) and acting (or pretending to act) in accordance with the public image they wish to foster. This raises ethical and legal issues (Chapter 9). There are many examples of individuals and organisations becoming notorious for their hypocrisy and criminal behaviour, having benefited from social esteem whilst pursuing their selfish interests.

In some circumstances, reputation is paramount. Organisations that rely heavily on their reputation to maintain a strong market position are likely to react strongly to threats to their public image. Organisations that are not held in such high esteem can take more and greater risks with their reputation because they have less to lose in this respect. Larger companies have a wider involvement with the public and so need to invest resources in public relations to protect and enhance their reputation.

Corporate Image and Brand Image

The prominence of logos and slogans in the self-presentation of organisations is based on the belief that they encapsulate in a simple, memorable form the central attribute or attributes of the organisation. They are supposed to trigger the appropriate associations and responses. Examples abound in newspapers, magazines, street hoardings and company literature.

The word 'image', as used in the terms 'public image' or 'brand image', has two meanings. First, there is the literal image (name or icon) that symbolises the organisation, product or service, for example the Shell symbol and party political symbols. Second, there is the pattern of beliefs and feelings associated with the literal image that give it its meaning or psychological significance.

The pictures that accompany other information about an entity convey information and influence. For example, the illustrations in a firm's annual report or in an advertising brochure are intended to convey or to reinforce a message. The message is that the firm is engaged in these kinds of activities and is managed by these kinds of people. In newspaper and magazine pictures, the postures, gestures, facial expressions, settings and backgrounds contribute to the general impression formed by viewers of the persons portrayed.

Although logos are often stylised and abstract, they nevertheless evoke (or are designed to evoke) the appropriate associations. If people are asked to recall a particular logo, they sometimes produce something that is closer to the literal image than the stylised logo. It is difficult to design a corporate logo that cannot be ridiculed by the opposition or media commentators; but adverse reactions usually fade with time. The launch date for the new corporate identity should take account of the circumstances likely to arise then. Selame and Selame (1988) provide practical examples of corporate images, and note the legal aspects of trademarks.

The connection between a name or its icon on the one hand and its meaning on the other can be strong and durable. An organisation that wishes to change its public image will consider changing its name and logo, and will engage in considerable public relations work to change the public's view of the organisation. This is unlikely to be achieved without real and substantial changes in the organisation itself.

The relationships between an organisation's self-image, the image it wishes to portray, and the real public image that evolves are complicated. Thus a political party that has undergone radical change, or the merging of two organisations, creates a situation in which the existing public image no longer corresponds to the new entity. For a time there might be considerable confusion and conflict between the old and the new image before the new entity establishes a distinct public image (social identity), as with the Liberal Democratic Party in the UK. Even so, the old image could persist for a long time in some sections of the public (to the benefit or detriment of the new entity).

The distinction between brand image and corporate image can be blurred, especially if the 'brand' is a service or a range of products. Thus a company that specialises in a small range of products—perfumes or car parts for example—could have a common image for the products on offer. This image would be closely identified with the public image of the company providing the product or service. Brand image is tied closely to marketing and consumer behaviour (Chapter 13). Corporate image, on the other hand, especially in larger, more diversified organisations, is tied more closely to corporate identity than to the brand images of its products or services. Olins (1978) provides examples of the complications and confusions that can arise following the merging of companies that make different products. He points out that public relations and advertising that promote a particular product are not necessarily suitable for promoting a company image, and vice versa (see also Olins, 1990).

Some cities have attempted to improve their corporate image through public relations efforts. This could be a response to a flagging economy, bad publicity or competition to host a prestige event (Chapter 11).

Visual Identity

Visual identity refers to the visual features that identify an entity—a person's physical appearance or robes of office, a company's logo and livery, a product's packaging. These can express tradition, modernity, strength, or whatever. Auditory identity is rarely mentioned; this is the sound that identifies an entity—a manner of speaking, a catch-phrase, an advertising jingle, a theme tune. Nowadays, visual identity is a prominent feature of corporate advertising. The dominance of television in the media has made visual identity very important for politicians and others in the 'public eye'. Consequently, many are using professional advisors to make their appearance, voice and expressive behaviour more effective. A person's reputation for a particular attribute, such as aloofness or verbosity, could conflict with the wider reputation that a person wishes to develop. Hence the lengths that some public figures go to in modifying their public appearance and behaviour in the interests of reputation management.

The design process can be sophisticated, comprehensive and expensive. Complex organisations need to coordinate design proposals with corporate policies and practices. This maximises the benefits of their visual identity because the visual identity has to work effectively across divisions within the company, across products, across communications (stationery, packaging), across cultures and over a considerable period. One problem is to get a balance between conformity and diversity incorporate identity. That is to say, the visual identity should be flexible enough to adapt to variations in the context in which the organisation operates.

Corporate Personality

The word 'personality' is used very loosely in ordinary discourse, whether in connection with persons or organisations. It is best to think of corporate personality as that set of major attributes that truly characterises the organisation. Corporate identity is that set of attributes that distinguish an organisation from others with which it might be compared. Olins's (1978) *The Corporate Personality* is an entertaining review of the images that commercial companies project and the reality that lies behind them. His examples could probably be updated with little alteration to the argument that company success depends to some extent on having a well-defined social identity that reflects a coherent internal organisation.

Some organisations are founded or taken over by a dominant individual who imposes his or her ambitions, plans and style on that organisation. Not all succeed, but those that do succeed are closely identified with this dominant individual. As an enterprise develops and changes, however, the dominant personality need not be best fitted to manage it. The transition to a new identity depends on the availability of new managers and on the circumstances in which the company finds itself. An increase in size is likely to mean a more bureaucratic and conformist style of management and identity. The reason is the increased complexity and sophistication of the organisation and the need for internal coherence. The equivalent need regarding personal identity is for internal consistency (Maddi, 1980). Olins (1978) argued that, in this secondary phase of its development, an organisation has to move away from an intuitive or natural identity to one that is more deliberate, more contrived. That identity should reflect the organisation's changed existence, and affect its marketing, its morale, its market value, and so on.

Personification and Corporate Identity

In some circumstances, the individual who controls an organisation *personifies* the organisation, as for example the head of an industrial organisation or political party. The character of a leader is likely to influence the character of an organisation; conversely, the character of the organisation is likely to influence the character of its leader. This interdependence helps to explain how persons come to personify their organisation, and why allegiance to a person can substitute so easily and effectively for allegiance to a cause. It helps to explain why personality is so important, not only in politics, but in every sphere of public life, even in scientific affairs. Political ideologies, economic policies and scientific theories are somewhat abstract and open to different interpretations. By contrast, the persons who espouse the ideologies, policies and theories can be understood in much the same way as other people in daily life can be understood. Consequently, a favourable public attitude towards the *person* is likely to bring about a favourable reception of the ideology, policy or theory that person espouses.

Public Impressions of Corporate Entities

A rational account of impression formation explains that interested parties judge the behaviour of an organisation by the extent to which it appears to further the organisation's aims. Interested parties, however, often have different preconceived ideas about an organisation, and so make different judgements. Consequently, different observers form different impressions based on the same or different information; they can agree about some of the attributes of an organisation but disagree about others. These attributions constitute the content of an entity's reputation and are typically distributed in a reversed-J form (Chapters 1 and 14). For example, the reputation of a charity includes some shared beliefs about what the charity is for and how it is supposed to conduct its business. Its reputation does not consist of a set of attributions shared by everyone. As we have seen, some attributes are central and widely shared, others are peripheral and held by only a few people. The total array of attributions could contain invalid and contradictory items. A charity that is judged by its publics to be spending too much on overheads—offices and administration—will suffer a loss of esteem (and donations) unless the impression can be quickly countered by good public relations. A firm that makes high profits and provides an efficient product or service is likely to enjoy a favourable reputation. That will help it to attract investment, expand its operations, retain and recruit staff, and improve its competitiveness. In other words its 'ecological niche' will be better protected and more capable of expansion.

The two main points to remember are as follows. First, corporate reputations have multiple attributes, and these attributes vary in importance depending upon circumstances. Second, reputation is only one factor in the general ecology (social, political and economic environment) in which a firm is operating. For example, a local firm could have a good local and national reputation, but other circumstances—technological and demographic changes—could lead to its decline. In some circumstances, reputation is only marginally important compared with all the other factors that affect a firm's success; in other circumstances reputation exercises a critical effect. A person's reputation has multiple attributes too, and here, more obviously perhaps, factors other than reputation—mood, illness, or other circumstances—affect the individual's success.

Even if the person or organisation remains unchanged, the reputation can change simply because of changes in the composition of the relevant interest groups. For example, infiltration of a political party by activists can result in derogation of the existing leadership and subsequent loss of support generally. Reputations, whether at the individual, organisational (corporate) or national level, reflect the effects of competition in their particular field. One reputation's gain is another reputation's loss. Public awareness and esteem are limited commodities. The rise and fall of public awareness or popularity is shown in the charts for popular music, in audience figures, in voting figures and in the extent of media coverage, for example. Serial changes in personal reputation are dealt with in detail in Chapter 14.

Individuals, organisations and nations try to convince their publics that they possess certain desirable characteristics, namely those that the public wish them to have. This maximises public esteem and support. In some circumstances, an organisation's behaviour misleads its public, and is intended to mislead. A 'cover story' is used to hide or disguise the organisation's underlying aim. Putting on an act is a common enough performance in daily life for us to recognise the distinction between what is genuine and what is simulated. There is, however, a considerable danger to reputation in not being what you seem. If the discrepancy is recognised, then the reputation as a whole suffers, not just the attribute that was simulated or hidden from public view. In politics, for example, public disclosure of sexual or financial immorality is likely to lead to a general loss of trust and respect.

The performance of a person or firm is not the only source of information that contributes to reputation. The behaviour of other people or other firms also provides information. Deliberately spreading false information to enhance or diminish a reputation is a direct intervention. Offering or withholding support sends signals to other people that they should adjust their attitude to a person or organisation. The performance of others can be used for comparison, as in league tables.

An industrial firm is likely to generate interest in many sections of the public. These interest groups include owners or shareholders, employees, subsidiary and dependent organisations, customers, suppliers, financial institutions, and possibly the media, the local authority and pressure groups of one sort or another. Consequently, the firm's reputation can be defined in several ways. It can be defined as the *set* of reputations in these interest groups, or as the *intersection* of these reputations (Chapter 1). The chances are that there will be a fair amount of agreement even across quite disparate groups about a few central attributes of the company. Differences and disagreements are likely to be about characteristics of a technical sort or characteristics of special interest to a particular group.

A firm's reputation is partly a function of its behaviour (including its public relations performance), and partly a function of the behaviour of those sections of the public that take an interest in it or have some involvement with it. These sectional interests have their aims and ways of fulfilling them that may or may not conflict with the aims and operations of the firm in question or with each other. The result is a widespread, complicated, interdependent network of individuals and social organisations whose interactions constitute the flow of information and influence that produce the phenomenon we call reputation or public image.

Opinions and inclinations that are at first fairly diffuse and heterogeneous can gradually coalesce into a more focused and uniform attitude towards a person, object or organisation. We perhaps over-estimate the extent to which a public image is focused and uniform. We under-estimate the diversity of interest groups, the diversity within interest groups, and the complexities and uncertainties of the general ecology. There are unpredictable shifts in reputation over time, and complex interactions between entities and between their reputations.

An entity's image is built up from inferences based on direct contact, and inferences based on other people's inferences. The balance between direct and indirect inferences (both of which can be mistaken) varies from person to person. Once the image has been formed, it is difficult or impossible to trace its origins or to examine the evidence on which it was based. Much information and influence is accepted passively and uncritically, unless it poses a threat to existing beliefs and practices.

Some people have a lot of information, others have little or none. People can choose to pass the information on to, or withhold it from, others. To some extent, people can choose to believe what they hear or not, or to construe it one way rather than another. Similarly, influence can be exercised or not; and, to some extent, people can accept or resist influence. In this complicated, serial, process of social interaction, some information is lost, transformed and invented; some influences are misdirected and counterproductive.

Objective and Subjective Factors

Well-established corporate reputations impose constraints on, but create opportunities for, action. The constraints include the norms and sanctions that govern the behaviour of individual members of the organisation, limits on the policies it is free to pursue, and limits on the means it is permitted to use in pursuing its policies. Consider, for example, public reactions to the police following misconduct by individual policemen. The opportunities include the freedom to act without constantly referring back to 'stakeholders' for permission. A well-established reputation implies trust among various interest groups. The organisation and the various interest groups have shaped each other's identity and behaviour over time, so that their values and requirements have converged. The constraints and opportunities associated with established reputations contribute to the success of firms operating in a competitive environment. This affects the wider economy and society as a whole.

In bureaucratic, centrally controlled societies, the reputations of individuals and organisations are formed in a different way. The State has a virtual monopoly on the mass communication media, so there is less freedom of speech and action. The important images are those formed at the higher levels in the social hierarchy, and there is less reciprocity of communication and influence. Unfortunately, there appears to be little or no comparative (cross-cultural) research on this aspect of reputation.

People's actions are governed by their subjective perceptions of the world; the consequences of their actions are governed by objective circumstances in the real world. These consequences are perceived as having a particular pattern of meaning, which may or may not correspond well with events and circumstances in the real world. This is what is meant by the 'social construction' of a belief system. For example, witchcraft as a belief system lacks scientific credibility, but has exerted a powerful influence on reputation in some cultures. Similarly, we form impressions of entities that, even if widely shared, sometimes prove to be erroneous.

It is possible, and widely believed, that predictions about a firm's future based on reputation are better than predictions based on independent objective data. If so, this would contradict the well-established finding in psychology that subjective (clinical) judgements are not as accurate as objective (actuarial) judgements (Meehl, 1954). The information conveyed by reputation is useful if it combines several independent sources, attaches due emphasis (weight) to evidence, and incorporates important subjectivities that influence people's actions. Sometimes, a good approximation to an objective assessment can be got by pooling several independent subjective assessments. This was a basic assumption in early attempts to assess personality (Chapters 2 and 4).

In situations where factual, objective data are scarce, subjective evidence of reputation is likely to be used to supplement it, and vice versa. The sorts of objective evidence one might consider in assessing the worth of a company include fixed assets, fluid assets, liabilities, profitability, market indicators, demographic factors, management experience and performance, and its 'track record'. Various signals indicate how well a firm is performing. Within a given industrial, commercial or public sector, the current signals about a particular organisation can be examined in historical perspective, or in terms of short-term or long-term forecasts, in comparison with similar organisations. Signals indicating that an organisation has improved, is continuing to improve and performs better than many of its competitors, are signals that make for a favourable public image. Naturally, different interest groups attend to different signals, or attach different degrees of importance to them. The same principle applies to personal reputation.

Professional expertise is needed to assess performance in many areas of public life. Corporate reputations depend heavily on the opinions of political, financial and industrial analysts (who must themselves have developed a favourable reputation through their work, or through other means). Sport and entertainment have their experts, critics, and commentators, as do science, literature and the arts. Reputations are made and unmade in these areas too by the processes of communication and influence already described (Chapter 6).

The subjective elements in a company's reputation might include its likely reaction to technological change, its ability to compete with newcomers in the market and workforce morale. As we shall see, in the world of industry and commerce at least, an organisation's reputation incorporates a great deal of objective evidence that has been processed by experts and communicated to interested parties. A possible drawback to what are, in effect, 'clinical' rather than 'actuarial' assessments of a company is that relevant criteria are ignored or weighted incorrectly, or irrelevant criteria are used in the decision process.

Reputations are built up over time; so, unless there have been deliberate and successful attempts to mislead the public, current reputation should provide a good estimate of the worth of a firm, given that circumstances continue as before. The importance of reputation varies from case to case, and from one occasion to another. A firm's current reputation influences onlookers' assessment of and reactions to that firm, which has the effect of modifying the firm's environment and performance. These changes, with those brought about by non-reputational factors, then feed back to influence reputation, and so the cycle continues. It is difficult if not impossible to establish the causal connections between performance and reputation, but recent developments in time-series analysis, longitudinal research, and path analysis might make it possible to carry out sophisticated investigations using field data (Magnusson et al., 1991).

Reputation is susceptible to influence from many sources. Costs in time, money and effort are incurred in building a favourable corporate reputation. Similarly, reputation management by individuals, through self-presentation, incurs costs and risks (Chapter 7). Such costs are worthwhile in anticipation of the long-term benefits of an enhanced reputation. However, even after a reputation has been established, costs are incurred in protecting and enhancing it.

This brings us back to the question of how performance and reputation are related. The well-informed, objectively based, impressions developed by experts and opinion leaders are converted into forms of information and influence that act upon less well-informed members of interest groups and the wider public. These derivative impressions are sometimes superficial and distorted versions of conclusions based on empirical evidence and rational argument. Information and influence spread through the interest groups and the wider public. The public image of a company then comprises all the explicit and implicit beliefs in circulation in the various 'publics' at a particular time. A firm's reputation, however, is more important in some areas than in others. This affects its actions and its success.

At the corporate level, the costs of building and maintaining reputation can be met by charging the higher prices that customers are prepared to pay for goods and services that seem 'guaranteed' by the company's reputation. Many large stores offer customer services—credit, home delivery, return of unsatisfactory purchases—that have costs but contribute to the firm's favourable image, and to customer loyalty—a long-term objective. Thus the price of a product is a signal of quality to consumers and others. Prices, however, can be misleading, as shown by objective assessments carried out by consumer research organisations. A trade-off is sometimes possible between short-term material losses and longer-term gains in reputation or 'goodwill', as with 'loss leaders'. This is a strategy of selling cheap in the short term to attract customers and overtake competitors. Goodwill is the social esteem and support built up over time by, say, a shop, service or manufacturer. It is an asset tangible enough to be taken account of in the purchase price of a firm, and in legal claims (Chapter 9). Davis (1992) looked at goodwill from an accounting perspective. Davis described business reputation as 'ethereal', but some of the factors suggested as constituting goodwill look similar to the attributions that make up corporate reputation (see Chapter 11). Factors of interest to accountants include copyrights, secrets, strategic location, cash reserves and potential for acquisition.

Some organisations try to enhance their reputation in a wide array of publics. This means engaging in activities and relationships that go well beyond their basic functions of producing goods or providing services. These extramural activities create the impression that the company upholds the values of the wider society, and so generate social approval and support. Donations to charity, sponsorship, competitions, exhibitions and other events are typically used to increase a company's public esteem. Firms publicise their contribution to popular issues, such as the environment, crime prevention or road safety. Successful exercises in public relations improve the organisation's morale, this being the collective expression of the increased confidence of the workforce.

Organisations try to find favour with other organisations, with the Government and with the media. Here, the influence is more direct; it is to help find means to achieve an organisation's main aims. Lobbying is the name given to the actions of representatives as they try to convince people who have authority, resources or influence that their organisation's aims and methods warrant support. Naturally, ethical standards could suffer in the process—malpractice can range from small favours to bribery and corruption on a massive scale.

People can engage in activities that confirm their adherence to ethical standards (sometimes set out in a formal code of conduct), for example by accepting them as a condition of membership of an organisation or licence to trade, by being prepared to cooperate with inquiries into apparent malpractice, and by revealing malpractice by others. In so far as a high ethical standard of behaviour is regarded as an important attribute of reputation, most people are reluctant to engage in malpractice unless the temptation is strong. On the other hand, what is regarded as malpractice in one sector of society is tolerated, or even accepted as normal, in another. Consider, for example, the point at which a gift becomes a bribe or an appointment nepotism. Cultural and subcultural norms exert a powerful influence on conduct.

Spread of Information and Influence

The media play a major role in forming the public image of some individuals and organisations. The media do not simply passively record events through unbiased reporting; they report selectively and interpret what they observe according to their sectional interests. Information can be omitted and biases introduced. The UK Government is now introducing legislation to ensure 'impartiality' in broadcasts. Journalistic ethics recommend that report and comment should be clearly distinguishable, but issues are often complicated and susceptible to different interpretations, and nowadays there is severe competition regarding coverage and timing. Consequently, report and comment are frequently indistinguishable, especially for uncritical readers and viewers. Media organisations themselves are subject to the effects of reputation. Like other entities, they develop favourable or unfavourable reputations, restricted or extended reputations, and reputations for specific attributes, such as impartiality, sensationalism or investigative ability.

There are limits to the amount of information that members of the various publics (interest groups) are willing or able to absorb. Some areas of information are related, so that under one set of news conditions a person or an organisation receives considerable publicity. In other news conditions, however, the person or organisation is not mentioned. The result is a certain amount of turbulence in the flow of information that affects reputation. The word 'turbulence' is chosen advisedly, to draw attention to the largely chaotic and unpredictable spread of information and influence through a large communication network that is subject to influences of many kinds.

The idea of turbulence in the spread of information and influence about an entity is related to the idea of the 'availability' of information about that entity, i.e. its 'visibility', for individuals in the communication network. To the extent that the entity (person, organisation, product, service) is associated with several areas of public interest—health, welfare, living standards, security, and so on— information about it is likely to be readily available because it is constantly in the news for one reason or another. Consider, for example, leading politicians, the public services, and large industrial or commercial organisations. Other entities that have newsworthy reputations are royalty, top people in the world of popular entertainment, music and sport, and so on, and entities temporarily in fashion or of public concern, such as developments in medicine, science or technology, or a criminal, or a new social movement.

The relationship between important social issues and the prominence of certain people or organisations can be influenced by pressure groups that manipulate public opinion—through their media contacts, through 'leaks' of confidential information, and through rumour, gossip and innuendo. Public opinion can be influenced through independent, objective investigation that reveals scandals about corruption in public affairs, the maltreatment of people in institutions, and so on (Doig, 1990). The main point, however, is that members of the public are likely to accept as important just those issues that their main sources of information and influence in the media—their daily newspaper, the nine o'clock news, their favourite chat show—tell them are important.

Reputations are made both in the public generally and in specialised sectors of the public—professional groups, readerships, market sectors—although these reputations interact to a greater or lesser extent, so that prominence in one sector of the public easily spreads to other sectors. Consequently, persons and organisations with a large, well-established reputation are normally at an advantage over those with a small or less well-established reputation. The reason is that they are likely to be involved in a wider array of activities of interest to one sector of the public or another, and so are more likely to enjoy more publicity. This decreases publicity for lesser known people and smaller organisations. Wider recognition depends on mobilising new sectional interests or generating newsworthy events and issues. This is done by canvassing for support, by resort to violence or by other sorts of conspicuous behaviour that attract public attention. The reputations of large corporate entities and 'celebrities' are virtually self-maintaining.

The collapse or failure of an organisation is not usually attributable directly to a loss of reputation. Rather, the initial loss of reputation is because an organisation fails to fulfil the expectations of interested parties. This initial loss then leads to a cycle of decline unless improved performance or public relations activities can repair the damage. In some instances, however, individuals and organisations are victims of malicious comment and fail to get adequate redress.

A widespread, well-established public image (brand image) is the holy grail of firms promoting a particular product or service (Chapter 13). The aim is to establish a consumer habit that makes it difficult for competing products or services to catch the attention and hold the interest of consumers. The dominant images come to mind, for example, when members of the public are asked about domestic appliances, motor cars, insurance or beverages.

It is sometimes said that there is no such thing as bad publicity. Bad publicity can provide opportunities for good publicity and rehabilitation—the right of reply, explanations and justifications, the expression of favourable attributes, opportunities to derogate opposing parties. This raises ethical issues about how persons and organisations should deal with failures to perform as expected. Ethical issues require careful handling in public relations, as for example with lapses in local government, hopsital treatment, industrial waste disposal, and air and maritime safety.

In theory, an entity's reputation is best served by a simple, generalised, favourable image. This maximises the extent to which the image is shared by members of the public. The extent to which reputational attributes are shared, however, is not as large as one would expect, at least when reputation is assessed from explicit, spontaneous opinions (free descriptions). Probe techniques can be used to explore the minor features of reputation by eliciting opinions and judgements (rankings, ratings, magnitudes) that might otherwise remain implicit or latent (Chapter 16).

In practice, entities have multiple attributes, and multiple reputations, so that overall their reputation tends to be diffuse. The problem in marketing is to promote a public image that is clear and widely shared. Some attributes are less salient than others for some sectors of the public, and there may be nothing about which the public can be said to be 'generally agreed' (Chapter 1).

11 Corporate Reputation: Empirical Studies

Introduction: Economic Aspects of Reputation

Interest in the economic effects of reputation on firms and products seems to have developed particularly in the 1980s (see Shapiro, 1982, 1983; Firth, 1990; Goldberg and Hartwick, 1990; Haas-Wilson, 1990). Readers interested in the economic technicalities are referred to Milgrom and Roberts (1982) and Sobel (1985). The basis of Sobel's economic model of reputation is that reputation based on reliable behaviour can substitute for a binding contract. Davis (1992) gives a semi-technical account of 'goodwill'—a well-known attribute of corporate reputation.

Some firms invest resources directly in reputation through advertising and public relations work. Other firms enjoy a reputation for high-quality goods and services at competitive prices without substantial direct investment in reputation. A well-established reputation offers protection against competition, provided goods and services continue to be of high quality. Firms with a good reputation take a risk if they sell a low-quality product at a high price because the adverse effect on their reputation affects other products, reducing sales and profitability. The assumption is that information about low-quality products spreads quickly and widely among potential consumers.

The development of a good reputation in commerce and industry can be regarded as an investment of resources. The assumption is that a good reputation provides a return on that investment by keeping prices at a profitable level, maintaining brand loyalty and attracting customers. Of course, if the venture fails the investment is lost, whereas if the resources had been deployed differently some of the investment might be recovered. Promotional ventures that fail are doubly damaging in the sense that the firm's pre-existing reputation is damaged by what is seen as mismanagement.

In commercial terms, a firm's reputation can be regarded as an asset, closely associated with 'goodwill'. Its reputation offers consumers a guarantee of quality that justifies a high price, especially if consumers cannot easily verify the quality of the goods or services.

Firth (1990) surveyed the effects of loss of reputation on firms of auditors that have been criticised by the British Department of Trade. The criticisms included lack of independence from a client firm, insufficient audit work, lack of support for audit staff by senior partners, and insufficient examination of a client's prospectus. Firth pointed out that such criticisms adversely affect the firm of auditors and the client firm whose accounts are not properly represented. They cast doubt on the auditor's other clients, since there is some risk that the accounts of these firms are misleading. The importance of the reputation of auditors is reflected in a league table. The reputation of a firm is enhanced by appointing auditors at or near the top of the league table.

Changes in reputation may be followed by changes in financial circumstances associated with share price, staffing or consumer behaviour. Empirical tests of these expected consequences are difficult to carry out because of the number and complexity of the variables involved—size of firms, trading conditions, market information, the time factor, and so on. Nevertheless, Firth's results show a tendency for the stock market to downgrade companies that are clients of the criticised auditors, and increased difficulty for the criticised auditors in attracting and keeping clients.

Corporate Characteristics

The adjective 'corporate' can be used in at least two ways. It can be used to refer to a particular firm or organisation, such as a small business, or a department in a larger organisation. It can also be used to refer to an organised system of firms or organisations, such as a University, a multinational firm or a national government. 'Corporate reputation' in the second sense refers to the public image of the higher-level organisation—the body that attends to the business of coordinating the diverse, and possibly conflicting, interests and activities of its various departments or subsidiaries. Of course, each of the lower-level organisations has its public image, and its 'internal image'. It may have different reputations *within* sections of the wider system of organisations to which it belongs. These reputations are likely to interact with each other in complex and unpredictable ways.

By definition, an organisation must have an internal structure, the function of which is to govern the organisation's activities. The organisation of company behaviour includes setting goals, making decisions, allocating resources, taking action and learning from experience. This requires some degree of reflexivity; the organisation must have an internal representation of itself—an image of its own make-up, resources, aims and strategy. Corporate culture is an aspect of corporate identity and is ideally reflected in the corporate code of conduct.

Fombrun and Ginsberg (1990) drew attention to the distinction between corporate strategy and business strategy. Corporate strategy includes the allocation of resources, which then helps to determine business, or departmental, strategies. Fombrun and Ginsberg investigated corporate 'aggressiveness' (note the analogy with the attribute of personal aggressiveness), a distinctive characteristic that is likely to feature prominently in both corporate and personal reputation. Corporate aggressiveness is shown by the extent to which resources are committed to risky enterprises. Aggressiveness enables an organisation to compete more effectively—to move faster and more freely, to take a larger share of the market, to weaken competitors and to enjoy the fruits of success.

Fombrun and Ginsberg (1990) drew attention to inertia that hinders development and resists change in established practices. The inertia is generated by organisational policies and procedures based on ideology, custom and corporate subculture generally. The analogy with political and personal reputation is obvious. Inertia leads to lack of aggressiveness or to aggressiveness that is excessive or unduly prolonged, leading to mounting debt or diminishing returns. Uncertainty inhibits aggressiveness. On the other hand, good performance and internal improvements encourage corporate aggressiveness.

It is possible to categorise corporate entities just as it is possible to think in terms of 'personality types'. Such categories are usually convenient simplifications (stereotypes) that ignore differences between individual entities within the same category. Fombrun and Abrahamson (1990) made the point that it is difficult to categorise organisations, because they differ widely in size, structure, activities and membership. Some firms compete or cooperate with each other, yet do not belong in the same business sector. Nevertheless, organisations within a category, such as Universities, football teams or pop groups, can be ranked on a variety of characteristics (possibly without sufficient account being taken of their comparability).

Corporate Performance

According to Fombrun and Shanley (1990), financial markets respond to information about profit, debt, advertising; institutional investors respond to information about risks (and dividends, of course); the media respond to information about larger, more profitable firms, and firms with philanthropic aims (support for charitable or cultural activities). The media also respond vigorously to corporate scandals and to activities that are against the public interest.

Economists argue that under certain conditions markets tend to be efficient. Relevant information quickly becomes available to those engaged in market transactions, so that realistic values are assigned to firms, stocks, and so on. This is analogous to the way information and influence in daily life affects personal reputations.

Given the diversity of sectional interests in business and financial markets, the diversity of individuals operating in them and the different circumstances affecting the markets, considerable variations are likely in the kinds and amounts of information available, and in the speed with which it is transmitted and put to use. Insider information and manipulation are the most glaring examples of variation in market information. These sorts of malpractice, and other deviations from ethical and legal standards, affect the reputation of the 'market' itself as a political and economic entity.

In any event, individuals are selective in attending to information, and interpret it according to their individual frame of reference. Computerisation helps to manage large amounts of information. Without such help, the 'effort after meaning' leads to simplified strategies for reaching conclusions and making decisions, especially if fast responses are required (see Nisbett and Ross, 1980; Kahneman, Slovic and Tversky, 1982).

Information that comes directly from source is processed by intermediaries—market analysts, financial correspondents—before it reaches most other people in the market. Information, including rumour, gossip and mischief-making, circulates through the market's social networks—by word of mouth, by example, by internal reports, by the business media, by the public media. The reluctance of banks to lend more to a company leads creditors to press more strongly for settlement, which weakens the firm's bargaining position, and leads employees and shareholders to look elsewhere. In addition, the business and financial markets operate within a wider social, now global, environment. The people who operate in them are subject to a variety of constraints, opportunities and contingencies, associated with national and international affairs, public opinion and pressure groups.

Fombrun and Abrahamson (1990) described the sorts of information and influence brought to bear on firms by the financial markets, the media, government, education, training agencies, professional organisations, and trade unions. They showed that the relationship is reciprocal—information and influence flow to and from firms internal to the business sector and organisations external to it. Their account describes the considerable complexity of the networks connecting a great number and variety of organisations. Reputation management, through public relations or other means, is a major factor determining a firm's survival and success in this complex and competitive environment.

The nature and scope of a firm's reputation are described by the total array of information about it in a particular group at a particular time. Fombrun and Shanley (1990), however, considered reputation to be just one of many corporate attributes that include size, profitability, risk and leverage (debt). What Fombrun and Shanley had in mind was the 'common factor' of reputation, the generalised attitude that the public or the market sector has towards a firm, based on a variety of facts and opinions. From their operational point of view, corporate reputation is an index derived from the within-sector ratings of eight attributes: quality of management, quality of products and services, long-term investment value, innovation, financial soundness, personnel, use of assets and public responsibility. The scientific assessment of personal reputation also requires a set of operationally defined attributes, and a measure of the extent to which they are assigned to a target person by a high proportion of members representing an operationally defined community.

Fombrun and Shanley (1990) drew attention to serial changes in corporate reputation. They noted that such changes can have an effect on the way a firm is assessed by the market, particularly if the change signals a departure from an established trend. This notion has its counterpart in personal reputation when observers become aware that a person's usual characteristics or patterns of behaviour have changed sufficiently to warrant comment and explanation.

From Fombrun's and Shanley's point of view, reputation crystallises a variety of facts and opinions into a manageable, well-defined image with several facets. The various facts and opinions come from different sources—from within the market (market indicators and opinions) and from the wider society (media reactions, pressure groups)—and are not necessarily entirely coherent or consistent. Nevertheless, information about reputation is important to institutional investors because it adds to their information base.

Firms cooperating or competing in the business and industrial sectors are affected by what they call the 'symbol-producing sectors'—financial markets, mass media, government and education. These sectors help to establish frameworks of understanding and evaluation, and contribute to the formation of corporate reputations.

Corporate Environment

The general environment—the wider culture—in which firms operate can be looked at from 'ecological' and 'evolutionary' points of view. A firm occupies a niche in the market, and has to defend and exploit it. Firms change over time and are faced with changes in market conditions; if they can adapt, then they survive and possibly grow and diversify.

The point is that the market sector is part of a wider culture, so firms have to engage in activities not directly related to the production of goods and services. Their support for charitable, cultural, sporting and other activities in the wider community involves costs. The question is whether the benefits of such support contribute indirectly to the firm's viability and success, or reflect genuine philanthropic motives. Naturally, support for activities that are highly valued by the wider community is likely to generate public esteem and goodwill. That, in turn, improves internal morale.

Although business activities include responses to the challenges of diversity and change, there is nevertheless a measure of conformity about standards and practices. This arises from a 'business ethic' that is internal to the sector, and from ethical and legal requirements in the wider society.

The complexities of a large-scale socio-economic system lead to regularities and predictable effects arising from well-established norms and practices. They also lead to irregularities and unpredictable effects, or turbulence, arising from unforeseen and unintended consequences of even small changes in one or more parts of the system. Although chance plays an important part, successes are usually attributed to the firm, failures to circumstances beyond the firm's control, as illustrated by company reports and public relations announcements. This is the 'self-serving bias', described in Chapter 6, that helps to maintain self-esteem.

Fombrun and Abrahamson (1990) went on to review the implications that the macro-culture of a business community has on such things as innovation, business strategies and adaptation. They aimed to show the extent to which business culture is 'socially constructed' at the collective level, based on cognitive processes operating at the level of interpersonal communication and influence. This ties in with our concern to examine the *collective* character of reputation, the social construction of persons and other entities, based on psychological processes at the interpersonal level.

Fortune International Surveys

Fombrun and Shanley (1990) referred to the 'market signals' that provide information to interested parties about a firm's performance and prospects. Many recipients of these market signals have professional knowledge and skills that enable them to interpret their significance and to act appropriately, for example, by trading shares, setting up a contract or making a forecast. Organisations that seem to be performing well and seem to have a secure future have a favourable reputation; that reputation usually applies to the whole organisation—its personnel, products, services, and so on. Corporate reputations, being large and complex, are likely to have subreputations that apply to, say, its board of directors or its after-sales service.

Fombrun and Shanley (1990) examined and refined the results of a survey of the reputations of nearly 300 firms carried out by the *Fortune* magazine around 1985 and reported by Hutton (1986). The respondents were executives, securities analysts and outside directors. They rated firms in the business sectors with which they were familiar, and used eight attributes of reputation (see later). Data were obtained from various sources on several characteristics—accounts, market performance, institutional ownership, media citations, charitable contributions, advertising expenditure and diversification.

Fombrun and Shanley reported that the availability of data varied from one firm to another, so that it was not possible to make comparisons on every characteristic for every firm. Also, organisational size was associated with a variety of other characteristics that made matching difficult.

Multiple regression techniques showed that reputation was significantly predictable from measures of profitability, size and visibility, and accounted for 27–35% of the variation in reputation. The causal relationships have to be worked out by other means.

The reputation attributes specified in the *Fortune* survey were as follows:

- quality of management
- quality of products and services

- long-term investment value
- innovativeness
- financial soundness
- ability to attract, develop and keep talented people
- community and environmental responsibility
- use of corporate assets.

Respondents were asked to nominate leading firms in a particular sector and then to rate them on each of the above attributes using an 11-point scale from 'poor' to 'excellent'. Earlier studies apparently had focused on one attribute, such as social responsibility, rather than on several. The question is whether these eight attributes measure one 'common factor' that would define corporate reputation in a more general way.

Attributes that are not carefully defined can be interpreted in different ways. For example, an attribute such as 'social responsibility' can refer to conferring immediate benefits on the local community or to adopting long-term strategies to benefit society. Moreover, the sort of 'social responsibility' that one organisation exhibits can be different from that of another. In other words, reputational attributes can be conceptualised in different ways, and the same concept can be operationally defined in different ways. A comparable problem arises with the assessment of personality characteristics.

Fombrun and Shanley factor-analysed the correlations between the eight attributes of reputation, and extracted a common factor that accounted for 84% of the variance. Factor analyses on comparable data confirmed the stability of their solution. They then carried out a time-series analysis on the results obtained from technical indices appropriate to the analysis of corporate character:

- size
- economic performance
- riskiness
- extent of institutional ownership
- favourability of media exposure
- differentiation (advertising and charitable contributions)
- diversification.

The data on these indices were derived from documentary sources, and are different in this respect from the a priori subjective attributes used in the *Fortune* survey and mentioned previously.

The three variables most highly correlated with reputation were profitability ($r = 0.44$), market value ($r = 0.49$) and risk ($r = -0.39$). The only statistically insignificant variable was yield (dividend/price ratio). The investigators were able to contrast firms with high profitability but low reputation with firms with low profitability but high reputation, thus showing that in some circumstances profitability and reputation are not associated.

The time-series analysis indicated that reputation was influenced favourably by prior profitability, advertising intensity and size, and was influenced unfavourably by riskiness. Further analyses using statistical regression supported the view that market value, dividend yield and institutional ownership influenced reputation when the other factors were held constant. Surprisingly, visibility (media exposure) seemed to have an unfavourable influence when these other factors were controlled. If this was not a statistical artefact, the effect might be that close media scrutiny indicates some suspicion about a firm's operations. The effect of charitable contributions was significantly favourable only for firms that funded charitable foundations.

Fombrun and Shanley summarised their results with a rank order of variables in order of importance for their effects on reputation:

1. profitability and risk
2. market value
3. media visibility
4. dividend yield
5. size
6. charitable foundations and contributions, and advertising

The analysis was complicated because firms differ in the extent to which they are diversified, and their reputations are therefore influenced differently by the above variables. Diversification as such appears to have an *unfavourable* influence. The apparent effect of diversification is to encourage an increase in the sorts of information examined when forming an impression of the organisation; this could result in a less clear image.

The most surprising finding by Fombrun and Shanley was that close examination by the media appeared to have adverse effects on reputation, apparently contradicting the cliché that there is no such thing as bad publicity. They found that neutral or favourable media assessments had a positive effect on diversified firms. They suggested that the negative effect of media coverage can be explained by the media's preference for bad news (but see below), by stakeholders' preference for stability and predictability (no news is good news, perhaps!), or, more subtly, by media coverage having its main effect on those who are already predisposed to make adverse judgements.

It would be interesting to test this view of the effects of media coverage on the fortunes of political parties. There is a case for arguing that political publicity is usually about mistakes and failures rather than about routine performance and successes, and that higher levels of publicity are followed by a decline in popularity. We must take care, however, not to be misled by a statistical artefact known as regression to the mean, in which initially high values tend to fall and initially low values tend to rise on a subsequent occasion of measurement.

Different aspects and sectors of society have different levels of media coverage. In Fombrun and Shanley's study of business firms, only 13% of media item titles were rated negative. The media coverage of politics, science, religion and entertainment probably have their different levels of negativity. Some media coverage goes beyond headlines, pictures and 'word slices'; the 'quality' sections of the media try to deal with important issues in depth and in a balanced way. Nevertheless, readers, listeners and viewers are likely to notice and remember whatever is emphasised and repeated rather than the reservations and details.

Fortune International Survey 1991

The *Fortune International* corporate reputations survey reported by Sprout (1991) comprised 306 large companies (sales of not less than US$500 million) in 32 industrial groups. Over 8000 senior executives, outside directors and financial analysts were asked to rate the companies in their sector on eight attributes of reputation on a scale from 0 (poor) to 10 (excellent). The attributes were as follows:

- quality of management
- quality of products and services
- innovativeness
- long-term investment value
- financial soundness
- ability to attract, develop and retain talented people
- responsibility to the community and environment
- wise use of corporate assets.

The report carries no further details of the sample or the procedures used to collect the data. The survey, however, is the latest in a series, and similar to the one reported in the previous section.

A consistent finding from the *Fortune* surveys is that more than 80% of respondents regard 'Quality of management' as the most important characteristic of a corporation, followed by 'Quality of products and services'. The importance of the attributes varied between the 32 industrial sectors, and changed over time because of changes in circumstances and prevailing attitudes and values. For example, mergers and acquisitions can move a company from one industrial sector to another, and so expose them to a different 'audience', i.e. a different set of interested parties and commentators.

The report shows that some companies held their position in terms of an overall league table of admiration and esteem, whilst others moved up or down. Year-to-year changes in earnings, profits, new products, market conditions and expectations, and so on, altered respondents' assessments of companies. The respondents themselves changed, as did the composition of the respondent samples within sectors. For these and other reasons, the order of merit overall is different from the order of merit within sectors.

The report gives no information on the extent to which the eight attributes of reputation were related. It is unlikely that they were independent of each other [see the analysis by Fombrun and Shanley (1990) of an earlier survey, summarised earlier]. Companies that ranked high or low on one attribute, however, did not necessarily obtain similar ranks on other attributes.

Corporations, like other sorts of entity, exhibit serial changes in reputation, and have different reputations in different sections of the public. The report gives no information on the comparability of ratings between sectors. For example, one company was reported to have ranked first in all eight measures of reputation and in its sector. Its average rating was 7.42, well below the 8.86 of another company that ranked first in its sector and first overall. One company ranked first in its sector with a score of 6.78, but ranked 86th overall. It is possible that a more sophisticated method of scaling, one in which attributes are weighted differently according to their importance in the different sectors, might produce different results. The number of companies in a sector affects the meaning of a rank position. No information was given about the number of companies in each sector, or the spread of ratings for each company. Consequently, it is not possible to test whether a difference between two ranks (associated with a difference in ratings) might be statistically significant.

Private and Public Enterprises

In a mixed economy, one finds both free-market competition and publicly funded services. They work under two contrasting conditions: one is competitive efficiency, the other is equal access. The reputation of organisations in a free-market economy is largely based on the attributes thought to reflect its competitiveness—its size, profitability, efficiency, and so on. The reputation of public service organisations is based more on their average level of performance, and on some notion of expected standards. In the absence of competition, there is some risk of low standards or inefficiency, or both. Free-market competition too has its disadvantages. The attributes of reputation for public service organisations include, for example, availability, quality, cost and responsiveness. Commercial and public service organisations thus have some reputational attributes in common.

Different sorts of organisation are interlocked in all sorts of ways in a large-scale modern economy, so they contribute to each other's reputation. The resulting accumulation and diversity of experience, together with the flow of information and influence, generates some widely shared attributions at the inter-organisational level. These can include estimates about key people in those organisations, particularly the people who 'represent', 'embody' or 'personify' an organisation.

At the organisational level, size is an important factor, as is the way productivity is defined and measured. Scientific productivity is affected by many factors, including organisational size. The size of university academic departments, for example, can affect their research reputation adversely by obscuring the research productivity of individuals. Baumert, Maumann and Roeder (1990) investigated the status of German university departments of economics and business studies. They were interested to see whether departments differed in public esteem (prestige, status, reputation) as they do in other countries, such as the USA, where free-market competition is greater. External evaluations, reflected in reputation fulfil an important social function in maintaining or raising standards of performance, provided such evaluations result in a competitive advantage for organisations that operate efficiently and effectively.

Baumert et al. (1990) obtained objective performance indicators—number of staff, publications, and so on—for 52 university departments. Opinions and ratings were obtained from a sample of staff. The criteria used to measure departmental reputation were average peer rating, the extent to which a department was known externally, and nominations as 'best' department. Baumert et al. found clear differences in departmental reputations. The *extent* to which a department was known was positively associated with the *degree of esteem* in which it was held. It is worth noting that the extent or size of a reputation, which is the total amount of information in circulation or the total number of people interested, is probably associated either with a high level of esteem or with a low (negative) level of esteem. That is to say, a widespread reputation can be associated with fame and honour or with infamy and dishonour.

Baumert et al. developed a structural model (causal network) revealing substantial relationships between departmental characteristics, funding, productivity, scientific impact and reputation, with other causal influences being less important.

The common factor that accounts for the relationships between the variables that contribute to reputation would be the overall capacity of an organisation to make itself visible through the impact its performance has on those sections of society where its reputation matters. This notion can be applied, by analogy, not only to organisations in the public or private sector but also to other entities—persons, products and services. Their reputations are a function of the extent to which the impact of their performance makes them visible to those sections of the public that have an interest in entities of that sort.

Images of Cities

Fortune commissioned a survey of 600 business executives, and interviewed many business leaders and other experts. According to Huey (1991) wrting in *Fortune*, the main attributes that business executives regard as most important for a city in the USA were, in order:

- a flexible high-quality workforce
- proximity to markets
- favourable local attitude towards business
- a good public education system
- convenient air services to key cities
- low costs—housing, labour, facilities, taxes
- efficient highways
- quality of life

The research methodology was not reported in detail. Although no city was best on every attribute, the outcome, based on all the above attributes, showed the folowing rank-order of merit:

1 Atlanta
2 Dallas/Fort Worth
3 Pittsburgh
4 Kansas City
5 Nashville
6 Salt Lake City
7 Charlotte
8 Orlando
9 Austin
10 Phoenix

The results seemed to confirm that some better-known cities had lost favour with the business community. Another set of respondents might have been given a different set of attributes, or might have produced a different ranking of cities. The magazine went on to give a pen-picture of the 'top ten' cities for business, mentioning matters such as population, office rentals, tax rates, average salaries, access to good workers and local attitudes to business. For some cities, the attributions mentioned included crime, food, race relations, culture and entertainment. Forty other cities were reviewed briefly. The survey is another illustration of how the reputation of entities other than persons can be investigated.

Some aspects of people's mental representations of cities can be studied by asking them to draw a map of a city or to give directions for a journey from one part of the city to another. Cities have attributes other than their physical layout. This is revealed even in the maps people draw (Milgram, 1974). Our image of a city is a social representation in that we share some aspects of it with other people. It incorporates some social attributions, and is influenced by our cultural upbringing. The social attributions may refer to the city's inhabitants, their life-styles, its political and economic characteristics, and so on. Our cultural upbringing provides a frame of reference within which different cities can be compared and contrasted. Our image of a city helps to govern our attitudes and reactions to it—whether we like it, whether we choose to live or work there, and so on. Cities can be compared using the Repertory Grid method (see Riley and Palmer, 1976).

Coopers & Lybrand Deloitte (1991) produced a brief report on how London compared with New York, Tokyo, Paris, Berlin and Frankfurt. The research methods were not described, but they included 'desk research', interviews and surveys. The report is in part a summary of London's reputation, compared with other cities, among business people, planners and others involved in the commercial and cultural aspects of major cities. Comparisons and contrasts between entities are important in reputation; so too are the social networks or 'audiences' that collectively represent the reputation. The report shows that for cities, as for other entities, it is possible to collect objective data, for example population or the distribution of employment. Such data may or may not be widely known among interested parties. The main attributes considered in the report concerned the creation of wealth, jobs and income, and quality of life. These are interdependent and depend on an 'enabling infrastructure', i.e. inter- and intra-city transport and communication, domestic and occupational accommodation, education and training facilities. By analogy, one can think of a person's abilities and dispositions (personality) as the 'enabling structure' that makes certain kinds of performance possible. Thus, reputational attributions may include statements about a person's possible, as opposed to actual, capabilities.

Of particular interest is the report's emphasis on London's future prospects compared with those of other cities. The future prospects that feature as reputational attributions are uncertain. Respondents may bolster their subjective predictions with objective data, for example extrapolations from past trends. The interesting general point is that an entity's future prospects (as contrasted with current attributes) may be a prominent feature of its reputation. This may have important consequences in terms of collective reactions. Obviously, a city that is *expected* to become less 'user-friendly' is less likely to attract users. Similarly, a person who is *expected* to become less influential is less likely to be approached by people seeking influence. Such expectations become self-fulfilling prophecies unless they can be counteracted quickly and strongly. For cities, according to the report, this means having a strategy and institutional framework that will plan land-use, transport and communications, control funding, develop the city's regional, national and international policies, and promote attractive images of the city in key publics.

Professional Reputation

Haas-Wilson (1990) surveyed the effects of reputation on the fees charged by professional social workers in the USA. She distinguished between (a) recommendations (impressions) conveyed to potential clients by well-informed sources (social workers and other professionals) and (b) those conveyed by less well-informed sources (friends and relatives). The distinction rested on the expectation that a reputation for high-quality service based on well-informed sources would raise the fee for that service, and thus contribute to market forces that relate price to quality of service. In the absence of information about professional reputation, consumers have no way of deciding which service provider to choose, so the market would not be efficient. Referrals even from professionals, of course, can be biased or ill-informed, and the number of referrals need not reflect any general agreement between professionals regarding the quality of a provider's service. Nevertheless, Haas-Wilson's results showed that well-informed recommendations are associated with higher professional fees. Furthermore, the results showed that where there are more service providers fees are lower. This illustrates the point made elsewhere that reputations in a given area are relative to each other. For a contrasting study of the negative effects of a poor reputation, see Goldberg and Hartwick (1990).

Common Factors in Reputations

It is not always possible to make comparisons between organisations on the same basis. Even when comparable information is available, different assessors use different frames of reference for selecting, weighing and interpreting the evidence. Assessment and comparison are much more difficult if one has to take account of historical trends and future prospects. If it is possible to make comparisons, then statistical methods may be used to identify one 'general' factor or a small number of 'common factors'.

The general factor (or set of factors) common to most or all the attributes of reputation provides a valuable, quantitative, operational definition of reputation for making comparisons between entities. The idea of a common, general factor of reputation, with different loadings on each attribute, extends the dictionary and common-sense definition of reputation as, 'What is generally believed about a person or thing'. The reversed J-curve of conformity— illustrated by the frequency of occurrence of categorical attributes—is probably linked to the existence of a common factor. It would not be surprising to find that attributes with high loadings on the common factor were attributes with a high frequency of occurrence in a free-description exercise, or a high average in a rating exercise.

The derivation of a general factor, or common factors, in studies of reputational entities of the same sort—industrial firms, university departments, local authorities or orchestras—is a function of the attributes initially chosen for examination. Investigators have a shrewd idea, based on common knowledge or previous research, about the characteristics of interest to particular groups. There are two advantages in deriving one or more common factors. The first is to show that different attributes of reputation vary in the extent to which they contribute to the overall effect, at least in a particular investigation. The second is to show that different entities can be compared with reference to a single index, or to a few basic indicators.

12 Public Relations and Organisational Behaviour

PUBLIC RELATIONS

Introduction

Public relations refers to the organised efforts of a corporate body to convey information and exert influence on its own members and on members of other sections of the public, often including the wider public. These efforts are supposed to meet accepted moral values and appropriate practices, but they sometimes fall short for the usual reasons. The aim of public relations, as its name implies, is to establish good relationships with the public, especially those sections of the public with whom its 'fate' is intertwined. For example, a manufacturing company needs to establish and maintain good relationships with its workforce, its customers and clients, the public in the region where it is located, and so on. The corporate body should be seen to be acting in the public interest as well as in its own interests.

Most aspects of an organisation's affairs have public relations implications. The UK Institute of Public Relations defines public relations as 'The deliberate, planned and sustained effort to establish and maintain goodwill and mutual understanding between an organisation and its publics.'

Public relations work has strategic and tactical aims. The strategic aims are to occupy and exploit the niche that the organisation occupies in its particular sector of society and the economy, to optimise its position and function in the 'market'. The tactical aims are to deal with public relations problems if they arise unexpectedly or as they unfold within the strategic plan. Public relations (strategic and tactical) are to corporate identity and behaviour what reputation management and impression management are to individual identity (Chapter 7).

Public relations work includes intelligence gathering, education, advertising and propaganda. The last three are not easily distinguished unless one can discover the motivation that lies behind the methods of communication and influence being used. All three can be used in the management of reputation. Education means presenting facts and objective opinions, with the aim of improving a public's rational understanding of and sensible dealings with an issue, for example the dangers of excessive drinking. Advertising means trying to persuade a public to believe and act in certain ways, without necessarily operating at a rational level; many forms of persuasion are used, including nonverbal materials—pictures, music—that operate at an emotional level.

Propaganda means using almost any method, fair or foul, to persuade a public to adopt a particular point of view. Propaganda is a form of persuasion used in conflict situations, where important issues are at stake, as in war or commercial rivalry. Intelligence gathering means collecting relevant data systematically, to get a better understanding of the problem to be solved and a better appreciation of the proposed solutions.

Effective corporate action normally requires a mutually supportive relationship between an organisation and its public(s). Using the ecology analogy, the relationship is symbiotic. If the organisation does not live up to society's expectations, society suffers; if the public fail to respond properly to the organisation's efforts, the organisation suffers.

Public relations work is an integral part of the business of any organisation, large or small. Large organisations usually have a department of public relations staffed by peope with professional training. In small organisations relationships with the public are usually carried out informally without much reference to the theory and practice of professional public relations.

The essential functions of public relations can be summarised as follows. First, intelligence has to be gathered on matters of interest to the organisation that affect its relationships with various publics. Public relations staff have to work closely with other departments within the organisation—personnel, sales, and so on. They have to deal with important external bodies—trade unions, local authorities, competitors. Intelligence has to be gathered on organisational morale—working conditions, pay, fringe benefits—even though responsibility for these matters may lie elsewhere. Second, the intelligence (information) gathered has to be processed. It has to be interpreted with regard to the organisation's aims, strategies and tactics. This takes time and demands close involvement of management and other departments within the organisation. Third, decisions have to be taken on what actions, if any, are required, and what resources are to be made available. Fourth, the necessary actions have to be taken, and their consequences evaluated. The whole process is an exercise in problem-solving, with constant reference back to the nature of the problem in case it needs to be reformulated.

The functions listed above are largely 'reactive', i.e. responses to changing circumstances and crisis management; 'proactive' functions are designed to prevent undesirable circumstances from arising, and to promote desirable states of affairs.

Some public relations activities are largely 'expressive' and not geared to specific aims or directed at narrowly defined audiences. These might include donations to charities, contributions to local festivities, open days, and so on. They are intended to show the organisation's 'social concerns' and its moral values. Most activities are directed towards specific aims in the interests of the organisation. These could include lobbying, and support for pressure groups or political organisations, apart from all the other, more routine, activities designed to protect, enhance and exploit the public image (reputation) of the organisation. Public relations work can contribute to the organisation's internal morale (self-esteem, pride, confidence), and, of course, to its 'corporate identity'—a critical factor, especially in the early stages of an organisation's development.

The kinds of work carried out by public relations people vary widely, depending upon the nature of the organisation, its size, the resources available, and the problems that arise. So, for example, there is a wide range of educational services, advertising material and propaganda techniques. Surveys are carried out, exhibitions are mounted, conferences are held. There is considerable word-of-mouth communication with influential opinion leaders (Chapter 6) and media contacts. Managerial experience and skills are necessary at the higher levels of public relations work, for example, in arranging exhibitions or special events, in publishing company reports, in arranging advertising, and, of course, in deciding what action to take in response to changing circumstances.

Keen and Greenall (1987) provided a method for prioritising public relations factors in order to make rational decisions about courses of action. They offered the equation:

$$\text{Overall Rating (OAR)} = \frac{\text{Relevance} \times \text{Accessibility}}{\text{Impact}}.$$

Ratings are made of how relevant a particular section of the public is, how accessible they are to information and influence, and how much impact the course of action is likely to have on them. The overall ratings combine these factors and show the priorities for several possible courses of action. This could have methodological implications for decisions about impression management (Chapter 7).

A public relations department has its own administrative, staffing and resource requirements, which we need not consider. It is of interest, however, to consider some of the actual skills required in public relations (reputation management) work. Data collection and analysis are fundamental; these range from large-scale social surveys and information retrieval to what amounts to detective work. Records have to be written and filed; reports have to be composed, edited and circulated. Arrangements have to be made for information to be published—in various forms for different audiences. Choices have to be made about which media to use, and how to use them. Computers and other forms of technology provide a variety of ways of reaching the public, or sections of the public. Computers are increasingly used to collect and analyse data, for example in connection with identifying target audiences, and in direct mailing. Some individuals within the organisation embody or represent the organisation; these people have to learn how to deal with the public, and are briefed on public relations issues as they arise. This is particularly important with regard to the 'style' or 'manner' in which information of interest to a public is presented, and how influence is exercised. The same message can be presented in different ways; persuasion can take many forms. Certain personal qualities are needed to create a favourable impression; temperamental qualities that are effective in one set of circumstances are not always effective in another set.

The content and form of communication and influence are important, so too is the medium used. Word of mouth in face-to-face situations is generally regarded as the most effective means of communicating with and influencing someone, especially if the communicator is a recognised authority or opinion leader. Other means include group meetings, the media, personalised letters, and so on. Besides the spoken word and the printed word, successful communication and influence may be achieved through pictorial means—posters, illustrations, films and television. In some circumstances, the whole range of means can be used—at a conference or exhibition, for example.

There is an extensive literature on public relations, advertising and propaganda. This goes well beyond our concern with reputation, and interested readers are referred to Center and Walsh (1981), Dyer (1982), and Engel, Blackwell and Miniard (1986).

The ways in which communication and influence operate at the group level are fairly well known because of the research work carried out on techniques of persuasion. The results are worth summarising because they indicate not only how communication and influence operate for corporate reputation, but also how they operate at the level of personal reputation.

Ideally, the message should appeal to the recipient's self-interest, and preferably serve a wider, public interest. The message should be credible, as should the source of the message (hence the importance of respected opinion leaders). The form and content of a message should be tailored to fit the audience to which it is directed; this means attending to the characteristics and circumstances of the audience, as well as to the 'comprehensibility' of the message. Messages have 'discourse features' that affect their persuasiveness, such as humour, or what can be read 'between the lines', or even by what is left unsaid. A message should enable and persuade recipients to think, feel and act in certain ways, by telling them what to do, why they should do it and how to do it. Communication and influence need not have an immediate effect, and care has to be taken not to produce the opposite effect to that intended, especially if one is dealing with people whose initial attitude is negative. The same basic message, repeated in different ways over a period, may eventually overcome initial resistance, as with campaigns designed to shift ingrained public habits regarding sex, alcohol and diet. These forms of persuasion seem to work best when they can be applied gently, moving a person's attitude and behaviour gradually in the desired direction.

Advertising

Advertising is a pervasive feature of a modern, large-scale market economy. It has become an important cultural influence, attracting substantial resources— financial, human and material. Its essential function is to draw the attention of potential consumers to the availability of products and services, from kittens for sale to the promotion of a multinational corporate image. This has the effect of encouraging consumption by stimulating desires and raising expectations. The techniques used in advertising do not rely much on rational persuasion (this is the province of education), but on consumers' suggestibilities. Thus, the suggestion that a desirable product or service can be obtained easily and cheaply could prevent consumers from realising that the product or service is not worth buying at that price. They may not realise that purchase will bring undesirable late-acting consequences, for instance debt, maintenance costs, or whatever.

Advertising, education, propaganda and public relations are overlapping areas of communication and influence. All play a role in the political economy of a country (and globally), and in a country's cultural life, which includes its prevailing beliefs, values, attitudes and life-styles. The arts, religion, science, sport, entertainment, and so on, are all affected, directly or indirectly, and in their different ways, by advertising and related techniques of communication and influence.

Advertising can be used to promote any entity that can have a reputation: a person, a social organisation, a product or a service. Some advertisements rely on associating a particular product or service with another entity that has a well-known, favourable reputation, as with advertisements for a product recommended by a famous person. It is not easy to evaluate the effects of advertising; this is a technical problem in market research, and the methods used vary from one area to another. Marketing and advertising are also dealt with briefly in Chapter 13.

Some advertisements (and other reputation management actions) are counter-productive because the people who produce them are insensitive to the possible consequences. Some advertisements are vulgar and offensive, some express out-moded social prejudices, some have undesirable effects because the designers do not understand the subtleties of human communication and influence. They rely too much on invalid 'common-sense' assumptions, intuition or 'expert' opinion, instead of objective research. Advertising is likely to be more effective when it is not discounted as such. Propaganda fails if it is perceived to be propaganda.

There are indirect and subtle ways of promoting names, goods, services and other entities. Older films illustrate how smoking and drinking were promoted strongly but indirectly by presenting them as aspects of interesting or desirable life-styles—as reflecting conviviality, poise, modernity, and the like. Similar examples can be found of direct advertising and indirect promotion of behaviours and reputations in today's media.

Advertising and propaganda can reduce or amplify the positive or negative aspects of an entity's reputation. Consider, for example, the public image of nuclear power, or the state propaganda that supports an authoritarian regime. Advertising can retard or accelerate trends in public attitudes and behaviour. For example, the taboos on sex, aggression, homosexuality and foul language have been reduced in recent years. Thus the reputation of people who exhibit these characteristics is affected to a lesser extent nowadays. Advertising blurs the distinctions between fiction, fantasy and real life. The reputation of actors can become confused with the roles they play.

Public Relations and Advertising

Public relations activity is designed to protect and enhance an entity's reputation, possibly by derogating competitors' reputations. Advertising is just one aspect of public relations activities. The importance of advertising in promoting a company's image and selling its products is shown by the resources devoted to advertising.

Advertisements, including 'self-advertisements' are designed to communicate an entity's 'identity' to its publics (audiences), and to enhance and enlarge the image that those publics have of it. Advertisements help to identify entities by distinguishing them from other entities with which they might be confused, or with which they can be unfavourably compared. Another aim is to generate active support—by encouraging people to purchase goods and services, to vote in particular ways, or to adopt certain attitudes, values and life-styles. In the process, advertising can lead people to develop habits, and reduce their exposure to other opportunities and courses of action. When successful, advertising makes it possible for organisations, or persons, to operate more efficiently (at a low cost–benefit ratio). This means doing the things they are good at—making soap, transporting people from one place to another or selling insurance.

Goldberg and Hartwick (1990) carried out a classroom experiment to investigate the effects of a company's reputation, and the extremity of its advertising claims, on the way respondents judged the company's product and the associated advertisement. From research into attitudes, it was expected that a company with a good reputation (high credibility) would have a positive effect on respondents' reactions. A company with a poor reputation (low credibility) would have a negative effect. The further expectation was that, within limits, a more extreme claim in an advertisement would have a greater effect than a weak or moderate claim. Moreover, company reputation (credibility) and extremity of advertising claim might interact. Naturally, contextual factors could obscure these effects, especially in real-world circumstances.

Goldberg and Hartwick (1990) presented subjects with either a brief positive or a brief negative 'image' of a company, and then showed them one of four advertisements differing only in the extremity of the claim made for the product.

The subjects were asked to rate the honesty and sincerity of the advertisements, and to predict how well the company's product would do in a test similar to the one portrayed in the advertisement. The company's reputation and the extremity of the claim each had an effect on respondents' assessment of the credibility of the advertisement and their evaluation of the product. Those respondents who formed a negative image of the company gave consistently lower product evaluations, especially for the most extreme advertising claim. They found the advertisements less credible at all four levels of extremity, again especially the most extreme level. In other words, both the product and the advertisement can be adversely affected by a combination of a negative reputation and an extreme advertising claim. The implication is that extreme advertising claims are likely to be heavily discounted by potential consumers to the extent that they are not made by companies with a good reputation. For a study of the positive economic effects of a good reputation, see Haas-Wilson (1990).

Public relations efforts can be directed inwards, towards improving the identity, morale and internal workings of an organisation. An analogy can be drawn with the way an individual can try to improve his or her personal qualities and self-confidence, possibly by resort to external help for advice and training. By analogy, one can think of internal public relations as optimising a company's 'internal environment' by regulating the factors that affect its efficiency. For example, from time to time it is necessary to lose staff, adopt new pay and working conditions, close departments, transfer resources, and so on. Unless these changes are made with due regard to public relations *within* the organisation, they may have adverse effects on morale and output, as well as on external relations.

Fombrun and Ginsberg (1990) argue that successful firms engage in various activities to promote their interests. They invest in reseach, in advertising and in public relations generally. They cultivate a coherent business culture. They stabilise relationships with suppliers and consumers. They try to optimise productivity through improved technological and human resources. They develop better manangement strategies and techniques. When these activities become effective, the firm's history of success is reflected in its public image, and its public image becomes an increasingly important factor in its continuing success.

Different sectors of the public respond differently to one or other of the several characteristics attributed to an organisation. For example, a school has attributes of interest and concern to staff, other attributes of interest to pupils, and yet other attributes of interest to parents, governers and suppliers. Communication across these membership boundaries brings about a measure of commonality, but the sectional images are likely to remain distinct. The reason is that these different groups are interested in different aspects of the school; each group has sectional interests that do not overlap much with those of another group.

These sectional interests lead members of one group to form a collective image that is different from that of another group. This means two things. First, the behaviour of an interest group towards an entity (target person or organisation) depends upon the information available and the influences to which the group is exposed. Second, an entity can send out different sorts of information to and exert different kinds of influence on different audiences with little risk of seeming inconsistent. For example, a firm may signal to shareholders that they can expect good dividends, and signal to employees that they can expect better pay and working conditions, knowing that it is unlikely, although possible, that both promises can be fulfilled. Subsequently, of course, the firm may have to explain why one or the other of both promises cannot be kept—this is a public relations problem.

ORGANISATIONAL BEHAVIOUR

Organisational Behaviour and Status

Promotion to higher status in an organisation has its dangers because it disturbs a person's existing network of communication and influence. Other people might resent the change, suspecting favouritism or fearing some loss of control. Some individuals avoid higher-status positions for various reasons, including the fear that one's reputation would be adversely affected by people's resentment. Some of the dangers to reputation inherent in high-status positions can be dealt with by doing things 'by the book' and according to agreed rules. This has the effect of shifting the blame for adverse consequences from the person (manager, supervisor) to the system. This is a weakness of bureaucratic systems that depersonalises decisions and actions, and protects the reputation of those who operate the system.

Personal Reputation in Organisations

Supervisors (or other middle-level staff in organisations) normally monitor the impression they make on others, especially their managers and others in authority over them. They may, however, misinterpret other people's reactions, and others sometimes act, deliberately or not, in ways that create an unfavourable impression.

Different sorts of organisation—businesses, universities, military establishments, professional organisations—have their different ways of communicating (or not communicating) interpersonal impressions. The development of personal appraisal schemes and requirements for professional status is making the process more open, explicit and formal. Even so, there is a considerable amount of reputational information that is not captured in formal appraisal schemes. This can have considerable influence on the behaviour of those who see their reputation inside and outside the organisation as important for their future career. They are sensitive, perhaps over-sensitive, to what they see as signals of their standing within the organisation and in related areas outside it.

Tsui (1984) argued that effective managers are aware that people in one part of an organisation have different expectations, and react differently to situations, from people in another part of the organisation. They need to look after the interests of members in their 'role set'. The ability to form a favourable reputation in different sections of an organisation, and in related audiences outside, is associated with managerial success. A good reputation restricted to one section of a business is less promising.

Managers have reputations outside the organisation in which they are employed, so there could be a relationship, not necessarily direct, between reputation within a company and reputation outside. An improved reputation within an organisation might lead to improved performance and greater loyalty. On the other hand, it might lead to a search for advancement outside. A loss of reputation within an organisation need not lead to a loss of reputation outside; in some circumstances it could have the opposite effect. Reputation is an important factor in career advancement internally as well as externally. This is seen in the extensive use of referees and advisors when organisations are making appointments to middle-level and higher-level positions.

Several investigations have examined professional reputation. McLaughlin and Butler (1973) found that the job characteristics regarded as most important by US Army officers were concerned with reputation (status, recognition, respect). This finding would no doubt apply to many other types of occupation. Gregory (1980) saw reputation as a factor leading some scientists to engage in fraud. Rowney and Zenisek (1980) provided evidence that among a group of authors, reputation was associated with increased likelihood of their manuscripts being published in journals of the Canadian Psychological Association. Long (1984) showed how cultural factors help to explain the low public image that nurses have in Japan. Sewell (1984) drew attention to the adverse effects that a negative public image can have on campus police officers, and presumably on other occupational groups. Seiler and Pearson (1984–85) identified recognition and reputation as factors in the work environment of university staff. Parker and Chan (1986) compared the public prestige of 13 types of health professionals ranked by occupational and physical therapists. Such rankings or 'league tables' are a common method of assessing reputation. Occupational therapists ranked themselves fourth with undertakers and labour union officials! This illustrates the limited value of undifferentiated league tables.

Kydd, Ogilvie and Slade (1990) reported an investigation into reputation using the responses of middle-level managers to hypothetical situations. Reputation was defined by the feedback managers received from their organisations. This could affect managers' search for other employment or their intention to leave the organisation. For the purposes of their experiment, Kydd et al. (1990)

compiled a series of scenarios in which managers received messages (feedback) under different conditions: public or private, and favourable or unfavourable. Favourable messages should enhance reputation, unfavourable messages should lower it. Messages delivered publicly have greater visibility, and therefore greater impact on reputation and self-esteem.

Scenarios are hypothetical situations imitating real-life situations; they are commonly used in consumer research. For example, consumers are asked how they think they would react to a product or service with such-and-such characteristics. Hypothetical questions of a similar sort are used in several areas of social and personality research. In the study by Kydd et al. (1990), subjects were asked to react to each scenario by rating how they thought it would affect their reputation inside the company, and in outside organisations. Subjects were asked to rate the effect that the circumstances depicted in each scenario would have on their search for employment elsewhere, and on their intention to leave the company.

The results showed that under these simulated conditions a favourable public message was thought to have a positive effect on internal and external reputation. A favourable private message, however, was viewed more negatively than an unfavourable private message. The explanation is that failure to convey a favourable message publicly raises doubts about its genuineness, or about its favourableness compared with the private messages other managers receive. An unfavourable public message, by contrast, might have the effect, in some circumstances, of improving one's external reputation. Messages given privately would have no direct effect on external reputation. Supervisors might not realise that approval given privately conveys the wrong impression, because one can give the same or a different message to others. On the other hand, selective public praise can be divisive.

Intention to leave was unrelated to internal or external reputation. Reputation is just one of many factors affecting critical career decisions. An improved external reputation appears to increase the likelihood of looking for career advancement in another company. Failure to get an expected promotion reduces self-esteem, and possibly reduces internal reputation, and so increases interest in career prospects elsewhere. In real-life, there are many factors to consider— family circumstances, age, the general state of the economy. Career planning is likely to be based on complex cost–benefit considerations, with reputation (or rather assumed reputation) affecting the career level aimed at. Actual reputation, as judged by independent external evidence, can affect the outcome.

Publicity is important in career advancement, but it is difficult to get and liable to produce unwanted side-effects, especially in large organisations and external bodies. By comparison, gaining approval within an organisation is easy—by meeting the normal requirements of the job. Publicity is got by exceeding performance expectations, and by reaching higher levels of esteem in competition with others.

At higher levels of management, external reputation becomes increasingly important as a factor in selection, because most applicants for posts will be at or close to the top of their current organisation. Their reputation and performance within that organisation are probably well established. External reputation then becomes a criterion for selection, apart from being an indication of ability to operate at an inter-organisational level.

Gioia and Sims (1983) used a videotape of a manager's behaviour and showed that prior information about a manager's reputation has a significant influence on observers' perceptions of that behaviour. For studies in impression management in organisational settings, see Giacalone and Rosenfeld (1989).

Organisational Morale, Commitment and Socialisation

One would expect high morale to be associated with high commitment to an organisation by its members. Such commitment would be expressed by strong motivation and personal involvement in the organisation's affairs, by satisfaction with, and loyalty to, the organisation, and by high levels of performance, cooperation with other members of the organisation and continuing membership.

Expressions of commitment—opinions and actions—are seen by others, they encourage conformity and increase the organisation's collective confidence and internal esteem. Such esteem is normally justified by the organisation's place in the wider society to which it belongs. This brings internal esteem into line with external (public) esteem—an aspect of corporate reputation. Criminal organisations, of course, distance themselves from the values and norms of the wider society, although they too experience many effects of organised social life.

Commitment to an organisation is a form of socialisation. It combines with the personal characteristics and situational factors that lead individuals to seek membership, or be recruited into membership, in the first place. The methods used to select members and to establish commitment vary widely, from the 'take it or leave it' treatment in loosely organised, casual associations, to the sometimes stressful initiation or intensive indoctrination procedures of authoritarian political, religious or military organisations. Whatever methods are employed to secure commitment, commitment means that individuals comply with the organisation's requirements, identify with the organisation and think of it as an extension of the self—'My firm', 'My club' or 'My school'. They internalise the organisation's beliefs and values, and are thus committed to promoting and defending its reputation.

The scientific assessment of corporate morale and individual commitment is difficult. There is the problem of defining the variables operationally, and the various methodological problems associated with sampling, self-report measures, response biases and data analysis. Caldwell, Chatman and O'Reilly (1990) reported a strong positive effect of recruitment practices and selection, and corporate values on individual commitment to and identification with an organisation. Well-defined systems of reward encourage compliance, but not necessarily commitment.

Corporate Codes and Conduct

Codes of conduct are relevant to reputation (whether corporate or personal) because reputation is largely evaluative. There are two aspects of social evaluation. One concerns competence; the other concerns conformity to accepted practices, i.e. morality. Corporate morality is a measurable aspect of corporate image (Lydenberg, Marlin and Strub, 1986).

Among an organisation's attributes are those that relate to its main aims and business practices, and the standards of behaviour expected of members and sanctioned by the organisation.

The clearest indication of a collective conscience (an agreed set of ethical rules) is a corporate code of conduct (see Raiborn and Payne, 1990). This is an explicit guide for members, setting out in general terms the kinds of conduct that are required or forbidden, and specifying the action to be taken against those who fail to comply. A corporate code of conduct usually assumes that members will not break the laws of the wider society. It is primarily concerned with regulating the internal order of the group, and ensuring the group's position and status in the wider society; it proscribes acts such as bribery, corruption and making false claims.

A code of conduct lays down ethical guidelines, telling members what is right or wrong. Its definitions and rules are fairly general, because it is difficult to specify exactly what actions would contravene the code. Following a complaint or charge, individual cases are usually dealt with by members specially appointed to administer the code. Sometimes it is possible to 'bend' the rules by choosing one interpretation rather than another, or by observing the letter rather than the spirit of the code.

Organisational morale and commitment are strongly influenced by the corporate subculture—its agreed beliefs, values, attitudes and practices. The corporate subculture might be inconsistent, and might conflict with the personal value system of some of its members. The powerful influence exerted by an organisation's internal subculture is easily illustrated by reference to delinquent reputation, indoctrination in political and religious organisations, and socialisation practices at school and at home.

Within organisations, there are leading members whose ideas are taken up, whose opinions shape collective beliefs, and whose actions set an example for others to follow. The effects of prestige and majority conformity, together with the effects of interpersonal communication and influence, usually bring about considerable agreement. Individuals who fail to conform are subjected to sanctions of one sort or another—neglect, ostracism, ridicule, hostility—and risk being ejected from the organisation.

A criminal organisation has to insulate itself somehow from external ethical and legal constraints. This is achieved through participation in a criminal subculture. Some organisations engage in unethical and illegal activities, in what are seen to be in the interest of the organisation—its survival or expansion. These are condoned or even encouraged in some corporate subcultures. Corporate socialisation makes clear the extent to which, and the manner in which, the organisation's code of conduct, and its internal culture, apply. An organisation's subculture, of course, includes more than a formal code of conduct for its members. It includes modes of address, appearance, styles of behaviour, customs and practices, attitudes and values, and so on.

A code of conduct is designed to protect an organisation's public image, and to a lesser extent to enhance it, by declaring its moral standards to others. This is particularly important for organisations offering professional services to the public. The code should incorporate protection for individual members who draw attention to breaches of the code. The reason for this is that revealing misbehaviour breaches another implicit code, namely, that one should protect and support one's group and its individual members even if they are in the wrong. There are cases of severe persecution of 'informers' or 'whistle-blowers'—the terms are pejorative.

Ideally, a corporate code of conduct should be clear, comprehensive, realistic and enforceable. There should be benefits to be gained from compliance, and penalties for non-compliance. The code should be practicable; it should be possible for members to fulfil its requirements without endangering their position in society.

There are usually sectional interests within an organisation, so that differences arise about the nature and scope of the code itself, and about its implementation. Differences arise concerning other aspects of the organisation's subculture—its policy, for example. Different sorts of organisations have different sorts of subcultures and different codes of conduct, whether explicit or implicit. Normally, these codes are compatible with, and derived from, the ethical standards that prevail in the wider community.

13 Brand Image and Consumer Behaviour

Introduction

The products and services most often dealt with in the study of consumer behaviour are those commonly encountered in the ordinary activities of daily living in a large-scale, industrial, market economy. They include motor vehicles, washing machines, foodstuffs, clothes, medical and dental care, legal services, financial advice, entertainment, and so on. These goods and services are normally purchased by people who have a certain amount of choice in a competitive market, hence the importance of marketing. The study of marketing and consumer behaviour deals with the factors that affect the purchase and use of goods and services, for example price, availability, advertising, image and consumer characteristics (Engel et al., 1986). Marketing tries to optimise the consumption of particular goods and services in the interests of the producer. Some advertised messages are concerned with the public interest—public health warnings, road safety advice, crime prevention, and so on.

There is no guarantee that consumers will respond positively even to substantial promotion of a particular product, service or message. In situations where consumers have a choice in how they behave, their behaviour is governed by many factors. These include their needs and desires, their attitudes and expectations, their understanding of what is available, their financial resources, and their decision processes. Some consumer actions are impulsive and lack a rational basis, other actions are based on careful consideration of the associated costs and benefits. These factors are important and well-known areas of psychology in their own right and do not need detailed discussion here. They probably affect consumer behaviour in the way that they affect other sorts of behaviour.

Consumer behaviour, broadly defined, refers to those cycles of behaviour that start with some motivational state and proceed through successive stages of information processing to decisions and actions related to the purchase or use of economic goods and services. This definition includes non-purchase and non-use of commercial products. People's reactions to public service messages can be analysed as a form of consumer behaviour. Consumer behaviour, narrowly defined, is the response consumers make to specified marketing efforts.

Some products and services satisfy basic human needs and desires, such as food, shelter and health; others make life more convenient, safer and more enjoyable, such as transport, communication, entertainment. Some are trivial or ostentatious, such as car stickers and executive toys. Regarding goods of the latter sort, however, we must not neglect their symbolic or expressive function—signifying status or a means of self-presentation (Chapter 7). Through technological and cultural change, we come to accept the 'need' for a variety of material goods and amenities.

Brand Image

The term 'brand image' has two meanings. First, it means the familiar visual symbol of a product, for example Rolls-Royce's Silver Lady, or the Coca Cola sign. Second, it means a characteristic or a small set of characteristics commonly attributed to a product, for example those attributed to a brand of coffee or whisky, or to a domestic appliance. A combination of iconic and lexical features is desirable from a marketing point of view. Advertisers attempt to establish a strong brand image for a product, so that consumers are inclined to prefer that product to less familiar ones.

In marketing jargon a 'service' is a product; so the term 'brand image' is used to refer to both material products and services. The distinction between these was introduced in Chapter 8 because there are reasons for supposing that the attributes assigned to products are somewhat different from the attributes assigned to services. This distinction is regarded as important in political marketing (Harrop, 1990). Service images, like product images, can be represented lexically and iconically, as with services such as water, power, transport, education and medical care. These representations are usually similar to or identical with the images, the logos and slogans, that identify the organisations providing the services. A company's name, badge and colours (its livery) often adorn its buildings, equipment, products, packaging and stationery.

The impressions people form of products and services make up consumers' image of the brand, and contribute to the reputation of the person or organisation that produces the product or provides the service. The main difference is that services are more closely identified than products with the corporate body that provides them. Corporate bodies are social organisations that have human-like characteristics—reliability, honesty, responsibility—attributed to them. Some organisations provide *both* services and products, although the images need not be closely associated.

Information about products and services is probably distributed over a social network in the familiar reversed-J type of distribution, in much the same way as information about personal reputation is distributed. Similarly, products and services are likely to have reputations that vary from one section of the public to another, and that change over time.

Different providers offer similar products or services that develop a reputation, as with a particular make and model of car, medical treatment or perfume.

Reputation (brand image) influences the price consumers are prepared to pay; it is a sort of guarantee of quality or exclusiveness (Allen, 1984). Some professional practitioners, such as those in dentistry, cosmetic surgery or psychotherapy, develop a reputation that attracts certain kinds of client and affects a client's sense of having benefited from a treatment or service—a 'placebo' effect. Reputation can enhance or diminish the effectiveness of managers and supervisors in a similar way, because people adjust their behaviour in anticipation of expected reactions.

Brand images are important for major varieties of goods and services, the sorts that are used widely and regularly, and need considerable investment by commercial organisations. Marketing becomes necessary to penetrate a market in the first place, then to protect the product's share of the market, or to increase its share, and make the product profitable. A well-established brand image gives some security and continuity to business operations.

A brand image is not simply an attribute or set of attributes describing a product. It is a statement about what the product or service *means* to consumers. So, for example, the brand image of a motor car might symbolise comfort, status and reliability. The image of a brand is likely to vary across different types of consumer, just as personal reputation varies from one group to another. If we think of the image as consisting of an array of attributes, then some attributes will attract one type of consumer, other attributes will attract other types. There are limits to the number and types of attributes that can be incorporated in a brand image. Advertisements and other sorts of promotional activities are likely to present simple images tailored to appeal to different audiences. Advertisements for Rolls-Royce cars appeal to wealthy consumers with expensive tastes, not to motorists who worry about the price of petrol.

Kwon (1990) reported that national brands of women's clothing are preferred to private brands. Kwon surveyed women's reactions to 14 well-known brands of women's daytime clothing. Six pairs of bipolar adjectives were used to describe the brands; these were career–leisure, dressy–casual, daring–conservative, trendy–classic, urban–country and young–old. The adjective pairs are a further illustration of how reputational attributes can be selected and standardised for research purposes (Chapters 15 and 16). Kwon included a self-rating that separated those women for whom brands were important from those for whom they were not. It is important in research into reputation to establish which sectors of the population are interested in the target entity. Kwon demonstrated differences between brands in respondents' awareness of them, and differences in the attributes assigned to them. This would affect respondents' likely behaviour as consumers influenced by style, price, fit, and so on. The general point is that attribution affects our reactions to entities represented by reputation.

Practitioners in marketing try to 'project' the desirable attributes of products. The most important product attributes are 'unique selling points' (USPs) that differentiate their product from its competitors. Price, packaging and sheer weight of publicity can be important. It is sometimes possible to distract attention from negative attributes of a product, for example the initial cost of a vehicle, by emphasising attractive but unimportant attributes, for example maximum speed. A similar process is found in political marketing. Commercial and political advertising is constrained by the sources and amounts of money available. There are also cultural constraints on the kind of advertising that are permitted.

By analogy, USPs in personal reputation are equivalent to identifying the personal characteristics that make someone uniquely suitable for a particular role, in a political leadership contest or as a potential business partner or other associate, for example.

Brand Loyalty

Brand loyalty is the tendency to prefer a particular product habitually without considering other possibilities. It applies not only to products but also to organisations and people. Brand loyalty reflects economy of effort and inertia. Such loyalty could be difficult to estabish initially, but easy to maintain subsequently, as in religious and political allegiance, company loyalty and personal loyalty. Brand loyalty for a product or service arises because purchases are reinforced by satisfying consequences, as with soap, the window cleaner or a make of car. If for some reason the preferred product is not available, then consumers become more aware of the alternatives and respond to other images. Such changes come about because of shortage of stock, distribution difficulties, price changes, the availability of competing brands, promotional pressures, social pressures, and changes in consumer characteristics—their attitudes, values and life-styles.

Although there are undoubtedly differences between the attributes we associate with, and the loyalties we feel for, say, a club, a brand of bread, a colleague or the city we inhabit, there are family resemblances between them that make 'brand image' a useful concept in the study of reputation.

Brand Image and Product Sales

The effects of a product's reputation and a firm's reputation on consumer behaviour appear to have been more thoroughly investigated than have the effects of reputation on interpersonal behaviour. The effects of product reputation on price and sales are not simple or direct.

McNeil and Miller (1980) saw the reputation of a product as a factor affecting consumer behaviour. Shimp and Bearden (1982) showed the effects of warrantor reputation on consumer behaviour. Bearden and Shimp (1982) showed that product warranty and manufacturer's reputation increased consumers' confidence in new products. LaBarbera (1982) showed that enhancing the credibility of information about a product could overcome a firm's handicap in not having an established reputation. Lumpkin (1984) reported that elderly consumers rely on brand image rather than on retailer's reputation.

Esfahani (1991) examined the reasons why product quality, such as for soap, rice and milk, is often low or variable in apparently competitive markets in less developed countries. Why does reputation (brand image) appear to have little or no effect in such markets? Esfahani's explanation was that, where there are many small producers of goods, costs and sales are uncertain, so commitment to high-quality, high-cost production is weakened. The costs of establishing product reputation seem too high. Large producers taking a large share of the market are more likely to have an established reputation and to be able to smooth out their costs over a long period, so that the investment in reputation pays off eventually. Even here, however, substantial or sustained reductions in quality are likely to have an adverse effect on reputation and therefore on demand.

Consumer Information

Maute and Forrester (1991) examined the factors affecting consumers' search for information about products and services. Their views may have implications outside the area of commercial marketing. They argued that a simple cost–benefit relationship does not explain the way consumers' use information and experience in making their choices. Much information is given freely, for example in advertisements and political advice, but it is discounted as biased. Maute and Forrester adopted an 'attribute qualities framework' for their research. Search attributes are those that consumers can assess reasonably well prior to purchase. Experience attributes are those that consumers can assess after using the product or service for a time. Credence attributes are those that consumers know of, but cannot assess because they lack the necessary expertise or resources. Independent consumer reports provide information on all three attribute categories, but at some cost in terms of time, money and effort.

Most products and services have a number of attributes. So, consumers may use different strategies when searching for different sorts of information that will help them to make a choice. For example, medical, legal and financial services are difficult for non-professionals to evaluate, even after using them. Voters may find it difficult to decide between the records of political parties. Seeking information and gaining experience help to reduce the risks and costs associated with poor choices. Sometimes, however, the costs of seeking information and gaining experience seem to outweigh the risk of making a poor choice.

One would expect consumers to consider the differences between the available products and services, and to take account of the importance of the various attributes. Apparently, however, consumers generally spend little time or effort searching for the best option and consider only a limited range. Naturally, different sorts of consumers are likely to use different decision strategies.

Maute and Forrester (1991) examined students' ratings of banking service attributes. Students rated attribute importance, differences between banks, attribute qualities, and the time and effort spent in the search for information. Surprisingly, they found that attribute importance was negatively related to search costs. The reason could be that the costs of examining important attributes seemed too high, or that such attributes were too difficult to evaluate. Consumers seem more likely to search more when the differences between brands are wider. What is not clear is how consumers establish the relative costs and benefits of gaining information and experience on different sorts of attributes. The practical implication is that, where attribute information is facilitated, consumers are more likely to choose a product or service that has competitive advantages. Other factors, of course play a part—brand loyalty, social pressures, and so on.

Market Research

Market research is a set of techniques designed to assess the nature and extent of factors thought likely to influence the uptake of goods and services by the public or sections of the public. Its methods include public opinion polling, attitude surveys, panel studies, in-depth interviews, focus groups (small discussion groups), direct observation, unobtrusive observation, participant observation, psychometric measurement and case-studies. These techniques can provide objective data about important political and economic issues. Such data can replace assumptions and subjective estimates in the formulation of political policies.

Marketing techniques are designed to inform and influence potential consumers so that they purchase this or that product or service rather than another, or use more of it, or pay more for it. The techniques range from broad image building through public relations work to 'point-of-sale' tactics. Marketing techniques have to take account of brand image, advertising, price, availability, and so on. Consumer rights and environmental considerations are becoming increasingly important. Some environmental or 'green' issues have been used to promote a brand image, even though they are irrelevant.

Marketing tries to cope with unexpected long-term consequences, such as complaints about the side-effects of drugs, hazards arising from component failure, legislation restricting the ingredients of foodstuffs, changes in fashion and competition. Consumer behaviour has to be monitored, so that tactical adjustments can be made to a marketing strategy, or so that the strategy itself can be revised.

Consumers differ in their psychological make-up and in their circumstances, so not surprisingly they differ in their response to the opportunities and constraints in the market for goods and services. Much depends upon their needs and desires, how soon they need to act, how well they discriminate between the available options and, of course, their susceptibility to persuasion. Much depends upon the 'images' they have of the products and services on offer. Some products and services have a clear, well-established image, others are vague, possibly confused. Clear images provide possible solutions to consumers' problems; they represent targets or goals towards which behaviour is directed. They promise consummations that will satisfy desires. It is common for advertisements to carry images of desirable things—sex, wealth, status—to excite interest in products such as alcohol, gambling, perfume and motor cars.

Social factors are important in consumer behaviour. Word-of-mouth information is highly influential. Social pressures within primary and secondary groups exert considerable influence on people's behaviour. We are inclined to emulate the behaviour and life-style of people in the reference groups we admire or aspire to. Marketing techniques take account of these social factors in their use of advertising and sales techniques. For example, well-known persons of high social status (celebrity spokespersons) recommend products, and parties are arranged to exploit the influence of conformity. Advertising can be designed for and targeted at certain kinds of family groups, socio-economic groups, or age groups.

Market research investigates consumers' sources of information, their spending habits and the factors affecting decisions to purchase. Marketing is directed not only at classes of individual consumers, but also at large-scale consumers—distributors, fleet owners and any organisation that uses substantial resources, including national and local government interests. Purchasing departments and buyers involved in bulk buying are normally more thorough in their decision-making and negotiate special terms with producers. Comparable care is taken in assessing personal reputation when it is important to take the right decision, as in selection for high office.

It does not follow that the image promoted by marketing techniques is the image formed by consumers. Advertising can produce unforeseen effects; advertising is only one of many factors affecting a brand's image and the behaviour of consumers. Counter-advertising (knocking copy), which used to be regarded as breaking the rules, may have an effect, as may the reports of independent assessors—consumer organisations, opinion leaders, government advisors, media correspondents, and so on. Consumers differ in the extent to which they are exposed to and influenced by these sources. Brand images are susceptible to alteration at any time; for example, one's image of a newspaper can be changed by hearing a friend's opinion of it, or by disagreeing with its leader column one day.

The image of a brand usually includes its name, its main physical features and appearance (including the packaging and logo), and its main function or functions. These make up its social identity, rather like the attributes that define a person's social identity (reputation), or an organisation's public image. As explained above, a brand image directs consumers' behaviour towards a particular goal or target. This is particularly important if the consumer is short of time, or lacks objective ways of assessing the merits of competing products. This applies to many commercial products—high-technology equipment, packaged foods and medicines. A good product reputation, i.e. a strong, favourable image, widely shared by consumers, reduces a purchaser's sense of risk by signalling that other people are behaving in the same way. In situations where products are objectively indistinguishable, a strong brand image is a distinct marketing advantage and sustains a higher price.

For some products and services, the image promoted has to be broad enough to appeal to a wide range of potential consumers, but flexible enough to permit different categories of consumer to form their selective impressions (images). It is likely, in view of the limitations on everyday cognitive functions, that brand images formed by consumers are simple impressions comprising only a few attributes, such as name, appearance, function, cost and acceptability. Advertising material that contains considerable detail is scanned selectively according to an individual consumer's interests and background experience. Much of what is noted is quickly forgotten, leaving a residue of information that constitutes the individual's image of the product. The extent to which consumers share the same image defines the product's reputation. It is important, then, to distinguish between the product image that advertising promotes, and the product image formed and shared by consumers.

The public images of products and services, like those of persons and organisations, need to be monitored and adjusted where necessary to fulfil their marketing, or social, function. Public images can be monitored in various ways, provided the problems associated with sampling (or other methods of 'representing' the population of interest) can be solved. Content analysis (Chapter 16) can be applied to subjects' free descriptions of a product. Social surveys use standardised methods—questionnaires, rating scales, check-lists, and so on. Multi-dimensional scaling can be used to make comparisons between products on several attributes thought to account for consumer preferences. Small group discussions uncover motivations and reactions not revealed by other methods.

Careful monitoring should reveal any mismatch between the image the promoters' are trying to create and the impressions created. It should also reveal favourable and unfavourable aspects of the product that were not anticipated at the design stage. The analogy with self-promotion (reputation management) is that we need to monitor the impressions other people form of us, because the impressions they form need not correspond to the impression we are trying to create (Chapter 7).

It is sometimes possible to move a product 'up market' or 'down market' in response to the findings of market research. This means modifying the product itself, 'packaging' it differently, changing the price, targeting a different sector of the market and promoting a different image. The analogy with personal reputation is that we can modify our appearance and behaviour to gain acceptance in different social circles.

Market researchers are interested in consumers' decision processes. Some decisions are based on reasoned argument, perhaps by an approximation to subjectively expected utilities (SEUs; see Phillips, 1980). Louviere (1988) described a complex statistical technique known as conjoint analysis that can be used to model consumers' decisions. The idea of weighing up the probabilities and values of possible outcomes is familiar in daily life, but everyday thinking is liable to several biases and heuristics that work against rational decision-making (Nisbett and Ross, 1980; Kahneman, Slovic, and Tversky, 1982).

One peculiarity of decision-making in consumer behaviour is that image attributes can be selected and combined in different ways. For example, a decision based on a weighted check-list of 12 attributes might be different from a decision based on the three most important attributes. Similarly, our assessments of other people might depend not on everything we know about them, but on just those characteristics that we regard as relevant and important. One assumes that the reason some attributes of personal reputation have a high frequency of occurrence in a social network is that many members regard them as relevant and important. Attributes interact with other attributes in a set, magnifying or diminishing their effects. Problems of this sort are dealt with under the general heading of multi-attribute analysis. Decision models can be used to infer the basis of consumers' preferences. For example, for some consumers and some products, price outweighs all other considerations. For other consumers and other products, fashionability or health have a strong influence on choice.

The sorts of characteristics attributed to or associated with a product (or service) naturally vary from one product to another, and even between products of the same kind—toothpaste, say, or interior decorators. However, products of a similar sort can be compared on a *specified* set of attributes—reliability, convenience, or whatever. This makes comparison much easier. Specified attributes can be ranked or otherwise quantified for importance.

Using specified attributes to make comparisons between people has a long history in personality assessment (Chapters 2 and 4). We can make a distinction between (a) subjective beliefs (about people, products or other entities) that are distributed across a particular social network in the ordinary circumstances of daily life, and (b) subjective assessments, such as ratings, formally elicited from specially selected samples or panels of respondents under standard conditions. The former corresponds to *actual reputation*, whereas the latter, depending upon the aim of the exercise, is either an *estimate of reputation* or a *substitute for objective assessment*, hence the connection with personality assessment.

In making inferences about people or products, attributes often have the effect of triggering implications or associations. For example, the price of a product brackets it with comparable products of a similar price, as with motor cars, jewellery, clothes, restaurant meals or a visiting speaker. From the consumer's point of view, price indicates quality. Consumers who have paid a high price for a product are likely to rationalise their decision subsequently by exaggerating the merits of the product they have purchased. A similar sort of effect is seen in social situations where people have to justify the lengths they have gone to to obtain membership of an exclusive group or a high-status role. High entry fees and stressful initiation ceremonies are used to signal exclusiveness and status of membership.

Consumer behaviour does not end with the purchase or use of a product or service. This is followed by secondary reflective appraisals, perhaps spread over a long period. We commonly reflect on the psychological and social significance of our social interactions, even long after the event, as a result of which our attitudes change. Similarly, consumers' experiences with a product or service shape their impressions of its worth, reliability, and so on. The main point is that first-hand acquaintance with a product, person, service or organisation, is likely to have a profound effect if the consequences are different from those expected from prior reputation. The effect can work both ways, changing a favourable to an unfavourable impression, and vice versa. Personal impressions based on hearsay usually give way under the impact of direct contact with the entity.

There are differences in the way we react to people as compared with inanimate objects (Bromley, 1977). People are active agents, and interaction usually involves negotiation. Our occasional bouts of pleading with or blaming inanimate objects are temporary lapses into juvenile forms of animistic thinking. The differences in the way we react to products as compared with services are perhaps more subtle. The argument in Chapter 8 is that services are more closely associated with, or identified with, their providers than products are with their manufacturers. Thus, if we are dissatisfied with a pair of shoes we have bought, our complaint is usually directed at the distributor (who provided the service) rather than the manufacturer. We blame the distributor for poor service; we cannot blame the shoes! The distinction is said to be important in political marketing because political policies are about providing services, and politicians are held responsible for the success or failure of the policies.

It is not necessary to deal in any detail with sales techniques in marketing. Sales techniques appeal to preferences and aversions, and make use of incentives, samples or trials, gradual involvement and even harassment. There is a 'sales' aspect to personal and corporate reputation, in the sense that clients (consumers) need to be persuaded to 'subscribe' to what the person or organisation has to offer, which is a service or product; it is a 'benefit' (convenience, comfort, security) that 'costs' something (time, effort, money, or whatever). Consumer reactions to products and services are more likely to be favourable if certain conditions are met: adequate information about the product is provided; assurances (guarantees) of quality and reliability are given; expectations are fulfilled. Sales techniques in marketing are analogous to impression management techniques in interpersonal relationships.

Market Segmentation

Market segmentation means dividing consumers into sectors. Each sector has distinctive characteristics that affect its perceptions of and reactions to a product. It also has its distinctive network of communication and influence. A product, or other kind of entity, is likely to have different reputations in different sectors of the public, hence the notion of 'multiple reputations'. For example, personal reputation is not usually a matter for the public at large, but for particular groups or 'audiences'; these are people who, for one reason or another, take an interest in that individual.

Marketing goods and services of a commercial sort can benefit by applying different promotional methods to different categories of people. People can be categorised in various ways—by demographic characteristics (age, sex, occupation, and so on), life-style (domestic and leisure activities, use of time and money), personal qualities (traits, values, attitudes). The aim is to identify people or organisations that share a particular set of characteristics; these are the ones most likely to want a particular type of product—security alarms, camping equipment, four-wheel drive cars or filtered water.

In practice, there may be no clearly identifiable category of consumer. Or if there is, it is sometimes difficult to target them with the usual marketing and advertising methods. Those engaged in marketing and advertising invent their prototype or stereotype consumers—young career women, pre-retirement men, first-time house buyers, and so on. Having identified and located a potential group of consumers, the problem is how to inform and influence them through marketing techniques of the sort already discussed.

Difficulties arise because the end-user of a product or service is not necessarily the purchaser or the person who provides money for the purchase. In other words, consumer behaviour is often the result of social interactions between several people—members of a family or a social group, members of a commercial organisation, or representatives of several organisations. Some people act as opinion leaders or advisors, others emphasise this or that aspect of the issue, others have to find the financial resources or take ultimate responsibility for the decision to purchase. Marketing has to take account of these and other influences on consumer behaviour, but normally it concentrates on what are thought to be the main influences, for instance mothers buying children's clothing, husbands making long-term financial plans. Sales promotion could involve high-level financial and legal arrangements. Monitoring the market means taking note of likely shifts in consumer behaviour consequent upon technological, demographic and cultural changes. There are two implications for personal reputation. One is that reputation management may require the use of intermediaries; the other is that performance may need to be adjusted to changes in circumstances in order to maintain reputation.

Social Class

Social class distinctions—based largely on socio-economic status, upbringing, values and life-style—are important in segregating people. This is clearly important for social network boundaries because of the way information and influence spread through a stratified and segregated society (Chapter 6). The relevance of social class to consumer behaviour is that it segregates the market. Appropriate goods and services are directed towards those most likely to want them, and appropriate methods of persuasion can be brought to bear. Social segregation limits people's social contacts and increases intra-class conformity (see later).

Social class is strongly associated with status. Roles in the economy are associated with status differences. Status refers to the esteem assigned to a social position, such as physician, policeman or bricklayer, because of the importance attributed to that position. The esteem assigned to social positions depends upon various factors, including cultural beliefs and values, and context. There is, of course, some variation in status within these positions associated with seniority or rank. Within a given community there is usually considerable agreement about the status of social positions.

Some groups have low social status and low financial resources. Consequently, little marketing effort is applied to them. This further degrades their status, because they are rendered almost invisible by their absence from the mass media. Ethical standards are sometimes breached by the negative social implications of some advertisements, for instance those that appeal to youth by derogating the elderly. Advertisers try to avoid associating their products with people of inappropriate status.

Interestingly, the method by which respondents rank social positions according to their status was known originally as the 'reputational' method. The assumption, presumably, was that public esteem is a prominent feature of reputation, and that higher-ranked positions (or the people occupying such positions) would be accorded a more favourable reputation. They could therefore be regarded as likely opinion leaders, and some aspects of their behaviour would set standards for others to aim at.

Advertising

East (1990) summarised some aspects of the effect of advertising on commercial sales. Apparently, the social and psychological factors that operate in practice are not well understood, and even laboratory studies of persuasion show little effect, at least on pre-existing attitudes, and presumably on attitudes for which there is separate independent justification. In practice, many factors, such as the availability of products, price, habit, competing brands, and so on, affect sales. Field studies of the long-term effects of advertising suggest that sales increase rapidly at the beginning of a campaign and gradually level off. When the campaign ends, there is at first a fairly sharp decline in sales and then a more gradual decline to a level somewhat higher than the original baseline. This sequence need not apply in all circumstances.

Opinion Leaders in Advertising

Chan and Misra (1990) examined the characteristics of opinion leaders in advertising and promoting commercial products. What they had to say relates to opinion leadership generally. The background literature confirms that the transmission of opinions in direct social interaction is generally more effective than advertising through the media, although it lacks the scale attained through the media. This fact is important if advertisers, or other communicators, wish to influence a small section of the public, namely those most likely to respond favourably to their product, service or message. For example, some highly specialised products—psychology textbooks, navigation equipment, model aeroplanes—are of interest to few people. Consequently, advertising needs to be focused on the sectional interest groups. It is likely that the individuals within interest groups such as these communicate with and influence each other directly, or at least through informal channels of communication (society memberships, conferences, house magazines, journal articles, trade papers).

The first problem for advertisers and advocates generally is how to identify likely opinion leaders in those sections of the public that they wish to influence. The second problem is how to get opinion leaders to use their influence in promoting a particular person, organisation, product, service or point of view. Part of the problem is that the characteristics of opinion leaders are likely to vary with circumstances, as with leadership generally. Another part of the problem is that effective advocates are likely to make equally effective opponents.

Chan and Misra (1990) proposed a characteristic they called 'public individuation' as one of several characteristics that contribute to effective advocacy. Public individuation refers to a person's sense of being different from other people, and being prepared to act in ways that attract attention. It contrasts with the more common characteristic of feeling similar to others and conforming socially. Advocacy or opinion leadership is normally needed to *change* people's opinions and behaviour; hence the need for opinion leaders to stand out somewhat from the conforming majority.

Being different—whether in appearance, political opinion, religious belief, diet, or whatever—has its advantages and disadvantages. It attracts attention, it expresses other ways of thinking and behaving, it can attract approval or ridicule and hostility. We choose to be different in some ways but not others, depending on the associated costs and benefits.

It has not been possible to show that certain personality characteristics are necessarily or strongly related to 'being different' from others. One might expect confidence and self-esteem to play a part, or arrogance and insensitivity. One would not expect anxious, insecure people to draw attention to themselves deliberately, at least not in the sense of advocating a new or controversial view on a topic of public interest.

Whether a person is perceived as different from others depends upon one's point of view. Homosexual appearance and behaviour are different in some ways from the appearance and behaviour of most people, but are similar to the homosexual minority. It is well known that minority support is powerful in sustaining individual deviancy from social norms. Clearly, a homosexual opinion leader is not likely to have much influence outside the minority group, and could have the opposite effect to that intended. The same effect applies to people advocating minority opinions—paedophiles, political rebels, vegetarians.

Effective advocates and opinion leaders must exercise a certain amount of skill. They have to choose which people to influence, which occasions are suitable for conveying information and exercising influence, and particularly which ways of modifying people's views and behaviour are most appropriate. Failure to select suitable methods of persuasion leads to loss of interest, or rejection of the message, by the audience. Advocates whose appearance or social characteristics— age, sex, background, personal qualities, and so on—differ greatly from those of their audience are usually at a disadvantage. On the other hand, as we have seen, opinion leaders need to be different in some ways, and may need charismatic characteristics that set them apart from ordinary people (Chapter 8). An advocate whose behaviour appears to be incompatible with the position advocated, for example advocating healthy living but continuing to smoke and stay fat, is not likely to be convincing.

In advertising commercial products or services, opinion leaders are regarded as having several significant characteristics. They are supposed to be well informed about a product, to place a high value on it and to have had more experience with it than other people, so that their assessment of it is firm. In arriving at a firm judgement about a product or service, opinion leaders ideally have accumulated all the information they think necessary, and are satisfied that their personal values or standards are not compromised. This personal involvement with, and confidence in, the product satisfies one part of the requirements for effective advocacy, leaving open the question of the skills needed to communicate with and influence others.

People whose position in society inevitably brings them to the attention of the public, or a section of the public, are likely to be regarded as opinion leaders. Their views are likely to be heard more widely and taken more seriously than those of other people. Such people benefit from training in communicating with and influencing people. Considerable attention is paid by politicians nowadays to their 'image' presented via television. The danger lies in losing the spontaneity of expression and the naturalness of appearance that lends conviction to one's views, substituting a more mechanical, predictable and unconvincing performance.

The problem for advertisers is to recruit suitable opinion leaders for people in the social groups they wish to influence. These could be single people (for holiday companionship), people approaching retirement (for financial investment) or animal lovers (for pet foods). The normal processes of social life make it likely that, in most circumstances, the opinion leaders acceptable to these groups will have demographic characteristics similar to those of members of these groups.

What attributes of opinion leaders distinguish them from other people in that sector of the market? Several suggestions have been made about the personality characteristics of opinion leaders. They are what one would expect from common sense, but none are particularly important from a practical point of view.

Chan and Misra (1990) studied the effects on opinion leadership of six attributes: personal involvement with the product (wine), familiarity with the product, exposure to printed media, risk preference, dogmatism and 'public individuation' (see earlier). Opinion leadership and the six attributes were measured by separate inventories, and reached acceptable levels of reliability. Data from a large sample of undergraduate students were analysed, and found to show three significant effects—for familiarity with the product, personal involvement with the product and public individuation.

Chan and Misra emphasised the importance of public figures in opinion leadership; these are people who establish a reputation for good judgement and have access to the public via the media. They also draw attention to the reputation that a media source has as an opinion maker. For example, the consumer magazine *Which?* is an important source of opinion for its readers, and for the public at large when its views are broadcast by the media—as for example about the services provided by garages. Chan and Misra mentioned the use of 'house parties' through which agents acting as opinion leaders attempt to recruit interested people to examine and try out products with friends and acquaintances.

In many areas of social life, the support of eminent people is assumed to add credibility and status to an organisation—they sit on boards of directors, charity committees, university courts, and so on.

Celebrity Spokespersons

Celebrity spokespersons are people who are very well known for their achievements in their particular areas—entertainment, politics, sport, and so on—and publicly endorse products and services through advertisements in the media. They sometimes publicly endorse organisations or persons voluntarily for moral or ideological reasons. The use of celebrity spokespersons in advertising is frequent and widespread, and substantial fees are paid for the most sought-after names. They provide, or rather simulate, 'word-of-mouth' information. The assumption is that we attend more closely to and remember more of the information presented by a prominent person, especially if that person is closely associated with the product or service they endorse, for instance a famous driver recommending a new car. This means the informant is a credible source, and credibility is an important factor in persuasion.

Ohanian (1991) reminded us that credibility has three components—attractiveness, trustworthiness and expertise. These make independent contributions to celebrity spokespersons' effectiveness. Ohanian (1991) investigated respondents' reactions as potential consumers to products endorsed by four celebrities. Certain subsidiary attributes contribute to the three components of credibility in American culture. Attractiveness incorporates 'attractive, high-class, beautiful, elegant and sexual'; trustworthiness incorporates 'trustworthiness, dependability, honesty, sincerity and reliability'; expertise incorporates 'expertise, experience, skill, knowledge and qualifications'.

Ohanian found no age or sex difference between respondents in their responses. The four celebrities, however, were rated rather differently on each of the three components of credibility, and in terms of respondents' reactions as potential consumers of the products they endorsed. Moreover, the main effect on the likelihood of purchasing a product was produced by the perceived expertise of the celebrity, not by their attractiveness or trustworthiness. The reason attractiveness and trustworthiness had insignificant effects, according to Ohanian, is that these, and most, celebrity spokespersons were highly attractive; and trustworthiness was discounted because respondents are aware that spokespersons are paid for their services.

There are clear implications for advertising and public relations generally, provided the limitations of Ohanian's (1991) investigation are recognised, and provided contextual factors are considered. The implications for the study of reputation generally are as follows. First, common assumptions about the effect of reputational attributes on the credibility of informants need to be tested. Second, the attributes, for example age, sex and social role, of informants may interact in different ways for different people. Third, the effect of an attribute might vary with the context in which it occurs; for example, chronological age might contribute positively to an informant's credibility with older audiences, but negatively with younger audiences.

Misra and Beatty (1990) examined the importance of matching the characteristics of a celebrity spokesperson with the characteristics of the product being endorsed. In other words, they questioned the assumption of a generalised positive effect of fame on consumers' interest, memory and inclination to purchase an advertised product. The support of some well-known people is best avoided!

Misra and Beatty (1990) constructed advertisements in which products were endorsed either by a well-known person whose reputational attributes matched or did not match those products. They considered three theoretical models of the way attention and memory would be influenced by congruent or incongruent pairing of product and celebrity spokesperson. For example, a baby-food product would be congruent with a nursing mother but not congruent with a politically radical male. Misra and Beatty found that matching improved the recall of brand information and the transfer of affect (evaluation). The explanation could be that matching the spokesperson to the product helps to concentrate attention on common features, thus improving encoding and subsequent recall.

Related Issues

Marketing techniques can assess the characteristics of consumers (purchasers and users) without too much difficulty. These characteristics can be used to identify other potential consumers who can then be targeted in sales promotion.

The outcome of competition between products depends to some extent on promotional effort. Where consumers are able to make fair comparisons between competing brands, they are likely to be influenced by such things as cost–benefit ratios, the ease with which the product can be used in an existing life-style, opportunities to try out the product before making a commitment to it, and opportunities to observe or learn about other people's reactions to the product.

The consumer's image of the product is assumed to have some connection with consumer behaviour. However, other factors enter the causal pathways. Where no image is present initially, as with a newly introduced product, then an attractive image has to be injected, as it were, into the mind of consumers. This is achieved by marketing and advertising techniques. To be effective long term, to sustain consumption, the performance characteristics of the product must be seen to correspond reasonably well with the attributes promoted by the advertised image. If not, then dissatisfaction will lead consumers to search for alternatives that promise a more satisfactory cost–benefit ratio. Brand loyalty built up over a long period inhibits searches for and trials of alternative products. Brand loyalty can be weakened or overcome by sales pressure, and by consumers' awareness that a product does not deliver what it promises, or that another product is better able to meet the relevant criteria regarding price, appearance and performance. The parallels with personal reputation are easy to see.

14 Serial Changes: An Investigation

Introduction

Reputations have a life-history—they have a beginning, they develop and change, and eventually they cease to exist. The only reputations that seem to have been subjected to a life-history type of analysis are those of people who have been the subject of biographical studies. So, for example, certain figures in literature, the arts, science, religion and politics have been closely studied, and their reputation has sometimes been an integral part of their biography. Biographers have not investigated the reputation of their subject with the same diligence as they have investigated their subject's life-history (Chapter 15). The distinction between them is blurred.

Reputation is necessarily retrospective. Sometimes, the information can be quite out of date, as with the reputation of a reformed criminal or a company that has been reorganised. Entities benefit for a time from a good reputation that they no longer merit, or they have to 'live down' a reputation for a time.

An interesting aspect of the life-history of reputations is that reputations are not independent entities, they interact with each other. Judgements about one person are made by comparing him or her with another person. A less obvious form of interaction is that in some circumstances there is an ecological relationship. For example, as one reputation increases in extent it does so at the expense of another in the same area of public awareness. It is as if there were a limit to the amount of interest and information that a public can sustain. This would apply, for example, to competing commercial products and to political opponents.

Reputation is a collection of individual impressions, some of which are shared to a greater or lesser extent with other people. These impressions change over time even in a public with a constant membership. The public image fades, changes in one direction or another, gets shorter and simpler, or more extended and elaborate. Elements from one reputation are transposed to another, or confused in the 'public mind'. These aspects of reputation are related to early work by Bartlett (1932) on memory and Allport and Postman (1947) on rumour. Rumour involves embedding processes—shortening, sharpening, levelling and assimilation—especially if there is some turnover of membership in the group. Embedding processes are notions used in studies of serial reproduction. Rumour is often associated with gossip. Much gossip is about people and social incidents, and illustrates how information is transmitted and influence exerted in a social network (Chapter 6). Reputation can be enhanced or diminished by many kinds of comment. Thus, adverse comments about an author's book, a parent's child or a firm's product can have adverse effects on the author, the parent or the firm. Reputation can incorporate all sorts of information by association.

Reputations that are restricted in size are likely to be unstable. Small variations in the reputee's behaviour or in the communication network could be associated with rapid and substantial changes in the distribution of information. By contrast, a widespread reputation probably becomes ultra-stable because of the interdependence of its parts and because of inertia in the communication system. Negative feedback from others can cancel initial changes in an individual impression; a large reputation has probably taken considerable time to develop and has overcome early obstacles to its progress. On the other hand, it is commonly believed that reputation is fragile. A widespread reputation changes in response to public forms of communication—newspapers and television—that disseminate information widely and rapidly.

Changes in the content and structure of a reputation over time are responses to changes in the entity itself, in the context in which that entity operates, and in the audience that collectively produces the reputation. If a person achieves something socially important, suffers a significant failure, or undergoes an interesting change in circumstances, then this information has to be reconciled with the existing framework of beliefs about that person. If one or more influential members leave a network, their contributions to the flow of information and influence are lost. Either way, the content and structure of the reputation will change.

Serial changes in reputation are analogous to the evolutionary changes that take place in the history of ideas. Changes in an entity's characteristics and circumstances produce variations (changes) in its reputations. These reputations face selection pressures and compete for survival in the networks of information and social influence. Some reputations survive, others do not; some thrive (become wider and more detailed), others decline.

Interpersonal communication and influence are pervasive aspects of social life. This ensures that socially interesting and important information is circulated fairly quickly and fully through a network. In small, tightly knit groups, the information is confined to members; there are sanctions to prevent some information from passing to people outside the group. In larger, more loosely organised groups, the information is likely to spread widely if it is of general interest and to be communicated to people outside the group. It is difficult for a large organisation to hide something important from the public that is generally known within the organisation, for instance an industrial hazard or accident, or serious misconduct within the organisation.

Although there have been few experimental investigations of serial changes in or dependencies between personal reputations, the relationships between, and the serial changes in, two or more reputations can be studied under controlled conditions. For example, the reputation of a person who does not have direct or frequent contact with the experimental group is likely to change when that person does have direct and frequent contact with the group. Under the initial condition (little or no contact), one would expect the person's reputation to be small in extent and deficient in content. Under the subsequent condition (direct and frequent contact), one would expect the person's reputation to become more widespread and informative—probably more valid and more widely shared. The introduction of a person into a social group has effects on that group. These effects include shifts of attention and interest to new members, the introduction of new terms of reference and standards of judgement, and, therefore, alterations in the nature and extent of the reputations in circulation in the group. It is possible to conceive of a system of interrelated reputations in which changes in one part of the system have repercussions on other parts. The most obvious repercussions will be changes in content and changes in evaluation brought about by changes in members' frames of reference.

If a person with an established reputation leaves the group, one would expect that reputation to diminish and change in other ways over time. Where a person continues to interact with other members of the group, any tendency to shrinkage and distortion in reputation is likely to be offset by fresh learning, and by reinforcement of existing beliefs and relationships.

Reputation is both a product and a process: a product in the sense that, at any one time, it consists of some level of agreement of opinions; a process in the sense that there is a flow of information and influence in a social network. In some circumstances, reputation is complex, vague and shifting, and susceptible to many kinds of modifying influences. Reputation observed under controlled conditions is likely to contain artefacts created by the method used to collect the data and the conditions under which the investigation is carried out.

The investigation described in this chapter was related to other investigations concerned with classifying the 'contents' of free descriptions of personality and the 'modes of explanation' that people use to make sense of the information at their disposal. These investigations were connected with the author's interest in the nature and development of personality description in ordinary language (Livesley and Bromley, 1973; Bromley, 1977). The following investigation by the author illustrates one way of studying reputation, and it draws attention to some basic issues. The statistical analysis is carried further in Chapter 15. Some readers may find sections of that chapter difficult.

Method

Anonymous impressions of three lecturers were written by a class of university students on nine occasions over a period of two semesters. These protocols yielded a considerable amount of information about the size, distribution and contents of the reputations. The main aim was to study the relationships between, and the changes over time in, the reputations of the three target persons. Writing the reports occupied approximately 15 minutes on each occasion. The first five occasions occurred at 2-week intervals during one semester; the next four occasions took place in the following semester and after an interval of 6 weeks. The number of students attending the class varied between 16 and 23, with an average of 20.

The three lecturers who volunteered to have their reputations investigated will be called A, B and C. They differed from each other slightly in age and status but were otherwise comparable, except that A had frequent and direct contact with the students from the beginning, B had little or no contact on the first four occasions but frequent and regular contact subsequently, and C had little or no direct contact with them at any time.

The test conditions and instructions probably elicited fuller and franker statements (private opinions) than would occur in natural (public) conditions. The students were not using their opinions 'instrumentally' in a social situation as a way of showing agreement, superiority or emotional involvement (and were not getting reactions to them); so it seemed reasonable to suppose that their statements were unaffected by the censorship associated with natural prudence.

The fifth occasion of testing was administered by lecturer B (not by A as on earlier occasions), and, as the results show, this produced marked alterations in the form and content of B's reputation which had consequences, especially for A's reputation.

Quantitative Results

The average number of words per report over all nine occasions for each of the three target persons was 59. The output of the students as measured by the total number of words written varied slightly over the period of 5 months during which their opinions were being recorded. The fluctuations are probably attributable to practice, increased information, variations in interest and fluctuations in attendance.

Figure 14.1 shows the mean number of words for each reputation on each occasion, and the mean for the three reports. This figure gives an indication of the size of each reputation and the fluctuations in size from one occasion to another. It shows how the size of one reputation (A) complements that of another (B).

The results in Figure 14.1 can be interpreted as follows:

1 The output of words never exceeded an average of 115 words for one reputation. Most students had written all they wanted to write before the end of the 15-minute period. This suggests that opinions about people are expressed simply and briefly. Written English is generally more complex than spoken English, so it seems likely that statements about reputation that

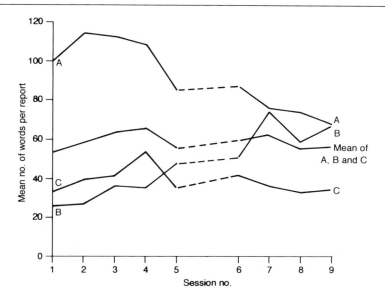

Figure 14.1. The mean number of words for each reputation A, B and C, separately and combined, over nine occasions of measurement

occur in everyday life are, if anything, shorter and simpler than those obtained in this investigation.

As far as reputation in general is concerned, statements about people we are not well acquainted with, and with whom we are not closely involved, are likely to be somewhat superficial. Clichés, stereotypes and hackneyed phrases are likely to be used.

2   The three reputations varied considerably in size, as measured by the number of words written about them. The number of words never fell below an average of 25, even for a person outside the group's acquaintance. Except for an inexplicable average increase on the fourth occasion, C's reputation remained fairly constant in size. The reputations of A and B, however, appeared to be complementary in size; in general, as one increased the other decreased. By the end of the series the two reputations A and B were almost the same size.

The time-limits imposed in this investigation were like natural time-limits, in the sense that we have to distribute our attention, interest, and interactions over many people. It is a simple matter of economics that the more we are occupied with one person the less we are occupied with another—our span of attention, our memory and our level of interest are limited. Consequently, an increase in the size of one reputation in a group may be offset by a decrease in the size of another.

The serial changes in reputation just described are similar to the phenomenon of ecological succession. We have a situation in which a change is induced in an ecological complex (a new person enters the social system, or a change occurs in the reputation of a person in the group). This change has repercussions throughout the system—new impressions are formed and communicated, and selective pressures (concerned with interest, topicality and ego-involvement) are exerted which 'shape' reputations and determine their size. Eventually, a sort of 'climax condition' is reached when the reputations reach a stable state. Thus, if there are no 'competitors', an individual enjoys a monopoly of interest and attention. If other individuals begin to attract attention, there is a strong possibility that interest in them will quicken, and interest and attention will spread. The first individual now attracts less interest and attention, because other individuals are taking their share of a limited resource; that reputation has waned. The effect is clearly shown in the decrease in size of A's reputation on the very first occasion when the students encountered B face to face. From that time onwards the two reputations become more alike in size. Average word output did not increase when two persons (rather than one) were 'known' to the group; output seemed to remain static, reflecting a limited resource. The risks to reputation created by competitors is well known, for example, in politics, entertainment and commerce; but even in the classroom, neighbourhood or factory, one person's gain in reputation is another person's loss.

The total number of words written is not entirely satisfactory as a measure of the size of a students's 'image' of a person. For reasons that are not entirely clear, the average number of words required to express an opinion (attribution or judgement) fell from approximately 11 on the early occasions in the series to between eight and nine on the later occasions. The simplest explanation is that as ideas become more familiar they find expression in shorter simpler forms. Descriptions and arguments are refined with practice, inessentials are omitted, until the final product is like a précis of the original material. The writing style becomes more 'telegraphic'—one-word sentences, omitted function words, and so on. The three reputations were differently affected. The mean number of words per attribution fell from nearly 12 to between seven and eight for A, and from 11 to eight for B, but fluctuated unpredictably for C, averaging between 10 and 11. The effect is shown in Figure 14.2.

In Figure 14.3, the size of the reputations is shown by the mean number of *attributions* per report. The mean number of attributions or opinions for the three reputations taken together rose steadily from five on the first occasion to seven on the last. The reputation of C, who was never directly involved with the class, was the same 'size' at the end of the series as it was at the beginning—an average of between three and four statements per report—although it fluctuated from over four on the fourth occasion to under three on the eighth. The reputation of A, which appeared to decrease fairly sharply in size when judged by the number of words, seems now to change little—from between nine and

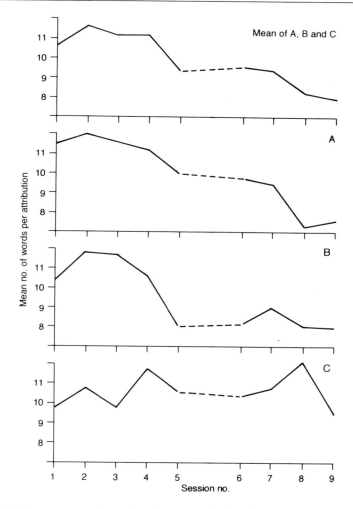

Figure 14.2. The mean number of words per attribution for each reputation A, B and C, separately and combined, over nine occasions of measurement

10 judgements per report early in the series to between eight and nine towards the end, although the fluctuations were inexplicably large on the seventh and eighth occasions. Person A was a familiar figure to the class throughout the series. The reputation of B, who became known at first hand to the students on the fifth occasion, increased abruptly from just over three judgements per report on the fourth occasion to nearly six on the fifth. It increased from nearly six after the interval to eight on the seventh occasion, eventually reaching a level comparable with that of A, between eight and nine judgements per report on the last occasion.

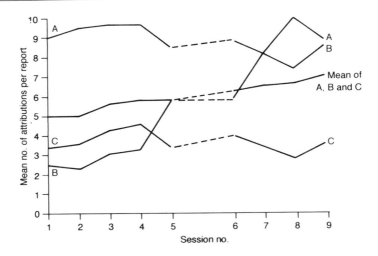

Figure 14.3. The mean number of attributions per report for each reputation A, B, and C, separately and combined, over nine occasions of measurement

These values suggest that the members of a social group can increase their fund of common knowledge about particular people. Although an upper limit to this fund of information must be presumed, it did not appear to be reached by the class of students because the average number of *attributions* per report rose steadily throughout the series, and 'slack time' was evident among students who had said all they wanted to say before the end of the allotted writing time.

Talk about people is a prominent feature of interpersonal communication; gossip and rumour are part of the 'politics of everyday life'. It is common experience, however, that opinions expressed about reputation are frequently dull and repetitive. There may be little to be said for want of fresh information. Information networks probably work well below full capacity most of the time. Information about individuals quickly becomes condensed and stereotyped and spreads quickly through a social group. Occasional transmissions are sent out, and these act to confirm or reinforce fading traces.

Although the information storage and transmission system of a communication network has an upper limit, it can bear a considerable increase, at least temporarily, above the amount of information normally in circulation. The storage and transmission of information about reputations, however, is only one call made upon the system, and it is normal for surges of interest in an individual to diminish later and to reach a stable state (climax condition). Social groups seem willing and able to respond with increased interest and attention to the stimulus of new personalities, but this cannot be sustained indefinitely. In time, competition, satiation, forgetting and other factors redistribute the information in response to changing circumstances. The resistance to information overload is illustrated by the complementary relationship in size between reputations A and B, and by the tendency of some respondents on some occasions not to use the full amount of time available.

There are several ways of representing a reputation as a distribution of opinions among a group of people. The opinions vary in kind and in the way they are distributed throughout the group. Opinions vary in the extent to which they are correlated with each other. Opinions, like personal qualities or words in sentences, usually form meaningful patterns, one opinion sustains another, as do statements in the structure of a description or argument.

The frequency of occurrence (PL or prevalence level) of opinions obtained from a group of people can range from 1, i.e. those that are idiosyncratic (expressed by one and only one person), to a maximum of n, i.e. those expressed by *all* members of a group. These opinions can be arranged in order of their frequency of occurrence from 1 to n, although some opinions may have the same frequency of occurrence. Typically, a few opinions are common to many members, while many opinions are common to a few members, or are held by just one member. This reversed-J frequency distribution reflects two contrasting effects: the effects of social conformity and the effects of individual diversity.

The data can be summarised by arbitrarily defining three PLs; (a) a 'high' level comprising all opinions stated by nine or more students; (b) a 'medium' level comprising all opinions stated by three to eight students; and (c) a 'low' level comprising all opinions stated by only one or two students. These PLs or frequencies correspond approximately to (a) 50% or more, (b) between 50 and 15% and (b) less than 15% of the group membership, respectively.

The three reputations can be compared in absolute terms by calculating the average number of opinions falling into each of the three prevalence levels during the second part of the investigation (sessions VI–IX), as shown in Table 14.1. The comparisons are also shown as percentages in Table 14.1. In this investigation,

Table 14.1. The average number of *different* attributions at the three prevalence levels (PLs)—high, medium and low—in the second part of the exercise (sessions VI–IX) for reputations A, B and C (percentages are given in parentheses)

| PL | Reputation | | |
	A	B	C
High	5.00 (3)	10.75 (8)	00.00 (0)
Medium	52.75 (32)	34.00 (24)	23.50 (36)
Low	108.50 (65)	93.75 (68)	41.25 (64)
Total	166.25 (100)	138.50 (100)	64.75 (100)

The aim is to compare and contrast the reputations of A, B and C; nothing is gained by averaging these figures.

about 65% of reputational attributions consisted of idosyncratic or low-frequency statements. About 30% consisted of medium-level statements. Only a small percentage (ranging from 0 to 8%) consisted of high prevalence level opinions, opinions that are widely shared. It appears, therefore, that the phrase 'What is generally said or believed about a person or thing' could be very misleading, since it was exceptional for more than half the students in the group to agree about a characteristic.

Towards the end of the series, A had the most extensive of the three reputations (in this class of students), as judged by the total number of opinions expressed. He was closely followed by B; and C's reputation was only two-fifths as large as A's, and only half as large as B's. A's extensive reputation was achieved not by greater agreement but by more widespread idiosyncratic and low-frequency opinions. B's reputation was similar, possibly a little more sharply defined by the number of high-frequency opinions. C's reputation appeared to have no features at all about which there was 'general agreement'; there were no high-frequency opinions.

The problem is complicated because there is a difference between what is 'recalled' or 'mentioned' by individuals, and what they would 'recognise' or 'agree to' if presented with a preformed opinion, as in an opinion survey. This is the interesting difference between the manifest content and the latent content of a reputation. It is one thing for people to have well-formed impressions that can be stated explicitly, but quite another to have vague impressions that are susceptible to influence, and capable of being formulated in different ways, or mapped onto a check-list or rating scale. We note in passing that high-frequency opinions are likely to be 'central' in the sense that they elicit associated opinions—a person who is judged to be 'intelligent' is assumed to be 'quick' and 'well informed', given an appropriate context.

Idiosyncratic attributions accounted for 51% and 48% of the total numbers of attributions for lecturers A, B and C, respectively. Attributions shared by

Table 14.2. Percentage distributions of attributions for the reputations of A, B and C, for the first part (sessions I–V) and second part (sessions VI–IX) of the investigation, categorised by three prevalence levels (PLs)—high, medium and low—corresponding to aproximately 50% or more, 15–49%, and less than 15%, respectively (see also Figure 14.4)

		Reputation					
		A		B		C	
	PL	I–V	VI–IX	I–V	VI–IX	I–V	VI–IX
High	9–16	8.1	3.0	20.2	7.8	21.2	—
Medium	3–8	30.7	31.6	21.7	24.4	15.6	36.5
Low	1–2	61.2	65.5	58.1	67.7	63.3	63.6

The table is read as follows: for A, sessions I–V, 61.2% of opinions occurred once or twice, 30.7% occurred between three and eight times, 8.1% occurred between nine and sixteen times.

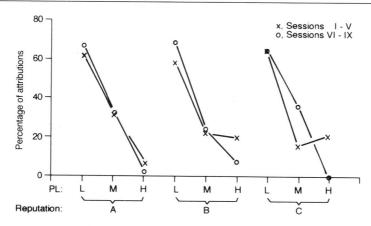

Figure 14.4. Graph of the percentage of attributions for the reputations of A, B and C, for the first part (sessions I–V) and second part (sessions VI–IX) of the investigation, categorised by three prevalence levels PL: H, high; M, medium; L, low) corresponding to approximately 50% or more, 15–49% and less than 15%, respectively (see also Table 14.2)

three or more members of the class each contributed only a small percentage of the total.

In Table 14.2 the data are grouped and summarised in percentages to simplify the results (see also Figure 14.4). Table 14.2 and Figure 14.4 show that for reputations A and B there was slightly *less* overall agreement between the students in the second half of the series than in the first. The difference between the first and second halves was greatest for C, for whom there were no 'high' prevalence attributions in the second half of the exercise (sessions VI–IX). As expected, the reputations of B and C were similar in the first half, and different from A in having a higher percentage of 'high' prevalence attributions. In the second half, C's reputation became, if anything, *more* diffuse than that of A or B, at least as regards attributions at 'medium' levels of prevalence, even though C's reputation was smaller than that of A or B.

Qualitative Results

The 'contents' or 'attributions' of the three reputations were examined. Except for a few characteristics found consistently on all or most occasions, the contents of the three reputations were unstable. Characteristics appeared on some occasions but not on others; some characteristics dropped out, whereas others made their appearance late in the series. This is compatible, however, with the theory of reputation already put forward. Reputation is a dynamic social and psychological process resulting from a combination of factors, such as the membership of primary groups, the social networks of communication and influence, the psychological characteristics of people (especially those directly involved with the person concerned) and situational factors. The behaviour and circumstances of the person concerned affect the impressions formed by the people with whom he or she interacts; but even at this stage, shared impressions do not provide an exhaustive account of the person. Primary impressions are selective and distorted by the personal biases of observers, and are therefore not wholly valid 'representations' of the person. The information that circulates beyond the primary groups is even more selective and biased, so that 'What is generally believed about a person' can hardly be regarded as a valid social representation. This echoes the original objection put forward by Allport (1937) to the proposal to define 'personality' as a person's 'social stimulus value'.

Perhaps the most important aspect of the results regarding the 'contents' of the three reputations is that they confirm the suggestion that psychological assessment in everyday life—even by people with some claims to intelligence and an interest in psychology—is superficial and unstable. The most frequent and most consistent characteristics did not distinguish between the three reputations, since each person was described as a pleasant young lecturer in the Department of Psychology. Sixty-eight characteristics were mentioned three or more times on at least one occasion, for example patient, neat, popular, humorous and tall. Contradictory attributions were rare.

Bland socially desirable characteristics are commonly attributed to people—the so-called Barnum effect. This sort of impression of others, however, is useful in social interaction. It is a convenient assumption (default value). It tells us that, in the absence of information to the contrary, the people with whom we are dealing have the characteristics appropriate to their position in society, and so appropriate to the role relationships that we have with them.

The social psychology of reputation has much in common with the processes that produce social norms, although the diversity of opinions about people seems at first to contradict this notion. The reversed-J distributions illustrate the 'collective' and 'conforming' character of reputation in the high-frequency opinions, and the spread of individual differences in the low-frequency opinions. This sort of distribution is a common feature of social behaviour.

What appears to happen is that 'general agreement' emerges only for a few obvious social and personal characteristics. In normal circumstances, these characteristics are socially desirable or at least acceptable. They provide a basis for routine social relationships. This 'general agreement' provides a common 'collective' anchorage point for members of a group, although individuals can form their idiosyncratic impression of a person. A personal impression is influenced by the perceiver's habits of psychological assessment, for example his or her 'personal construct system' (Kelly, 1955). It may have some 'ecological validity' if it is based on first-hand observation. If a person's impression of another is confirmed, or at least not contradicted, by other people's opinions, then it will seem valid to that person.

Some characteristics are difficult to state as adjectives in a check-list or rating scale. Consider the following items from the students' free descriptions: 'Knowledgeable about and interested in sex'; 'More at ease with small groups than with large classes'; 'His jokes occasionally go flat'. The aim of the student exercise was not to make precise comparisons and measurements with arbitrary scales, but to discover what *kinds* of characteristics are spontaneously attributed to people, and how they are *distributed* over subjects and occasions. Investigations like this make it possible to identify most of the personal characteristics that are of interest to a group of people, and make it possible to construct standardised check-lists or rating scales for use with comparable groups. The teacher evaluation forms used in many universities provide a group assessment of characteristics relevant to teaching, and thus estimate a person's reputation 'as a teacher'. Individualised scales, specially constructed to refer to a particular person, could be used to track serial changes in reputation.

As explained earlier, students wrote reports on nine occasions. Some of the statements made in their earlier reports were omitted from later reports, and some statements appeared for the first time late in the series. Variable attendance, with individual differences in exposure to information and influence in the social network, could explain these variations. Reduced interest as the exercise was repeated might have had some effect, but any such influence was not evident in terms of the total output of words and judgements.

One expects members of a social group to have similar ways of forming impressions of people. They share some common-sense notions, a common language, and similar attitudes and values. It is not surprising, therefore, to find some agreement in the impressions they have of a person. What is surprising is the range of differences between them. As we have seen, less than 10% of what the students said about a teacher was 'general', in the sense of being shared by approximately a half or more of the students in the class.

What is said about a person does not consist entirely of statements about personal qualities (traits). Many statements are factual, referring, for example, to the person's appearance, job, whereabouts, relationships with other people, health, achievements and failures, and all manner of other things, not excluding his circumstances, history and possible future (Bromley, 1977). So a description of traits is inadequate as an 'account' or 'representation' of a person. What is needed, and what people in everyday life recognise, is an account that describes people in a functional way. This means describing people as individuals with particular characteristics that explain how they interact with others, and how they deal with their particular circumstances. With the help of this account, the individual's 'personal qualities' are given a context that makes them meaningful and useful. For example, statements such as, 'He retains the attention and respect of students', 'He would be cantankerous in old age' and

'His illustrations are not apt', scarcely rank as personality traits or even habits. Nevertheless, they illustrate how students 'construe' teachers, and help to convey an impression. The opinions shared by a reasonably high proportion of the members of a group reveal the 'constructs' used collectively (by the group) to describe a person's social identity.

Selective Perception and Negative Attributes

Observers, because of their different interests and opportunities, are exposed to different samples of a person's behaviour. They interpret the 'same' behaviour differently by emphasising certain features or by taking account of different contextual factors. For example, some observers get the impression that the person has a good temper, others get the impression that he does not show his feelings. Some observers judge a person's behaviour to be neat, others judge it to be meticulous or even finicky.

In everyday life, we normally accept people at face value if there is no evidence of socially undesirable characteristics. People differ, of course, in the nature and extent of their criticism of others. Our reluctance to make adverse judgements could arise from several sources—genuine uncertainty and high standards of proof, insecurity and fears of being ill thought of oneself, doubts over the way listeners would receive such judgements, and so on. Although it is *safer* to attribute socially desirable characteristics to a person, very little is gained except economy of effort. If it is important to have a valid assessment of particular attributes, especially of attributes that can be masked, then one should observe the person closely, and canvass opinions widely and in some depth.

Negative opinions were rare in the student exercise described. They included attributions such as indecisive, conceited, keeps students in the dark, guarded, high opinion of self and easily embarrassed. These items were very infrequent, and more than outweighed by numerous 'positive' low-frequency items, statements attributing socially desirable attributes to the three teachers. The low-frequency positive and negative items in a reputation provide useful leads for further inquiry. Such attributions 'stand out' as deviant or interesting as compared with attributions that we take for granted. They can be interpreted as 'flaws' in the organisation of behaviour—when the person is off-guard, under stress, in unusual circumstances, or whenever the 'mask' slips. They illustrate failures in impression management.

There is some evidence that discussions took place among students about the persons A, B and C. So it is even more surprising that the high-frequency contents of their reputations were so small in comparison with the low-frequency contents.

The frequency with which social role characteristics were mentioned by students, and the overwhelming presence of socially desirable attributes, suggest that we normally adopt a simple strategy in forming impressions of people. The strategy is (a) to discover the person's social role and one's formal relationships with that person, and (b) to attribute the characteristics expected of a person in that role. If this simple strategy fails because our expectations are not fulfilled, or because our impressions conflict with those of other observers (i.e. the person's reputation), then we have to modify our impression to take account of these facts, and re-adjust our behaviour. A necessary feature of our normal strategy in forming impressions of people is to identify them as individuals—by name, location, appearance, and so on. Failure to do so can lead to confusing one person's reputation with that of another.

15 Methodology, Quantification and Research

METHODOLOGY

Introduction

Behavioural research employs a wide range of methods (Kerlinger, 1986) but is strongly biased towards the experimental and quantitative methods. The fact that there have been few experimental studies of reputation does not mean that there is no empirical evidence about the social and psychological aspects. It means that we have to look elsewhere for that evidence. Moreover, laboratory studies of social and psychological processes are greatly influenced by many contextual factors, and have to be treated with considerable caution. Adherence to formal design and analysis criteria is no guarantee that the results of a laboratory experiment are ecologically valid. The same rule, of course, applies to data derived from other sources—field studies, surveys and case-studies.

Personal reputation, corporate image, brand image and their associated attributes are difficult to define and quantify, and therefore are difficult to investigate scientifically. There are two approaches to this problem—quantitative and qualitative. The quantitative approach develops reliable and valid psychometric instruments—check-lists, Q-Sorts, rankings, rating scales, attitude scales, and so on (Chapter 16). Psychometric instruments are widely used in psychological research. It is important to appreciate the underlying measurement theory (Ghiselli, Campbell and Zedeck, 1981; Kline, 1986). The qualitative approach analyses descriptive data, as explained in the next section.

Psychometric scales have the advantage of standardising subjects' assessment of an entity's reputation, but they have the disadvantage of restricting and directing it. Open-ended, descriptive methods of assessment have the advantage of not restricting the range of subjects' responses, but they present the difficulty of developing standard methods of analysis. Social survey methods are widely used in the social sciences, and in public relations and advertising, and sometimes combine qualitative and quantitative methods. For information about methodology and measurement in research into reputation, see Craik (1985).

Qualitative Methods

In everyday life and in practical applications, the 'descriptive' or 'content' aspect of reputation is usually the most prominent and interesting aspect. There appears to be some misunderstanding about the relationship between qualitative and quantitative methods. Qualitative methods are methods of recording observational data in non-numerical form, as narrative accounts, archival records, diagrams, and video- and audio-recordings. Some of these qualitative data provide quantitative data as counts or can be converted into numerical scales. Qualitative data have to be processed (transcribed, edited) before they can be dealt with quantitatively (Ericsson and Simon, 1984). They include interview data, case-materials, ethnographic reports, projective test responses, and responses to sentence stems and open-ended survey questions. Fielding and Lee (1991) have reviewed a wide range of computer-assisted methods for analysing qualitative data. Regarding social knowledge representation in this area, see Fischer and Finkelstein (1991).

The processing usually consists in dividing the data stream into basic elements, then sorting these elements or items into a set of exclusive and exhaustive categories. This is the essential aim of content analysis (Chapter 16). The sorts of elements and categories used depend to some extent on the investigator's purpose and frame of reference; the system emerges gradually as the investigator puzzles over the data. Similar conclusions may be reached by investigators using different methods of content analysis. Once the data have been unitised and categorised, quantitative analyses can proceed in the usual way, although care must be taken to see that the variables identified have the characteristics necessary to meet the necessary statistical assumptions. Naturally, rendering data into a form that makes quantitative analysis possible does not guarantee that the results are meaningful.

The essence of qualitative data analysis lies in the initial scrutiny of the raw data—the identification of units and their assignment to categories. Interpreting raw data in this sense is like deciphering a code or a text in an unknown script. Intuitions about the data have to be tested against independent criteria or against new samples of data.

Qualitative analysis is supposed to generate insights and understanding, and trigger theories about the data. This is supposed to come about by perceiving (hypothesising) relationships, groupings and structures that would not otherwise be considered. These *post hoc* conclusions must be independently validated. Qualitative analyses rely on descriptive accuracy; quantitative analyses rely on statistical and mathematical accuracy. The problem is to show the effectiveness of the methods employed.

A person's actions, or reports of those actions, often lead observers to make inferences about the person's dispositions—abilities, motives, values, and so on. Inferences can be based on simple, context-free, behaviour statements, as in rating them as indicating intelligence, kindness or other traits (Fuhrman, Bodenhausen and Lichtenstein, 1989). In real life, however, the circumstances in which the behaviour occurs are likely to have considerable influence on what observers infer from a person's actions.

Ethnographic methods—systematic observation in real-life settings and the analysis of accounts from respondents—are also applicable. Anthropological studies reveal aspects of the social psychology of reputation that might be missed if attention were restricted to Western middle-class behaviour, for instance the ultra-conservatism of small close-knit communities (Bailey, 1971).

The case-study method was prominent in the early history of the social and behavioural sciences, but was eclipsed by the rise of experimental and survey methods. Bromley (1986) has shown how the method can be used to advantage in psychology and related disciplines, and has argued that it has a fundamental role in scientific work. The method is used extensively, although not necessarily rigorously, in a wide array of disciplines, and has considerable value as an instructional device. There are, however, few if any detailed case-studies of the *reputation* of individual persons or other entities. Many famous people, in the arts, science, literature, religion and politics, have been closely investigated, but these studies are biographical. They investigate the person rather than the reputation, although they make considerable use of the impressions of key informants, and comment on the person's reputation(s) (Chapter 3).

Given the permission of the target person, it would not be difficult to carry out a case-study of his or her reputation (Chapter 14). Even so, some respondents might be reluctant to disclose what they know or believe. Case-studies of the reputations of organisations and products would seem to present few difficulties, given the necessary resources and permissions.

Survey Methods

Survey methods lie at the intersection of quantitative and qualitative methods. The extent, content and structure of a person's reputation could be investigated using social survey methods. These methods are well-known and widely used, especially for public opinion about politicians and political parties, and about people who, for one reason or another, arouse widespread public interest. Social surveys are carried out in the interests of public relations (for individuals or organisations), and in the marketing and advertising of goods and services. Some references have been cited in earlier chapters, and Chapter 16 contains further information and deals briefly with sampling.

QUANTITATIVE ASPECTS

Introduction

In theory, each respondent in a group might assign attributes different from those of any other respondent, or conversely every respondent might assign the same attributes. In practice, the distribution of attributions falls between these two extremes. Respondents assign some attributes that many other respondents assign, but assign other attributes that are idiosyncratic, or shared by only a few respondents. An observed distribution depends upon the size of the sample and the method of eliciting attributes. There is a relationship, however, between the prevalence level (PL) of an attribution, which is the number of respondents citing that attribute, and the number of different attributions (DA) at that PL (Chapter 14).

Operational Definitions

Several different sorts of operational definition are used in the assessment of reputation. First, the boundaries of the relevant social group or network have to be defined. Second, if specific attributes of reputation are investigated, they have to be defined by how they are to be measured. Third, there has to be some definition of reputation itself. Reputation could be defined by a specified set of measured attributes, as with the corporate reputations described in Chapter 11.

A problem of definition arises in free-description studies of reputation because of the way opinions are distributed across members of a group. The characteristic reversed-J distribution means that some opinions are widely shared, others not. The question is whether reputation should be defined by the total number of opinions obtained from respondents (including those given by only one person), or by the high-frequency opinions only, or by those opinions (attributions) that are shared by two or more members of a group. The answer to this question depends on the purpose of an investigation; investigators can define reputation in different ways. For example, one could estimate the collectivity of opinions by identifying those held by members occupying central positions in the network of communication and influence.

From a theoretical point of view, there are advantages in defining reputation as the *total set* of statements about an entity obtained under specified conditions. This takes account of the possibility that reputation is a diffuse system of beliefs, some of which are crystallised (made explicit) as opinions under certain conditions. These opinions are normally expressed in negotiating social relationships—through gossip, advice and influence. Some opinions are based directly on personal experience and arrived at independently, some are based on hearsay or indirect influence, whilst others are suppositions or are expressed for ulterior motives. In social discourse, opinions that are regarded as important and central are disseminated, re-stated, elaborated or otherwise emphasised.

Collective Character of Reputation

Some opinions are shared by two or more respondents; so the 'collectivity' of these opinions can be measured by the number or proportion of respondents holding them. Maximum collectivity is achieved when an opinion is shared by *all* the members of a group. Idiosyncratic opinions are not 'collective' in this sense. Reputations, as sets of attributions, are collective representations. But how collective are they? It is possible to see the regression analyses described later as operational measures of the degree of their collectivity.

Idiosyncratic opinions that are not shared at one time are *potential* sources of sharing later in time. Conversely, opinions that are shared by only a few people can become restricted to individual opinions or disappear altogether. New opinions emerge from time to time because of changes in an entity's characteristics or changes in the social context or in circumstances generally, for instance in the membership of a group or in their current concerns. The processes of social assimilation and conformity make for stability and continuity within a group, as new members adopt the prevailing attitudes. New members, however, sometimes introduce different sorts of information and influence. The more widely shared opinions provide a frame of reference or feedback that enables individuals to check their personal impressions for relevance, accuracy and consistency.

In time, under stable conditions, the system of shared impressions and attitudes toward an entity should settle into a steady state. This corresponds to what is called an 'established' reputation, and is likely to resist change. The resistance to change comes from the conformity effects associated with negative feedback for contrary opinions, and from the commitment people have to their well-established points of view, as with brand loyalty or political loyalty. Some reputations are simple, convenient, stereotyped images that are not easily modified.

Other reputations are complex and change over time. Serial changes are likely if the entity itself changes its character, if it interacts with another entity so that their reputations become interdependent or if circumstances change. If an entity ceases to exist, or if, say, a person leaves a particular social network, then reputation is likely to continue for a time but to undergo changes. Some of these changes are accounted for by loss of interest, a reduction in reinforcement, individual forgetting, and the losses and distortions associated with the serial reproduction of verbal material (Bartlett, 1932). In exceptional circumstances, a reputation persists or continues to grow long after the entity to which it refers has ceased to exist. This is true of certain historical figures and events— the stuff of myths and legends, fame and infamy (Middleton and Edwards, 1990).

As a social product, reputation is a system of impressions distributed in a social network so that some elements are shared widely, whilst others are shared less widely or not shared at all. These elements vary in several ways: (a) in their variety; (b) in their degree of concentration or density, as measured by their frequency of occurrence; (c) in their salience, as measured by their average rank order of appearance or priority in a series of elements; and (d) in their degree of association with other elements, as measured by the extent to which items are correlated.

Attributes that have a reasonably high frequency of occurrence may be intercorrelated in ways that form clusters or factors. This identifies some basic 'dimensions' of reputation. Alternatively, attributes may have different loadings on a single, common factor of reputation, for example esteem. Multi-dimensional analysis provides a way of defining the attributes of reputation, and measuring their centrality.

Representing the Distribution of Attributions

Unless their output is strictly controlled, subjects differ in the total number of attributions they make. Attributions differ in the number of subjects making them, i.e. their PL. The number of *different* responses, however, is usually considerably less than the total number of responses given by a group of subjects. Maximum agreement is reached when all the attributions are shared by all the subjects and there are no idiosyncratic responses. Minimum agreement is found when none of the attributions are shared and all the responses are idiosyncratic.

Two possibilities illustrating near maximum and actual minimum agreement are shown in Table 15.1, where subjects are numbered from 1 to n in the first column, and the different responses (attributions—DAs) are labelled a, b, c, and so on. The number of responses for each subject is given in the final column of the table. For ease of comprehension, the number of subjects is limited to six and the number of responses to a maximum of five. Obviously, the amount of agreement depends on the number of responses produced by each subject.

Table 15.1. Hypothetical examples showing the maximum and minimum extent of agreement between subjects in the distribution of different responses (attributions; DAs) about a target entity. Each letter a, b, and so on, represents a *different* attribution (see text for further details)

Subject	Response type	No. of DAs
Maximum agreement		
1	a b c d e	5
2	a b c d	4
3	a b c	3
4	a b	2
5	a b	2
6	a	1
$n = 6$	Total DAs $= 5$	$\sum_{i=1}^{n} DA = 17$
Minimum agreement		
1	a b c d e	5
2	f g h i	4
3	j k l	3
4	m n	2
5	o p	2
6	q	1
$n = 6$	Total DAs $= 17$	$\sum_{i=1}^{n} DA = 17$

For the maximum agreement case in Table 15.1, it could be argued that four different attributions (a, b, c and d) are shared among six respondents, giving a mean of 0.33 shared attributions per respondent. Alternatively, it could be argued that 16 out of a total of 17 responses are shared (response 1e is idiosyncratic). For the minimum agreement case in Table 15.1, no attributions are shared among the six respondents (all the responses are idiosyncratic), giving a mean of zero shared attributions per respondent. These ratios express the extent to which reputation reflects 'What is generally known or believed' about an entity among members of a group. Idiosyncratic attributions contribute to reputation in one sense but do not form part of the 'collective representation', which comprises the more widely shared attributions.

A more revealing way of showing the extent of agreement between subjects is to calculate the regression of the logarithm of the frequency of occurrence of the different responses (DAs) on the logarithm of the number of responses at the various PLs, i.e. levels of frequency of occurrence. The higher the intercept and the steeper the negative slope, the greater the agreement within the group. The calculations and figures in the sections that follow are based on the empirical data summarised in Chapter 14.

The distribution of reputational attributes among a group of respondents can be represented in various ways. One way is to construct a Respondent × Attribution matrix; this represents the raw data. (The Respondent × Attribution matrices for the data summarised in Chapter 14 are too large to be reproduced here.) This raw data matrix can be arranged so that respondents are ranked according to the number of attributions they make, i.e. their score, and so that attributions are ranked according to how frequently they are mentioned. This is the extent to which opinions are shared—their prevalence. However, tied ranks for subjects' scores and PLs, and the existence of many attributions at the lower levels of prevalence (and especially idiosyncratic attributions), mean that the row and column orders of a Respondent × Attribution data matrix are only approximations. The relationship between the frequency with which attributions are mentioned (PL) and the number of *different* attributions (DA) mentioned at each level of frequency can be plotted as a graph with DA as the ordinate and PL as the abcissa. The relationship is typically negative and logarithmic as shown in Figure 15.1.

The number of different attributions (DA) at the lower prevalence levels (PL) decreases steeply from a maximum (usually associated with the number of idiosyncratic attributions in a free-description exercise), then decreases asymptotically as the number of different attributions approaches a maximum PL. That is to say, the numbers of different attributions at the lower PLs are relatively large; at higher PLs the number of different attributions decreases sharply at first and then more slowly to its lower limit of 1. The maximum PL, of course, cannot exceed n, the number of subjects in the group, and is usually

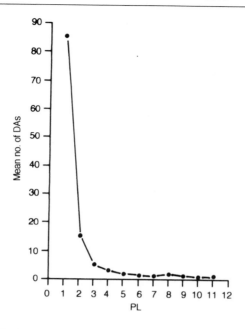

Figure 15.1. The relationship between mean number of different attributions (DA) and the prevalence level (PL) for teacher A's reputation averaged over 20 respondents and nine occasions of measurement

much lower. By contrast, the maximum number of different attributions is usually greater than *n*, because subjects usually produce several responses, some of which are idiosyncratic.

Another way of looking at the frequency with which attributions are mentioned (their prevalence) and the number of different attributions at each PL is to see it as expressing tension between the contrasting pressures social conformity and individual diversity. That is to say, attributions vary in the extent to which they are shared among members of a group. The nature of this variation is determined by several factors, but particularly by the effects of communication and influence (conformity) and by individual differences in knowledge, interest, and so on (diversity).

It is important to understand (a) the relationship between, and (b) the difference between, the curve in Figure 15.1 and the other reversed-J curve of conformity described in Chapter 1. This was obtained by plotting a graph of the frequency of *each* attribution, where the attributions are arranged in order of frequency of mention, as in Figure 1.1. The reason for making PL the abcissa and DA the ordinate is explained below. The DA refers to the *number* of *different* attributions reaching a given PL.

Measuring Collective Representations

If PL and DA are both transformed to a logarithmic scale, then the relationship between PL and DA becomes more linear, and can be most conveniently expressed by a regression equation of the form:

$$\log DA = a + b(\log PL),$$

where a is the intercept and b is the slope. The relationship can also be described in a regression equation of the form:

$$\log PL = a + b(\log DA).$$

The correlations between DA and PL were very high, so that it makes little difference whether DA or PL is used as the predictor variable. The results for Lecturer A, in the study described in Chapter 14, averaged over nine occasions are represented by the negative logarithmic relationship in Figure 15.2, which shows the effect of transforming DA and PL to a logarithmic scale.

In raw-score terms, the ordinate is DA, the number of *different* attributions; the abcissa is PL, the prevalence level, the number of respondents making the *same* attribution. Each point represents a number of DAs at a given PL. The scales in subsequent figures are also transformed into logarithmic scales; this has the effect, as explained above, of making the relationship between log PL and log DA linear. The explanation for this relationship is that where the level of prevalence is at a minimum each attribution is idiosyncratic. If n is the number of respondents, and k is the number of attributions each is required to make (or the average number of responses made), then the total number of attributions is $n \times k$. Many of these attributions are idiosyncratic, reflecting each respondent's special knowledge of the target, his or her attitude to the target, and the accidents of mood, circumstances, associative memory, and so on.

The number of idiosyncratic attributions is unlikely to reach the maximum possible value of $n \times k$ because some of the knowledge and beliefs about the target are usually shared by two or more respondents. This is the result of respondents forming similar impressions of the target independently, and of social pressures that produce the typical reversed J-curve of conformity. In practice, as we have seen, the extent to which attributions are shared, even in homogeneous groups whose members are well acquainted with the target, is not large. So the number of attributions that are shared by larger numbers of respondents becomes vanishingly small at a PL well below the theoretical maximum, which is n, the number of respondents in the group. For the sorts of reputations described in Chapter 14, the observed value of DA typically reduces to 1 ($\log 1 = 0$), giving the most general agreement for 1 attribution at a prevalence level of about 50%, for example 10 students out of a class of 20.

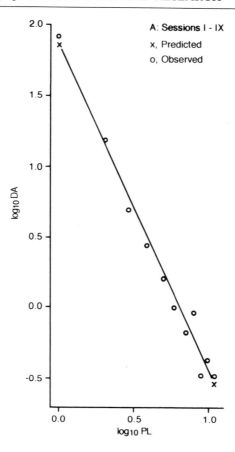

Figure 15.2. The relationship between log PL and log DA for reputation A for occasions I–IX combined (PL, prevalence level; DA, number of different attributions)

The relationship between log PL and log DA makes it possible to predict one from the other. If the size (n) of the sample (social group) is known, it follows that the levels of prevalence can vary between 1 and n, although not every PL need be occupied. The unknown quantities are the *numbers* of *different* attributions at each possible PL. A regression equation based on a small sample can be used to predict the size of sample needed to reach a given PL or a given number of idiosyncratic attributions.

A more complex equation is needed to describe the untransformed curvilinear relationship (least squares, closest fit) illustrated in Figure 15.1. The logarithmic transformation has no social or psychological significance. It is simply a familiar mathematical method of fitting data points to a straight line rather than to a curve of the sort shown in Figure 15.1. The transformation facilitates comparisons between different sets of data (see below). The main reason for adopting a regression analysis is not to predict one variable from the other, but to use simple quantitative indices (intercept and slope) to make comparisons between reputations.

The number of observed data points is determined by the number of PLs for which there are one or more DAs. DAs can range from one to the total number of idiosyncratic attributions made on a particular occasion. The negative values of log DA (fractional values of DA) are the result of averaging measurements when some attributions do not have high PLs on every occasion of measurement.

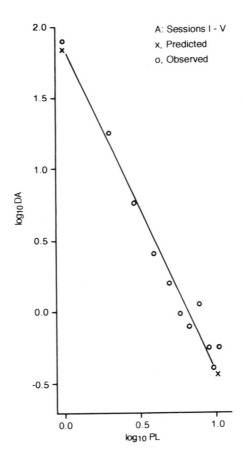

Figure 15.3. The relationship between log PL and log DA for reputation A for occasions I–V combined (PL, prevalence level; DA, number of different attributions)

Methodological and Theoretical Considerations

The method used to collect the data influences the results. Thus, provided they are similarly acquainted with the target, an investigation in which only a few attributions are elicited from respondents is likely to yield a distribution in which the number of *different* attributions is small. An investigation in which many responses are elicited from respondents is likely to yield a distribution in which the number of *different* attributions is large.

A further influence on the relationship between PL and DA is produced when the respondents are not well acquainted with the target of the reputation. In these circumstances, the relationship between log PL and log DA is still linear. The slope is parallel with but lower than that obtained for respondents who

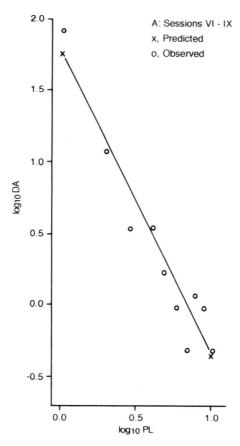

Figure 15.4 The relationship between log PL and log DA for reputation A for occasions VI–IX combined (PL, prevalence level; DA, number of different attributions)

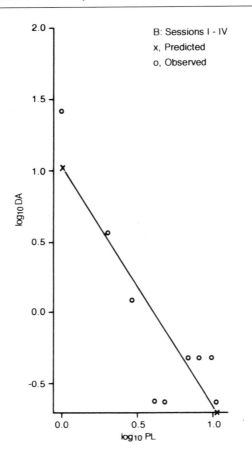

Figure 15.5. The relationship between log PL and log DA for reputation B for occasions I–IV combined (PL, prevalence level; DA, number of different attributions)

are well acquainted with the target, meaning that the intercept (representing the number of attributions mentioned once) is lower, and the maximum PL (representing the attribution mentioned by the highest number of respondents) is also lower. This is shown by comparing the graphs of the relationship between log PL and log DA obtained under different conditions (Figures 15.3 to 15.8).

The typical finding, as explained elsewhere, is that many different attributions are mentioned by one or a few respondents, whereas only one or a few different attributions are mentioned by many respondents. The words 'few' and 'many' are used relative to the number of respondents and the number of attributions. It is unusual for each respondent in a group to report the same set of attributes, or for each respondent to report a completely different set of attributes

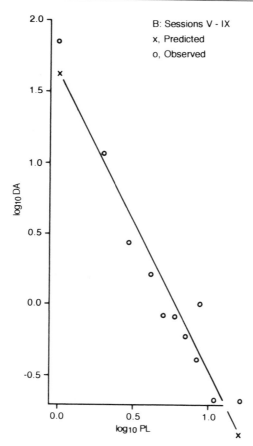

Figure 15.6. The relationship between log PL and log DA for reputation B for occasions V–IX combined (PL, prevalence level; DA, number of different attributions)

(see Table 15.1). Of course, such a result or some approximation to it, is possible given a particular group of respondents, a particular method of eliciting attributions, or a target with a particular sort of reputation among the respondents.

The results of the investigation into serial changes in reputation show that for Lecturer A (Figure 15.2) the intercept for sessions I–IX combined would have to increase from log 1.86 to log 2.36 (that is to say, the number of idiosyncratic attributions would have to increase from 72 to 229) to be confident of observing at least one attribution with a PL of 11. Using a free-description method, in similar circumstances, this would mean increasing the sample size from 20 to 64. Maintaining a sample size of 20 but allowing more time, thus

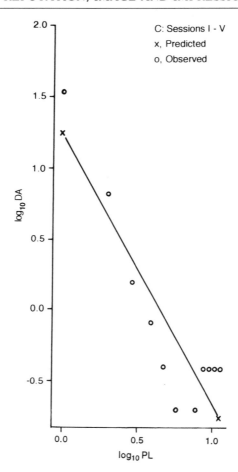

Figure 15.7. The relationship between log PL and log DA for reputation C for occasions I–V combined (PL, prevalence level; DA, number of different attributions)

increasing the number of free-description attributions per respondent, might not have the same effect. It might increase both the intercept and the slope of the regression line, which means that it would increase the number of idiosyncratic responses without having much effect on the maximum PL. This possibility, however, remains to be tested empirically.

Empirical Results

Figure 15.2 shows the relationship between log PL and log DA for Lecturer A's reputation averaged over nine sessions of observation as reported in the

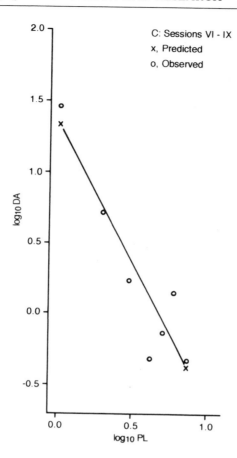

Figure 15.8. The relationship between log PL and log DA for reputation C for occasions VI–IX combined (PL, prevalence level; DA, number of different attributions)

study of serial changes in reputation in Chapter 14. Figure 15.2 shows the same data as in Figure 15.1 but uses logarithmic scales. This result summarises an average of 180 attributions (111 *different* attributions) elicited from an average of 20 students on each of nine occasions of measurement.

The results that follow further describe and illustrate the regression of log DA on log PL. The aim is to facilitate comparisons between different reputations or the same reputation under different conditions.

The regression equation for the data for Lecturer A, averaged over sessions I–IX, was:

$$\log DA = 1.857 - 2.28 \ (\log PL).$$

In a class of 20 students, on an average occasion of measurement for Lecturer A, one could expect over 70 different attributions to be mentioned once, 15 twice, 6 three times, and so on. Thus the predicted number of different attributions at the minimum or 5% (1 out of 20) PL is 72, compared with an observed value of 82. The predicted number of different attributions at the maximum or 30–35% (6–7 out of 20) PL is between 1 and 2, compared with an observed value of 1.

The size of the sample would have to be increased by a factor of three or four to elicit an attribution that is common to 11 respondents. With a sample size of 20, the maximum predicted prevalence is approximately 6 (30%), bearing in mind that the method of free description was used to elicit attributions.

The differences between the observed values and those predicted from the regression equation, known as residuals, indicate the extent to which the regression equation fits the empirical data. In the studies reported here, the relationships between log PL and log DA are based on 7 to 11 data points. Each data point is an average of 20 students. The data points, however, are too few to justify a statistical analysis of the residuals. Visual inspection of Figures 15.2 to 15.8 seems to confirm that the logarithmic transformations and the associated regression equations provide a sensible way of analysing reputational data.

The different occasions of measurement for Lecturer A produced higher or lower maximum levels of prevalence. They went as low as 5 and as high as 11 over the nine sessions in the study of serial changes for Lecturer A. The study of serial changes in reputation comprised one series of five occasions of measurement separated by an interval of 6 weeks from a subsequent series of four occasions of measurement. Figure 15.2 averages the results for Lecturer A over all nine occasions. Figure 15.3 averages the results for the first five occasions. Figure 15.4 averages the results for the next four occasions. Figures 15.2, 15.3, and 15.4 produce very similar results. For the first five occasions combined the correlation between log PL and log DA is -0.98, the intercept 1.83 and the slope -2.16. For the next four occasions combined the correlation is -0.96, the intercept 1.75 and the slope -2.08. Lecturer A was in full and frequent contact with the students throughout the investigation. His reputation was formed early, even before the start of the investigation; it appears to have reached a stable state as there is no discernible change in the distribution of attributions between the two sets of observations.

The results for Lecturer B are shown in Figure 15.5 and Figure 15.6. Lecturer B came into contact with the class of students for the first time on the *fifth* meeting of the class. The comparison here is between the first *four* occasions (Figure 15.5), when students were unacquainted with Lecturer B, and the next *five* occasions (Figure 15.6), when B was in face-to-face contact with students. The intercept for the second set of occasions is higher, at 1.61, than for the first set, at 1.02. The slope at -2.10 is steeper for the second set of occasions, being − 1.67 for the first set. The correlation between log PL and log DA, at − 0.96, is higher for the second set than for the first set, at − 0.86.

This seems to imply that as Lecturer B's reputation developed over sessions V–IX it did so by increasing the number of attributions that were idiosyncratic or had a low PL. The maximum PL was approximately 4 averaged over the first four occasions, and approximately 6 averaged over the next five occasions. By comparison, the predicted number of idiosyncratic attributes rises from between 10 and 11 averaged over the first four occasions to approximately 42 averaged over the next five occasions. This illustrates the increased diversity of attributions associated with increased acquaintance with the target. This applies even when the number of respondents remains the same or nearly the same, and even when there is some increase in the extent to which attributions are shared.

The results for Lecturer C are shown in Figure 15.7 and Figure 15.8. Lecturer C had no direct contact with the students in class during the period of the investigation or before it. The relationship between log PL and log DA averaged over the first five occasions looks remarkably similar to the relationship averaged over the next four occasions. The intercepts are 1.24 and 1.33, respectively; the slopes − 1.85 and − 1.33, respectively; the correlations − 0.90 and − 0.92, respectively. However, the maximum PL has declined from 12 over the first five occasions to 7 over the next four occasions. In other words, there was *less* agreement about Lecturer C's reputation later in the series than earlier.

The number of respondents varied irregularly between 16 and 23 over the nine occasions. Figure 15.9 shows the serial changes in the mean number of attributions per respondent for each of the Lecturers A, B and C. The attributions

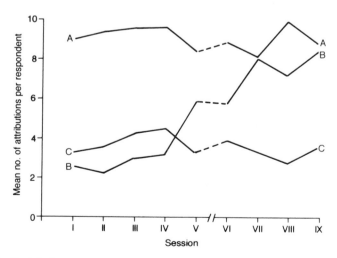

Figure 15.9. Serial changes over occasions I–IX in the mean number of attributions (DA) per respondent for reputations A, B and C (also shown in Figure 14.3)

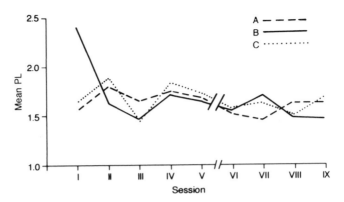

Figure 15.10. Serial changes over occasions I–IX in the mean prevalence level (PL) of attributions for reputations A, B and C (see text for further details)

for A were consistently high and showed little or no change; the attributions for B increased considerably from the earlier to the later occasions; the attributions for C remained low throughout the series. Figure 15.10 shows the serial changes in the mean PL for attributions. The PL for B showed a sharp reduction from the first to the second occasion; this was possibly because only the barest facts about B were known to most of the students on the first occasion, but by the second occasion more was known and more diversity was apparent. There is little to choose between the three reputations as regards the average PL of attributes as the series progressed, although there appeared to be a slight decline overall. The similarity between A, B and C in serial trends for the mean PL was presumably a function of the skewed (reversed-J) distribution typical of reputational attributions, and the prevalence of low-frequency attributions.

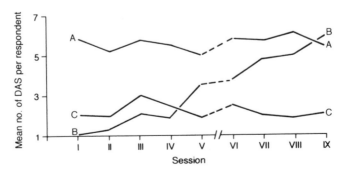

Figure 15.11. Serial changes over occasions I–IX in the mean number of different attributions (DA) per respondent for reputations A, B and C

Figure 15.11 shows the serial changes in the average number of *different* attributions per respondent for Lecturers A, B and C. As expected, the mean number of different attributions for A started at a high level and continues at more or less the same level throughout the series. The mean number of different attributions for B started at a very low level and, with one exception, increased on each subsequent occasion, particularly on the fifth when B met the class for the first time. By the end of the series, the mean number of different attributions for B reached the same level as that for A. The mean number of different attributions for C started at a low level, and continued at that level throughout the series, except for an unexplained small increase on the third occasion.

16 Assessment: Techniques and Issues

Introduction

This chapter describes a selection of techniques for the assessment of reputation, and comments on their advantages and disadvantages in basic research and in practical applications. It suggests what each technique is likely to tell us about the nature of reputation. Examples of assessment techniques are also given elsewhere in this book; measurement and quantification are dealt with more specifically in Chapter 15. The assessment and measurement of reputation require operational definitions of the variables under investigation. As explained elsewhere, there are several varieties of reputation, and one entity can have several different reputations. These reputations, or aspects of these reputations, can be defined and assessed in different ways. The problem is to work out which method is likely to give the best results. Measurements can be made of (a) the extent or size of a reputation; (b) the level of esteem (amount or rank order of merit) of reputations; (c) the contents of a reputation; and (d) the degree of similarity between reputations, or between a reputation and the entity it represents, or between a reputation and a prescribed standard.

Where possible, several independent methods of assessment should be used to cross-check findings. Most of the methods described below are familiar to psychologists and are well documented. They will not be described in detail, since we are concerned only with their suitability for investigating reputation. The study of social judgement raises a number of difficult methodological issues (Eiser, 1990).

Nominations

Members of a group can be asked to nominate, i.e. to mention by name, one or more persons (or other entity) they think fit a particular category—as in calling for nominations in an election, or in a consumer-preference study. Nominations can be obtained in different ways, for example by individual proposals, by proposals that are seconded or have the required number of supporters. The number of nominations received, assuming equal opportunities for members to nominate, is one measure of the extent to which nominees are known and believed to have the attributes appropriate to the specified role, such as chairperson or representative. Nominations can be made for achievement or bravery awards, for beauty contests, or for most-preferred co-worker. Naturally, the results depend on the circumstances under which the nominations are made.

Nomination is a basic method of assessing reputation. It reflects the extent to which identities and impressions are available to members from memory, and it is likely to reflect the importance of opinion leaders in the social network of communication and influence. If there is more than one nominee, then the number of nominations received for each is the first approximation to (a) the group's interest in the issue and (b) the nominees' standing in the group. For example, suppose a group of 150 people are invited to nominate someone to represent them, or to name the best worker for the year. The results might show that five different names were received, as follows:

Nominee	No. of nominations received
A	13
B	7
C	3
D	2
E	2

Clearly, the vast majority of the group did not nominate anyone, perhaps because of lack of interest, or because no one they knew fitted the prescribed category.

If members were invited to nominate up to, say, three people, this would probably increase the number of nominees, but would still provide a comparative measure of each nominee's reputation. Thus, nominations are one indication of the extent to which persons (or other entities) are known and believed to fit a specified category. Nominations are usually a preliminary to a more systematic vote (see later). Members can be asked to put their nominees in rank order of preference. It complicates the arithmetic slightly but improves the accuracy of the results.

The advantages of nomination for assessing reputation are that it is simple and reflects the natural, manifest (salient or spontaneous) level of awareness and interest in a particular reputation-related issue. The disadvantages are that it is crude and fails to take account of latent reputation, i.e. the opinions that people would form if they were made aware of the possibilities and encouraged to make a choice. The method is widely applicable. People can be asked to nominate not only persons but also organisations and commercial products, for awards for example. Stating a preference is a form of nomination.

Votes

Voting is a well-known procedure widely used in a variety of settings as a measure of support and esteem (Newland, 1972). As with the franchise in political affairs, voting in studies of reputation has to take account of the various qualifications and rules that determine who is eligible to vote, i.e. the electorate, and how votes are to be registered. This means defining the social boundaries of the reputations under investigation, and making the method of data collection explicit.

Voting means exercising a choice between candidates by casting a vote for one rather than another. The simplest voting measure is a count of the number of votes cast for each candidate. A table of results shows how many people voted out of the total eligible to vote, how many votes each candidate received, how many votes were spoiled (by not abiding by the procedure for recording a vote) and how many abstained. These numbers can be converted to percentages for the purposes of comparison. Under the 'first past the post' system, the candidate who secures a simple majority of votes is elected. Under the alternative vote (AV) system, voters rank several candidates in order of preference. If no candidate secures a simple majority of first preferences, then the candidate with the fewest first preferences is eliminated, and the votes redistributed among the remaining candidates. The process continues until a candidate obtains a simple majority.

Under the single transferable vote (STV) system, voters rank candidates in order of preference. A calculated quota of votes is needed for election; votes surplus to the quota are redistributed among candidates who have not reached the quota. If necessary, the lowest ranking candidate is eliminated, and those votes are redistributed. The more modern systems of voting use some form of proportional representation, such as the STV. Proportional representation is designed to secure a result that reflects the proportional distribution of votes cast.

In the list system of voting, the number of nominees elected depends upon the proportion of votes cast for each list or for each party or organisation putting forward a list. The list system of voting could be used to assess *sets* of attributes. For example, in market research, consumers are asked to vote or state their preferences for products, described in terms of various attributes—price, appearance, taste, and so on. As explained elsewhere, consumer decisions are influenced by their perceptions of these attributes. In political research, voters could be asked to state their preferences for *sets* of politicians in an attempt to discover which particular *combination* has the most electoral appeal. Similarly, voters could be asked to state their preferences for sets of policy options; this might bring home to voters the costs as well as the benefits of various policy options. The point is that people (or attributes) *in combination* interact with each other to produce a combined effect that is not obvious when each person (or attribute) is considered in isolation.

Votes provide a ratio scale and so show, for example, that one candidate received no votes and that one candidate received twice as many votes as another. Many psychological measures, and most measures of reputation, are not ratio scales. The numbers 'do not remember where they came from', and non-ratio measures are often used in parametric statistical analysis. Investigators should consider, however, whether the nature of their measures imposes limits on the conclusions they draw from their results.

These voting systems can be used to study reputations. Preferences can refer to any sort of entity (persons, organisations, products, events, places) and any sort of attribute (trust, beauty, taste, reliability, comfort). A simple count of votes can be used to identify the most preferred candidate, or to arrange several candidates in order of merit. Proportional representation is likely to provide reasonably accurate estimates, and to discriminate between candidates. In research into reputation, it is not necessary to use the election procedure described above, since what is usually required is a rank order of merit of the entities under investigation.

The advantage of these voting systems as measures of reputation is that they reflect, to some extent, latent reputation. That is to say, the attention of members of the voting group (electorate or audience) is drawn to all candidates (entities) by the ballot paper (in research, the record form). Without this cue or reminder of who or what is eligible, they may not know or may have forgotten the names of one or more of the candidates. The related disadvantage is that it leads to votes that have little or no psychological or social significance. This could lead to errors of measurement and to the loss of ecological validity, because the numbers of votes are supposed to indicate aspects of reputation. Another advantage is that votes can be counted to show the level of interest in the reputation issue and the magnitude of the preferences associated with that issue.

The disadvantage of voting as a measure of reputation is that the voting list is usually shorter than the nomination list, especially if the procedure for nominating has restrictive conditions. Thus, even proportional representation produces only an approximation to the true distribution of preferences. The way out of this difficulty is to permit unrestricted nominations, and invite members of the 'electorate' or 'audience' to rank-order as many candidates as they sensibly can.

In a political context, compulsory voting raises ethical issues. In the contexts of basic and applied research, however, participation is voluntary; non-response raises methodological rather than ethical issues. The ethical aspects of research into reputation are governed by the law, and by the codes of conduct enforced by society and by professional bodies.

Guess Wh? Method

The Guess Who? test was developed as an adjunct to sociometry (Chapter 6), and has often been used to study reputation in schoolchildren (see, for example, Brieland, 1952). The procedure is simple, it is a variation of the nomination method described above. Children are asked to answer questions such as 'Who is the cleverest child in the class?', 'Who is the most popular child in the class?', 'Who is the most helpful?' or 'Who would you prefer not to sit next to?'

Shigetomi, Hartmann and Gelfand (1981) assessed schoolchildren's reputation for altruism from teacher ratings and a classroom sociometric test. Altruism was assessed behaviourally on six classroom tasks. Girls had a much higher reputation for altruism than boys, although the behavioural differences were smaller. Zarbatany et al. (1985) argued that the reputation for altruism in girls is explained by the sorts of test items used and by gender differences in response to item content.

Masten, Morison and Pellegrini (1985) revised the class play method of assessing peer reputation. It requires respondents to assign peers to the positive or negative role they would play best. Positive reputation was associated with competence; social isolation was associated with difficulties at school. Masten (1986) examined the positive relationships between children's humour, academic and social competence, peer reputation, and teachers' ratings of classroom behaviour. Peer reputation meant popularity, gregariousness, happiness and leadership.

The procedure raises ethical issues. The information obtained by the Guess Who? method helps teachers to identify influential children, and possibly children who are socially isolated or disliked, and in need of help. The method can be adapted to deal with personal reputations other than those of schoolchildren, and with entities other than persons, hence the 'Guess Wh?' title. For example, the questions can be phrased as 'Guess Where?', 'Guess When?', 'Guess What?' or 'Guess Which?' to investigate people's ideas about places or historical events or other entities about which there are socially shared representations.

The advantages and disadvantages of the Guess Wh? method are the same as those of the nomination method. It is simple, and it reflects salient (available) ideas, but it is crude and neglects the latent aspects of reputation.

Duncan (1966) used a sociometric measure of reputation, called the Personality Integration Reputation Test (PIRT), to identify 'integrated' persons. The measure consisted of seven 'Guess Wh?' questions. Subjects nominated three members of their fraternity who best exemplified the behaviour mentioned in the questions. This was behaviour such as expressing their feelings without hurting others, having an open mind and not jumping to conclusions. The measure was internally consistent and reliable over time. Data were also collected on subjects' self-concept, locus of control and grade-point average. Six of the seven items in the PIRT proved to be associated in the sense that the nominations were distributed over a few members of the fraternity. The item asking about people who stick to their opinions, even when they are unpopular, did not give the same distribution of nominations. It was dropped from the subsequent analysis.

It is worth noting that the phrasing of Guess Wh? questions can make a difference to the way subjects interpret them. Those people identified as integrated were compared with a representative sample of fraternity members.

They appeared to have a more positive self-concept, a higher internal locus of control, and a wider range of interests and activities. The integrated people had a significantly higher grade-point average, but not significantly higher levels of intellectual capacity or creativity. The study illustrates that the distribution of reputations, as measured by sociometric nominations, is highly skewed, i.e. some people receive many more nominations than others. It also illustrates that social consensus for some attributions is associated with attributes other than those specified in the Guess Wh? questions.

Check-lists

A check-list is simply a list of words or phrases referring to a particular issue. In studies of reputation, respondents mark those items on the check-list that they think characterise the entity under examination, such as traits for persons, attractions for television programmes, facilities for holiday resorts, conveniences for supermarkets, and so on. The instructions can vary: respondents can be asked to mark all or as many items as they can, or to mark a specified number, or to assign a rank order of importance to selected items. The results depend upon the items in the check-list, and how they are presented to respondents.

These methods are similar to nominations and voting. The advantages and disadvantages are much the same. The main advantage of check-lists is that they are simple, and record responses in a standardised way. One can use them to explore a wide array of entities and attributes, and to compare two or more entities of the same sort. The main disadvantages are that they are crude, and that each response is categorical rather than numerical. Some check-list items may not be salient or relevant for some respondents.

Rating Scales

Rating scales enable respondents to quantify their judgements. For example, instead of marking the items they agree with, as in a check-list, they can indicate the strength of their agreement (or disagreement) with a statement, such as, 'This supermarket usually has a slow check-out.' A typical nine-point rating scale is as follows:

Strongly agree								Strongly disagree
1	2	3	4	5	6	7	8	9

It is possible to substitute phrases for the numbers in a rating scale, or to provide one or more anchorage points between the two extremes. The number of points in rating scales varies, usually from five to 11. Scales of this sort are known as Likert scales.

One advantage of rating scales is that judgements can be summed and averaged to give a combined score, or set of scores, that reflects the strength of respondents' responses. It may be necessary, by statistical analysis, to prove that items are independent of one another, or conversely that they are measuring the same underlying factor. For the measurement of reputation, this means investigating the extent to which the attributes in a set are associated. The outcome determines whether the responses can be combined as a measure of, say, esteem, leadership or entertainment value, or whether the responses should be grouped into subsets indicating several independent aspects of esteem, leadership or entertainment value.

The main disadvantage is that rating scales are susceptible to some response biases. Some respondents prefer average or extreme ratings, and responses to earlier items can affect subsequent responses (Poulton, 1975). The physical features of the scale—its length, the number of scale points, labels, and so on— are likely to affect subjects' responses.

Lynch, Chakravarti and Mitra (1991) examined subjects' ratings of cars varying in price and fuel consumption. They concluded that the ratings were affected by contextual factors, i.e. by the spread in price and fuel consumption. They also concluded that prior experience helps to determine the extent to which context affects the underlying mental representation rather than the way ratings are assigned. Subjects who know more about the objects being rated appear to be less influenced by current context, i.e. their mental representations are more firmly established. It seems likely that ratings of persons and other reputational entities are liable to similar influences.

Preferences

Preference measures consist of sets of ratings of characteristics attributed to entities, for example persons, television programmes and towns. The ratings are usually made on five or 11-point scales contrasting pairs of bipolar adjectives. The adjectives are derived from prior investigations, and respondents are instructed to base their responses on their personal experience of the entities being investigated. They have been used to characterise least-preferred and most-preferred co-workers (LPC and MPC, respectively; Fiedler, 1967). They can be used in industry or the Armed Forces, for example, to identify the sorts of characteristics that are important in identifying potential leaders or forming teams to maximise social cohesion. They can be used in market research to reveal the characteristics of liked and disliked foods, branded products, newspapers, music, and so on.

Preferences scaled in this way can be averaged over a group of respondents to show the level and spread of scores for each attribute, and to assess the degree of association between the observed and the expected or desired outcome. The advantages and disadvantages of preference measures are the same as those of rating scales.

Magnitude Scales

Magnitude scales can be used to assess the seriousness of crimes, the attractiveness of faces, the stressfulness of life-events, and so on (Lodge, 1981). Respondents are told to assign a particular numerical value to one or more specified items (anchorage points) in a list. They are then asked to assign values to the other items so that the values are in proportion to one another. For example, if the reference item has a value of 15, then an item that a respondent thinks has twice the value of the reference item is assigned a value of 30. Respondents review the magnitudes they have assigned to items until they are satisfied that they are proportionately correct. One could use the magnitude scaling method to investigate the 'worth' or 'esteem' assigned to people or other entities, or the 'importance' of each of several attributes for entities of a given sort. As with other methods of measurement, magnitude estimates can be summed and averaged over respondents to give a collective or group result.

The main advantage of magnitude measures is that they can be regarded as ratio scales, and so have a true zero point. This eliminates some difficulties in the interpretation of measures of social and psychological variables. The main disadvantage is that respondents need some instruction and practice in the procedure, whereas the other methods described so far are easier for respondents to understand.

Questionnaires and Structured Interviews

Many different sorts of questionnaire can be constructed. Like other methods, they provide a standardised way of collecting data from respondents. They can be administered individually or collectively. They can be administered in a direct, person-to-person way, or sent by mail, or dealt with over the telephone or through a VDU and keyboard. They can be answered personally, or on someone else's behalf. Items can be answered 'True', 'False', or 'Don't know', or on Likert scales. Items can be paired for social desirability or other characteristics. There is a considerable literature on the construction and administration of questionnaires, and on survey methods generally. The best-known examples are personality questionnaires, social survey and public opinion instruments, and market research interviews. In some circumstances, observations can be made, and brief questionnaires administered, without respondents being aware of the fact (Webb et al., 1966).

Structured interviews are direct person-to-person conversations that follow a systematic scheme of interrogation similar to that of a questionnaire, with the advantages of flexibility, and additional inquiries and observations by the interviewer, possibly using a recording device. They can incorporate open and closed questions.

Questionnaires and structured interviews are widely used in the social and behavioural sciences. The responses to them are reactions to the demand characteristics of the situation. Consider how the following questions might elicit different attributions about an entity: 'What do *you* see as the three most important characteristics?' versus 'What do *most people* see . . .?' Or 'What attributes are important to you?' versus 'What attributes are important to *people like you* [or to specified classes of people]?' The answers do not necessarily correspond to what respondents believe; still less do they correspond to how respondents behave.

Although reputation is defined by the nature and extent of people's ideas (beliefs, opinions) about an entity, this does not mean that the subjective character of questionnaire responses is no longer a difficulty. Knowledge of an entity's reputation is only useful, from a theoretical and practical point of view, if it enables us to understand, predict, and possibly control people's behaviour towards that entity, or to understand the nature or the behaviour of the entity itself. To put the matter another way: a reputational measure should be a valid measure of reputation, but the reputation need not be a valid representation of the entity to which it refers.

The advantages of questionnaires and structured interviews are that they provide an economical way to investigate large samples of subjects, and to investigate issues that virtually preclude direct observation, for instance sexual behaviour or deviance. The disadvantages relate to their imperfect reliability, and more importantly to the difficulty of proving their validity. Sometimes, investigators are interested in the validity of a reputation as a representation of an entity, as they are for example when they use reputation to assess personality.

Questionnaires and structured interviews are familiar instruments for assessing reputation, and need no further elaboration. Examples of their use are given throughout this book. Unstructured interviews can be used by observers as a basis for making quantitative judgements, but the main point is that structured interviews are standardised and designed to provide categorical or quantitative measures.

Measures of reputation based on surveys of public opinion regarding politicians or commercial organisations are of limited use because such opinions are highly derivative and superficial, and so presumably susceptible to change if exposed to new information or influence.

Attitudes

It might be supposed that reputations are better represented by collective attitudes than by collective beliefs, because of the assumption that attitudes are dispositional characteristics closely related to behaviour. This supposition, however, runs counter to the accepted definition of reputation in terms of 'What is generally believed'. Moreover, Ajzen and Fishbein (1980) have drawn attention to limitations in the traditional approach to attitudes, and have introduced their theory of reasoned action. In view of the complex relationships between beliefs and actions described by Ajzen and Fishbein, it is interesting to note that the law on defamation (Chapter 9) assumes that loss of social esteem threatens adverse *behavioural* consequences—avoidance, ridicule, hatred—not merely negative beliefs and attitudes.

It is not necessary to go into the technicalities of attitude measurement. There is an extensive literature on the construction, administration and analysis of data derived from attitude scales (for example, see Oskamp, 1991). Ajzen and Fishbein (1980) have briefly reviewed the area (see also Ajzen, 1988). It is not difficult to construct scales for the measurement of attitudes towards reputational entities. However, the link between attitudes towards entities and actions related to entities is indirect, and attitudes measured in the traditional way may not predict behaviour very well.

Sampling

Representative samples of people are used to assess primary reputation in the marketing of goods and services to consumers, and in corporate public relations work in key areas, and in public opinion polling. Sampling of a less systematic kind is used in compiling a biography. Sometimes 'soundings' are taken when appointing people to posts in a political party or other 'representative' body.

Assessments of reputation can be based either on samples of people who have had direct contact with the target entity, or on samples of people who know the entity only by hearsay. The former shows what is meant by 'primary reputation'; the latter shows 'extended' or 'secondary' reputation.

In studies of communication networks (Chapter 5), 'snowball' samples have their uses, but are not representative in the statistical sense. The 'snowball' method of sampling can be used to study reputation. It has the advantage of recruiting people who are more closely related and homogeneous than those in a random sample. Snowball samples are not equivalent to random samples. A snowball sample starts with a small random sample or a single individual. Members of this initial sample then nominate other possible respondents. For example, an inquiry into the brand image of a car would begin by asking a small sample of potential car buyers to nominate other potential car buyers. These nominees in turn would be asked to take part and to nominate other potential buyers. Gradually, the number of new nominees decreases (as the number of repeat nominees increases), and at some stage recruitment stops. This sort of sample will have average characteristics similar to or different from another snowball sample, depending upon the characteristic of the initial sample and the accidents of recruitment. Snowball samples are more likely than random samples to reveal social relationships that underlie communication and influence. Some features that are rare and difficult to detect in random samples may be magnified in snowball samples. The sampling method used, and the inferences drawn from the data, must be justified and made explicit.

Q-Sorts

Q-Sorts are similar to ratings. The main difference is that Q-Sorts are *comparative* ratings (Stephenson, 1953). That is to say, the items are rated relative to each other over a fixed distribution, whereas items rated in the usual way are rated on an *absolute* scale. Respondents are given cards or slips of paper with statements printed on them, such as, 'Is reliable', 'Looks good' and 'Expensive'. They are required to sort these, according to their salience, into an obligatory normal distribution, ranging from, say, 'Strongly agree' to 'Strongly disagree' on a 9-point scale. Q-Sorts can be used to assess virtually any kind of entity—the self, other people, the Government, works of art. For a nine-point scale and 101 items, the distribution would be approximately:

Rating:	1	2	3	4	5	6	7	8	9
Items:	1	4	12	21	25	21	12	4	1

The ratings assigned to Q-Sort items, given their positions in the obligatory normal distribution, are recorded and analysed. The distribution for one person can be compared with that of another person by correlating the two Q-Sorts. If the items that are sorted can be classified in some way, then one can test whether the mean score for one set is significantly different from the mean score of another set. Q-Sorts are normally used in the study of individual cases, but the results from a group of individuals can be combined.

A respondent's sorting can be compared with a criterion Q-Sort based on theoretical expectations or on the judgements of competent observers—for example clinicians or other types of expert. For example, the organisers of a political party wish to know how the public image of the party compares with the party's ideal image of itself, or how the public image of their party compares with another party's image. The statements to be sorted might include the following:

- can be relied upon
- has a good political record
- neglects minority interests
- attracts women voters
- needs more talented people.

These and other attributes would cover a range of desirability. Respondents would be asked to arrange 80–100 such items in a normal nine-point distribution from most to least salient or applicable, for one or more political parties.

A criterion sorting could be agreed between the party managers and their public relations advisors. They would hope to have a distinctive public image, and to find that members of the electorate shared their ideal image in that respondents' sortings would correlate well on average with the criterion Q-Sort.

The advantages of Q-Sort measures, like some other measures, are that they can be adapted to different kinds of investigation, and are easily scored. A disadvantage is the time it takes to explain the procedure and to monitor respondents' compliance with instructions.

The Q-Sort method was originally developed to assess the relative salience of personal characteristics, so it can be used to assess personal reputation. It can be used to assess the self-concept—the subject arranges the statements in a normal distribution from 'Most like me' to 'Least like me'. Consequently, a Q-sort method might be appropriate if we wished to compare a person's self-image with his or her actual or imagined public image using the same standard set of attributes. The similarity of the two images would be measured by correlating the two sets of ratings. Assessing the actual public image assumes that the Q-Sorts made by members of a 'public' could be averaged in a meaningful way.

Ordinary ratings can be normalised, but this would not necessarily give the same result as a Q-Sort. The main advantage of the Q-Sort is that the procedure obliges subjects to make comparative ratings of statements, whereas ordinarily ratings are made sequentially, which could result in order effects.

Repertory Grids

This method is widely used. It has a variety of forms and applications (Adams-Webber, 1979). The outline that follows gives only a brief indication of the nature and scope of the method, which is designed to investigate the mental constructs people use in giving meaning to the world around them. For example, in comparing and contrasting one person with another we think of some people as sociable in contrast with others who are solitary, and think of some as sensitive in contrast with others who are thick-skinned. These polar opposites are examples of the sorts of personal constructs one might use to categorise people—personal in the sense that there are differences between individuals in their constructs.

The procedure is to provide or elicit a number of 'elements', such as 'Myself', 'My best friend', 'The person I work with most', and so on. The standard, traditional way of eliciting personal constructs is to ask respondents in what way two of these people are alike and different from a third. The people selected for comparison and contrast are sampled repeatedly so that a fairly comprehensive list of bipolar constructs is obtained. The various elements are then rated on each of the constructs. The resulting matrix makes it possible to correlate the constructs over elements, or the elements over constructs. The way the data are collected and processed depends upon the purpose of the investigation, and on the assumptions necessary for legitimate statistical analysis. The constructs often fall into clusters, as do the elements. This reveals the underlying personal construct system.

One advantage of the method is that respondents usually find the task interesting, and the results informative. It provides measures that can be analysed in sophisticated ways. It can be adapted to different kinds of inquiries. One disadvantage is the complexity of the administration, and the time it takes to complete the exercise.

Repertory Grids could be used to study reputation by standardising the elements and constructs. This would have to follow preliminary inquiries to determine what sorts of constructs were prevalent in a particular community, and which entities were to be compared and contrasted. The results should reveal the average structure of the belief system of a social group about a particular set of entities. For example, the method could be used to examine the constructs used by a section of the adult female population to compare and contrast various types of clothing (Kwon, 1990) or forms of part-time employment. This should indicate the public image of each type of clothing or each form of employment within that section of the population. It should identify the underlying constructs these women use in giving meaning to these aspects of their environment.

The Repertory Grid Technique is useful because the 'constructs' elicited from respondents correspond to reputational attributions, and the 'elements' correspond to entities. The method was originally developed to investigate personal, i.e. individual, constructs. If the same constructs and elements are used by members of a group of respondents, then analysis of the data will show the extent to which members agree in the way they categorise the attributes and entities. This method imposes the same frame of reference on respondents although, as we have seen, reputational attributions usually vary widely in their level of prevalence. Group constructs are those that members agree are meaningful and relevant—the sorts of attributions that would have a high level of prevalence in a free-description exercise. The aim of a group Repertory Grid would be to establish the average value for each attribution (construct) for each entity (element), and to compare the various entities on those attributions or on the underlying dimensions.

Orley (1976) used the Repertory Grid Technique to examine the attributions made by Gandan villagers about spirit entities. Riley and Palmer (1976) used it to investigate respondents' representations of seaside resorts. They considered how qualitative and quantitative methods are combined in the Repertory Grid Technique. They dealt with the problem of differences in the extent to which constructs (attributions) are shared by weighting constructs according to their frequency of occurrence. They did not report the frequencies, but it is possible that they were distributed in the familiar reversed-J form, and included idiosyncratic constructs. They solved the problem of having many different constructs from a medium-sized sample of subjects by grouping the resorts (entities) and finding the constructs that best described them.

Klion and Leitner (1991) reported that students use personal constructs differently in forming impressions of new as compared with familiar acquaintances. They conclude that investigations into impression formation must take account of the relevance of personal constructs (attributions) to the elements (entities) being considered. So, for example, it might be a mistake to judge a new political movement in terms of the attributes of familiar political movements, or to use the same attributes when judging male and female politicians.

The Repertory Grid Technique can be used to calculate a collective representation for a sample of subjects, or for subgroups within a sample. Cluster analysis applied to the matrix of correlations between subjects across constructs can be used to test for the existence of subgroups within a sample. The data for the subgroups can be analysed separately. For details of measurement by Repertory Grid Technique, see Slater (1976).

Bipolar attributions (constructs) obtained by the traditional method of triads can be converted into ratings (or into rankings if there are only a few elements, i.e. entities). These can then be averaged across subjects within a sample or subgroup. The average ranks or ratings provide a consensus grid that can be analysed in the usual way. Individual deviations from the consensus (collective) grid can be calculated.

Semantic Differentials

Some words overlap in meaning. Factor analytic studies suggest that three semantic factors account for much of the variance in associations between words (Osgood, Suci and Tannenbaum, 1957). These factors are evaluation, potency, and activity. Bipolar pairs of words—warm–cool, strong–weak, quick–slow, and so on—are used to construct a series of rating scales. These scales provide a standardised method of attributing characteristics to an entity. Evaluation is an important attribute of reputation for many sorts of entity, including people, commercial products, social movements and cities. Potency might be an important attribute in the reputation of political leaders or drugs. Activity might be an important attribute in the reputation of children or the elderly. Words change their meaning according to context, so care has to be taken in selecting relevant bipolar pairs of adjectives, in assigning them to their appropriate semantic category, and in assigning the positive and negative poles. It is possible to define semantic categories other than the three most often used (evaluation, potency, activity).

The Semantic Differential (Agrawal and Sharma, 1977) can be used to measure or compare public images. A Semantic Differential Test is easy to construct and administer. The method is well documented. The analysis is the same as

Table 16.1. Sets of bipolar semantic scales (see text for further details)

Evaluation	*Anxiety*
Fair–unfair	Afraid–unafraid
Clean–dirty	Anxious–calm
Good–bad	Disturbed–undisturbed
Honest–dishonest	Nervous–restful
Pleasant–unpleasant	Tense–relaxed
Positive–negative	Upset–quiet
Successful–unsuccessful	
Sweet–sour	*Potency*
Valuable–worthless	Hard–soft
Wise–foolish	Heavy–light
	Large–small
	Masculine–feminine
	Rugged–delicate
	Severe–lenient
	Strong–weak
Activity	Thick–thin
Active–passive	
Busy–lazy	*Familiarity*
Excitable–calm	Clear–confusing
Hot–cold	Familiar–unfamiliar
Impetuous–quiet	Predictable–unpredictable
Quick–slow	Simple–complex
Sharp–dull	Understandable–mysterious
Tense–relaxed	Usual–unusual

for other methods of rating. Its disadvantage, perhaps, is its limited theoretical basis.

Table 16.1 lists some bipolar semantic scales. It is obvious that, with the help of a thesaurus, other scales could be constructed. The problem, however, is to develop reliable and valid scales that are theoretically interesting or of practical use, for example leadership attribute scales (Chapter 8).

Behaviour Description Scales

Behaviour description scales are designed to minimise subjective judgements by getting observers to report what they observe, or rather to match an observed action with one of several options listed on a record form or coded for machine recording. Instruments devised for the observation of people and animals in natural settings, for example, use a keyboard or stylus to record each of several kinds of defined behaviour, their time of onset, and duration. Thus teachers can code a pupil's actions in specified situations, observers can code participants' contributions to a discussion or problem-solving task. Individuals can keep records of their own behaviour. Data collected in machine-readable form can then be analysed automatically.

Behaviour records are widely used in occupational settings, such as work study. The forms used for performance evaluation in occupational settings are designed to provide a summary account of the individual's performance and achievements. Teacher evaluation measures invite students to record their impressions of a teacher by responding to a list of performance characteristics. These characteristics are not actions in the strict sense, but achievements such as 'Maintains the interest of the class', 'Provides useful handouts' and 'Deals properly with students' problems'. In personality research, attempts have been made to define traits by the frequency of certain actions.

Behaviour records are clearly valuable, and are thought to be superior to judgements of a more subjective sort. They are, however, subject to errors and biases, especially if made unsystematically and unrepresentatively. Like other measures, behavioural measures are not ends in themselves but indices of whatever is under investigation—aggressiveness, competence, family relationships, or whatever.

The advantage of behavioural measures is that they can be used to test the extent to which measures based on reputation (collective, subjective estimates) provide a valid representation of the target entity. It is well known that subjective estimates are liable to various errors and distortions. The disadvantage of behavioural measures is that some interfere with the behaviour being observed, they are time-consuming and difficult to carry out.

Projective Tests

Projective tests present vague or ambiguous stimuli so that subjects have to draw on their imagination and feelings in making sense of them. Stimulus materials, such as the names or pictures of entities, could be used to elicit associations. Subjects could be asked to complete sentence stems (incomplete sentences) containing a reference to an entity. Their responses to such tests could be content-analysed. Free descriptions may involve some 'projection', i.e., self-revealing attributions, when subjects are not well acquainted with an entity.

Content Analysis

Content analysis is central to the study of reputation and will be dealt with here in some detail. Measures can be derived from a content analysis of ordinary language descriptions of people, organisations, products, events and other entities. The contents of descriptions are unitised, classified and counted. Content analysis is used to classify and measure the amount of space that newspapers and periodicals devote to an entity, or the amount of time occupied by it on radio or television. An exploratory study of newspaper coverage of the late Robert Maxwell showed considerable variations in the amount of space devoted to him, and in the numbers and kinds of attributions made, showing the typical reversed-J distribution. Such results show how much and what kinds of information and influence come from different sources. The types and amounts of media coverage are useful indices of reputation at a national level. Content analysis can be applied to archival documents in the study of reputations that have historical interest.

It is convenient to describe reputation by the main characteristics attributed to an entity by members of a defined group. Attributions are simply statements (words, phrases, sentences) that refer to the supposed characteristics of an entity. Persons can be described by their physical appearance, personality characteristics and social relationship; organisations can be described by their size, functions and management; products and services can be described by their price, function and reliability.

Content analysis is a procedure for identifying and classifying the characteristics attributed to entities. The results can be quantified, statistically analysed, and interpreted. Latent variables—variables not apparent in the surface structure of the data—can be identified. Content analysis has a wide range of applications—in advertising and propaganda, and in the social and behavioural sciences generally (George, 1959; Stone et al., 1966; Holsti, 1969; Ogilvie, Stone and Kelly, 1980; Rosengren, 1981; Weber, 1983; Gottschalk, Lolas and Vinex, 1986; Zuell, Weber and Mohler, 1989; Weber, 1990).

The basic aim is to sort the available data, for instance people's accounts of persons, organisations, products or services, into an exhaustive and exclusive set of categories. This means assigning every item to one category or another. This is often difficult. It may require a 'miscellaneous' category, and rules for dealing with items that can be assigned to more than one category.

Attributes can be assessed by examining documents—case-materials, letters, newspaper articles, transcripts of discussions, and so on. It is possible to apply content analysis to pictorial material—advertisements, films. Where attributions are elicited formally, by a check-list for example, the content categories are determined beforehand and are implicit in the items. This eliminates one major problem in content analysis, namely, classifying raw data, when there is little in the way of prior expectations about the sorts of data obtained from free descriptions or historical records, for example. Pilot inquiries provide useful guidance.

The amount of raw data available for content analysis is usually considerable— hundreds or thousands of units of analysis. The first step, therefore, is to reduce the data to manageable proportions. Texts can be coded (analysed) at various levels; single words, phrases, sentences; segments of text or paragraphs, or complete texts. The level adopted depends upon the purpose of the inquiry; the same material can be analysed at different levels. Computer software can be used to carry out complex analyses quickly and objectively once the data— continuous text or test responses—have been coded, and the procedures have been properly defined and carried out (Weinreich et al., 1989).

Texts usually have to be carefully edited before the analysis proper begins, especially if they are naturally occurring texts or transcripts of verbal accounts. This is because of individual differences in language usage—differences in fluency, vocabulary, grammar and style. The same attribution can be expressed in a variety of ways, and contextual factors alter the meaning of words and phrases. Editing is necessary because the referents of pronouns have to be identified, and because words and phrases may be used ironically. It follows that care taken at the editing stage reduces errors and distortions that would otherwise contaminate the text eventually converted into machine-readable form.

Current developments in computer software are making it possible to carry out sophisticated analyses of qualitative data. This gives greater descriptive precision. Computer software, such as the Micro-OCP (Oxford University Computing Service, 1988), the General Inquirer III (Zuell, Weber and Mohler, 1989), or Nudist 2.2 (Richards and Richards, 1991), will generate indexes, word-lists, concordances, word-counts, and other results from texts. Word-lists are useful as a preliminary step. They reveal the way words are distributed—their frequencies of occurrence over different data sources. High-frequency function words, such as 'of' or 'the', can be eliminated; attention can be focused on selected high-frequency content words. With the help of a thesaurus or other literary aids, investigators can identify synonyms, antonyms and other lexical relationships. There are special content-analysis dictionaries (see Bullard and Crossing, 1989; Zuell, Weber and Mohler, 1989; Weber, 1990) that show how words can be grouped under various headings, such as 'certainty', 'wealth', 'causality' and 'power'. This enables different investigators to use the same framework for their analyses.

Computer-assisted content analysis is advantageous in large-scale studies, and for longitudinal studies of serial changes, and repeated measures. One might wish to group or to separate different sets of data—from males and females, for example, or over different periods of time. Computer-assisted methods make it possible to develop complex cross-references that would otherwise be missed.

Words derive their meaning from the context in which they occur, so that concordances are essential for ascertaining word meanings, and making sections of text unambiguous. For example, the meaning of the word 'efficient' depends upon whether it is preceded by 'not' or 'very', or followed by 'at present' or 'at that time'. Key words in context (KWIC) are those that are important in giving the gist of a document, and occur frequently in the text as a whole.

The coding (classification) of data in content analysis depends upon having some initial understanding of or a theory about the material under examination. Different observers have different ideas about the sorts of categories needed, and particularly about the classification of individual items. This raises problems of reliability. Inter-coder reliability refers to the extent to which *different* coders code the same items in the same way. Intra-coder reliability refers to the extent to which the *same* coder codes the same items on different occasions.

When enough items have been assigned to a category, it is possible to compare the items within the category with each other. This makes it much easier to see the similarities and differences between them. Some items stand out as different from the others, and have to be moved to another category; or the category itself has to be subdivided. Sometimes, categories can be arranged hierarchically, with minor categories grouped into major categories. This may be necessary either to get the level of detail required, or to obtain a high level of reliability (Bilsbury, 1977).

It is often difficult to get reliable results in content analysis. Disagreements between coders have to be resolved in one way or another, preferably by reference to clear criteria and many agreed exemplars. This means setting up a standard coding scheme, an essential feature of content analysis. It is usually established by extensive pilot studies or through successive revisions of the scheme as the analysis progresses. The scheme finally arrived at should be explicit enough (defined and exemplified or completely catalogued) to enable other investigators to use it. Two or more different but valid schemes could produce compatible results.

One approach to construct validity for content analysis is to set up standards against which a particular analysis can be assessed (Holsti, 1969). For example, Davies et al. (1989) have compiled a dictionary of life-events that contains many life-events with specified characteristics (attributes). This helps to overcome some of the methodological difficulties associated with the study of ageing and life-stress. The Lasswell and Harvard dictionaries (Zuell, Weber and Mohler, 1989; Stone et al., 1966) attempt to deal with basic difficulties such as ambiguity, idioms and proper nouns; they make it possible to group together items that are superficially different but basically similar. For example, in a content analysis of personality descriptions, the phrases 'likes to be with people', 'enjoys the company of others' and 'friendly', could all be grouped under the category SOCIABLE. In a hierarchical scheme 'sociable' might be a subcategory of TRAITS, and 'traits' might be a subcategory of DISPOSITIONS. For corporate reputation, company addresses might be categorised as LOCATION, the number of male employees as MALE, the age structure of employees as AGE; these three categories might be grouped under DEMOGRAPHY. The main advantage of content dictionaries is that they provide different investigators with an accepted common framework, thus eliminating the need to invent another scheme.

It is not difficult to work out an *exhaustive* set of content categories. Difficulties arise with *exclusiveness*. For example, should 'likes people' be classified as MOTIVATION, TRAIT, HABIT or ATTITUDE? One has to lay down rules governing the assignment of items to categories; these rules define the kinds of item assigned to the various categories, or catalogues/dictionaries that list items under their appropriate heading. One may have to resort to split or multiple codings, which complicate the analysis.

We have seen that in free descriptions the attributes of personal reputation are often distributed as a reversed-J curve. The more frequently occurring attributes are easily identified in a content analysis. Some of the more interesting aspects of reputation, however, might be discernible in the less frequently occurring attributes. Low-frequency categories might suggest ways in which a reputation might develop, or a potential subreputation. Content categories that contain only a few items, however, are not useful from a statistical point of view. Two or more low-frequency categories can be combined into a larger single category, provided it can be made meaningful.

The results of a content analysis are not self-explanatory. They have to be related to the investigator's theoretical framework, although this can be simple and informal. The investigator usually has ideas about the effects of age, gender, socio-economic status and other subject variables, on the distribution of attributes, or ideas about the effects of experimental conditions. The methods used to collect data will certainly have some influence on the results. If the data are derived from diaries, dispatches, correspondence, or other documentary sources, the analysis would normally check for effects attributable to those sources, for example date, author and type.

The basic quantities in content analysis are 'counts' of the number of items falling into various categories. It is possible to weight items differently, but this requires a rationale. For example, words and phrases describing attributes can be weighted differently because of their importance or frequency.

Problems arise about the way counts are used in calculations—as absolute numbers or as proportions—and about the transformations required to meet statistical assumptions. For example, texts vary in length, so a word frequency of 50 in a text of 1000 words would be equal to 5%, whereas in a text of 500 words it would be equal to 10%. The means and variances of distributions of proportions are not independent, so an arcsine transformation is recommended.

Categories can be grouped into sets or themes. Themes are sometimes used at the outset to identify complex issues that are not apparent in short sections of text—for example themes to do with marketing policy, social relationships, performance or reliability. This means ignoring material irrelevant to the main themes. More usually, however, themes are defined as sets of categories.

Some interesting variables are not apparent in the surface structure of texts, or even in the descriptive statistics. These are latent variables—factors or clusters— that have to be extracted from the data by complex statistical manipulation.

The ultimate aim of content analysis in the study of reputation is to explain how and why a reputation has its particular content and structure.

Metric and Statistical Issues

Data obtained by psychological methods of measurement have limitations for statistical interpretation. Ratings, for example, may be distorted by range effects (Poulton, 1975), and by other response biases that affect level and spread (Cronbach, 1955). Cronbach (1958) described how data derived from studies in social perception could be analysed. Attribute variables may be related to each other in different ways, making it necessary to segregate or to combine them in order to avoid obscuring true effects and relationships. Effects may not be independent, for example those attributable to the 'difference' between two variables; and relationships between variables may not be linear. Unequal units of measurement and awkward distributions may introduce the need for transformations of scales. Combining the results obtained from different observers may conceal systematic effects associated with age, sex, personality or other demographic or 'subject' variables. Exploratory data analysis helps to identify the most appropriate statistical techniques.

References

Abelson, R. P., Kinder, D. R., Peters, M. D. and Fiske, S. T. (1982). 'Affective and semantic components in political person perception.' *Journal of Personality and Social Psychology*, **42**, 619–630.

Abrams, D. and Hogg, M. (eds) (1990). *Social Identity Theory*. Brighton: Harvester Wheatsheaf.

Adams-Webber, J. R. (1979). *Personal Construct Theory. Concepts and Applications*. Chichester: John Wiley.

Agrawal, K. G. and Sharma, B. R.(1977). 'Four traditional professions: a comparative study.' *Indian Educational Review*, **12**, 49–60.

Ajzen, I. (1988). *Attitudes, Personality and Behaviour*. Milton Keynes: Open University Press.

Ajzen, I. and Fishbein, M. (1980). *Understanding Attitudes and Predicting Social Behavior*. Englewood Cliffs, NJ: Prentice-Hall.

Albright, L., Kenny, D. A. and Malloy, T. E. (1988). 'Consensus in personality judgments at zero acquaintance.' *Journal of Personality and Social Psychology*, **55**, 387–395.

Allen, F. (1984). 'Reputation and product quality.' *RAND Journal of Economics*, **15**, 311–327.

Allport, G. W. (1937). *Personality*. London: Constable.

Allport, G. W. (1955). *Becoming: Basic Considerations for a Science of Personality*. New Haven, CT: Yale University Press.

Allport, G. W. and Odbert, H. S. (1936). 'Trait names: a psychological study.' *Psychological Monographs*, **41**, 1–211.

Allport, G. W. and Postman, L. J. (1947). *The Psychology of Rumour*. New York: Holt, Rinehart & Winston.

Argyle, M. (1975). *Bodily Communication*. London: Methuen.

Argyle, M. (ed) (1981). *Social Skills and Health*. London: Methuen.

Arluke, A. and Levin, J. (1984). 'Another stereotype: old age as second childhood.' *Aging*, No. 346, 7–11.

Arthur, G. L., Sisson, P. J. and McClung, C. E. (1977). 'Domestic disturbances: a major police dilemma, and how one major city is handling the problem.' *Journal of Police Science and Administration*, **5**, 421–429.

Bailey, F. G. (1971). *Gifts and Poisons: The Politics of Reputation*. Oxford: Basil Blackwell.

Banks, L. and Zil, J. S. (1980). 'Perverse polymorphic sociopathy in Ibsen's *Peer Gynt*.' *Corrective and Social Psychiatry and Journal of Behavior Technology, Methods and Therapy*, **26**, 168–171.

Barker, D. and Miller, D. (1990). 'Hurricane Gilbert: anthropomorphising a natural disaster.' *Area*, **22**, 107–116.

Barry, B. (1984). 'Perceptions of suicide.' *Death Education*, **8**, 17–25.

Bartlett, F. C.(1932). *Remembering*. Cambridge: Cambridge University Press.

Bartlett, J. (1980). *Familiar Quotations* (15th edn). London: Macmillan.

Baumeister, R. F. (1982a). 'Self-esteem, self-presentation, and future interaction: a dilemma of reputation.' *Journal of Personality*, **50**, 29–45.

Baumeister, R. F. (1982b) 'A self-presentational view of social phenomena.' *Psychological Bulletin*, **91**, 3–26.

Baumert, J., Maumann, J. and Roeder, P. M. (1990). 'Reputation—a hard-currency medium of interchange. A structural equation approach.' *Scientometrics*, **19**, 397–408.

Bearden, W. O. and Shimp, T. A. (1982). 'The use of extrinsic cues to facilitate product adoption.' *Journal of Marketing Research*, **19**, 229–239.

Bem, D. J. and Funder, D. C. (1978). 'Predicting more of the people more of the time: assessing the personality of situations.' *Psychological Review*, **85**, 485–501.

Benham, Sir G. (1948). *Benham's Book of Quotations, Proverbs and Household Words* (revised edn). London: Harrap.

Bennett, M. and Yeeles, C. (1990). 'Children's understanding of the self-presentational strategies of ingratiation and self-promotion'. *European Journal of Social Psychology*, **20**, 455–461.

Bernard, H. R., Johnsen, E. C., Killworth, P. D., McCarty, C., Shelley, G. A. and Robinson, S. (1990). 'Comparing four different methods for measuring personal social networks.' *Social Networks*, **12**, 179–216.

Bernard, H. R., Johnsen, E. C., Killworth, P. D. and Robinson, S. (1991). 'Estimating the size of an average personal network and of an event subpopulation—some empirical results.' *Social Science Research*, **20**, 109–121.

Bienenstock, E. J., Bonacich, P. and Oliver, M. (1990). 'The effect of network density and homogeneity on attitude polarization.' *Social Networks*, **12**, 153–172.

Biggs, S. J., Rosen, B. and Summerfield, A. B. (1980). 'Video-feedback and personal attribution in anorexic, depressed and normal viewers.' *British Journal of Medical Psychology*, **53**, 249–254.

Bilsbury, C. D. (1977). 'Person perception in educationally subnormal children.' Liverpool: University of Liverpool, unpublished Ph.D. thesis.

Block, J. (1978, originally 1961). *The Q-Sort Method in Personality Assessment and Psychiatric Research*. Palo Alto, CA: Consulting Psychologists Press.

Bloom, L. J., Schroeder, D. H. and Babineau, W. (1981). 'Reputation, training, fee, and androgyny: their comparative effects on impressions of therapist credibility.' *Journal of Clinical Psychology*, **37**, 90–95.

Boissevain, J. (1974). *Friends of Friends: Networks, Manipulators and Coalitions*. Oxford: Basil Blackwell.

Bond, C. F. (1982). 'Social facilitation: a self-presentational view.' *Journal of Personality and Social Psychology*, **42**, 1042–1050.

Bond, M. H., Chiu, C. and Wan, K. (1984). 'When modesty fails: the social impact of group-effacing attributions following success or failure.' *European Journal of Social Psychology*, **14**, 335–338.

Bowers, T. A. and Pugh, R. C. (1973). 'Factors underlying college choice by students and parents.' *Journal of College Student Personnel*, **14**, 220–224.

Breaugh, J. A., Klimoski, R. J. and Shapiro, M. B. (1980). 'Third-party characteristics and intergroup conflict resolution.' *Psychological Reports*, **47**, 447–451.

Brieland, D. (1952). 'A variation of the "Guess Who" technique for the study of the adjustment of children.' *Journal of Educational Research*, **45**, 385–390.

Brody, R. A. (1991). *Assessing the President—The Media, Elite Opinion, and Public Support*. Stanford: Stanford University Press.

Bromley, D. B. (1977). *Personality Description in Ordinary Language*. Chichester: John Wiley.

Bromley, D. B. (1986). *The Case-Study Method in Psychology and Related Disciplines*. Chichester: John Wiley.

Broughton, R. (1990). 'The prototype concept in personality assessment'. *Canadian Psychology*, **31**, 26–37.

Bryman, A. (1992). *Charisma and Leadership in Organizations*. London: Sage.

Bullard, C. G. and Crossing, E. E. M. (1989). 'Validation of the General Inquirer Harvard IV Dictionary.' In C. Zuell, R. P. Weber and P. Mohler (eds), *Computer-assisted Text Analysis for the Social Sciences: The General Inquirer III*. Mannheim, FRG: Center for Surveys, Methods, and Analysis (ZUMA).

Burroughs, W. J., Drews, D. R. and Hallman, W. K. (1991). 'Predicting personality from personal possessions—a self-presentational analysis.' *Journal of Social Behavior and Personality*, **6**, 147–164.

Burt, M. R. and Albin, R. S. (1981). 'Rape myths, rape definitions, and probability of conviction.' *Journal of Applied Social Psychology*, **11**, 212–230.

Burt, R. S. (1982). *Toward a Structural Theory of Action: Network Models of Social Structure, Perceptions and Action*. New York: Academic Press.

Burt, R. S. (1990). 'Detecting role equivalence.' *Social Networks*, **12**, 83–97.

Burt, R. S. and Minor, M. J. (eds) (1982). *Applied Network Analysis: Structural Methodology for Empirical Social Research*. Beverly Hills, CA: Sage.

Buss, D. M. and Craik, K. H. (1983a). 'The dispositional analysis of everyday conduct.' *Journal of Personality*, **51**, 393–412.

Buss, D. M. and Craik, K. H. (1983b). 'The act frequency approach to personality.' *Psychological Review*, **90**, 105–126.

Buss, D. M. and Dedden, L. A. (1990). 'Derogation of competitors.' *Journal of Social and Personal Relationships*, **7**, 395–422.

Byrne, R. W. and Whiten, A. (eds) (1988). *Machiavellian Intelligence: Social Expertise and the Evolution of Intellect in Monkeys, Apes and Humans*. Oxford: Clarendon Press.

Caldwell, D. F., Chatman, J. A. and O'Reilly, C. A. (1990). 'Building organizational commitment: a multi-firm study.' *Journal of Occupational Psychology*, **63**, 245–262.

Carter-Ruck, P. F. and Walker, R. (1985). *Carter-Ruck on Libel and Slander* (3rd edn). London: Butterworth.

Center, A. H. and Walsh, F. E. (1981). *Public Relations Practices: Case Studies* (2nd edn). Englewood Cliffs, NJ: Prentice-Hall.

Chan, K. K. and Misra, S. (1990). 'Characteristics of opinion leaders—a new dimension.' *Journal of Advertising*, **19**, 53–60.

Cheek, J. M. (1982). 'Aggregation, moderator variables, and the validity of personality tests: a peer-rating study.' *Journal of Personality and Social Psychology*, **43**, 1254–1269.

Chen, C. C. and Meindl, J. R. (1991). 'The construction of leadership images in the popular press: the case of Donald Burr and People Express.' *Administrative Science Quarterly*, **36**, 521–551.

Cialdini, R. B., Borden, R. J., Thorner, A., Walker, M. R., Freeman, S. and Sloan, L. R. (1976). 'Basking in reflected glory: three (football) field studies.' *Journal of Personality and Social Psychology*, **34**, 366–375.

Coleman, S. R. (1982). 'B. F. Skinner: systematic iconoclast.' *Gamut*, **6**, 53–75.

Conger, J. A. (1989). *The Charismatic Leader—Behind the Mystique of Exceptional Leadership*. San Francisco: Jossey-Bass.

Cooley, C. H. (1922). *Human Nature and the Social Order*. New York: Scribner.

Cooley, R. S. and Seeman, J. (1979). 'Personality integration and social schemata.' *Journal of Personality*, **47**, 288–304.

Coopers & Lybrand Deloitte (1991). *London: World City. Summary Report*. London: Coopers & Lybrand Deloitte.

Cottle, S. (1991). 'Reporting the Rushdie affair: a case study in the orchestration of public opinion.' *Race & Class*, **32**, 45–64.

Covington, M. V., Spratt, M. F. and Omelich, C. L. (1980). 'Is effort enough, or does diligence count too? Student and teacher reactions to effort stability in failure.' *Journal of Educational Psychology*, **72**, 717–729.

Craik, K. H. (1985). 'Multiple perceived personalities: a neglected consistency issue.' In E. E. Roskam (ed), *Measurement and Personality Assessment*. New York: Elsevier (North Holland).

Craik, K. H. (1986). 'Personality research methods: an historical perspective.' *Journal of Personality*, **54**, 18–51.

Craik, K. H. (1989). 'Personality and reputation: a conceptual re-examination.' Berkeley, CA: University of California, draft mimeo.

Crick, B. (1980). *George Orwell: A Life*. London: Secker & Warburg.

Cronbach, L. J. (1955). 'Processes affecting scores on "understanding of others" and "assumed similarity".' *Psychological Bulletin*, **52**, 177–193.

Cronbach, L. J. (1958). 'Proposals leading to the analytic treatment of social perception scores.' In Tagiuri, R. and Petrullo, L. (eds), *Personal Perception and Interpersonal Behaviour*. Stanford: Stanford University Press.

Cronbach, L. J. and Gleser, G. C. (1953). 'Assessing similarity between profiles.' *Psychological Bulletin*, **50**, 456–474.

Cronshaw, S. F. and Ellis, R. J. (1991). 'A process investigation of self-monitoring and leader emergence.' *Small Group Research*, **22**, 403–420.

Crowne, D. P. and Marlowe, D. (1964). *The Approval Motive: Studies in Evaluative Dependence*. New York: John Wiley.

Danheiser, P. R. and Graziano, W. G. (1982). 'Self-monitoring and cooperation as a self-presentation strategy.' *Journal of Personality and Social Psychology*, **42**, 497–505.

Davies, A. D. M., Wilkinson, S. J., James, O. and Newton, J. T. (1989). 'Life stress in the elderly: a dictionary of life events and difficulties.' Liverpool: University of Liverpool, Department of Psychology, unpublished ms.

Davis, D. L. (1984). 'Medical misinformation: communication between outport Newfoundland women and their physicians.' *Social Science and Medicine*, **18**, 273–278.

Davis, M. (1992). 'Goodwill accounting—time for an overhaul.' *Journal of Accounting*, **173**, 75–86.

Davison, W. P. (1983). 'The third-person effect in communication.' *Public Opinion Quarterly*, **47**, 1–15.

Deluga, R. J. (1991). 'The relationship of upward-influencing behavior with subordinate-impression management characteristics.' *Journal of Applied Social Psychology*, **21**, 1145–1160.

DePaulo, B. M., Kenny, D. A., Hoover, C. W., Webb, W. and Oliver, P. V. (1987). 'Accuracy of person perception: do people know what kinds of impressions they convey?' *Journal of Personality and Social Psychology*, **52**, 303–315.

Diamond, D. W. (1991). 'Monitoring and reputation: the choice between bank loans and directly placed debt.' *Journal of Political Economy*, **99**, 689–721.

Doig, A. (1990). *Westminster Babylon: Sex, Money and Scandal in British Politics*. London: W. H. Allen (Allison & Busby).

Dorn, P. J. (1986). 'Gender and personhood: Turkish Jewish proverbs and the politics of reputation.' *Women's Studies International Forum*, **9**, 295–301.

Duncan, C. B. (1966). 'A reputation test of personality integration.' *Journal of Personality and Social Psychology*, **3**, 516–524.

Durkheim, E. (1898). 'Individual and collective representations.' In E. Durkheim, *Sociology and Philosophy* [D. F. Pocock, trans, 1965]. London: Cohen & West.

Dyer, G. (1982). *Advertising as Communication*. London: Routledge.

East, R. (1990). 'Advertising and sales.' *The Psychologist*, August, 362–364.

Easterby-Smith, M. (1980). 'The design, analysis and interpretation of repertory grids.' *International Journal of Man-Machine Studies*, 13(1), 3–24.

Eiser, J. R. (1990). *Social Judgement*. Milton Keynes: Open University Press.

Ekman, P. (1985). *Telling Lies*. New York: Norton.

Ekman, P. and Friesen, W. V. (1974). 'Detecting deception from the body or face.' *Journal of Personality and Social Psychology*, 29, 288–298.

Ekman, P. and Friesen, W. V. (1975). *Unmasking the Face*. Englewood Cliffs, NJ: Prentice-Hall.

Emler, N. (1984). 'Differential involvement in delinquency: toward an interpretation in terms of reputation management.' In B. A. Maher and W. B. Maher (eds), *Progress in Experimental Personality Research*, vol 13. New York: Academic Press.

Emler, N. (1990). 'A social psychology of reputation.' In W. Stroebe and M. Hewstone (eds), *European Review of Social Psychology*, vol 1. Chichester: John Wiley.

Emler, N. (1992). 'The truth about gossip.' *Social Psychology Section Newsletter*, Number 27. Leicester: British Psychological Society.

Engel, J. F., Blackwell, R. D. and Miniard, P. W. (1986). *Consumer Behavior* (5th edn). Chicago, IL: Dryden Press.

Ericsson, K. and Simon, H. A. (1984). *Protocol Analysis: Verbal Reports as Data*. Cambridge, MA: MIT Press.

Erikson, R. S. (1990). 'Roll calls, reputations, and representation in the U.S. Senate.' *Legislative Studies Quarterly*, XV, 623–642.

Esfahani, H. S. (1991). 'Reputation and uncertainty. Toward an explanation of quality problems in competitive LDC markets.' *Journal of Developmental Economics*, 35, 1–32.

Farr, R. and Moscovici, S. (eds) (1984). *Social Representations*, Cambridge: Cambridge University Press.

Faulks Committee (1975) *Legal Aspects of Reputation, Report of the Committee on Defamation. Cmnd. 5909*. London: HMSO.

Feldman, D. C. and Klich, N. R. (1991). 'Impression management and career strategies.' In R. A. Giacalone and P. Rosenfeld, (eds), *Applied Impression Management. How Image-making Affects Managerial Decisions*. London: Sage.

Fiedler, F. E. (1967). *A Theory of Leadership Effectiveness*. New York: McGraw-Hill.

Fielding, N. G. and Lee, R. M. (eds) (1991). *Using Computers in Qualitative Research*. London: Sage.

Firth, M. (1990). 'Auditor reputation: the impact of critical reports issued by government inspectors.' *RAND Journal of Economics*, 21, 374–387.

Fischer, C. S. (1982). *To Dwell Among Friends: Personal Networks in Town and City*. Chicago, IL: University of Chicago Press.

Fischer, M. D. and Finkelstein, A. (1991). 'Social knowledge representation: a case-study.' In N. G. Fielding and R. M. Lee (eds), *Using Computers in Qualitative Research*. London: Sage.

Fiske, A. P., Haslam, N. and Fiske, S. T. (1991). 'Confusing one person with another— what errors reveal about the elementary forms of social relations.' *Journal of Personality and Social Psychology*, 60, 656–674.

Fiske, S. T. and Taylor, S. E. (1991). *Social Cognition* (2nd edn). New York: McGraw-Hill.

Fombrun, C. J. and Abrahamson, E. (1990). 'Producing cognitive environments: the macro-cultures of business communities.' New York: New York University, Graduate School of Business, Working Paper (mimeo).

Fombrun, C. J. and Ginsberg, A. (1990). 'Shifting gears: enabling change in corporate aggressiveness.' *Strategic Management Journal*, 11, 297–308.

Fombrun, C. J. and Shanley, M. (1990). 'Keeping score: institutional assessments of corporate performance.' New York: New York University, Graduate School of Business, Working Paper (mimeo).

Fombrun, C. J. and Shanley, M. (1990). 'What's in a name? Reputation building and corporate strategy.' *Academy of Management Journal*, **33**, 233–258.

Footman, R. (1986). 'How the world has changed. The public image of the universities 1961–1986.' In S. Bosworth, *Beyond the Limelight*. Reading: University of Reading, Conference of University Administrators.

Fox, R. (1977). 'Suicide prevention in Great Britain.' *Mental Health and Society*, **4**, 74–79.

Fraser, C. and Gaskell, G. (1990). *The Social Psychological Study of Widespread Beliefs*. Oxford: Clarendon Press.

Fuhrman, R. W., Bodenhausen, G. V. and Lichtenstein, M. (1989). *Research Methods, Instruments & Computers*, **21**, 587–597.

Funder, D. C. (1980). 'On seeing ourselves as others see us: self-other agreement and discrepancy in personality ratings.' *Journal of Personality*, **48**, 473–493.

Funder, D. C. (1987). 'Errors and mistakes: evaluating the accuracy of social judgment.' *Psychological Bulletin*, **101**, 75–90.

Funder, D. C. and Colvin, C. R. (1988). 'Friends and strangers: acquaintanceship, agreement, and the accuracy of personality judgment.' *Journal of Personality and Social Psychology*, **55**, 149–158.

Galam, S. and Moscovici, S. (1991). 'Towards a theory of collective phenomena: consensus and attitude change in groups.' *European Journal of Social Psychology*, **21**, 49–74.

Galton, F. (1869). *Hereditary Genius: An Inquiry into Its Laws and Consequences*. London: Macmillan.

Gangestead, S. and Snyder, M. (1985). '"To carve nature at its joints": on the existence of discrete classes in personality.' *Psychological Review*, **92**, 317–349.

George, A. L. (1959). *Propaganda Analysis*. Evanston: Row, Peterson.

Gergen, K. J., Hepburn, A. and Comer, D. (1986). 'The hermeneutics of personality description.' *Journal of Personality and Social Psychology*, **6**, 1261–1270.

Gerth, H. H. and Mills, C. W. (eds) (1991). *From Max Weber: Essays in Sociology*. London: Routledge.

Ghiselli, E. E., Campbell, J. P. and Zedeck, S. (1981). *Measurement Theory for the Behavioral Sciences*. San Francisco: W. H. Freeman.

Giacalone, R. A. and Riordan, C. A. (1990). 'Effect of self-presentation on perceptions and recognition in an organization.' *Journal of Psychology*, **124**, 25–38.

Giacalone, R. A. and Rosenfeld, P. (eds) (1989). *Impression Management in the Organization*. Hillsdale, NJ: Lawrence Erlbaum.

Giacalone, R. A. and Rosenfeld, P. (eds) (1991). *Applied Impression Management. How Image-Making Affects Managerial Decisions*. London: Sage.

Gilbert, G. R., Collins, R. W. and Brenner, R. (1990). 'Age and leadership effectiveness: from the perceptions of the follower.' *Human Resources Management*, **29**, 187–196.

Gioia, D. A. and Sims, H. P. (1983). 'Perceptions of managerial power as a consequence of managerial behavior and reputation.' *Journal of Management*, **9**, 7–26.

Glassman, R. M. and Swatos, W. H. Jr. (eds) (1986). *Charisma, History, and Social Structure*. New York: Greenwood Press.

Goffman, E. (1959). *The Presentation of Self in Everyday Life*. New York: Doubleday.

Goffman, E. (1963). *Behavior in Public Places*. Oxford: Basil Blackwell.

Goldberg, M. E. and Hartwick, J. (1990). 'The effects of advertiser reputation and extremity of advertising claim on advertising effectiveness.' *Journal of Consumer Research*, **17**, 172–179.

Golden, C. J., Kuperman, S. K. and Osmon, D. C. (1980). 'Productivity ratings of psychology programs based on publications in clinical journals.' *Professional Psychology*, **11**, 797–806.

Gottschalk, L. A., Lolas, F. and Vinex, L. L. (eds) (1986). *Content Analysis of Verbal Behavior*. New York: Springer-Verlag.

Goumaz, G. (1982). 'The social integration of the mentally handicapped child.' *Early Child Development and Care*, **8**, 131–145.

Graber, D. A. (1988). *Processing the News* (2nd edn). White Plains, NY: Longman.

Gregory, A. (1980). 'Why do scientists engage in fraud?' *Parapsychology Review*, **11**, 1–6.

Guillebeaux, F., Storm, C. L. and Demaris, A.(1986). 'Luring the reluctant male: a study of males participating in marriage and family therapy.' *Family Therapy*, **13**, 215–225.

Gunther, A. (1991). 'What others think. Cause and consequence in the third-person effect.' *Communication Research*, **18**, 355–372.

Haas-Wilson, D. (1990). 'Consumer information and providers' reputations. An empirical test in the market for psychotherapy.' *Journal of Health Economics*, **9**, 321–333.

Hamilton, D. L. (1992). 'Perceiving persons and groups.' Paper presented at the annual conference of the British Psychological Society, Scarborough, UK, April 1992.

Harrop, M. (1990). 'Political marketing.' *Parliamentary Affairs: A Journal of Comparative Politics*, **43**, 277–291.

Hartshorne, H., May, M. A. and Shuttleworth, F. K. (1930). *Studies in the Nature of Character,* vol 3. *Studies in the Organization of Character*. New York: Macmillan.

Hastie, R., Ostrom, T. M., Ebbesen, E. B., Wyer, R. S. Jr., Hamilton, D.L. and Carlston, D. E. (eds) (1980). *Person Memory: The Cognitive Basis of Social Perception*. Hillsdale, NJ: Lawrence Erlbaum.

Hearnshaw, L. S. (1979). *Cyril Burt: Psychologist*. London: Hodder & Stoughton.

Henry, E. O. (1977). 'A North Indian healer and the sources of his power.' *Social Science and Medicine*, **11**, 309–317.

Hepworth, M. (1975). *Blackmail. Publicity and Secrecy in Everyday Life*. London: Routledge & Kegan Paul.

Hewstone, M. (1989). *Causal Attribution. From Cognitive Processes to Collective Beliefs*. Oxford: Basil Blackwell.

Holsti, O. R. (1969). *Content Analysis for the Social Sciences and Humanities*. Reading, MA: Addison-Wesley.

House, R. J., Spangler, W. D. and Woycke, J. (1991). 'Personality and charisma in the United-States Presidency: A psychological theory of leader effectiveness.' *Administrative Science Quarterly*, **36**, 364–396.

Howard, G. S., Cole, D. A. and Maxwell, S. E. (1987). 'Research productivity in psychology based on publication in the journals of the American Psychological Association.' *American Psychologist*, **42**, 975–986.

Huey, J. (1991). 'The best cities for business.' *Fortune International*, **124** (11), 4 November, 38–62.

Hultberg, P. (1988). 'Shame: a hidden emotion.' *Journal of Analytical Psychology*, **33**, 109–126.

Hutton, C. (1986). 'America's most admired corporations.' *Fortune International*, **113** (1), 6 January, 32–43.

Huxley, A. (1932). *Brave New World*. London: Chatto & Windus.

Ichheiser, G. (1943–44). 'Misinterpretations of personality in everyday life and the psychologist's frame of reference.' *Character and Personality*, **12**, 145–160.

Ichheiser, G. (1949–50). 'Misunderstandings in human relations. A study in false social perception.' *American Journal of Sociology*, **55** (suppl), viii + 70.

Ickes, W. J., Reidhead, S. and Patterson, M. (1986). 'Machiavellianism and self-monitoring: as different as "me" and "you".' *Social Cognition*, **4**, 58–74.

James, W. (1890). *The Principles of Psychology*, vol. 1. London: Macmillan.

Jaspars, J., Fincahm, F. D. and Hewstone, M. (1983). *Attribution Theory and Research: Conceptual, Developmental and Social Dimensions*. New York: Academic Press.

Johnson, A. M. (1990). 'The "Only joking" defense: attribution bias or impression management?' *Psychological Reports*, **67**(R1), 1051–1056.

Jones, E. E. (1990). *Interpersonal Perception*. New York: W. H. Freeman.

Jones, E. E. and Pittman, T. (1982). 'Toward a general theory of strategic self-presentation.' In J. Suls (ed.). *Psychological Perspectives on the Self*. Hillsdale, NJ: Lawrence Erlbaum.

Jones, E. E., Schwarts, J. and Gilbert, D. T. (1983–84). 'Perceptions of moral-expectancy violation: the role of expectancy source.' *Social Cognition*, **2**, 273–293.

Jones, M. C. (1958). 'A study of socialization patterns at the high school level.' *The Journal of Genetic Psychology*, **93**, 87–111.

Kadushin, C. (1968). 'Power, influence, and social circles: a new methodology for studying opinion makers.' *American Sociological Review*, **33**, 685–699.

Kahneman, D., Slovic, P. and Tversky, A. (eds) (1982). *Judgement Under Uncertainty: Heuristics and Biases*. Cambridge: Cambridge University Press.

Kanekar, S., Nanji, V. J., Kolsawalla, M. B. and Mukerji, G. S. (1981). 'Perception of an aggressor and a victim of aggression as a function of sex and retaliation.' *Journal of Social Psychology*, **114**, 139–140.

Kaplan, R. E. (1984). 'Trade routes: the manager's network of relationships.' *Organizational Dynamics*, **12**, 37–52.

Keen, C. and Greenall, J. (1987). *Public Relations Management: In Colleges, Polytechnics and Universities*. Banbury: Heist Publications.

Kelley, H. (1991). 'Unwed mothers and household reputation in a Spanish Galician community.' *American Ethnologist*, **18**, 565–580.

Kelly, G. A. (1955). *The Psychology of Personal Constructs*. New York: Norton.

Kenny, D. A. and Albright, L. (1987). 'Accuracy in interpersonal perception: a social relations analysis.' *Psychological Bulletin*, **102**, 390–402.

Kenny, D. A. and LaVoie, L. (1984). 'The social relations model.' In L. Berkowitz (ed), *Advances in Experimental Social Psychology*, vol 18. Orlando, FL: Academic Press.

Kenrick, D. T. and Funder, D. C. (1988). 'Profiting from controversy: lessons from the person–situation debate.' *American Psychologist*, **43**, 23–34.

Kerlinger, F. N. (1986). *Foundations of Behavioral Research*. New York: Holt, Rinehart & Winston.

Kimmel, A. J. and Keefer, R. (1991). 'Psychological correlates of the transmission and acceptance of rumours about AIDS.' *Journal of Applied Social Psychology*, **21**, 1608–1628.

Kinder, D.R. and Fiske, S. T. (1986). 'Presidents in the public mind.' In M. G. Herman (ed), *Handbook of Political Psychology*. San Francisco: Jossey-Bass.

Kinder, D. R., Peters, M. D., Abelson, R. P. and Fiske, S. T. (1980). 'Presidential prototypes.' *Political Behavior*, **2**, 315–337.

King, D. G. and Blaney, P. H. (1977). 'Effectiveness of A and B therapists with schizophrenics and neurotics: a referral study.' *Journal of Consulting and Clinical Psychology*, **45**, 407–411.

Kline, P. (1986). *A Handbook of Test Construction*. London: Methuen.

Klion, R. E. and Leitner, L. M. (1991). 'Impression formation and construct system organization.' *Social Behavior and Personality*, **19**, 87–98.

Knight, S. (1984). *The Brotherhood: The Secret World of the Freemasons*. London: Granada.

Knoke, D. and Kuklinski, J. H. (1982). *Network Analysis*. Beverly Hills, CA: Sage.

Kwon, Y.-H. (1990). 'Brand name awareness and image perception of women's daytime apparel.' *Perceptual and Motor Skills*, **71**, 743–752.

Kydd, C. T., Ogilvie, J. R. and Slade, L. A. (1990). '"I don't care what they say, as long as they spell my name right." Publicity, reputation and turnover.' *Group and Organization Studies*, **15**, 53–74.

LaBarbera, M. and Wolfe, T. (1983). 'Characteristics, attitudes and implications of fentanyl use based on reports from self-identified fentanyl users.' *Journal of Psychoactive Drugs*, **15**, 293–301.

LaBarbera, P. A. (1982). 'Overcoming a no-reputation liability through documentation and advertising regulation.' *Journal of Marketing Research*, **19**, 223–228.

Lang, G. E. and Lang, K. (1990). *The Building and Survival of Artistic Reputation.* Chapel Hill, NC: University of North Carolina Press.

Lazar, A. L. (1973). 'Reasons cited by college students in teacher training for taking an elective course on the education of the gifted.' *Gifted Child Quarterly*, **17**, 274–278.

Lehman, H. C. (1953). *Age and Achievement.* London: Oxford University Press.

Leventhal, L., Abrami, P. C. and Perry, R. P. (1976). 'Do teacher rating forms reveal as much about students as about teachers?' *Journal of Educational Psychology*, **68**, 441–445.

Leventhal, L., Abrami, P. C., Perry, R. P. and Breen, L. J. (1975). 'Section selection in multi-section courses: implications for the validation and use of teacher rating forms.' *Educational and Psychological Measurement*, **35**, 885–895.

Lewis, K. N. and Lewis, D. A. (1985). 'Pretherapy information, counselor influence, and value similarity: impact on female clients.' *Counseling and Values*, **29**, 151–163.

Lewis, T. H. (1974). 'An Indian healer's preventive medicine procedure.' *Hospital and Community Psychiatry*, **25**, 94–95.

Lindholm, C. (1990). *Charisma.* Oxford: Blackwell.

Little, W., Fowler, H. W. and Onions, C. T. (1984). *The Shorter Oxford English Dictionary on Historical Principles*, (3rd edn). Oxford: Clarendon Press.

Littrell, J. M., Caffrey, P. and Hopper, G. C. (1987). 'Counselor's reputation: an important precounseling variable for adolescents.' *Journal of Counseling Psychology*, **34**, 228–231.

Livesley, W. J. and Bromley, D. B. (1973). *Person Perception in Childhood and Adolescence.* Chichester: John Wiley.

Lodge, M. (1981). *Magnitude Scaling. Quantitative Measurement of Opinions.* Beverly Hills, CA: Sage.

Long, S. O. (1984). 'The sociocultural context of nursing in Japan.' *Culture, Medicine and Psychiatry*, **8**, 141–163.

Longmore, P. K. (1988). *The Invention of George Washington.* Berkeley, CA: University of California Press.

Lord, C. G., Desforges, D. M., Chacon, S., Pere, G. and Clubb, R. (1992). 'Reflections on reputation in the process of self-evaluation.' *Social Cognition*, **10**, 2–29.

Louviere, J. J. (1988). *Analyzing Decision Making: Metric Conjoint Analysis.* Beverley Hills, CA: Sage.

Lukes, S. (1973). *Individualism.* Oxford: Basil Blackwell.

Lumpkin, J. R. (1984). 'The effect of retirement versus age on the shopping orientations of older consumers.' *Gerontologist*, **24**, 622–627.

Lydenberg, S. D., Marlin, A. T. and Strub, S. O. (1986). *Rating America's Corporate Conscience.* Reading, MA: Addison-Wesley.

Lynch, J. G. Jr., Chakravarti, D. and Mitra, A. (1991). 'Contrast effects in consumer judgments: changes in mental representations or in the anchoring of rating scales?' *Journal of Consumer Research*, **18**, 284–297.

McKinlay, A. and Potter, J. (1987). 'Social representations: a conceptual critique.' *Journal of the Theory of Social Behaviour*, **17**, 471–488.

McLaughlin, G. W. and Butler, R. P. (1973). 'Perceived importance of various job characteristics by West Point graduates.' *Personnel Psychology*, **26**, 351–358.

McNeil, K. and Miller, R. E. (1980). 'The profitability of consumer protection: warranty policy in the auto industry.' *Administrative Science Quarterly*, **25**, 407–427.

Maddi, S. R. (1980). *Personality Theories: A Comparative Analysis* (4th edn). Homewood, IL: Dorsey Press.

Magnusson, D., Bergman, L. B., Rudinger, G. and Torestad, B. (eds) (1991). *Problems and Methods in Longitudinal Research—Stability and Change*. Cambridge: Cambridge University Press.

Manstead, A. S. R. and Semin, G. R. (1981). 'Social transgressions, social perspectives, and social emotionality.' *Motivation and Emotion*, **5**, 249–261.

Martink, M. J. (1991). 'Future directions: toward a model for applying impression management strategies in the workplace.' In R. A. Giacalone and P. Rosenfeld (eds), *Applied Impression Management. How Image-Making Affects Managerial Decisions*. London: Sage.

Masson, J. M. (1985). *The Assault on Truth. Freud's Suppression of the Seduction Theory*. Harmondsworth: Penguin.

Masten, A. S. (1986). 'Humor and competence in school-aged children.' *Child Development*, **57**, 461–473.

Masten, A. S., Morison, P. and Pellegrini, D. S. (1985). 'A revised class play method of peer assessment.' *Developmental Psychology*, **21**, 523–533.

Maute, M. F. and Forrester, W. R. Jr. (1991). 'The effect of attribute qualities on consumer decision making: a causal model of external information search.' *Journal of Economic Psychology*, **12**, 643–666.

May, M. A. (1932). 'Foundations of personality.' In P. S. Achilles (ed). *Psychology at Work*. New York: McGraw-Hill.

Mead, G. H. (1934). *Mind, Self, and Society*. Chicago, IL: University of Chicago Press.

Meehl, P. E. (1954). *Clinical Versus Statistical Prediction*. Minneapolis: University of Minnesota Press.

Middleton, D. and Edwards, D. (eds) (1990). *Collective Remembering*. London: Sage.

Milgram, S. (1974). 'The small-world problem.' In J. B. Maas, *Readings in 'Psychology Today'*. Del Mar, CA: CRM Books.

Milgrom, P. and Roberts, J. (1982). 'Predation, reputation, and entry deterrence.' *Journal of Economic Theory*, **27**, 280–312.

Miller, A. H. (1990). 'Public judgments of Senate and House candidates.' *Legislative Studies Quarterly*, **XV**(4), 525–542.

Misra, S. and Beatty, S. E. (1990). 'Celebrity spokesperson and brand congruence. An assessment of recall and affect.' *Journal of Business Research*, **21**, 159–173.

Moreno, J. L. (1934). *Who Shall Survive? Foundations of Sociometry, Group Psychotherapy, and Sociodrama*. Washington, DC: Nervous and Mental Disease Monograph, No. 58.

Morrant, J. C. (1985). 'In defence of Sigmund Freud against Masson's charge of cowardice.' *Canadian Journal of Psychiatry*, **30**, 395–399.

Morrison, E. W. and Bies, R. J. (1991). 'Impression management in the feedback-seeking process—a literature review and research agenda.' *Academic Management Review*, **16**, 522–541.

Newland, R. A. (1972). *Only Half a Democracy*. London: Electoral Reform Society.

Nisbett, R. and Ross, L. (1980). *Human Inference: Strategies and Shortcomings of Social Judgment*. Englewood Cliffs, NJ: Prentice-Hall.

Nokes, G. D. (1957). *Cockle's Cases and Statutes on Evidence* (9th edn). London: Sweet & Maxwell.

Ogilvie, D. M., Stone, P. J. and Kelly, E. F. (1980). 'Computer-aided content analysis.' In R. B. Smith and P. K. Manning (eds), *Handbook of Social Science Research Methods*. New York: Irvington.

Ohanian, R. (1991). 'The impact of celebrity spokespersons' perceived image on consumers' intention to purchase.' *Journal of Advertising Research*, **31**, 46–54.

Olins, W. (1978). *The Corporate Personality. An Inquiry into the Nature of Corporate Identity*. London: Design Council.

Olins, W. (1990). *Corporate Identity: Making Business Strategy Visible Through Design*. New York: McGraw-Hill.

Olson, K. R. and Johnson, D. C. (1991). 'Individual differences in self-presentational styles.' *Journal of Social Psychology*, **131**, 495–510.

Orley, J. (1976). 'The use of grid technique in social anthropology.' In P. Slater (ed), *Explorations of Intrapersonal Space: The Measurement of Intrapersonal Space by Grid Technique*. London: John Wiley.

Orpen, C. and Bush, R. (1974). 'The lack of congruence between self-concept and public image.' *Journal of Social Psychology*, **93**, 145–146.

O'Shaughnessy, N. (1989). *The Phenomenon of Political Marketing*. Basingstoke: Macmillan.

Osgood, C. E., Suci, G. J. and Tannenbaum, P. H. (1957). *The Measurement of Meaning*. Urbana: University of Illinois Press.

Oskamp, S. (1991). *Attitudes and Opinions* (2nd edn). London: Prentice-Hall.

Over, R. (1982). 'The durability of scientific reputation.' *Journal of the History of the Behavioral Sciences*, **18**, 53–61.

Oxford University Computing Service (1988). *Micro-OCP*. Oxford: Oxford University Press.

Oxford University Press (1979). *The Oxford Dictionary of Quotations* (3rd edn). Oxford: Oxford University Press.

Park, B. (1986). 'A method for studying the development of impressions of real people.' *Journal of Personality and Social Psychology*, **51**, 907–917.

Parker, H. J. and Chan, F. (1986). 'Prestige of allied health professionals: perceptions of occupational and physical therapists.' *Occupational Therapy Journal of Research*, **6**, 247–250.

Peretti, P. O., Brown, S. and Richards, P. (1979). 'Perceived value-orientations toward premarital virginity of female virgins and nonvirgins.' *Acta Psychiatrica Belgica*, **79**, 321–331.

Perry, R. P., Abrami, P. C., Leventhal, L. and Check, J. (1979). 'Instructor reputation: an expectancy relationship involving student ratings and achievement.' *Journal of Educational Psychology*, **71**, 776–787.

Phillips, L. D. (1980). 'Introduction to decision analysis.' Tutorial Paper 79–1 (mimeo). London: The London School of Economics and Political Science, University of London.

Potter, J. and Litton, I. (1985). 'Some problems underlying the theory of social representations.' *British Journal of Social Psychology*, **24**, 81–90.

Poulton, E. C. (1975). 'Observer bias.' *Applied Ergonomics*, **6**, 3–8.

Pozo, C., Carver, C. S., Wellens, A. R. and Scheier, M. F. (1991). 'Social anxiety and social perception: construing others' reactions to the self.' *Personality and Social Psychology Bulletin*, **17**, 355–362.

Preston, J. D. and Guseman, P. B. (1979). 'A comparison of the findings of different methods for identifying community leaders.' *Journal of the Community Development Society*, **10**, 51–62.

Putnam, S. L. and Stout, R. L. (1985). 'Evaluating employee assistance policy in an HMO-based alcoholism project.' *Evaluation and Program Planning*, **8**, 183–194.

Raiborn, C. A. and Payne, D. (1990). 'Corporate codes of conduct—a collective conscience and continuum.' *Journal of Business Ethics*, **9**, 879–890.

Raub, W. and Weesie, J. (1990). 'Reputation and efficiency in social interactions: an example of network effects.' *American Journal of Sociology*, **96**, 626–654.

Richards, L. and Richards, T. (1991). 'The transformation of qualitative method: computational paradigms and research processes.' In N. G. Fielding and R. M. Lee (eds), *Using Computers in Qualitative Research*. London: Sage.

Riley, S. and Palmer, J. (1976). 'Of attitudes and latitudes: a repertory grid study of perceptions of seaside resorts.' In P. Slater (ed), *Explorations of Intrapersonal Space: The Measurement of Intrapersonal Space by Grid Technique*. London: John Wiley.

Ritter, G. (1973). 'Epilepsy and social prejudice in the light of history [in German].' *Psychiatrie, Neurologie and Medizinische Psychologie*, **25**, 754–761.

Rogers, E. M. and Kincaid, D. L. (1981). *Communication Networks: Toward a New Paradigm for Research*. New York: Macmillan.

Rose, S. M. (1985). 'Professional networks of junior faculty in psychology.' *Psychology of Women Quarterly*, **9**, 533–547.

Rosen, S., Cochran, W. and Musser, L. M. (1990). 'Reactions to a match versus mismatch between an applicant's self-presentational style and work reputation.' *Basic and Applied Social Psychology*, **11**, 117–129.

Rosenberg, M. J. (1965). 'When dissonance fails: on eliminating evaluation apprehension from attitude measurement.' *Journal of Personality and Social Psychology*, **1**, 28–42.

Rosenfeld, P. (1990). 'Self-esteem and impression management explanations for self-serving biases.' *Journal of Social Psychology*, **130**, 495–500.

Rosengren, K. E. (ed) (1981). *Advances in Content Analysis*. Beverly Hills, CA: Sage.

Rosenthal, R. W. and Landau, H. J. (1979). 'A game-theoretic analysis of bargaining with reputations.' *Journal of Mathematical Psychology*, **20**, 233–255.

Rosnow, R. L. and Fine, G. A. (1976). *Rumour and Gossip. The Social Psychology of Hearsay*. New York: Elsevier.

Rost, M. G. (1990) 'Review of J. Bergmann, *Gossip—About the Social Form of Discreet Indiscretion*.' *Language and Society*, **19**, 569–571.

Rowney, J. A. and Zenisek, T. J. (1980). 'Manuscript characteristics influencing reviewers' decisions.' *Canadian Psychology*, **21**, 17–21.

Rudd, R. (1986). 'Issues as image in political campaign commercials.' *The Western Journal of Speech Communication*, **50**, 102–118.

Ruiz-Ruiz, M., Serrano, V., Padilla, P. and Pena, J. M. (1986). 'The public image of suicide: attitudes toward suicide and mental illness.' *Crisis*, **7**, 84–88.

Salancik, G. R. and Meindl, J. R. (1984). 'Corporate attributions as strategic illusions of management control.' *Administrative Science Quarterly*, **29**, 238–254.

Sande, G. N., Goethals, G. R. and Radloff, C. E. (1988). 'Perceiving one's own traits and others': the multifaceted self.' *Journal of Personality and Social Psychology*, **54**, 13–20.

Scheier, M. F. (1980). 'Effects of private and public self-consciousness on the public expression of personal beliefs.' *Journal of Personality and Social Psychology*, **39**, 514–521.

Schlenker, B. R. and Weigold, M. F.(1990). 'Self-consciousness and self-presentation: being autonomous versus appearing autonomous.' *Journal of Personality and Social Psychology*, **59**, 820–828.

Schlenker, B. R., Weigold, M. F. and Doherty, K. (1990) 'Coping with accountability.' In C. R. Snyder and D. R. Forsyth (eds), *The Handbook of Social and Clinical Psychology*. New York: Pergamon.

Schlenker, B. R., Weigold, M. F. and Hallam, J. R. (1990). 'Self-serving attributions in social context.' *Journal of Personality and Social Psychology*, **58**, 855–863.

Schneider, D. J., Hastorf, A. and Ellsworth, P. C. (1979). *Person Perception* (2nd edn). Reading, MA: Addison-Wesley.

Schudson, M. (1990). 'Ronald Reagan misremembered.' In D. Middleton and D. Edwards (eds), *Collective Remembering*. London: Sage.

Schwartz, B. (1990). 'The reconstruction of Abraham Lincoln.' In D. Middleton and D. Edwards (eds), *Collective Remembering*. London: Sage.

Schwartz, B. (1991) 'Social change and collective memory—the democratisation of Washington, George.' *American Sociological Review*. **56**, 221–236.

Scott, J. (1991). *Social Network Analysis. A Handbook*. London: Sage.

Seiden, R. H. and Spence, M. (1983–84). 'A tale of two bridges: comparative suicide incidence on the Golden Gate and San Francisco–Oakland Bay Bridges.' *Omega, Journal of Death and Dying*, **14**, 201–209.

Seiler, R. E. and Pearson, D. A. (1984–85). 'Dysfunctional stress among university faculty.' *Educational Research Quarterly*, **9**, 15–26.

Selame, E. and Selame, J. (1988). *The Company Image. Building Your Identity and Influence in the Marketplace*. New York: John Wiley.

Semin, G. R. and Gergen, K. J. (eds) (1990). *Everyday Understanding, Social and Scientific Implications*. London: Sage.

Semin, G. R. and Manstead, A. S. R. (1981). 'The beholder beheld: a study of social emotionality.' *European Journal of Social Psychology*, **11**, 253–265.

Sewell, J. D. (1984). 'Stress in university law enforcement.' *Journal of Higher Education*, **55**, 515–523.

Shapiro, C. (1982). 'Consumer information, product quality, and seller reputation.' *Bell Journal of Economics*, **13**, 20–35.

Shapiro, C. (1983). 'Premiums for high quality products as returns to reputations'. *Quarterly Journal of Economics*, **98**, 659–679.

Shapurian, R. and Hojat, M. (1985). 'Sexual and premarital attitudes of Iranian college students.' *Psychological Reports*, **57**, 67–74.

Shaver, K. G. (1975). *An Introduction to Attribution Processes*. Cambridge, MA: Winthrop.

Sherif, M. (1936). *The Psychology of Social Norms*. New York: Harper & Row.

Shigetomi, C. C., Hartmann, D. P. and Gelfand, D. M. (1981). 'Sex differences in children's altruistic behavior and reputations for helpfulness.' *Developmental Psychology*, **17**, 434–437.

Shimanoff, S. B. (1985). 'Rules governing verbal expression of emotions between married couples.' *Western Journal of Speech Communication*, **49**, 147–165.

Shimp, T. A. and Bearden, W. O. (1982). 'Warranty and other extrinsic cue effects on consumers' risk perceptions.' *Journal of Consumer Research*, **9**, 38–46.

Shotland, R. L. (1985). 'A preliminary model of some causes of date rape.' *Academic Psychology Bulletin*, **7**, 187–200.

Simonton, D. K. (1991). 'Latent-variable models of posthumous reputation: a quest for Galton's G.' *Journal of Personality and Social Psychology*, **60**, 607–619.

Sindelar, P. T. and Schloss, P. J. (1987). 'A citation analysis of doctoral-granting programs in special education and relationships among measures of program quality.' *RASE: Remedial and Special Education*, **8**, 58–62.

Skanes, G. R. (1984). 'Eighteen eighty-four.' *Canadian Psychology*, **25**, 258–268.

Slater, P. (ed) (1976). *Explorations of Intrapersonal Space: The Measurement of Intrapersonal Space by Grid Technique*. London: John Wiley.

Smith, M. B., Bruner, J. S. and White, R. W. (1956). *Opinions and Personality*. New York: John Wiley.

Snyder, M. (1974). 'The self-monitoring of expressive behavior.' *Journal of Personality and Social Psychology*, **30**, 526–537.

Sobel, J. (1985). 'A theory of credibility.' *Review of Economic Studies*, **LII**, 557–573.

Spear, J. C. (1984). *Presidents and the Press. The Nixon Legacy*. Cambridge, MA: MIT Press.

Spinrad, W. (1991). 'Charisma: a blighted concept and an alternative formula.' *Political Science Quarterly*, **106**, 295–311.

Sprout, A. L. (1991). 'America's most admired corporations.' *Fortune International*, **123** (3), 11 February, 38–55.

Stephenson, W. (1953). *The Study of Behavior*. Chicago, IL: University of Chicago Press.

Stevenson, B. (1949). *Stevenson's Book of Proverbs, Maxims and Familiar Phrases*. London: Routledge & Kegan Paul.

Stevenson, B. (1974). *Stevenson's Book of Quotations* (10th edn). London: Cassell.

Stone, P. J., Dunphy, D. C., Smith, M. S. Ogilvie, D. M. and associates (1966). *The General Inquirer: A Computer Approach to Content Analysis*. Cambridge, MA: MIT Press.

Sullivan, J. L. and Feldman, S. (1979). *Multiple Indicators. An Introduction*. London: Sage.

Swann, W. B. Jr. (1984). 'Quest for accuracy in person perception: A matter of pragmatics.' *Psychological Review*, **91**, 457–477.

Sykes, J. B. (ed) (1976). *The Concise Oxford Dictionary of Current English* (6th edn). Oxford: Clarendon Press.

Tajfel, H. (1981). *Human Groups and Social Categories. Studies in Social Psychology*. Cambridge: Cambridge University Press.

Taylor, G. (1989). *Reinventing Shakespeare*. London: Weidenfeld & Nicolson.

Tedeschi, J. T. (ed) (1981). *Impression Management Theory and Social Psychological Research*. New York: Academic Press.

Tedeschi, J. T. and Reiss, M. (1981). 'Verbal strategies in impression management.' In C. Antaki (ed), *The Psychology of Ordinary Explanations of Social Behaviour*. London: Academic Press.

Tetlock, P. E. and Manstead, A. S. R. (1985). 'Impression management versus intrapyschic explanations in social psychology: a useful dichotomy?' *Psychological Review*, **92**, 59–77.

Thibaut, J. W. and Kelley, H. H. (1959). *The Social Psychology of Groups*. New York: John Wiley.

Thoreson, R. W., Cox, J. G. and Krauskopf, C. J. (1975). 'Reputation, halo, and ratings of counseling programs.' *Journal of Counseling Psychology*, **22**, 446–450.

Tsui, A. S. (1984). 'A role set analysis of managerial reputation.' *Organizational Behavior and Human Performance*, **34**, 64–96.

Tuddenham, R. D. (1951). 'Studies in reputation, III. Correlates of popularity among elementary schoolchildren.' *Journal of Educational Psychology*, **42**, 257–276.

Tuddenham, R. D. (1952). 'Studies in reputation, I. Sex and grade differences in schoolchildren's evaluations of their peers. II. The diagnosis of social adjustment.' University of California: *Pychological Monographs*, **66**, No. 333, pp. 1–58.

Tunnell, G. (1984). 'The discrepancy between private and public selves: public self-consciousness and its correlates.' *Journal of Personality Assessment*, **48**, 549–555.

Turner, J. C. (1991). *Social Influence*. Milton Keynes: Open University Press.

Turner, J. C., Hogg, M. A., Turner, P. J. and Smith, P. M. (1984). 'Failure and defeat as determinants of group cohesiveness.' *British Journal of Social Psychology*, **23**, 97–111.

Ungar, S. (1981). 'The effects of others' expectancies on the fabrication of opinions.' *Journal of Social Psychology*, **114**, 173–185.

Uribe, V. M. (1988). 'Short-term psychotherapy for adolescents: management of initial resistances.' *Journal of the American Academy of Psychoanalysis*, **16**, 107–116.

Villanova, P. and Bernardin, H. J. (1991). 'Performance appraisal: the means, motive, and opportunity to manage impressions.' In R. A. Giacalone and P. Rosenfeld (eds), *Applied Impression Management. How Image-Making Affects Managerial Decisions.* London: Sage.

Vonk, R. and Heiser, W. J. (1991). 'Implicit personality theory and social judgment: effects of familiarity with a target person.' *Multivariate Behavioral Research*, **26**, 69–81.

Wall, J. A. Jr. (1991). 'Impression management in negotiations.' In R. A. Giacalone and P. Rosenfeld (eds), *Applied Impression Management. How Image-Making Affects Managerial Decision.* London: Sage.

Wallace, A. F. C. (1956). 'Revitalization movements.' *American Anthropologist*, **58**, 264–281.

Watkins, A. (1990). *A Slight Case of Libel: Meacher v Trelford and Others.* London: Duckworth.

Webb, E. J., Campbell, D. T., Schwartz, R. D., and Sechrest, L. (1966). *Unobtrusive Measures. Nonreactive Research in the Social Sciences.* Chicago: Rand McNally.

Weber, R. P. (1983) 'Measurement models for content analysis'. *Quality and Quantity*, **17**, 127–149.

Weber, R. P. (1990). *Basic Content Analysis* (2nd edn). Newbury Park, CA: Sage.

Weinreich, P., Northover, M., McCready, F., Asquith, L. and Liu, W. (1989). *IDEXPC User-Guide.* Belfast: University of Ulster at Jordanstown.

White, A. (1985). 'Factors in applicant choice of a counselor education program.' *Counselor Education and Supervision*, **24**, 372–383.

Whobrey, L., Sales, B. D., and Elwork, A. (1981). 'Witness credibility law.' *Applied Social Psychology Annual*, **2**, 189–210.

Wilson, R. (1985). 'Reputations in games and markets.' In Roth, A. E. (ed), *Game-theoretic Models of Bargaining.* Cambridge: Cambridge University Press.

Wilterdink, N. (1992). 'Images of national character in an international organization—5 European nations compared.' *Netherlands Journal of Social Sciences*, **28**, 31–49.

Wright, J. C. and Dawson, V. L. (1988). 'Person perception and the bounded rationality of social judgment.' *Journal of Personality and Social Psychology*, **55**, 780–794.

Wylie, R. (1979). *The Self Concept.* Lincoln: University of Nebraska Press.

Young, H. S. (1984). 'Practising RET with lower-class clients.' *British Journal of Cognitive Psychotherapy*, **2**, 33–59.

Zarbatany, L., Hartmann, D. P., Gelfand, D. M. and Vinciguerra, P. (1985). 'Gender differences in altruistic reputation: are they artifactual?' *Developmental Psychology*, **21**, 97–101.

Zubin, J., Steinhauer, S. R., Day, R. and Van Kammen, D. P. (1985). 'Schizophrenia at the crossroads: a blueprint for the 80s.' *Comprehensive Psychiatry*, **26**, 217–240.

Zuell, C., Weber, R. P. and Mohler, P. (eds) (1989). *Computer-assisted Text Analysis for the Social Sciences: The General Inquirer III.* Mannheim, FRG: Center for Surveys, Methods, and Analysis (ZUMA).

Author Index

Subject Index